# METHODISM DIVIDED

*A Study in the Sociology*
*of Ecumenicalism*

# SOCIETY TODAY AND TOMORROW

General Editor: A. H. Halsey
*Fellow of Nuffield College and Head of the Department
of Social and Administrative Studies, Oxford*

\*

# METHODISM DIVIDED

A Study in the Sociology of Ecumenicalism

ROBERT CURRIE
*Wadham College, Oxford*

FABER AND FABER
24 Russell Square
London

*First published in mcmlxviii*
*by Faber and Faber Limited*
*24 Russell Square London WC1*
*Printed in Great Britain by*
*Western Printing Services Limited, Bristol*

*Standard Book Number:*
*571 08467 2*

© Robert Currie 1968

# Contents

7

# CONTENTS

# Tables, Figures and Graphs

## TABLES

# TABLES, FIGURES AND GRAPHS

## GRAPHS

10

# Introduction

The most widely acclaimed development in modern Christianity is the ecumenical movement. In western societies, the churches have been moving towards unification ever since the industrial revolution. Even today when organized religion is declining, the potential effects of ecumenicalism are considerable. The amalgamation of the Methodist Church and the Church of England into a disestablished English episcopalian church is probably imminent. The ultimate amalgamation of this new denomination with the Roman Catholic Church is a possibility that many would welcome and few would dismiss. The likelihood of such developments indicates the magnitude of recent changes in Christianity: the emergence of coalescent tendencies in a hitherto highly divisive religion; the rapid transformation or surrender of certain beliefs and practices; and the obsolescence and supersession of many denominations.

Historical and sociological analysis of these developments is at a preliminary stage. Even straightforward histories of specific unions are rare. Where available, they lay most stress on formal theological aspects and give little attention to social and organizational factors. Critical discussion of ecumenicalism encounters other difficulties than lack of information. Most religious organizations are now 'ecumenical', at least in principle. Since they have accepted ecumenicalism as orthodoxy, most pronouncements on the subject suffer from a certain tendentiousness. Ecumenicalism is assumed to be the will of God, and is less discussed than eulogized. Ecumenical projects are interpreted in lofty terms of 'mission', with little reference to their specific motivation and origin. Much emphasis is placed on enthusiastic international conferences, while the practicalities of everyday church life are often overlooked. Since ecumenicalism asserts unity, peace and concord between all Christian people, ecumenicalists dwell on the harmony of the coming great Church, not on the conflict of ideas, personalities and policies involved in ecumenical activity. In

11

belittling old conflicts and veiling new, the ecumenical movement obscures past and present alike.

This book examines some of the ecumenical movement's assumptions, through a study of the divisions and unification of Methodism: the dominant sector of Nonconformity, the most dynamic religious movement in industrialized Britain and the pioneer of English ecumenicalism.

Methodism and Methodist ecumenicalism display many particular characteristics special to Methodist history. In the past too little attention has been paid to this history. Above all, very little work has been done on the history of Methodism since Wesley's death in 1791. Valuable monographs and articles have appeared, but a general history has been lacking. The present study attempts to remedy some of this deficiency. Many subjects have thus been treated for the first time and much previously unused material has been analysed. This is particularly true of the sections of this book which deal with the numerical growth of Methodism; the organization of Methodist denominations; interchurch relations in the Methodist world; the transformation of Methodist culture in the nineteenth and early twentieth centuries; and the processes by which the Methodist Church has been formed. Partly because of the impossibility of referring the reader to other works on many of these subjects, partly because of the wide implications of division and union, it has been necessary, in presenting the major theme of this book, to give a picture of Methodism as a whole.

But this study is not only concerned with the particulars of Methodist history. Few individual religious organizations tell us nothing about the movements of which they are a part. The community of Methodist denominations tells us a good deal about Christianity in an industrialized society, and, indeed, about Christianity as a whole. In some ways Methodism is an accelerated microcosm of Christianity. Large slow movements of great complexity affecting Christianity as a whole can be seen happening on a small scale, at great speed, and in a relatively simple way, in Methodism. Methodism has already had its 'reformation' period (approximately 1791–1855) and its overlapping ecumenical phase (approximately 1797–1932). Its divisions have been caused, and its reunification hindered, by those conflicts of laity and hierarchy, and those debates about church government, freedom of belief and administration of sacraments, that have dominated the history of Christianity.

Methodism has known, in rapid succession, remarkable success and severe chronic recession, a change of fortune which other churches have only experienced slowly and in milder form. The evangelistic ethos of Methodism, its sensitivity to statistics, and its lack of state authentication or great historical tradition, have made it peculiarly responsive to pressures felt by Christianity as a whole, but ignored or dismissed by slower moving and more protected churches.

Although conclusions from the Methodist experience of ecumenicalism do not inevitably apply everywhere else, the Methodist case has considerable general relevance. Significant growth of church unity will come not from the work of the World Council of Churches or the British Council of Churches, or from developments such as the Church of South India, but from the efforts of denominational leaders to unify long-established churches in the context of advanced industrial societies. Methodism offers the two leading English examples of such union churches: the United Methodist Church (1907) and the Methodist Church (1932). At the very least, study of these two bodies may suggest lines of enquiry into those similar church unions which provide the solid advance of ecumenicalism. In this book, such general comment is confined to the major current ecumenical project in England, the attempt to join a reunited Methodism to the Church of England from which it divided.

In the investigation of these developments, due emphasis must be given to ideas and ideals, but these do not occur in a vacuum. Many writers on religious movements interpret their members and leaders as pale saints whose more mundane and vigorous acts stand out as startling and inexplicable deviations from sanctity. But this study concerns itself not with the highest experiences of the few but with the general experiences of the many. It attempts to set high religious aims in the context of the ordinary concerns and conflicts of chapel life and the struggles of rival leaders, denominational realities whose life and interest may compensate for what they lack of the moral symmetry of the theological textbook.

This is a relatively unusual approach to the discussion of religion. But this study does not assume that the members and leaders of Methodist denominations were or are fundamentally unusual, except in so far as Methodism long occupied the frontiers of Christianity in England. Methodist experiences, policies and personalities may generate criticism, but such criticism is often more widely relevant also. Nor does this study assume, with those who feel able to discount Nonconformity as a mere passing phase in the history of the Church, that the reversals Methodism has recently suffered are peculiar to it alone. If–as some may fear–the most exposed provinces of the Church have fallen, the hinterland should also beware.

This book examines a number of problems. It studies the conflict between lay and ministerial elements in both division and union; and interprets the former as basically a lay, the latter as basically a ministerial activity. It seeks to show how patterns of growth are related to the development of union policies, and suggests that ecumenicalism is always partly a response to adversity–more specifically, in this case, a response to numerical decline. It illustrates the replacement of older ideas and practices by liberal theology, culture and churchmanship, a development of the greatest significance in forwarding the union of churches. It considers how far a group of divided and antagonistic denominations converge in organization and in their doctrine of the ministry before they finally unite. It discusses different types of 'polemical ecumenicalism', and the 'ecumenicalism of mission', and shows that high policy often clashed with commitments to chapel, denomination or class. It shows how a series of united churches comes into being, and critically examines their record in fulfilling the promises made by ecumenicalists.

Although the subject matter of this book is largely historical, the arrangement is topical and analytical rather than chronological. The first part deals with the causes and character of the division of Methodism. After this introductory section, parts two and three are parallel and complementary analyses of the unification of Methodism. Part two deals with the factors at work in the ecumenical process. Part three shows how interdenominational negotiations developed as a result of these factors. Part four is a critical discussion of the Methodist experience of ecumenicalism.

By electing me first to a research studentship and then to a research fellowship, the Warden and Fellows of Nuffield College enabled me to carry through this study. I am grateful to the Rev. C. A. French and Mr. R. M. Rattenbury for permission to cite papers in their possession; to Dr. Eric Baker for permission to use the minutes of the Methodist union committees; to the Methodist Publishing House for permission to reprint clauses 30 and 31 of the Deed of Union; and to the author for permission to publish the letter quoted on p. 302. Didsbury and Hartley Victoria Colleges and the Methodist Archives kindly provided facilities and materials for study. I have also had the benefit of comment and information from many people. I have been particularly fortunate in receiving much assistance, advice and criticism from Professor H. A. Clegg, Mrs. P. Currie, Dr. John Walsh and Dr. B. R. Wilson.

# Part One

# Conflict and Crisis in Methodism

# CHAPTER ONE

# Ethic and Authority from Wesley to Bunting

## The Development of the Methodist Movement

By 1791 Methodism contained many of the elements which divided it repeatedly in the next seventy years. The basic disagreement among Methodists at this date was one common to Christians. Some Christians, usually members of the hierarchy or men very closely connected with it, interpreted the Christian life in authoritarian terms. Such people were intellectuals and leaders, whose commitment to their theology and ethic was both strong and abstract. They had principles, and these principles were to determine their lives and those of their followers in every particular.

Others, usually laymen, tended to interpret the Christian life in freer terms of the autonomy of the individual believer, under God, gathered in the fellowship of the Christian community. Such people did not have the abstract commitment of their leaders. Instead of high principles they had deep loyalties, to persons and to a community. When and if they formulated their faith, they did so in terms of individual freedom and fellowship, rather than obedience to a theological and ethical code.

The conflict between these different viewpoints was intensified in Methodism, a movement which began as a search for a 'method' to bring believers to 'perfection'. The search led to the formulation and imposition of an uncompromising world-rejecting ethic, demanding subordination of secular interests to the total pursuit of perfection under the direction of a total authority. This 'method' originates in the psychology and theology of John Wesley (1703–91). Wesley founded and dominated Methodism, and his unique position in the movement has led to excessive historical emphasis on his life and thought. But the development of Methodism owes much to Wesley's personality.

Wesley's early life was dominated by a very powerful mother, whose concept of education was to teach children, 'When turned a year old

17

(and some before)' to 'fear the rod and cry quietly'.[1] Her influence over Wesley was very strong throughout his life. Even his most radical innovation–the appointment of laymen to ministerial functions–was made under the influence of his mother. All the Wesley children, with the exception of Charles, had unhappy sexual experiences.[2] Charles' poetry is full of sexual imagery, often of an allegedly regressive type. John's relationships with women were not successful, and late in life he suddenly and secretly married a widow who treated him with violence and abuse. It has been argued that he was sexually retarded.[3]

Such tensions and influences contribute to the intensity of Wesley's genius. They may be associated with his demand for strong external discipline and its fulfilment. In this respect Wesleyanism deviates from Luther's ideal of faith in the justifying love of God. Luther separated 'faith' and 'works' and held that 'Doctrine is heaven: life is earth'.[4] The mature exposition of this theology dismayed Wesley who closely associated assurance of divine love with performance of the divine command. For Luther, faith itself is the 'works' of religion; for Wesley, works are faith.

Wesley was greatly influenced by writers, such as Thomas a Kempis and William Law, who demanded fulfilment of high ethical standards. These theologians disturbed Wesley: 'I was . . . very angry at Kempis for being too strict.'[5] But instead of rejecting discipline in frustration, Wesley made renewed efforts to secure success and divine approval by the 'method' of the Oxford 'Holy Club'. 'By my continued "endeavour to keep his whole law" inward and outward, "to the utmost of my power", I was persuaded that I should be accepted of him.' On 24 May 1738, the day of Wesley's conversion, he learned that we *may* 'be partakers of the divine nature', that we are 'not far from the kingdom of God', and that God *does* work a 'change . . . in the heart through faith in Christ'. Wesley felt his heart 'strangely warmed. I felt I did trust in Christ, Christ alone, for salvation; an assurance was given me, that he had taken away *my* sins, even *mine* and saved *me* from the law of sin and death.' Although Wesley's experience derives

---

[1] John Wesley, *Journal*, London, 1930, vol. 1, p. 388.

[2] See Maldwyn Edwards, *The Astonishing Youth*, London, 1959, *passim*.

[3] E. P. Thompson, *The Making of the English Working Class*, London, 1963, pp. 370 ff; G. E. Harrison, *Son to Susanna*, London, 1944, pp. 183 ff; V. H. H. Green, *The Young Mr Wesley*, London, 1961, pp. 210–11.

[4] Martin Luther, *A Commentary on St Paul's Epistle to the Galatians*, London, 1956, pp. 13, 476.

[5] Wesley, *op. cit.*, vol. 1, p. 97.

much from Luther's, conversion did not liberate Wesley from ethical requirements, *but enabled him to fulfil them*.[1]

The central item of Wesley's theology is 'Christian Perfection'. Wesley clarifies the idea almost incidentally in a pamphlet, *Farther Thoughts on Christian Perfection*, published in 1762:

> 'One commends me. Here is a temptation to pride. But instantly my soul is humbled before God; and I feel no pride; of which I am as sure as that pride is not humility.
>
> 'A man strikes me. Here is a temptation to anger. But my heart overflows with love. And I feel no anger at all; of which I can be as sure as that love and anger are not the same.
>
> 'A woman solicits me. Here is a temptation to lust. But in the instant I shrink back. And I feel no desire or lust at all; of which I can be as sure as that my hand is cold or hot.'

The examples chosen–pride, which his mother had 'insisted upon conquering' in a child, bodily pain or corporal punishment, and sexual desire–are themselves significant. So is the response, which is nothing, non-response, a suitable ethic for one brought up in a house where, in his mother's words, 'the family usually lived in as much quietness as if there had not been a child among them'.[2]

This ethic demanded self-improvement under authority, to be embodied in the elaborate and powerful Methodist 'Connexion' of societies. Central to the Connexion is the 'Class Meeting', whose members met 'To confess their faults one to another, and to pray one for another, that they may be healed'. Such an organization largely rejected Lutheranism, and Wesley felt obliged to defend it against 'Luther in the fury of his solifidianism'.[3] The Class Meeting required conformity to the Methodist ethic of self-improvement and sober continence. Apparent democracy in the Class is delusive. Wesley controlled the classes, if indirectly, ran them on inquisitorial lines, and expelled many for failure to conform.[4]

But Wesleyanism, being a subsection of Christianity, was not uniformly authoritarian. Christian theology presents a recurrent antithesis of Law and Gospel, the Law demanding conformity to the divine will and the earthly organization which speaks with the divine voice; the Gospel justifying a wide range of free relationships of

---

[1] *Ibid.*, vol. 1, pp. 96–102; Green, *op. cit., passim.*

[2] John Wesley, *A Plain Account of Christian Perfection*, London, 1952, pp. 75–6; Wesley, *Journal*, vol. 1, pp. 388, 390.

[3] *Ibid.*, vol. 1, p. 185.

[4] *Ibid.*, vol. 1, p. 185.

individuals, and even rejection of the prevailing norms, in response to the dictates of the *inner* voice of conscience or faith. Wesley accepted the general framework of Christian mythology, its 'three-storey universe',[1] and its rewards and punishments in terms of salvation from 'the pit . . . the fire that never shall be quenched', for the kingdom of heaven, where 'sorrow and sighing flee away'.[2] He also adopted the antithesis of Law and Gospel, and the consequent appeal to the dictates of Gospel, or Christ, to justify deviant behaviour.

Despite his hostility to Luther, Wesley also accepted a great deal of Lutheranism. Wesleyan theology, with its themes of the 'Witness of the Spirit' and 'Assurance',[3] is closely connected with Lutheran thinking–Wesley was an Arminian who rejected Calvin's predestinarianism. Wesley used Arminian theology to show that all could achieve the Methodist goal of 'perfection'. But the Arminian promise of spiritual progress for all might also suggest that achievement of perfection did not depend on obedience to ecclesiastical authority. Wesley condemned and punished deviance, but his theology could justify deviance.

Wesley needed such justification himself, to vindicate his conduct towards the Church of England. Wesley frequently reiterated his attachment to the Church of England. But his relationship with it was ambivalent. His father left the Dissenters, became an Anglican clergyman and engaged in polemic against them. Mrs. Harrison speaks of the 'deeply hidden discord' in his personality.[4] John Wesley's mother's father was a prominent Nonconformist, and she herself broke important Anglican conventions and encouraged Wesley to break them.[5] Wesley's Arminianism explicitly rejected the Calvinism underlying the Thirty Nine Articles. Towards the end of his life, Wesley, having established a separate religious body outside the Church of England, rejected the doctrine of episcopacy on which that body is founded and himself ordained 'Superintendents' (i.e. bishops).[6]

Wesley justified his relationship with the Church of England on the ground of divine call and private judgement adopted by Reformation

---

[1] Rudolf Bultmann, *Jesus Christ and Mythology*, London, 1960, pp. 14–15.

[2] John Wesley, *Sermons on Several Occasions*, London, 1956, pp. 81, 83.

[3] *Ibid.*, pp. 111–33.

[4] Harrison, *op. cit.*, pp. 20 ff.

[5] John Kirk, *The Mother of the Wesleys: A Biography*, London, 1864, pp. 1–16.

[6] Wesley, *Journal*, vol. 1, pp. 386–8; Edgar W. Thompson, *Wesley: Apostolic Man*, London, 1957, *passim*.

leaders. The view that a man must belong to that Church into which he was born was 'attended with such difficulties as no reasonable man can ever get over,' said Wesley. 'Not the least of which is, that if this rule took place, there could have been no Reformation from Popery; seeing it entirely destroys the right of private judgement on which that whole Reformation stands.'[1]

But Wesley deplored the revolutionary strain in Reformation thought resulting in quietism, antinomianism, mysticism, millennarianism. 'Christianity is essentially a social religion,' he declared. The statement indicates his theological position on the far right of the Reformation. He taught a close and unbreakable bond between the inward experience of faith and the outward works of goodness. 'It is most true', he wrote, 'that the root of religion lies in the heart, in the inmost soul. . . . But if this root be really in the heart, it cannot but put forth branches. And these are the several instances of outward obedience which partake of the same nature with the root; and, consequently, are not only marks or signs, but substantial parts of religion.'[2]

These works exist in the context of, and conform to, a conventional pattern of social morality. But 'works' particularly means loving relationships with each other and the non-religious; and, a characteristic Wesleyan note, 'obedience' to the appropriate, corporate, and allegedly divinely sanctioned morality. Christianity is a 'social religion': it appears in and cannot be divorced from the context of human society; and it creates a community of love and 'obedience' within this society, which aims to expand until it is co-extensive with society. The rationale of classical Methodism is to require 'obedience' of believers, and to make all men believe. 'I look upon all the world as my parish', said Wesley.[3]

The world he was born into was one of mass illiteracy and few voluntary organizations. Within this world he chose a smaller sphere, composed of remote areas of ignorance and irreligion which had survived a millennium of Christianity. Sixty per cent of Wesley's converts came from the eleven counties where organized Christianity was weakest.[4] His greatest successes were in two areas where pre-

---

[1] Wesley, *Sermons*, p. 447.
[2] *Ibid.*, pp. 237, 245.
[3] Wesley, *Journal*, vol. 1, p. 201.
[4] Cheshire, Cornwall, Cumberland, Durham, Lancashire, Middlesex, Northumberland, Staffordshire, Surrey, Warwickshire and the West Riding. In the eighteenth century, churches were most thinly distributed relative to population in these counties.

Christian religion survived at its strongest, Cornwall and the Isle of Man. The population which responded most readily to Wesley knew little of religion. They were poorly educated and even illiterate. Popular mass movements were unknown in eighteenth-century England. Wesley attempted his unprecedented task with the least promising materials available. The necessities of this task influenced the organization of Methodism; but, although pressures and needs shaped much of the Methodist structure, large parts of this structure are simply organizational embodiments of Wesley's doctrine or reflections of Wesley's psychology.

Wesley said the purpose of Methodism was 'to spread scriptural holiness over the land', to convert all men to obedience to the Wesleyan norm. But even among the converted, Wesley concluded, 'Personal religion . . . is amazingly superficial.'[1] Hence, he believed, the necessity for that 'spirit of mutual inquiry' which 'runs through and colours the whole system,' as a later Wesleyan put it.[2] The 'mutuality' of the enquiry was not evident. In the small groups–'bands' or 'classes'–which were the essential units of Wesley's system, each member was indeed 'To speak . . . the true state of our soul, with the faults we have committed . . . and the temptations we have felt since our last meeting.' But it was the leader of the group who asked 'searching questions' on these matters. The leader, Wesley wrote, had to make 'particular inquiry into the behaviour of those whom he saw weekly. . . . Many disorderly walkers were detected. Some turned from the evil of their ways. Some were put away from us. Many saw with fear, and rejoiced unto God with reverence.'[3]

The inquisitorial element in classical Methodism arose from Wesley's doctrines. Its dictatorial elements arose from his character. Wesley was Methodism's executive, legislature, and judiciary combined. The Methodist Conference was, during Wesley's lifetime, no more than 'Several Conversations between the Rev. John Wesley, A.M., and the Preachers in Connexion with Him'. The members of Conference were mere counsellors. 'I myself sent for these of my own free choice,' declared Wesley. 'And I sent for them to advise, not to govern me. Neither did I at any time divest myself of any part of the

[1] *Minutes of the Methodist Conferences from the First, Held in London, by the late Rev. John Wesley, A.M., in the Year 1744*, vol. 1, London, 1862, pp. 449, 457.

[2] *Memorials Literary and Religious of Thomas Garland*, London, 1868, p. 348.

[3] Frank Baker, *Methodism and the Love-Feast*, London, 1957, p. 14; John B. Dyson, *Methodism in the Isle-of-Wight*, Ventnor, 1865, p. 48.

power . . . which the providence of God had cast upon me.'[1] The acts of Conference were simply the acts of Wesley.

When preachers needed to be appointed, said Wesley, 'I commenced my power to appoint each of these, when, and where, and how to labour'; and this system of centralized direction of the 'travelling preachers', known as 'itinerancy', characterized Wesleyanism. When stewards were needed to manage the affairs of the localities, Wesley declared, 'it was I myself, not the people, who chose these Stewards, and appointed each the distinctive work wherein he was to help me, as long as I desired.' When Methodists were in conflict with Methodists, Wesley judged the case.[2]

The incautious Cheshire Methodist who invited Wesley to give *his* testimony in class, profoundly misinterpreted the nature of Methodism. 'We are no republicans,' said Wesley, 'and never intend to be.' The simple if curious explanation was that, though Wesley spent his lifetime offering his followers perfection, in his eyes none ever achieved it. In defence of his autocracy, he wrote,

'If you can tell me any one, or any five men, to whom I may transfer this burden, who can and will do just what I do now, I will heartily thank both them and you. But some of our Helpers say, "This is shackling free-born Englishmen" and demand a free Conference . . . wherein all things shall be determined by most votes. . . . It is possible after my death something of this kind may take place; but not while I live.'[3]

The exigencies of 'experimental religion' required both the face-to-face group in which religious commitment could be expressed and thus known; and the enquiry into thoughts and deeds which confirmed the reality of this commitment. Wesley's authoritarianism demanded that benevolent despotism, or theocratic centralism, which characterized his system. But the system did not grow overnight. Nor did it co-exist easily with that other Methodism which Wesley's efforts stimulated, but of which he knew little.

Methodist historiography gives great prominence to Wesley's reluctant abandonment of Anglican 'decency and order' for 'field-preaching'. At Bristol, on 2 April 1739, Wesley writes, 'At four in the

[1] George Smith, *The Polity of Wesleyan Methodism, Exhibited and Defended: or, a Historical Record of the Rise, Progress, and Present State of the Government of That Religious Body; and a Careful Comparison of All Its Leading Peculiarities with the Explicit Teaching of Holy Scripture*, London, 1851, p. 14.
[2] *loc. cit.;* John Wesley, *Letters*, London, 1931, vol. 8, p. 196.
[3] Baker, *op. cit.*, p. 33; *Minutes of the Methodist Conferences*, vol. 1, p. 505.

afternoon I submitted to be more vile and proclaimed in the highways the glad tidings of salvation, speaking from a little eminence in a ground adjoining to the city, to about 3,000 people.'[1] The occasion is historic, as Wesley clearly meant it to be; and it began half-a-century of field preaching. But the history of Methodism is not the biography of Wesley; and, while Wesley spent his life in travel, ruling and guiding the denomination he founded, the Methodist people lived a quiet and settled life, grouped in 'societies', and, as soon as possible, quit the field for the chapel.

At once the vertical chains of command, from member to leader, to preacher, to Wesley, became entangled with a horizontal pattern of Methodist life and Methodist chapels. The itinerant Wesley was a stranger to this emergent localized culture, but he was aware of its dangers. With an earlier Christian leader he could say, 'Here we have no lasting city, but we seek the city which is to come',[2] the heavenly Jerusalem. But the Methodist people created an earthly 'lasting city' of their own, the chapel, and increasingly regarded Wesley's prose-lytizing theocracy as a distraction or an intrusion. Wesley's response was to extend his own sovereignty.

The proprietors of Methodist chapels were trustees, whose trust included control of the pulpit. The trustees of the New Room in Bristol, for example, could exclude what preachers they chose. In theory this power was reasonable and useful: Wesley, in London or Newcastle, could hardly determine whether a preacher was uttering heterodoxy in the New Room pulpit. In practice, the power was desirable, from the congregation's point of view, since it soon developed its own views on preaching, which were quite as strong as Wesley's. But Wesley 'vehemently objected' to the exercise of his followers' new found faculties, and required alteration of the New Room trust deed to give Wesley and his appointees exclusive power to appoint and dismiss preachers for the New Room pulpit. Later, when a chapel was built by subscription at Dewsbury, its trustees refused to accept a Methodist deed unless they had the power to appoint and dismiss. The Conference, on Wesley's direction, built another chapel. 'No Methodist trustee,' declared Wesley, 'if I can help it, shall after my death, any more than while I live, have the power of placing and displacing the Preachers,' for 'if the Trustees of Houses are to displace Preachers, then itinerancy is at an end.'[3] The preachers, according to

[1] Wesley, *Journal*, vol. 1, p. 184.
[2] Heb. 13.14: *Revised Standard Version*.
[3] Thomas Cooper, *A Treatise on the Rights, Duties and Liabilities of Trustees of Wesleyan Methodist Chapels*, London, 1850, pp. 9–10, 12.

Wesley, had nothing to do but to save souls, i.e. to preach in the chapels; the trustees had nothing to do but to keep up the chapels.

## The Problems of an Elite

When Wesley died, in 1791, Methodism had developed a complex structure influenced by Wesley's doctrines and personality, by the growth of chapel society, and by the demands of a mass movement in uneducated populations. Wesley, as President in the annual Conference (or indeed out of it) appointed, formally recognized, and dismissed preachers. He ordained some to administer sacraments and others, as 'Superintendents', to act as bishops and ordain others. He controlled denominational funds such as the Contingent Fund, the building of chapels, and the filling of pulpits. Once 'Superintendents' were ordained in 1784, a complete hierarchy emerged. But uncertainty remained. Wesley was obviously the fount of Methodist orders, except in the case of ordained clergymen of the Church of England who were also Methodists. But it remained unclear who, under him, and after his death, could exercise this power: the Superintendents, primarily appointed to serve in America, or the Conference collectively.

Below Wesley, Conference and Superintendents, and unquestionably subject to Wesley-in-Conference while Conference sat, and Wesley alone when it did not, were the varying grades of preachers. 'Travelling preachers', directly appointed by Conference, were divided into Wesley's 'Assistants', and their 'Helpers'. Travelling preachers were appointed on a short-term basis, first one, later three years. They were almost invariably paid by the local quarterly meeting; *although they were directed by and responsible to Wesley-in-Conference.* This system paralleled the division of power in the chapel between trustees and Conference. The constitutional doctrine of Wesleyanism was that he who pays the piper does *not* call the tune. The travelling preachers, through the assistant, were in charge of the 'local preachers', unpaid laymen, who remained in secular employments, but preached locally at the majority of services, as the assistant directed them.

The entire denomination was thus a 'connexion' of parts under the sovereignty of Wesley. From 1746 it was subdivided into 'circuits' of chapels and other preaching places. In 1791 there were about seventy circuits, ranging in size from the London Circuit of 2,950 members to the Sussex Circuit of 260. Travelling preachers were appointed to circuits, and each circuit was under an assistant.

Question 23 of the *Large Minutes* asked, 'What is the office of a

Christian minister?' to which the answer was, 'To watch over souls as he must give account.' In the circuit the assistant watched over souls. He grouped the members in bands, or in more flexible groups, called classes, which superseded bands. He appointed leaders of the classes and met them regularly and frequently to supervise their work. He had charge of the travelling preachers of the circuit, and appointed the local preachers, directing them to conduct services as and when he saw fit. He alone admitted members by administering a quarterly class ticket, the passport to chapel life. He presided over the quarterly meeting which did the business of the circuit, and probably, as Wesley's representative, frequently appointed both circuit and society stewards who were responsible for circuit and chapel business respectively. The assistant also adopted Wesley's judiciary function. The assistant heard cases involving members or lay officials, and pronounced sentence, subject to Wesley-in-Conference. The assistant could suspend lay officials, and he could expel members by the simple device of withholding class tickets. He might also be initially responsible for cases involving other travelling preachers. Under the assistant and the other travelling preachers, the lay officials conducted the business; the local preachers filled the pulpits; the leaders had charge of the members, and remitted their weekly and quarterly 'class money' to the assistant.[1]

Just before his death in 1791, Wesley wrote of Christian Perfection, 'This doctrine is the grand *depositum* which God has lodged with the people called Methodists; and for the sake of propagating this chiefly He appears to have raised us up.'[2] Wesley remained faithful to his youthful beliefs which, through the elaborate 'method' of his polity, he hoped to inculcate in his followers, guiding and directing them in the way of truth. When he died, the Wesleyan Societies in the United Kingdom numbered 72,476 members.

Wesley's chief concern was the preservation of his highly successful evangelistic organization. He had failed to come to terms with the problem of relationships with the Church of England, professedly living and dying a Church of England man, despite his schismatic orders and sacraments. He also failed to provide any guidance on the location of power after his death. But he did provide very carefully for the continuation of the Wesleyan organization, appointing the 'Legal

[1] *Minutes of the Methodist Conferences*, vol. 1, pp. 567, 573, 609, 617; Edgar Thompson, *op. cit., passim*; *Minutes of the Methodist Conferences*, pp. 455, 479, 489, 493, 533–5, 539.

[2] Quoted in Frank Baker, *A Charge to Keep*, London, 1954, p. 106.

Hundred' by the Deed of Settlement in 1784. These 100 named preachers, and successors whom they could appoint, constituted the legal Conference after Wesley's death, controlling the other ministers and organizing the system of annual deployment of ministers known as 'Stationing'. This settlement provoked jealousies among the 135 ministers excluded[1] and the Hundred allowed other ministers beside themselves to attend Conference, concerning themselves with mere legal ratification of the larger body's decisions.

Wesley's death was immediately followed by a struggle for power among the ministers. Alexander Mather and Thomas Coke sought to become the new Wesley. To the end of his life, Coke 'never quite dispossessed himself of the notion . . . that he was the true successor of Wesley'.[2] But the small group of ministers led by Coke failed to establish an episcopacy of Superintendents and the term 'Superintendent' was rapidly downgraded to apply to the old ' "Assistants" in charge of Circuits'. Collective leadership won the day; William Thompson, 'a safe and trustworthy man, moderate in his opinions', was elected President of the 1791 Conference on the platform of the 'Halifax Circular'–annual appointment to offices, promotion to the Legal Hundred by seniority alone, and devolution of executive powers to District Committees.[3] The authors of the Halifax Circular hoped to prevent seizure of power by an individual or small group, to all intents and purposes by Coke.

Their success was limited. Coke was given a new office, Secretary of Conference, in 1791. The London District Meeting, chaired by Coke, illegally proscribed the reformer Kilham before the 1796 Conference had even met to hear his case. The Meeting repudiated a current allegation that the preachers were 'a company of whining Jesuits, and consequently atrocious knaves'. But it had established the claim of the semi-permanent London secretariat–the publishing house or 'Book Room', Missionary Society, etc.–to direct the collective leadership. The Book Room was still described, sixty-five years later, as having 'assumed a very extensive and considerable influence in Wesleyan affairs' as 'a sort of minor conference'.[4]

---

[1] *Life of the Rev. Alexander Kilham . . . One of the Founders of the Methodist New Connexion in the Year 1797. Including a Full Account of the Disputes Which Occasioned the Separation*, London, 1838, pp. 93–5.

[2] T. P. Bunting and G. Stringer Rowe, *The Life of Jabez Bunting, D.D.*, vol. 2, London, 1887, pp. 156–7.

[3] *Life of Kilham*, pp. 188–9; J. Robinson Gregory, *A History of Methodism*, London, 1911, vol. 1, pp. 209–10, 211.

[4] *Life of Kilham*, pp. 243–4, 247–50; Joseph Beaumont, *Life of the Rev. Joseph Beaumont*, London, 1856, p. 126.

The struggle for power weakened the preachers at a time of considerable difficulty. Two main problems faced them. Wesley had restricted administration of sacraments by his assistant preachers. Many of his followers resented this. But the so-called 'Church Methodist' party in the denomination opposed any administration of schismatical Methodist sacraments. In this situation, the preachers confessed, 'We knew not what to do, that peace and union might be preserved' and, narrowing the number of possibilities to two, drew lots.[1] Their decision was to suspend the administration of sacraments for one year. But they could hardly repeat this technique indefinitely.

The second problem facing the preachers was even more serious than the sacraments. As early as June 1791, a meeting at Redruth indicated popular desire for some redistribution of power.[2] Such redistribution would challenge the centralized authoritarianism of Wesley's system and jeopardize the position of the preachers, whose priestly or ministerial status was not at all clear. The preachers resisted with peculiar success.

Demand for reform was divided among various groups, ranging from 'Church Methodist' trustees of chapels who feared capitulation by Conference to demands for Methodist sacraments, to radicals like Kilham who wanted a democratic Methodism with its own sacramental system. The preachers succeeded in playing off one section against another and in disciplining and then expelling Kilham.[3] Meanwhile they resolved some of the problems inherent in the vagueness of the Deed of Declaration, and placated most of the remaining opposition, by a series of legislative acts culminating in the Plan of Pacification of 1795 and the Leeds Regulations of 1797.

By these acts, the Legal Hundred was recognized as 'the only legal persons who constitute the Conference.' The sacramental controversy was resolved by the cautious formula, 'The Lord's Supper shall be administered by those only who are authorized by the Conference, and at such times and in such manner, as the Conference shall appoint.' District Meetings were created, linked directly to Conference by annual election of the Chairman of the District in the latter body. Districts were supposed to provide judicial decisions between Conferences as Wesley had formerly. But Coke and other Ministers probably regarded the districts as substitutes for dioceses, and hoped, in vain, that the Chairmen would eventually become bishops. The

---

[1] *Minutes of the Methodist Conferences*, vol. 1, p. 273.
[2] *Life of Kilham*, pp. 136–8.
[3] *Ibid.*, pp. 201, 203, 214–15, 326.

District Meeting, composed of all the ministers in the district, was to take decisions on new building, and to share in decisions on alteration or division of circuits in its own district; to determine, although 'Delegates' were specifically forbidden, which of its members should go to Conference, and to send ministerial representatives to the Stationing Committee of Conference, on which devolved Wesley's function of deploying ministers.

The main concession to lay demands for power concerned the local courts. Ministers and lay officials together were to appoint lay officials, to admit members (and to expel on charges of immorality), to propose candidates for the ministry, and to perform local judicial functions. Generally, the ministers, as represented by the superintendent of the circuit (i.e. the former 'assistant'), had power of initiation or nomination, the officials gathered in the appropriate meeting, that of confirmation or election, i.e. of veto. In disciplinary cases, officials acted as jury, pronouncing as to the facts, the minister as judge. The circuit quarterly meeting as a whole was given power to suspend the operation of new legislation in the circuit for one year, and to veto proposals for division of the circuit.

These concessions to the Methodist people were superficially striking. Laymen, who had only little and undefined existence in Wesley's system, were now admitted to new powers. But they were entirely excluded from Conference and the district meetings, and their power in the local courts was subordinate to the ministers, whose nominees all officials (and indeed members) continued to be. Conference announced, 'Thus, brethren, we have given up the greatest part of our government into your hands as represented in your different public Meetings.' In particular, Conference declared, 'The members of our Societies are delivered from every apprehension of clandestine expulsions; as that Superintendent would be bold indeed who would act with partiality or injustice in the presence of the whole Meeting of Leaders.'

These assurances satisfied many. Laymen would have been less satisfied if they had known that Coke, who deplored these concessions, prevented the insertion of the crucial Plan of Pacification and Leeds Regulations in the Conference Journal. Thus although the two documents were published in the printed Minutes, they did not become law till twenty years after Coke's death when, in 1835, the strange omission was revealed and hastily rectified. Laymen might have been disconcerted if they had grasped the significance of two resolutions of the Conference of 1796, evidently arising out of Kilham's case. The first read, '*no Preacher shall publish anything* but what is given to the Conference, and printed in our own press. The Book Room to determine what is proper to be printed.' The Conference, having given censorship of ministers into the hands of the London secretariat, resolved with great aplomb, 'Let no man, nor number of men, in our Connexion, on any account or occasion, circulate letters, call meetings, do or attempt to do anything *new*, till it has first been appointed by the Conference.' Despite its concessions, the Conference effectively announced its intention to replace Wesley's autocracy with a hierarchical rule if anything more rigid and far-reaching.[1]

But intention was not fulfilment. In the period from the death of Wesley in 1791 to the death of Coke in 1814, ministers increased from 235 to 685, members from 72,476 to 203,273. This massive expansion markedly weakened the ministerial elite. Their book-keeping was poor, as the published Minutes illustrate, and their general financial arrangements were feeble. By 1818, the all-important Contingent Fund had been 'very frequently embarrassed', and Conference had a debt of £5,000.[2] Especially as Methodism spread out from the larger centres of population, new members were increasingly hostile to the 'ECCLESIASTICAL DISCIPLINE' essential to Methodism.[3]

'In most of the country places, we are very low,' wrote Jabez Bunting in 1812. 'There is but little of Methodist discipline. . . . My fixed opinion is that the success of Methodism in these parts has been more rapid than solid.'[4] These new 'country' Methodists preferred their own freer forms of worship and shunned the older forms of Methodist services, based on the Anglican Prayer Book. A critic wrote in 1836, 'in the great majority of country circuits, where in my opinion the liturgy is most needed, it is never used. Why! Because its introduction would disturb the peace and possibly annihilate the very existence of these Societies.'[5] More than a century after Wesley's death, some claimed that 'country' Wesleyans demanded much greater power in chapel society than 'town' Wesleyans did. The Rev.

[1] *Minutes of the Methodist Conferences*, vol. 1, pp. 362, 364, 677–705.

[2] Valentine Ward, *Free and Candid Strictures on Methodism and Especially Its Finances*, Aberdeen, 1818, p. iii; T. P. Bunting, *The Life of Jabez Bunting, D.D.*, vol. 1, London, 1859, p. 126.

[3] *Ibid.*, pp. 425 ff.

[4] *Ibid.*, pp. 425–30; Bunting and Rowe, pp. 33–4.

[5] James Kendall, *Miscellaneous and Free Strictures on the Practical Position of the Wesleyan Connexion towards the Church of England, with Other Correlative Observations, Designed to Promote a Better Understanding and Permanent Friendship between Those Important Religious Communities*, London, 1836, p. 27.

Henry T. Hooper wrote in 1908, 'In the town . . . the minister represents the Connexion and takes over the chapel as his own. . . . In the
village the chapel belongs to the people . . . and the people take over
the minister as a newcomer to be attached to them.'[1]

The preachers, often undistinguished by class or education from
their members, endeavoured to control the people by rigid imposition
of discipline, and assumption of far-reaching pastoral prerogatives
that often degenerated into petty tyranny.[2] The contemporary reputation of Methodism for Jesuitism and intolerance, was not entirely at
variance with the realities of an authoritarian organization, driven by
the effects of its own growth, to assert its principles in ever more
extreme form.

But the hierarchy could not solve its problems by mere unco-
ordinated aggression against the laity. The preachers' fundamental
difficulty was the vacuum left by Wesley's death. John Pawson
observed, 'I am persuaded that from the creation of the world, there
never existed a body of men who looked up to any single person with
a more profound degree of reverence than the preachers did to Mr.
Wesley.'[3] But immediately after Wesley's demise mutual distrust had
prevented the preachers from appointing a second Wesley. Coke
attempted to play such a part nevertheless, but he was inadequate to
it, and ministers began to demand a new leader who could repair the
Methodist machine and re-establish the authority of the hierarchy.
For this they were prepared to pay a considerable price.

*The Theory and Practice of Buntingism*

The new leader was Jabez Bunting, born in Manchester in 1779, the
high Tory son of a radical tailor. He trained to be a doctor, but when
he was twenty, decided to enter the Wesleyan ministry instead. He had
'a constitutional aversion to talk about himself'. He had 'no disposition to sun himself in the smiles of the public'—instead Robert
Newton became orator, spokesman, and public fund-raiser for the
Buntingite party. Even at the great Leeds Missionary Meeting of
1813, which Bunting prepared, he spoke thirty-first out of thirty-nine

[1] *Methodist Times*, 27 August 1908, p. 719.

[2] E.g., Benjamin Gregory, *Autobiographical Recollections*, London, 1903,
pp. 247–8; William Wright, *The Practice of Wesleyan Priests a Violation of
Christ's Precepts; or, a Few Words of Explication Relative to the Unscriptural
Treatment of Messrs Wright and Christian of Stamford from Mr B. Gartside,
Wesleyan Superintendent*, London, 1842, pp. 12 ff.

[3] Luke Tyerman, *The Life and Times of John Wesley*, London, 1871, vol. 3,
p. 298.

speakers, 'but with a few words, chiefly affecting a detail of the organization'. He was dissatisfied with the rapid growth of Methodism, distrusting revivalism and evangelistic activities, and preferring 'smaller numbers, with more knowledge and depth of piety' to 'large societies'. So far from promoting the extension of Methodism he reduced its numbers by well over 100,000.[1]

Bunting's silence, and the hagiography surrounding him, have been broken only by the attacks of his enemies, and by Joseph Fowler's records of the secret Wesleyan Conferences. Many details of Bunting's career remain obscure. The early years of his ministry probably saw the establishment of a Buntingite party of ministers, the members of which subsequently occupied the major Connexional offices. In 1806 Bunting was dissatisfied with being appointed Assistant Secretary to the Conference of that year, and in 1821 he only took the Editorship on the understanding that it would be a temporary post. Neither office had ever been anything but a subordinate appointment, and Bunting was probably only interested in Missionary affairs, the preserve, since Wesley's death, of Coke. But few Buntingites showed enough interest in missionary affairs to become missionaries. 'A well organized missionary system' was simply a method of making Bunting 'a public man', as his son put it.[2]

Bunting's first attack was premature. By 1803–4, the missionary accounts, under Coke's control, had reached 'a state of almost unintelligible entanglement'. Coke was abroad and the twenty-four year old Bunting was called in to straighten them out. Older ministers were dissatisfied at this, and, on his return, Coke 'grieved at what had passed during his absence'. A decade in the provinces followed Bunting's period in London: Coke may have exiled him, via the Stationing Committee, for his temerity. But he contrived to remain active in Connexional politics during this period, acting chiefly by 'private suggestions'. In 1813, there was pressure for change in Missionary affairs, still languishing under Coke. In Leeds, Bunting organized and launched the first popular Missionary Society in Wesleyanism. At the following Conference he was elected Secretary. From this eminent position he proposed a solution to an acute

[1] Bunting, *op. cit.*, pp. 11, 21, 98, 110, 223; Thomas Jackson, *Recollections of My Own Life and Times*, London, 1873, p. 215; *Wesleyan Takings, or Centenary Sketches of Ministerial Character, as Exhibited in the Wesleyan Connexion during the First Hundred Years of Its Existence*, London, 1840, p. 4; Bunting and Rowe, *op. cit.*, pp. 33–4, 50, 77.

[2] Bunting, *op. cit.*, pp. 266, 280, 291, 312–16, 375–6; Bunting and Rowe, *op. cit.*, pp. 28, 38, 187–8.

constitutional problem. As the number of ministers rose, the Legal Hundred dwindled as a proportion of the whole, and as the Deed of Settlement and its list of names became more and more remote, the Hundred became the hundred oldest ministers unleavened by ability or youth. Bunting proposed and carried the *election* of a candidate to every fourth vacancy, from the preachers of fourteen years' standing. Since by this arrangement he was just eligible, he stood and was elected. Wesley's concept of the Hundred, and the doctrine of the Halifax Circular, were overturned.[1]

As a member of the Hundred, as champion of the younger preachers, and as annually re-elected semi-permanent Secretary of Conference, Bunting established himself as a leading figure. By the Conference of 1815, Coke was dead, 'removed', as Bunting put it.[2] For some time Bunting was at the Mission House. He also did a spell at the Book Room. But he was appointed permanent General Secretary at the Mission House in 1833.

The 'iron, menacing, shackling, browbeating, reign of Jabez Bunting'[3] drew its strength from his administrative ability. He rationalized the administrative procedures and finances of Wesleyanism. He was 'the grateful servant of the Conference' as he put it, ubiquitous, indispensable. By 1837 the Conference could not proceed if Bunting was absent from its sessions, for Bunting established 'a Conference within a Conference; and the latter forming only an outer circle . . . with little or no power, and with but a partial knowledge of the wheels that work the machinery'. The wheels in question were the Connexional committees, 'one of the chief secrets of his power'. In 1844, ten leading Buntingites held eighty-nine committee seats between them; six other leading ministers, more or less opposed to Bunting, seven. By controlling certain major committees, Bunting could determine Conference decisions. Edmund Grindrod proudly announced in 1842 that 'one master hand, for the last generation has framed the great majority of the acts of our Conference'.[4]

---

[1] Bunting, *op. cit.*, pp. 231–3, 311; Bunting and Rowe, *op. cit.*, pp. 70–4.

[2] *Ibid.*, p. 85.

[3] James Everett, '*Methodism As It Is*'. *With Some of Its Antecedents, Its Branches and Disruptions; Including a Diary of the Campaign of 1849. Protracted during a Period of Seven Years; with a Special Reference to the Character, Power, Policy and Administration of the 'Master Mind' of John Wesley's Legislative Successor*, London, 1863, vol. 1, p. 87.

[4] Benjamin Gregory, *Sidelights on the Conflicts of Methodism*, London, 1898, pp. 74, 251, 507; *All the Numbers of the 'Fly Sheets', Now First Reprinted in One Pamphlet*, London, 1849, pp. 19, 22; Jackson, *op. cit.*, p. 312; Edmund Grindrod, *A Compendium of the Laws and Regulations of Wesleyan Methodism*, London, 1842, p. xv.

Bunting exerted almost unlimited pressure within the ministerial body as a whole by his known and partisan control of the Stationing Committee. He would use this power to reward his party, to please a rich layman, to punish an opponent. 'Many of the preachers are under personal obligations to him, for special services as Stationing Secretary', wrote a critic in 1834. A year later another wrote contemptuously of the Minister who said ' *"we are afraid of Bunting"* ', and added 'in a lower tone of voice (lest some bird of the air should carry the tidings to Jabez) . . . *"He . . . will send us to bad circuits"* '.[2]

Despite his self-concealment, Bunting had an extensive propaganda system, culminating in the *Watchman* newspaper, which was designed to spread proper views of 'doctrine and discipline'. The Book Room was used to publish Buntingite material. The Theological Institution, of which Bunting was President and the two leading Buntingites tutors, was a seminary for producing Buntingite ministers. Bunting declared, 'The source of all our evils is this incompetent ministry. . . . It is necessary to teach a man how to administer our discipline'.[2]

Any constitutional opposition to Bunting had to be mounted in Conference. This Bunting dominated. So strong was the tendency to authoritarianism, to submission to the few leading men, that the *active* Conference was minute. In 1844, when there were 1,216 ministers in the Connexion, *twenty-seven*, that is, about 2 per cent, spoke at Conference. In Conference, 'the Platform', i.e. officials and ex-Presidents – largely Buntingites – could 'carry almost everything. It could dispose of the Presidency with something approaching to certainty.' Should opposition, or mere deviation, *still* arise, it was, no matter how small (or how reasonable), crushed by abuse and degradation. The greatest surviving veteran of Wesley's preachers was shouted down and demoted to an impoverished circuit for the last year of his ministerial life, for promoting schools for poor children without Conference approval. Another minister opposed to Bunting, was, for a technicality, given a solemn presidential censure, which carried with it 'a kind of stigma for the rest of a man's ministerial life'. An opponent would be continuously interrupted, silenced by a Buntingite President,

---

[1] Gregory, *op. cit.*, pp. 111–13, 528; Bunting and Rowe, *op. cit.*, p. 113; '*Fly Sheets*', p. 9; *A Catechism for Wesleyan Methodists, Particularly for Methodist Class Leaders and Local Preachers; Wherein the Various Points at Issue between the Conference and the People Are Taken up and Discussed in Familiar Dialogue*, Liverpool, 1834, p. 32; *The Watchman's Lantern*, 14 January 1835, p. 36.

[2] Bunting and Rowe, *op. cit.*, pp. 154, 169–70; *Wesleyan and Christian Record* 26 December 1844, p. 280; '*Methodism As It Is*', vol. 1, pp. 122–4; Gregory, *op. cit.*, p. 105.

informed by Bunting that he was 'not quite right in his mind'.[1]

But the hierarchy was not the whole of Methodism. As Samuel Warren put it, in 1827, 'the entire Body of Wesleyan Methodists is composed of two Orders–the CONFERENCE, and the people'.[2] Bunting's power among the people was never as strong as his power within the hierarchy. But he tried to control the people, partly by punitive forays into troublesome parts of the Connexion, partly by directing the preachers to exercise rigid authority over the members.

In theory Bunting respected lay power. 'I wish,' he wrote in 1816, 'all our pecuniary affairs were more submitted to our lay friends. Surely, if spiritual things belong, as we readily enough insist, to spiritual men, secular concerns as legitimately fall under the special cognizance of secular men.' Bunting was still urging 'the co-operation of our lay brethren' in 1850. But this did not mean that Bunting encouraged or promoted the rights of ordinary members and lay officials. The quarterly meeting theoretically had the right to memorialize Conference. 'There must not come a time', said Bunting, dismissing memorials protesting against his breaches of Methodist law, 'when we are to hear all the nonsensical memorials which some two or three queer individuals may get up in a meeting.' Bunting rejected any suggestion of lay representation. Benjamin Gregory wrote, 'The *representative principle* was by Dr. Bunting most resolutely resisted.'[3]

Instead Bunting proceeded in his government of the Connexion, as in his government of the hierarchy, by committee. Lay 'co-operation' meant mixed lay and ministerial committees dealing with various items of departmental business, though with no fundamental questions of policy. These committees were 'a strong sea wall against popular encroachment on pastoral prerogative', Gregory noted. The lay members of the committees were nominees of the Conference. They were usually very wealthy businessmen, often Londoners, often closely related to the ministers. They served on several committees each, often for decades. The views of these laymen were comparatively harmless to the hierarchy. Mr Farmer of London said contentedly, in 1851, when Wesleyanism was in confusion, 'Theirs was a kind of paternal system; and the people were accustomed to look up to the preachers with a degree of reverence, respect and love.' As a demon-

---

[1] *Ibid.*, pp. 108, 113–15, 195 ff, 233–4, 379; '*Fly Sheets*', p. 43; Beaumont, *op. cit.*, p. 123.

[2] Samuel Warren, *Chronicles of Wesleyan Methodism. First Department. A Digest of All Its Laws and Regulations with a Comprehensive Statement of Its Principal Doctrines*, London, 1827, p. 31.

[3] Bunting and Rowe, *op. cit.*, pp. 95, 353; Gregory, *op. cit.*, pp. 83, 497.

stration of lay participation, the mixed committees were, one fervent Buntingite noted, 'rather absurd'.[1]

Other aspects of Bunting's regime caused concern to the members. The Buntingite party was composed of 'ultras, exquisites, absolutists' who stood far to the right of the spectrum of Methodist opinion after the Napoleonic War. E. R. Taylor maintains that Bunting upheld 'the traditional Methodist isolation from politics', a curious judgement on one who injured a leg falling over a bench in the House of Commons. Dr. Bunting, who appeared on Tory hustings, and, with Newton, conducted a campaign against Lord John Russell, presumably sustained this injury during the course of his political work. Bunting persecuted and punished Wesleyan ministers who held deviant political views, the Radicals J. R. Stephens and William Griffith, the Liberals Thomas Galland and Samuel Dunn. The hierarchy as a whole sought to force Tory views on the laymen, 'the great majority' of whom were 'utterly opposed' to Toryism, and wanted 'radical reforms, both in Church and State'.[2]

Bunting's proceedings were often marked by manifest injustice. He told the Conference of 1842, 'Adapt your principles to your exigencies.'[3] Consolidation of Methodism meant action against the constitution of the 1790s, and Bunting both rewrote the constitution, e.g. on the question of the Legal Hundred, and worked 'outside' it, basing his power not so much on Conference but on the newer system of Connexional committees, many of which he originated. But his policies also involved such extensive breaches of rules, and such large-scale injustice, that his dictatorship can only be regarded as arbitrary.

The inquisitorial system was central to Methodism. Bunting used the system against opponents, and indeed extended it in 1834 and 1849 by tests of loyalty to himself, enforced under pain of expulsion. Bunting himself explicitly excluded his own conduct and that of his officials from examination. Connexional rules or decisions were applied capriciously. The aged veteran Clarke was exiled from London under a rule Bunting invented for the occasion and subsequently

[1] James Everett, *Supplement or Appendix to 'Methodism As It Is' with a Special Reference to the Character, Power, Policy and Administration of the 'Master Mind' of John Wesley's Legislative Successor*, London, 1868, pp. 6–14; *Wesleyan Vindicator and Constitutional Methodist*, August–September 1851, p. 149; *Memorials . . . of Thomas Garland*, p. 322.

[2] *'Methodism As It Is'*, vol. 1, p. 121; E. R. Taylor, *Methodism and Politics, 1791–1851*, Cambridge, 1935, p. 13; Bunting and Rowe, *op. cit.*, pp. 266–7; Gregory, *op. cit.*, pp. 150–67, 202, 237–8, 409 ff; *Wesleyan*, 19 September 1844, p. 9.

[3] Gregory, *op. cit.*, p. 331.

broke for nine years. Conference expelled two ministers for contributing to a Liberal newspaper, while giving the Buntingite Tory
paper a vote of thanks. Finally, the system of Special District
Meetings, designed to secure fair trial, was converted by Bunting into
machinery for prosecuting and punishing opponents.[1]

Bunting's excesses were so gross that few can have imagined them
necessary to rectify the marginal weaknesses of Wesleyan organization misdirected by Coke and his fellow preachers. Nor could they
seriously claim that the feebleness of Coke's leadership demanded the
vigour of Bunting's tyranny to redress the balance. Bunting's success
in establishing complete control over the hierarchy baffled many of its
members. The Rev. Joseph Beaumont wrote despairingly after the
1841 Conference:

> 'Oh it is a melancholy spectacle to see Dr. Bunting swelling there
> and trampling down every just principle, every manly sentiment,
> every honourable feeling, every delicate sensibility . . . but it is a
> still more melancholy spectacle to see 500 men sitting in conclave,
> suffering him to do so, permitting the outrage, tolerating the
> abomination, nay, confirming the audacious tyranny. And why is
> it so? . . . Is the system itself bad? Is it fatal to liberty, to independ-
> ence, to honour?'[2]

The 'system' of Wesley's autocracy vitalized and directed the new
hierarchy of Methodist preachers. But in his lifetime, Wesley 'was no
more to be classed with the preachers than with the private members
of the society'. He stood above both.[3] Bunting was the leader of the
hierarchy, which he disposed of much as his own property. But he
was also the champion of the hierarchy. He consolidated its power in
the new denomination while he crushed all attempts to challenge his
position within it. In this respect too he revealed what was latent in
Wesley's system. For not only did Wesley teach the preachers that
they should accept his decisions and directives without question but
he also taught them that the people should accept their decisions and
directives. While defying authority in the Church of England, Wesley
established an authority at least as great in his own denomination:
new preacher is but old priest writ large.

But this new priesthood could not flourish in Wesley's lifetime.
Wesley exercised absolute control over it. The people themselves

---

[1] *Ibid.*, pp. 55–6, 111–13, 124, 186–7, 193, 262–5, 281, 409 ff, 458, 469.
[2] Quoted in Richard Chew, *James Everett: A Biography*, London, 1875, p. 334.
[3] *Life of Kilham*, p. 46.

identified authority with Wesley, and even by 1810, as T. P. Bunting put it, 'had not yet been so fully trained as to recognize their "preachers" as having any distinct and Divine commission as ministers of Christ'. 'Dr. Bunting,' a later Wesleyan wrote, 'was chiefly responsible for turning Methodist preachers into Wesleyan ministers.'[1] Because he raised the status of the travelling preachers, confirming them as a new Methodist priesthood, his followers could overlook his manifest excesses and regard Wesleyanism with peculiar complacency, amid all the disasters that Bunting's regime brought it.

The more committed Buntingites could not allow that there were excesses. To them, the Buntingite system was the work of 'one master hand . . . one superior mind', and its operation was morally impeccable. 'The system as now established,' declared the Rev. Richard Watson, 'is hostile only to the guilty, protective only to the innocent.'[2]

The heart of this system was the assertion of the priestly power inherent in the 'pastoral office' of the Wesleyan minister. 'Never have the clergy claimed a more ample authority in virtue of the pastoral office than amongst the descendants of those primitive preachers whom the Wesleys summoned to their assistance,' wrote a critic. The justification of these claims remained confused. Sometimes special significance was attached to Wesley. The pastorate was 'the living John Wesley', said Bunting. Wesley's connexionalism was regarded as having inherent virtues. The New Testament Church showed a 'Connexionalism in principle,' said J. H. Rigg, 'union in doctrine, in object, in love and in commission of the apostles.'[3] Many Wesleyans agreed with him.

Appeal to Wesley and his system did not answer every question. Even if Wesley was the fount of Methodist orders, and the connexional system itself the divine *esse* of the Church, it remained obscure why some members of the connexion, the ministers, should lead it, and others, the laymen, should not. Some meaningful distinction between these two categories was needed. One way of doing this

[1] Bunting and Rowe, *op. cit.*, p. 104; J. E. Rattenbury, *Christian Union and Methodist Fusion*, London, n.d., p. 27.

[2] Grindrod, *op. cit.*, p. xv; Richard Watson, *An Affectionate Address to Those Trustees, Stewards, Local Preachers and Leaders of the London South Circuit, Whose Names Are Affixed to Certain Resolutions, Bearing Date, September 23, 1828*, London, 1829, p. 13.

[3] Beaumont, *op. cit.*, p. 118; Gregory, *Polity*, p. 185; James H. Rigg, *Congregational Independence and Wesleyan Connexionalism Contrasted*, London, 1851, pp. 10–11; George Smith, *op. cit.*, pp. 58–62.

was to appeal to the obvious distinction between the two, the fact that the minister was a full-time employee of the Church and the layman was not. Alfred Barrett declared that Christ intended 'to have men separated to the work of the Gospel, and supported by the offerings of the people.' John Beecham found 'An actual separation from secular business, and an entire dedication to the sacred calling', to characterize the ministry. Laymen were not so dedicated; therefore they were not ministers. Ministers could claim to govern the Church; laymen could not.[1]

This theory was curiously weak. 'Entire dedication' was difficult to interpret in any other sense than 'full-time employment'. If entire dedication meant full time employment, in the sense that the minister devoted his working day to church work in return for a salary, then he was merely a professional, and the layman (who paid him) an honorary, church worker. As an argument to show that ministers must govern the church, this was virtually useless. It might as well be argued that ministers were, by their profession, a sort of ecclesiastical civil service, which should be entirely subordinate to a lay government of the Church elected by the people.

The task of Buntingite theology was to justify hierarchical claims on stronger grounds than these. It was continually tempted by Catholic theories of apostolic succession and special grace in ordination, according to which the hierarchy, uniquely possessed of divine grace, imparted this grace in unbroken succession to all it ordained. George Smith, for example, rejected the idea of 'special grace' in ordination as 'unreasonable, unscriptural and truly monstrous', but sought to strengthen the feeble definition of the ministry as 'selected, chosen, separated men,' by claiming for them 'the special and abiding presence of the Lord Jesus.' 'Special grace' and 'the special . . . presence' of God are not easily distinguishable.[2]

In effect Buntingites, looking to Wesley's example, had to rely on special call, rather than special grace or presence. Wesley's position depended on a doctrine of his own *'extraordinary mission'* from God

---

[1] Alfred Barrett, *Essay on the Pastoral Office as a Divine Institution in the Church of Christ: Containing a Particular Reference to the Manner in Which It Is Exercised amongst the Wesleyan Methodists*, London, 1839, p. 14; John Beecham, *An Essay on the Constitution of Wesleyan Methodism, in Which Various Misrepresentations of Some of Its Leading Principles Are Exposed, and Its Present Form Vindicated*, London, 1851, pp. 103, 106, 113; George Smith, *The Doctrine of the Pastorate: or, the Divine Institution, Religious Responsibilities, and Scriptural Claims of the Christian Ministry, Considered with Special Reference to Wesleyan Methodism*, London, 1851, pp. 15 ff.

[2] Smith, *op. cit.*, pp. 9–10, 21.

which enabled him to do what he did. But such a doctrine led not to the ecclesiastical construct at which Buntingites aimed, but to ecclesiastical anarchy. Special call and the Church's commission had to coincide, and Buntingites had to reject the doctrine of private judgement which Wesley himself strongly maintained. Buntingite ministers insisted that they had a special call. Richard Watson stated that 'the preachers had no scriptural warrant to sit with closed doors, or to refuse the admission of lay delegates' to Conference, 'but on the ground of their extraordinary call to the work of the ministry.'[1]

Laymen denied this. Buntingites therefore authenticated the minister's special call by commission: asserting implicitly that those who received the special call were those who were appointed by the hierarchy, and none other. Conference, the body which appointed ministers, was 'the organ of Providence,' said Bunting, i.e. its acts were providential. His most successful opponent, James Everett, correctly adduced the meaning of this claim. The Conference, he wrote, 'proclaim themselves . . . heaven-appointed teachers and absolute rulers–whose right it is to do what they please–excluding whom they will–receiving–killing–making alive–lifting to honour, sinking to infamy'. The Buntingite John Scott advocated precisely the same doctrine, when he urged a Conference obituary condemning a dead opponent of Bunting's. The Conference, he said, was 'a court expressly called upon to "sit in judgement and pronounce a decision on the career of the departed"'.[2]

Buntingite theology demanded for the Conference that 'power of the Keys' characteristic of papal sovereignty. 'Bunting believed that God himself placed the local Methodist congregation in the charge of the pastor, who would have to answer for the souls of his people at the last day', writes Dr. Kent. The assumption is that those on whom the Wesleyan Conference lays pastoral responsibility, God lays pastoral responsibility. Bunting declared that the Superintendent of the Circuit 'is the man directly responsible to God . . . the father of the family . . . the general-in-chief', and that 'the Superintendent, as Angel of the Church, is responsible over all'. Since the Superintendent is only the administrative head for the time being of a particular group of chapels, their members, officials, and ministers, it must be assumed that the divine element in his responsibility, the accountability not

[1] John Kent, *Jabez Bunting: The Last Wesleyan*, London, 1955, p. 15.

[2] *The Rev. Robert Emmett's Declaration*, Preston, 1835, p. 1; Bunting, *op. cit.*, p. 240; '*Methodism As It Is*', vol. 1, p. 67; Gregory, *Recollections*, pp. 404–5.

merely for circuit discipline, but for human souls at the day of judgement, is imported by appointment of Conference, the *episcope*, which channels a divine grace amounting to episcopal ordination.[1]

Given such premises, Richard Watson argued that '*no checks of whatever kind*' could '*obstruct the legitimate and scriptural exercise*' of the '*power inherent in the Ministry*'. A body of Methodist law existed to provide some sort of balance, however unequal, between the different interests in the Church. But this law was binding on the people only. The hierarchy had power to override the law, since it was the hierarchy that was divinely appointed to administer it. Gregory observed that for Bunting 'the supreme authority of the Pastorate was, to all practical intents and purposes, *the Constitution* underlying all documentary elements. . . . If at any time such settlements, plans, regulations, enactments, precedents, or what else, should hamper or imperil that supreme authority, *they*, not *it*, must give way.' Bunting's lavish tyranny was firmly based upon an expansive theory of the ministry.[2]

But laymen still existed. They were divided into two groups. One was the lay aristocracy of wealthy men. In Wesleyanism, as in Parliament, Buntingites argued, power should be in the hands of those distinguished by their '*mind, character, station*, property and influence'. These shared with ministers in the temporal government of Wesleyanism, and fully acknowledged pastoral supremacy in the spiritual government. The other group was composed of the lay officials and private members. Participation by such in ecclesiastical government was absurd:

> For just experience tells, in every soil;
> That those who think must govern those who toil.

It was particularly absurd to think of participation by the inferior, uneducated laity of Wesleyanism, who were to be saved by, not to have the running of, the denomination. Rigg informed laymen that their ancestors were scarcely distinguishable for 'brutal ignorance' from 'South African troglodytes, or Ceylonese tree-lodgers, or Australian savages'. The descendants of these troglodytes were themselves not possessors of perfection.[3]

---

[1] Kent, *op. cit.*, p. 18; Bunting and Rowe, *op. cit.*, p. 252; Gregory, *op. cit.*, p. 192.

[2] Watson, *op. cit.*, p. 7; Gregory, *Sidelights*, p. 499.

[3] William Vevers, *A Defence of the Discipline of Methodism*, London, 1835, p. 55; Rigg, *op. cit.*, pp. 71–2.

The lay claim 'that the Local Preachers and Class Leaders shall be recognized as Co-Pastors with the regular Ministers', shocked Buntingites. Bunting rejected jurisdiction by local preachers over ministers. 'When I am tried, I will be tried by my peers,' he said. Laymen could of course be 'called' to be local preachers and class leaders. But the crucial question here as elsewhere was not so much the special call itself as its attestation by the hierarchy who alone could commission ministers. The minister was indeed called, but he had to hear his call in the right quarters. Similarly, no layman alone could discover call or indeed opinions. He must be appointed and directed to such as he was allowed to do by the hierarchy itself. Hierarchical approval of lay acts was an essential 'check to fanaticism', i.e. private judgement. Bunting declared, 'We do not hold . . . that every man who understands the Gospel has a right to preach it.'[1]

The role of the hierarchy in the Church was plain. 'I believe,' said Bunting, 'that we are teachers to instruct and pastors to *govern* our people.' The minister had an 'elevated' office and must be treated by the people with 'respectful deference and demeanour'. They were told by the Conference, 'The Minister of God is your judge as God's Minister, and you are not to judge him.' The lay role was also clear. The Rev. Edmund Grindrod commended 'patience to the suffering poor'. Bunting's son taught that 'the Christian duty of submission to authority, whatever that authority may be, is and must be binding and permanent'. Newton pointed out that the truly religious are 'full of self-abasement, and are even ready to condemn themselves', while it is only those who are '*losing religion*, or *have lost it*' that are 'full of self-confidence, and find their pleasure in censuring and condemning other persons'. Should anyone disagree with the hierarchy, he could only follow Wesley's advice and 'go quietly'. If he stayed, while remaining in disagreement, or even in conflict, with the hierarchy, he 'was guilty of a flagrant transgression of that morality of the New Testament, the observance of which was a principal condition of his admission to our society'.[2]

Bunting's rule and doctrine established a Wesleyan priesthood in conflict with the Wesleyan people. The pastors determined to defeat a popular movement whose claims they rejected and whose ideas they

---

[1] Beecham, *op. cit.*, p. 111; Bunting, *op. cit.*, p. 243; Barrett, *op. cit.*, pp. 44–5, 106; Bunting, *op. cit.*, p. 118.

[2] Gregory, *op. cit.*, p. 83; Barrett, *op. cit.*, pp. 149, 319; *Minutes of the Methodist Conferences . . . 1844–1847*, London, 1848, p. 569; Bunting and Rowe, *op. cit.*, pp. 114–15, 169; Jackson, *op. cit.*, pp 356–7; Kent, *op. cit.*, pp. 29 ff.

abhorred. Wesleyanism would 'grapple with and surmount the evils of popular democracy', wrote Charles Welch,[1] for, in Bunting's words, 'METHODISM was as much opposed to DEMOCRACY as to SIN'.[2] The people must accept the perfectionist ethic of Methodism, under the authority of the Methodist hierarchy. This was a theory for an ideal world. Unfortunately the real world presented obstacles to this theory, above all the chapel.

[1] Charles Welch, *The Wesleyan Crisis: or, the Co-existence of Wesleyan Methodism and the 'Central Association', Totally Incompatible*, London, 1835, p. 58.

[2] *An Appeal to the Members of the Wesleyan Methodist Societies in Great Britain*, Leeds, 1827, p. 6.

# CHAPTER TWO

# Chapel Community and Denominational Conflict

## *The Chapel*

The chapel is the central fact of Methodism. 'It is indeed,' writes a Methodist historian, 'almost impossible to exaggerate the part' it 'played in the lives of its adherents.'[1] Chapel created a largely self-contained community of wage earners and tradesmen, first in the social void of the eighteenth-century countryside, then in that of the nineteenth-century town, a 'low society' of the humble paralleling the high society of the educated and wealthy.

The strength of this new society appeared in its festivals, especially the Sunday School Anniversary, a characteristically chapel-centred and non-religious Methodist occasion, given a veneer of Christianity by association with Whitsuntide. The forms of this festival varied. The Sunday School dinner, 'Hot joint and vegetables–Yorkshire pudding–and plum pudding', a public tea and games on the green, services with solos, evening recitations and even dialogues, were common. At Mousehole, members and scholars processed through the streets to the chapel with band, banners, and flowers. In the north, Anniversary was the occasion for a display of finery. In Rawtenstall, Anniversary was known as 'Sitting up in White', for the girls, in white dresses and stockings, the boys in white waistcoats and blue jackets, appeared splendid on a stepped platform. In Brighouse, however, it 'was known as "Cap Day", because on that day the girls wore white frilled caps provided by the school, and crimped by a machine kept for that purpose.'[2]

Friends and neighbours swelled the Anniversary congregation. Sir

---

[1] E. E. Kellett, *As I Remember*, London, 1936, p. 121.

[2] H. J. Hayhoe, *Memories of a Village Chapel*, Layer-de-la-Haye, 1952, pp. 4–5; John J. Beckerlegge, *Two Hundred Years of Methodism in Mousehole*, Mousehole, 1954, p. 31; E. H. Taylor, *History of Longholme Wesleyan Chapel and Schools*, Rawtenstall, 1921, pp. 36–7; Joel Mallinson, *Methodism in Huddersfield, Holmfirth and Denby Dale*, London, 1898, p. 54.

# CHAPEL COMMUNITY

Harold Bellman writes that, in Paddington,

> 'Months of rigorous training followed the careful selection of festival music. . . . Old members came from near and far to hear the singing. New suits and dresses were timed to arrive for Anniversary Sunday. Extra seats blocked the aisles. After the services . . . were over, the congregation often showed no signs of moving and choruses had to be repeated again and again.'

Such occasions appealed to non-Methodists also: Shirley Redfern's landlady said she was ' "Church", but didn't mind going to the Methodists when there was anything special on.'[1]

Commitment to chapel was intense. The Rector of Ingoldsby, Lincolnshire, violently opposed the establishment of Wesleyanism in the locality. But 'Every farmer in the village sent a team to convey stones for the new chapel from a neighbouring quarry.' Even where such opposition was absent, the mere cost of building a chapel made it an enterprise of great importance. Opening day was 'the day of days. . . . Some had lived for that occasion from happy childhood. Grateful tears came into their eyes . . . at such a rich fulfilment of their dreams and desires–a chapel costing nearly a thousand pounds. . . . It was a *gold* letter day for the Methodists.' Members idealized the community of chapel and school: "tis there we all agree, all with happy hearts and free,' and:

> in the class I meet with friends I greet
> At the time of morning prayer.

Chapel was, in every sense, the great 'rallying point for the people'. It evoked the strongest sentiments. Sir Harold Bellman met his wife at Trinity Wesleyan Chapel, Fernhead Road, Paddington: 'We grew up in the old chapel. We loved to serve it. We were married there . . . our three children were Christened there, and we are always certain of a welcome when we pay a return visit.'[2]

Chapel ownership was a desirable if awesome responsibility, whether to Samuel Troutbeck, apothecary, of Mill Street, Congleton, who owned the first Methodist chapel in the town, built in 1761 at the back of his house, or to the proprietors of the Thorncliffe Iron Works,

---

[1] Harold Bellman, *Cornish Cockney. Reminiscences and Reflections*, London, 1947, p. 38; Shirley Redfern, *Methodist Journey*, London, 1950, p. 40.

[2] Thomas Dixon, *The Earnest Methodist: A Memoir of the Late Mr Thomas Dixon of Grantham*, London, 1871, p. 119; Lewis H. Court, *The Romance of a Country Circuit*, London, 1921, p. 104; Hayhoe, *op. cit.*, pp. 3–4; *United Methodist Magazine*, April 1922, p. 109; Bellman, *op. cit.*, pp. 43–4.

Rotherham, who zealously built a Wesleyan chapel in connection with their manufactory. Even the most radical Methodists shared the enthusiasm of such local notables. James Sigston, Joah Mallinson, and Zebulon Stirk divided Wesleyanism to form the Protestant Methodist denomination, treated the sacraments with indifference, abolished the separate ministry, and were full of 'the spirit of Radicalism'. But they strongly resisted any attempt to divest them of their property in Stone Chapel, Leeds. Still humbler men knew their feelings. The poor trustee of Quarry Hill Primitive Methodist Chapel, Leeds, and his wife, 'could not sleep at night owing to the debt for which they felt responsible.' But this was a citizenship worth a great price.[1]

To rule in this society was most desirable of all. George Waddington, fellmonger and leather-dresser, came to Newland, Hull, in 1849. Waddingtons ran Newland chapel for a hundred years. Many other families, such as the Whiteheads at Rawtenstall, and the Beecrofts at Luton, played a similar role.[2] But power was not confined to these dynasties. If all the offices in Methodism had been held singly, every other member could have been an office holder. In the event, one member in twelve was a local preacher or steward, one in ten a trustee, one in four a Sunday School officer or teacher.[3] This vast officialdom created an interior social mobility, within the chapel community, far more important than that exterior mobility, from rags to riches, of which Methodist historiography is so proud. Few could and did become great manufacturers, peers or cabinet ministers. But many became chapel officials and gained respectability and prestige thereby, at least within the chapel and, in certain parts of England, in society at large.

All was well in Methodism but for the minister, supported and paid by the chapel community—which he ruled for his own purposes. The position of the minister in Methodism created copious grievances.

[1] J. B. Dyson, *History of Wesleyan Methodism in the Congleton Circuit*, London, 1856, p. 56; Matthew Henry Habershon, *Chapeltown Researches*, London, 1893, p. 142; Benjamin Gregory, *Sidelights on the Conflicts of Methodism*, London, 1898, p. 71; *Protestant Methodism at Leeds; Being a Statement of the Proceedings Which Have Lately Taken Place in That Connexion; and Which Have Caused the Secession of a Number of Preachers, Leaders, Trustees and Private Members*, Leeds, 1832, p. 8; William Beckworth, *A Book of Remembrance. Records of Leeds Primitive Methodism*, London, 1910, p. 41.

[2] Frank Baker, *The Story of Methodism in Newland*, Hull, 1958, pp. 19, 26, 28, 31; Taylor, *op. cit., passim*; J. Douglas Tearle, *Our Heritage. Chapel Street Methodist Church, Luton, Centenary, 1852-1952*, Luton, 1952, p. 17.

[3] Calculations based on the various *Minutes*.

Under the itinerant system, he appeared briefly for three years, bringing his foreign opinions with him, carried out such policies as he chose, prohibited what he disliked, and departed to make way for another. Ministers were 'birds-of-passage', 'the shepherds stationed at present in the circuit', as opposed to the local lay leaders of many years' standing, who might find themselves slighted, thwarted and even disciplined by 'the stranger'.[1]

This never failed to shock the officials. 'Here I am,' said Mr. David Rowland, the Liverpool Methodist reformer, 'a member of your society from my boyhood–from ten years of age–a leader and a local preacher in your society for twenty years–here I am excommunicated, anathematized by the Rev. Samuel Jackson.' Ministerial power meant not only that the official's position in the chapel, but his position in society, were precarious. Mr Thomas Ormrod of Bolton, expelled by the Rev. John McOwan, said, 'He had been an inhabitant of the town thirty-three and a half years, and held responsible offices among his fellow townsmen; and he could not suffer his character to be injured by any one who was only a transient resident in the town.'[2]

Contempt for Methodist ministers was hardly the preserve of non-Methodists. Mr. J. A. Mason, a Birmingham Wesleyan, declared in 1841 that the 'majority of Conference . . . justify the often expressed opinion that, a little low cunning; much pride and impudence; stout lungs, plenty of harlequin grimace; a long dangling watch-chain; black coat; bible; and surtout over the arm, form the sum total of commodities necessary for a Methodist preacher.' Extravagance of dress and style of living among preachers deeply disturbed the laity, who paid their salaries. Mr Charles Houchen of Yarmouth wrote:

'O ye Wesleyan Methodist travelling preachers, I beseech you all in the name of God to come out in your public preaching faithfully against pride, first set the example, enforce it among your wives and

[1] Beckerlegge, *op. cit.*, p. 38; *The Laws of the Wesleyan Methodist Society on the Expulsion of Members: Reprinted from the Minutes of Conference for the Year 1835 with Condemnatory Remarks on the Same. By a Member of the Wesleyan Society Who Has Been Such for Twenty Years*, Birmingham, n.d., p. 17; *Report of the Trial and Expulsion of Mr Thomas Ormrod, Leader and Trustee; Mr James Raper, Leader; and Mr Robert Harrison, Ex-Local Preacher, with an Address to the Officers and Members of the Wesleyan Society in the Bolton Circuit; and a Letter to Robert Knowles, Esq.; Together with an Account of the Extraordinary Ejection of the Officers, Teachers and Scholars of the Fletcher Street Sabbath School, by the Trustees*, Bolton, 1851, pp. 3, 11.

[2] *Report of a Meeting Held at the Tabernacle, Hull, on Wednesday, Feb. 11, 1835, to Explain the Principles and Objects of the Wesleyan Methodist Association; Report of the Trial and Expulsion . . ., loc. cit.*

families yourselves; the mouth of the church is open, and the world, do not wonder at it to see some preachers turning the sacred pages of the bible over with their black gloves in the pulpit, with their starch collars on, and watchguards hanging across their breasts; its mocking God to his face with pride [sic].'[1]

Such sentiments were widespread: when Robert Eckett, later leader of the Wesleyan Methodist Association, spoke in Finsbury Circus Chapel, he was frequently interrupted by cries of approval from a man who said, 'I have been paying tithes, to those rascally church parsons for many years, and I am delighted to hear this Mr. Eckett blow up their whole concern.' But Methodists expressed these views with peculiar fervour and attention to detail. The disaffected delighted in calculating how much ministers cost. It was estimated in 1830 that the London South Circuit spent £926 9s. 0d. per annum on ministers. Mr. Russell, a leader and local preacher, in the London East Circuit, was, perhaps not surprisingly, expelled for asserting that the ministers cost the circuit £300 each a year, and that every service in the circuit could, anyway, be taken by local preachers, who were of course unpaid.[2]

Ministerial education also offended many laymen. College education would both identify ministers with 'the wealthy and the fashionable', and encourage their arbitrary proclivities. Ministers should not remain in their studies, but should be found 'in the *pulpit*, on the *highway*, and–' a significant touch–'near the *social hearthstone*'. Evangelistic fervour would be dampened. '*Whence are the people to look for their* REVIVALISTS?'asked James Everett. 'Not, alas! to a college.' That educated ministers were snobbish, alien and deficient in zeal, persisted in Methodist tradition for a century after the first Methodist theological college was founded. This distrust was expressed by the lay official who told Shirley Redfern that 'them professor chaps' in the colleges would 'spoil' ministerial candidates, and weaken their grip on 'the true faith'.[3]

[1] J. A. Mason, *The Glory of Methodism; or, August Will Come*, Birmingham, n.d., p. iii; Charles Houchen, *To the Wesleyan Methodist Conference Assembled at Bristol*, July, 1846, Yarmouth, 1846, p. 11.

[2] *The Watchman*, 11 November 1835, p. 357; *The Circular to Wesleyan Methodists*, 31 March 1830, pp. 17–19; 31 May 1830, p. 38.

[3] *Circular to Wesleyan Methodists*, 27 February 1830, pp. 13–16; *The Disputants; or, The Arguments in Favour of the Newly Established Theological Institution among the Methodists Brought to the Test; and the Institution Itself Proved to Be Un-Wesleyan, Un-Scriptural, Un-Necessary, Impolitic and Dangerous. By a Disciple of the Old School*, London, 1835, pp. 63, 76; Redfern, *op. cit.*, p. 46.

Other ministerial attributes aroused lay hostility. Ministers were believed to manipulate stationing to suit themselves: in particular, 'the kindness of DR BUNTING' to his favourites was believed to clash with the wishes and plans of the quarterly meeting which invited ministers to the circuit. It was peculiarly offensive too that ministers should obtrude their politics on the chapel, for, despite modern historians, comparatively few Wesleyan *laymen*–unlike their more vocal ministers–were Tory. Dr. William Small, a Boston Wesleyan, expelled by the Rev. Ralph Scurrah in 1841, declared that while the preachers were 'to a great extent *under the direction* of a powerful party, *wholly devoted to Toryism*', '*fifteen* out of every *twenty* Methodists are favourable to a liberal government'.[1]

Ministers were unpopular. Such popularity as they retained was frequently depleted by conflicts between themselves and the chapel. Congregations were often dissatisfied with ministers' want of enthusiasm. 'Revivalism,' so far from commending itself to the Wesleyan hierarchy as a means of channelling off incipient radicalism, as Mr. E. P. Thompson suggests, was suspect to many ministers, who deplored 'fanaticism and rant'.[2] Laymen were eager for such displays however. Even the 'middle-class Methodism' of Hinde Street Wesleyan Chapel, London, demanded revivals. At the love-feast on Christmas Day, 1842,

'Thirty-four persons spoke with much propriety and power. . . . During the prayer of Mr. T. an indescribable awe rested upon the assembly. . . . When Father Jones pleaded with God, Mr. James Richardson cried with a loud voice "I have got it! I have got it!. . ."' Every few seconds the affecting cries of penitence were lost amidst the bursting joys of triumphant faith.'

When metropolitan feelings were so strong, country Methodists were unlikely to be indifferent. In 1832, the Rev. William Davis tried to

---

[1] *Strictures in Defence of the Rev. J. Kendall, and of the Subscribers of the Testimonial of Respect to Him, on His Recent Removal from Market Rasen, in Reply to the Letter of 'A Wesleyan' Inserted in the Stamford Mercury of the 10th of Last Month*, Market Rasen, 1841, p. 4; John Field Smyth, *A Vindication of the Conduct of the Wesleyan Methodist Preachers Composing the Lincoln District, in Reference to the Examination of Some Young Men, Candidates for the Ministry, at Their Annual Meeting Held in Boston, May 1841, Being a Reply to Two Letters Signed 'A Hater of Priestcraft', and also to One Signed 'William Small', on the General Character of Wesleyan Methodism: All of Which Have Recently Appeared in the Stamford Mercury*, Boston, 1841, p. 27.

[2] E. P. Thompson, *The Making of the English Working Class*, London, 1963, pp. 350 ff; H. Owen Rattenbury and Gervase Smith, *Memorials of the Rev. John Rattenbury*, London, 1884, p. 38.

stop the 'various gymnastic exercises' of the Derby Wesleyans in their Band Meeting. The members who had long suffered his staid ministrations in silence, told him, 'this is the *People's Meeting*, this is *our* time for speaking'.[1]

Trustees and proprietors of chapels, though perhaps less impassioned, had grievances also. Buntingites frequently denied that the ministers possessed the chapels by virtue of the trust deeds. 'The truth is,' declared the *Watchman*, 'that the Wesleyan chapels in Great Britain are, strictly speaking, the property of no class of men.' Trustees were not powerless against ministers in their own chapels for they had 'tremendous powers, to shield themselves equally from false doctrine and immorality in their ministers'. But trustees doubted their ability to resist the preachers, fearing 'that when a Chapel is built, or made over, upon the Conference plan, it is theirs forever', and the trustees' alleged powers over the pulpit would be worthless.[2]

Ministers did little to allay these fears. The Rev. George Gibbon, Superintendent at Huddersfield in 1793, 'observed to the trustees, that they were no masters there, but the conference were. One of them asking him the question, What are we?–he answered, CYPHERS.' The Rev. Thomas Jackson, President of the Conference in 1849, allegedly told trustees, 'The Chapels are ours, and the Debts are yours.' This infelicitous epigram was largely true. Trustees could exclude preachers for immorality or heterodoxy. But such unlikely occurrences did not trouble them. They wanted at least an equal share in the government of the property which they held in trust and the preachers controlled. The *Watchman* summed up their opinion with rare candour when it wrote in 1835, '*The travelling preachers appointed to the circuit are virtually the owners of the chapels.*' Their rule was supreme and none could oppose them. If they did, they were soon expelled. Even proprietors were not safe. The reformer, Mr. Thomas Roseveare, of Barn Park, Cornwall, was expelled 'in his own freehold chapel at Boscastle,' by the Rev. Aquila Barber, a 'Jesuitical tool of the lords of Conference.'[3]

---

[1] Nehemiah Curnock, *Hinde Street Chapel, 1810–1910*, London, 1910, pp. 42, 76; George Brown Macdonald, *Facts against Fiction; Or a Statement of the Real Causes Which Produced the Division among the Wesleyan Methodists in Derby; Forming a Reply to the Account Published by an Anonymous Writer*, Derby, 1832, pp. 17–18.

[2] *Watchman*, 9 September 1835, p. 286; 11 November 1835, p. 356; James Douglas, *The System of Methodism Further Exposed; and the Wiles of Priestcraft Investigated*, Newcastle, 1814, p. 19.

[3] *An Appeal to Christians of Every Denomination; Respecting the Late Disputes among the Methodists by the Members of the New Connexion in Hudders-*

Chapel officials found ministers very troublesome. Many no doubt pondered the advice of the Bolton policeman to the 'astonished member' he was painstakingly excluding on ministerial orders from Fletcher Street Chapel: 'You can easily fix them; give them no more of your brass.' Laymen feared ministers, while ministers in turn distrusted and disliked the lay officials who paid them and opposed them. One minister characterized them in 1814 as '*Captious, Quibble,* and *Grumble. Dr. Slyboots . . . Corah Snarle, Achan Screwpenny,* and *Nabal Gruff.*' A century later, ministerial unease about officials persisted. A Superintendent gave a young minister with a mildly troublesome Norfolk leaders' meeting, 'one last word of advice: never let them know when you're beaten.'[1]

The attitudes of officials and ministers were at variance. Officials regarded the minister as a useful employee, who might, for example, 'relet the empty pews' by the quality of his preaching. They wanted to look on him 'somewhat as a proud owner might watch the action of his famous trotting cob'. Out of the pulpit they expected him to be found frequently and entertainingly at their '*social hearthstone*'. But the minister looked upon all he surveyed as '*particularly his own circuit*', which he was to rule, and direct to the higher things of religion.[2]

James Stacey, discussing divided Methodism in 1862, wrote, 'Such divisions are sure to recur under a system which fosters the popular element as Methodism does, training it to every sphere of religious activity up to the very highest, yet denying it all share in those legislative acts for which in this very training a certain preparation is given.' Stacey referred to Conference. But laymen were most disturbed by their weakness in their own chapels, and exclusion from Conference was resented mainly as preventing them from redressing the balance of chapel society. Wesley created a vast army of lay officials, whose efforts were essential to the expansion and survival of

*field and Its Neighbourhood,* Huddersfield, 1798, p. 4; Thomas Cooper, *A Treatise on the Rights, Duties and Liabilities of Trustees of Wesleyan Methodist Chapels,* London, 1850, p. 43; *Watchman,* 19 August 1835, p. 261; Matthew Baxter, *Methodism: Memorials of the United Methodist Free Churches, with Recollections of the Rev. Robert Eckett and Some of His Contemporaries,* London, 1865, p. 457.

[1] *Report of the Trial and Expulsion of Mr Thomas Ormrod . . .,* p. 5; Theophilus, *Methodism, or Despotism; an Interesting Case, Clearly Stated in a Recent Conversation between Diotrephes, Gaius and John,* Redruth, 1814, p. 16; Redfern, *op. cit.,* p. 44.

[2] Curnock, *op. cit.,* p. 81; W. Hargreaves Cooper, *In Methodist Byways,* London, 1914, p. 5; *The Disputants,* p. 63; Macdonald, *op. cit.,* p. 13.

Methodism, but he left them in complete subservience to the ministers, who, as one writer put it in 1814, 'make all arrangements in the societies.'[1]

The *abuse* of this constitutionally enormous ministerial power in the chapels obsessed reformers such as Rowland and Eckett. The hierarchy had 'invaded and trampled underfoot the local authorities of Methodism', said Rowland. Eckett looked aghast at the Conference imposition of an organ on the Leeds Methodists and its consequences:

'The RIGHTS of a leaders' meeting have been trampled upon. Official Members have been unjustly expelled! Several THOUSANDS of persons have been delivered over to Satan, so far as the pronouncing anathemas and "*Ecclesiastical censure*" could deliver them, and all this incalculable mischief perpetrated to maintain an arbitrary claim to act *independent* of, and contrary to Law.'[2]

Above all, ministerial power in the chapel alienated those who directly shared their pastoral work, the class leaders and the local preachers. These functionaries, particularly the latter, did approximately what ministers did, and were men of some education who could appreciate and criticize ministerial claims, and indeed speak against them. They stood outside the property system of the chapel. While trustees and stewards were businessmen, appointed as such to do the secular work of chapel society, leaders and local preachers were men appointed because of their zeal and character to perform a more spiritual and elevated role. All officials were ministerial nominees. But since the demand for the difficult and irksome task of local preaching far exceeded the supply, the local preacher was indispensable and virtually irreplaceable.

The economy of Methodism placed most services in the hands of local preachers. But the Superintendent deployed them without consultation, merely informing them through publication of the quarterly 'plan' of appointments. A variety of appointments was available since circuits usually consisted of a few large and prosperous central chapels and many small, outlying chapels, and morning service was far less important and well-attended than evening service. Local preachers were almost invariably planned for the largest chapels only

---

[1] James Stacey, *A Prince in Israel, or, Sketches of the Life of John Ridgway, Esq.*, London, 1862, p. 99; James Douglas, *Methodism Condemned, or, Priestcraft Detected*, Newcastle, 1814, p. 5.

[2] *Report of a Meeting . . . at the Tabernacle, Hull . . .*, p. 5; Robert Eckett, *Letter Addressed to the Rev. John Gaulter*, London, 1828, p. 6.

in the morning. Usually, and virtually always at night, they preached in small and remote country chapels. This encouraged some local preachers to regard themselves as drudges.

In their eyes 'the payed preachers' had become 'fine gentlemen'. They assumed airs of superiority such as 'the exclusive right to administer the Lord's Supper'. They excluded the local preachers from their councils, above all from Conference; and they adopted titles denied to the local preachers: 'when their names are published, the title *Revd* is attached to it; while on the same bill, a local preacher, who may be equally popular, is simply and consistently plain Mr.' Not surprisingly, some local preachers became convinced that they were 'often treated with as much contempt' by ministers 'as a wealthy pluralist in the Establishment shows to a poor curate.'[1]

In 1834–5, local preachers led lay resistance to ministerial claims, especially to the proposal to widen the gap between local and travelling preachers by providing college education to the latter. In the 1840s and 1850s, dissidents hoped, and Buntingites feared, much from the formation of the Local Preachers' Mutual Aid Association. The delegates who gathered in Albion Street Chapel, London, in March 1850 to organize the Wesleyan Reformers, were drawn to a large extent from local preachers. Many delegates were both 'pastoral' officials – leaders or local preachers – and 'business' officials – stewards or trustees. But nearly half the delegates were purely or mainly 'pastoral' officials, while less than a quarter were purely or mainly 'business' officials. Strong opposition to ministerial power in the chapel came from private members and from all ranks of officials. But this opposition was largely expressed and led by class leaders and local preachers who constituted an unofficial 'shadow' ministry in the chapel, ready to seize power and form a new ministry, and indeed new denominations.[2]

[1] An Old Local Preacher, *Thoughts on the Case of the Local Preachers in the Methodist Connexion*, Bristol, 1820, *passim*; *Lay Preaching Defended. A Few Plain Remarks for the Consideration of the People Called Methodists, Occasioned by the Conduct of Mr Charles Atmore, Superintendent of the London East Circuit, towards the Community Preachers*, London, 1820, pp. 6, 9; *A Catechism for Wesleyan Methodists Particularly for Methodist Class Leaders and Local Preachers; Wherein the Various Points at Issue Between the Conference and the People Are Taken Up and Discussed in Familiar Dialogue*, Liverpool, 1834, p. 7.

[2] *An Apology for those Wesleyan Methodists Who Dissent from the Conference Interpretation of the Law of Expulsion*, London, 1836, p. 41; Dyson, *op. cit.*, p. 158; *Wesleyan Delegate Takings: or Short Sketches of Personal and Intellectual Character, as Exhibited in the Wesleyan Delegate Meeting Held in Albion Street Chapel, London, on the 12th, 13th, 14th and 15th March, 1850, by Some of Them. Together with an Exposition and Defence of the Resolutions, Passed at That Meeting*, Manchester, 1850, pp. 178 ff.

## Offshoots and Secessions

These new denominations have been divided into 'offshoots': Band Room Methodists, Primitive Methodists, Bible Christians, Tent Methodists, Arminian Methodists; and 'secessions': Methodist New Connexion, Protestant Methodists, Wesleyan Methodist Association, and 'Wesleyan Reformers' (see Figure One).[1] The former generally

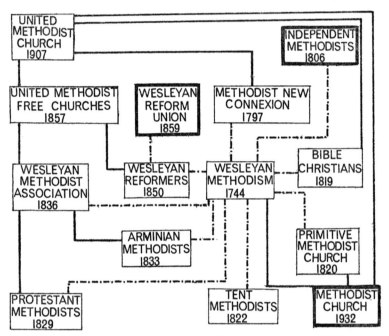

FIGURE ONE. *Major Divisions and Unions of British Methodism.*
*Note:* 1. Dotted lines indicate divisions; unbroken lines indicate unions.
2. Heavy lines indicate extant Methodist denominations.
3. Dates refer to the first Conference or comparable body.

materialized quicker than the latter; they were 'revivalist' in emphasis rather than 'constitutionalist'; and they developed a mass following round a very few ex-Wesleyans, unlike 'secessions', which were almost entirely composed of ex-Wesleyans, and did little recruiting in the outside world.

Other, less widely recognized, differences existed. 'Secessions' developed through extensive and prolonged propaganda on major

[1] e.g. F. W. Bourne, *The Bible Christians: Their Origin and History, 1815–1900*, London, 1905, p. 25.

denominational issues, involving constitutional–ecclesiastical quest-ions, especially as raised by Buntingite excesses. But even at its most successful, this propaganda needed local chapel grievances to cause mass divisions in Wesleyanism; and, when such grievances were available, local concerns tended to predominate over national and in effect, lay concerns over ministerial. 'Secession' denominations derived most of their strength from conflicts between officials and ministers.

'Offshoots' needed comparatively little propaganda, for they arose out of more immediately comprehensible issues. While 'secessions' used–though usually only briefly–ministerial leadership, but were essentially lay official movements, 'offshoots', using lay official leader-ship, were essentially movements of the lay membership. Hence while 'secessions' were especially concerned with those constitutional issues which interested officials, 'offshoots' were concerned more with matters of evangelism and revivalism which interested members.

'Offshoot' denominations were usually highly localized in origin. In most cases they arose from lay dissatisfaction with the Wesleyan hierarchy's feeble evangelism and distrust of revivalism. Hugh Bourne (1772–1852), founder of Primitive Methodism, declared, 'I never knew a Burslem circuit travelling preacher perform what Mr. Wesley calls "field-preaching" all the time I was a member. . . . This then was and is modern, not primitive Methodism, and I think there is a broad difference between the two.' John Pyer (1790–1859), the Tent Methodist, wrote in 1818, 'When I contrast Mr. Wesley's journals with the present apathy of preachers and people, I am pained exceedingly.'[1]

Such reactions to the respectable and unadventurous Wesleyanism of the early nineteenth century led to division when some relatively prosperous and determined lay leader was able to articulate dis-content. Most of the leaders of 'offshoots' were men of property. Hugh Bourne was a carpenter of sufficient means to build chapels, employ a missionary, and later to run a press. William O'Bryan (1778–1868), founder of the Bible Christians, had a farm which enabled him to spend 'hundreds of pounds in his efforts to extend Methodism'. George Pocock, founder of the Tent Methodists, financed the movement for several years, employed one or more missionaries, and built a chapel a year for seven years, at least one of

[1] H. B. Kendall, *The Origin and History of the Primitive Methodist Church*, London, 1909, vol. 1, p. 39; K. P. Russell, *Memoirs of the Rev. John Pyer*, London, 1865, p. 50.

which remained his private property for nearly a quarter of a century.[1]

Various misconceptions surround the history of the 'offshoot' denominations. Wesleyan authorities are often condemned for rigidity in dealing with evangelistic laymen. They were, said F. W. Bourne, 'blind . . . harsh and violent'.[2] In fact they were peculiarly tardy in acting against local revivalist leaders who ran their own denominations side by side with Wesleyan Methodism. Mr. Broadhurst led a group which, eager 'to assume the name of *Revivalists*', conducted large, enthusiastic and irregular band meetings in North Street, Manchester. Trouble came to a head in 1803, but Broadhurst and his followers remained Wesleyans until Bunting's arrival in Manchester in 1805. Bunting condemned the effect of 'promiscuous admission' of persons to band meetings. Broadhurst and others were expelled, to form the Band Room Methodists, who survived at least till 1821.[3]

O'Bryan began his evangelistic work in 1801. By 1810, he had established his own preaching places in five or more Cornish villages. He was expelled for these irregularities, but later readmitted. In 1814 he recommenced his personal itinerancy and was again and finally expelled. He now had twenty preaching places of his own. He extended his activities into Devon, and here, a characteristic element in the development of 'offshoots', he joined with an entirely separate group, led by James Thorne (1795–1872), a farmer of Shebbear. In 1815, these two groups formed the Bible Christian Connexion, in which they coexisted uneasily until 1829.[4]

George Pocock began the tent mission at Whitchurch near Bristol in April 1814. Services were conducted in Somerset, Gloucestershire and Berkshire. By 1820, in addition to the tent, Pocock's group had eight chapels. He recruited the services of John Pyer, with whom he eventually quarrelled, as O'Bryan and Thorne later quarrelled with each other. Pocock's circular letter of 1819, 'which invited Christians

[1] John Petty, *The History of the Primitive Methodist Connexion*, London, 1864, p. 10; H. B. Kendall, *The History of the Primitive Methodist Church*, London, 1919, p. 14; F. W. Bourne, *op. cit.*, pp. 18, 20; George Eayrs, *Wesley and Kingswood and Its Free Churches*, Bristol, 1911, pp. 215–16; Russell, *op. cit.*, p. 56; George Pocock, *A Statement of Facts Connected with the Ejectment of Certain Ministers from the Society of the Wesleyan Methodists in the City of Bristol, in February and March, 1820*, Bristol, 1820, *passim*.

[2] Bourne, *op. cit.*, p. 19.

[3] *A Statement of Facts and Observations Relative to the Late Separation from the Methodist Society in Manchester; Affectionately Addressed to the Members of That Body, by Their Preachers and Leaders*, Manchester, 1806, pp. 5–8, 10, 12, 18, 24.

[4] Bourne, *op. cit.*, pp. 13–23.

of all denominations to come up to the help of the Lord', and the employment of Pyer as full-time missionary in that year, indicated a new stage in the movement, which the local Wesleyan authorities could scarcely ignore. Pocock declined to put the tents 'under the direction of the Superintendents of those circuits where they might happen to be used', and various leaders of the movement were expelled in early 1820. The Tent Methodists lasted as a separate denomination about five years.[1]

The most important, largest and most complex of these developments was the emergence of the Primitive Methodist Connexion. After 1800, Hugh Bourne was active in north Staffordshire, and seems to have built and run a 'revivalist' Wesleyan chapel at Harriseahead. Bourne was interested in Quakerism, and knew Peter Phillips, the 'Quaker Methodist' leader of the Independent Methodists, a strange congeries of diverse chapels, established in 1806. Bourne and Phillips befriended Lorenzo Dow, an American, who conducted the evangelistic 'Camp Meetings' already popular in America. On 31 May 1807, Bourne conducted a Camp Meeting on Mow Cop. The Wesleyan Conference, with its characteristic distrust of 'fanaticism and rant', soon prohibited any more. In June 1808, after several infringements, Bourne was expelled, because he had 'set up other than the ordinary worship'.[2]

A year later, Bourne employed as a preacher James Crawfoot, leader of the Magic Methodists, a small group specializing in trances. Later he made a second alliance. William Clowes, who had been slightly associated with Harriseahead and with the camp meetings, was expelled in 1810 for irregular evangelism, and shortly afterwards became paid evangelist for a group known as Clowesites, who opened their first chapel in July 1811. Two months before, the followers of Bourne and those of Clowes had united; and in February 1812 they adopted the name 'Primitive Methodists'. The Magic Methodists had little influence on the new denomination, but the differences and conflicts between Bourne and Clowes persisted into the 1830s.[3]

'Offshoots' from Wesleyanism were alliances of evangelistic laymen who reacted against the apathy and formality of contemporary Wesleyanism as they saw it. Rejecting the hierarchy's restrained evangelism and aspirations for a more ecclesiastical Methodism, they salved their consciences by opting out of Wesleyan chapel society and,

[1] Pocock, *op. cit.*, pp. 3–4, etc.; Russell, *op. cit.*, *passim.*
[2] Kendall, *op. cit.*, pp. 11–29.
[3] *loc. cit.*; John T. Wilkinson, *William Clowes*, London, 1951, pp. 88–100.

simultaneously, out of the current rise in the educational and social standards of Wesleyanism. Only two of these denominations, the Bible Christians and the Primitive Methodists, survived for any great length of time. As is shown later, 'offshoots' largely recruited from poorer sections of the population than Wesleyans touched. They were more sectarian in character, adopting conservative positions on dress and morals and even, for some time, their own severe and abbreviated hairstyle. Throughout their separate existence, their denominational life was more deferential and less various than that of Wesleyanism. But it was considerably more fervent. The transports and 'gymnastic exercises' of the band meetings of Arminian and Band Room Methodists, of the tents, of the camp meetings, and of the interminable 'protracted meetings' which the Primitive Methodists later introduced, found few parallels in contemporary Wesleyanism outside Cornwall. Although by the end of the nineteenth century the Bible Christians and Primitive Methodists had largely abandoned these revivalistic activities, both denominations proved very successful. In 1901, more than a quarter of British Methodists adhered to one or other of them.

*Methodist Reform*

'Secessions' from Wesleyanism, seeking some kind of 'Methodist reform', began with the formation of the Methodist New Connexion in 1797. When Wesley died, many members and officials wanted formal recognition of Wesleyanism as a dissenting body entirely separate from the Church of England, administering its own sacraments, and reformed in constitution to provide lay delegation in Conference and much greater lay power in the chapel. Coke led resistance to these changes. They were championed by Alexander Kilham (1762–99), a travelling preacher who wanted a Wesleyanism which administered its own sacraments, and gave parity of denominational power to ministers and laymen.[1]

Kilham was assisted by general unrest in Wesleyanism which briefly led to unofficial conventions of lay delegates preceding Conference. Kilham sought the allegiance of the developing Methodist public in ways which set the pattern for the leadership of reform movements in Wesleyanism. He provided lay and official dissidents with the prestige and direction of ministerial leadership. He produced a series of circulars and pamphlets, and, for a time, a paper, the

---

[1] *Life of the Rev. Alexander Kilham . . ., One of the Founders of the Methodist New Connexion in the Year 1797. Including a Full Account of the Disputes Which Occasioned the Separation*, London, 1838, *passim*.

*Methodist Monitor.* After his expulsion he visited many places, especially in the north, speaking against Conference.

Thirty years later, a new generation of reformers were urged, 'In your respective Circuits spread information as widely as possible.'[1] But Kilham understood the need for propaganda as well as his successors. Reform movements required a conjunction between lay grievances against ministers, and conflict inside the hierarchy itself. Propaganda seeking to effect this conjunction was usually the work of ministers, who had the facilities and the education to produce it. Such propaganda, while appealing to localized lay dissidence, had to be respectable enough to justify action against the hierarchy, and generalized enough to merge grievances of a local and personalized nature into a conflict on the denominational level against the hierarchy as a whole.

Kilham appealed to the rights of Englishmen, and the doctrines of Protestantism. He linked his constitutional demands with specifically religious reforms, although while later reformers called for more revivalism, Kilham called for more sacraments. His incipient democracy and his concern with sacraments have perhaps impressed historians too much. The impetus of the first division of Methodism, as of later reform agitation, was lay demand for control of chapel society. 'Who can deny,' asked a meeting of laymen in 1796, 'that we are a society in which the people have no voice? in which they are not permitted to deliberate on the choice of their own officers, formation of their own laws, or distribution of their own property?'[2]

Despite Kilham's success in mobilizing Methodist opinion, the hierarchy largely succeeded in dividing and neutralizing opposition. The New Connexion was formed in 1797. Kilham died in 1799, and the Rev. William Thom subsequently led the new denomination. When members of the denomination conversed, a critic noted, 'the subject would generally be the excellency of the New Connexion system of Church government over that of the Old Connexion, or accounts of some additions to the body from the Old Connexion'.[3] But the separate denominational existence which enabled the New Connexion to apply the 'excellency' of reformed Methodist principles, also concluded the Kilhamite attempt to establish this 'excellency' inside Wesleyanism. Perhaps during Thom's regime, and certainly as he was displaced by younger and bolder men, New Connexionists

[1] *An Address to the Methodist Societies*, London, 1835, p. 3.
[2] *Life of the Rev. Alexander Kilham*, p. 246.
[3] J. T. Barker (ed.), *Life of Joseph Barker, Written by Himself*, London, 1880, p. 109.

tried to offset the disadvantage of their speedy expulsion from Wesleyanism by actively proselytizing that denomination with New Connexion propaganda.

During times of agitation in Wesleyanism, the New Connexion Book Room's output increased by 25–50 per cent, and a good deal of unofficial and anonymous pamphleteering accompanied official publications. When the Manchester Band Room controversy broke out in 1806, a New Connexion pamphlet, called *A New Pair of Scales,* promptly appeared. Its aim, a Wesleyan claimed, was '*to draw the old Methodists into the New Connexion*'. An anti-hierarchical and pro-New Connexion pamphlet published by a Manchester Wesleyan in 1815 was taken up by the New Connexion, and republished in Glasgow in 1816 for some reason, and in Bristol in 1820, to coincide with the Tent Methodist controversy there. The Leeds Organ Case of 1827–9 and the formation of the Protestant Methodists provided another opportunity for New Connexion propaganda. When conflict broke out over the Wesleyan Theological Institution, New Connexion pamphleteers were particularly active. Wesleyanism was denounced as 'the absolutism of Spain under the atrocious Ferdinand'. The New Connexion constitution was advertised: 'It is Scriptural, it is rational, it is beneficial'; and dissidents were warned not to think 'of adding another to the many sections of Methodist churches . . . but resolve to unite yourselves to that community which is most congenial with your principles', i.e. the Methodist New Connexion.[1]

But the most popular piece of New Connexion pamphleteering was *Wesley's Ghost*, published in Manchester in 1846. This started a

---

[1] William Baggaly, *A Digest of the Minutes, Institutions, Polity, Doctrines, Ordinances and Literature of the Methodist New Connexion*, London, 1862, pp. 127–30; Philalethes, *False Balances Detected; or, A Reply to a Pamphlet Entitled 'A New Pair of Scales, in Which Facts are Weighed'*, Manchester, 1806, p. 9; *An Exposition of the Proceedings of the Old Methodist Conference, with Reflections on the Nature and Tendency of Its System of Government; Illustrated by Some of Its Enactments. By A Member of the Old Methodist Society*, Glasgow, 1816, p. 2; cp. *An Exposition . . .*, Bristol, 1820; *A Letter to the Rev. Isaac Keeling, in Reply to His Letter Addressed to the Editors of the Leeds Mercury But Most Particularly in Reference to His Reflection on the Methodist New Connexion. By a Member of That Community*, Leeds, 1827, *passim*; T. Allin, *Letters to the Rev. John Maclean, Containing an Exposition of the Government of Wesleyan Methodism, with Practical Illustrations of Its Effects*, London, 1835, p. 55; James Leach, *Address, Delivered after Laying the Foundation Stone of a New Chapel in Great Dover Road, Southwark, on Monday, July 7th, 1834, for the Methodist New or Representative Connexion*, London, 1834, p. 16; A Lover of Methodism, of Liberty and Truth, *To the Delegates Representing the Wesleyan Methodist Association, Assembled in Manchester in Easter Week, 1835*, Manchester, 1835, p. 8.

'ghost' literature, usually provided with a fine inky illustration of the apparition denouncing the wickedness and decadence of Buntingite Wesleyanism. No overt New Connexion propaganda appeared in *Wesley's Ghost*–the only indication of its provenance being that it was printed and published by two firms who specialized in New Connexion business–and, rather like an over-clever advertising campaign, *Wesley's Ghost* simply developed an autonomous, and, from the New Connexion viewpoint, not very useful life of its own.[1]

New Connexion propaganda was perhaps most useful to dissident Wesleyan laymen in the years after 1797 when they were still recovering from Kilham's defeat. Local agitation for reform accompanied the great Cornish revival of 1813–14. Dissidents, centred on Ladock Chapel in the Truro Circuit, vainly asked, 'are not the people belonging to the chapels sufficient to manage their own concerns without the interference of the Preachers?'[2] London was the scene of later difficulties, in which, as in the Band Room controversy, Bunting was involved. A revival in the London West Circuit in 1816–17 led to conflicts between laymen and ministers, who 'endeavoured to put a stop to such a work of God, and to "crush it"'. Following an argument over a set of candlesticks, a leading layman was expelled. Suppression of an irregular order of 'community preachers' in the London East Circuit in 1820, caused considerable ill feeling.[3]

Revivalist zeal and strong local grievances combined in both Cornwall and London, but lacked ministerial leadership and the ideology it could provide. For a while the Rev. Daniel Isaac seemed likely to supply both. In 1815, he published his book *Ecclesiastical Claims* which attacked episcopacy and, implicitly, Buntingism. Bunting had it censured in Conference. Isaac replied with a pamphlet denouncing

[1] Vetus, *Wesley's Ghost*, Manchester, 1846.

[2] John Riles, *An Address to the Methodist Societies, Recommending the Proper Settlement of Their Chapels, So as to Secure Them to Their Original Design; With a Reply to the Objections Made against This Mode of Settlement*, Truro, 1813, p. 7; *A Letter to Mr John Riles, Occasioned by His Late address to the Methodist Societies; Recommending the Proper Settlement of Their Chapels, so as to Secure Them to Their Original Design. To Which Is Added, A Short Address to the Methodists. By a Member of That Body*, Truro, 1814, *passim*; William Aver, *A Letter to a Member-of-That-Body, Containing Some Strictures on His Letter to Mr John Riles*, Penryn, 1814, p. 6.

[3] J. P. Fesenmeyer, *An Appeal to the Wesleyan Methodist Societies throughout the Kingdom, against Acts of Injustice and Oppression. Calculated to Extinguish a Revival of the Work of God in the London West Circuit. Also a Defence of Revivals in General, and That Revival in Particular: with Observations on the Alarming Division and Rent in Ireland, Where Six and Twenty Chapels Have Been Closed against the Travelling Preachers. In a Letter to Jos. Butterworth, Esq., M.P.*, London, 1817, p. 43; *Lay Preaching Defended, passim.*

'Messrs Bunting and Co., and . . . their manner of doing business in Conference'. But Isaac declined to become Kilham's successor, and the danger of secession passed.[1]

The danger could not be eliminated. In 1803, the Rev. William Bramwell was stationed in Leeds. He became 'the nucleus and head of an ungovernable Revivalist party'. When he left the circuit, his friend, disciple and biographer, Mr. James Sigston, a schoolmaster, became leader of the revivalist *'imperium in imperio'*. Sigston's power dismayed Bunting. He determined to 'teach Leeds a lesson'. The opportunity came in 1827, when the Leeds district meeting decided against the installation of an organ, which was opposed by many of the Leeds trustees. Conference illegally overruled the district meeting. Matthew Johnston, a supporter of Sigston, organized an opposition meeting of local preachers. Sigston, who, like other evangelistic laymen, had forsaken circuit affairs 'for some years', later appeared as leader of the opposition. The Superintendent was Edmund Grindrod, a creature of Bunting's. He called a packed Buntingite special district meeting to try the culprits. The illegality of this meeting was compounded by the extraordinary appearance of Bunting himself as self-appointed 'Official Adviser to the President'. The desired expulsions and resignations followed. But this sensational display of tyranny – whose illegality Bunting frequently admitted – did far more than create the 3,000-strong Protestant Methodist denomination. It showed that Conference refused to accept the constitution, and was determined to attack both revivalism and the position of the laymen. Thirty years of comparative peace gave way to thirty years of hot and cold war.[2]

The immediate sequel to the Leeds Organ Case was the first Wesleyan reform paper since the *Methodist Monitor*. Mr. David Rowland of the Liverpool North Circuit organized a group of dissidents, dominated by two great concerns, 'the Leeds never-to-be-forgotten case', and the movement for parliamentary reform, whose principles they believed 'were applicable to ecclesiastical as well as to political institutions'. The refusal of the Superintendent of Liverpool North to pass resolutions on the Organ Case provided the occasion for anonymous publication by Rowland and Mr James Picton, in January 1830, of *The Circular to Wesleyan Methodists*.[3]

[1] Daniel Isaac, *Ecclesiastical Claims Investigated and the Liberty of the Pulpit Defended*, London, 1815; Daniel Isaac, *Remarks on a Minute of Conference*, Grantham, 1816, p. 2.    [2] Gregory, *op. cit.*, pp. 52–3, 55, 65–8, 72–3, 98.

[3] Baxter, *op. cit.*, pp. 209–10; J. Allanson Picton, *Sir James A. Picton*, London, 1891, pp. 130–1.

The *Circular*, a work, 'projected long before it actually commenced', ran fortnightly till the end of July 1833. In 1830, 1,700 copies were printed per issue, and about 220 sold. The *Circular* was quite widely available, except in southern and central agricultural counties. Bunting promptly came to Liverpool North as Superintendent in 1830, but he could neither expel Rowland nor stop the *Circular*, which survived Bunting's stay by nearly a year. The *Circular's* attacks on the hierarchy and advocacy of reform, marked a new stage in the reform movement.[1]

Sigston's revivalism and the reform ideology and propaganda of Liverpool were supplemented by a reformed theory of Methodist polity. This was the work of Robert Eckett (1797–1862), a Yorkshire stone-mason, who joined the London West Circuit, when Bunting was a minister there, about the time of the candlesticks affair. Eckett's views and personality symbolized nineteenth-century Methodism. In appearance he was:

'a man of low stature whose rotundity is pretty nearly equal to his height–whose eye speaks defiance to his antagonists–a man of . . . boundless self-reliance . . . with hair pointed in all directions but principally towards the zenith–with trousers halfway up his legs–coat half off his shoulders . . . his person anything but attractive, his manner aught but pleasing, and his voice . . . monotonous in a remarkable degree–his pronunciation often incorrect, though always measured and stately.'[2]

He may not have come into contact with the Leeds group before Sigston and Johnson came to London to proselytize local preachers in April 1828. But in July 1828, Eckett published a pamphlet on the Organ Case, and probably had a hand in several anonymous London pamphlets. Later he preached for the Protestant Methodists, and sat on the committee which drafted their Model Deed. By the end of 1830, he was also in touch with the Liverpool group.[3] Eckett's doctrine of 'circuit independence', which sought to combine the unity of Methodist Connexionalism with the chapel autonomy of Congrega-

[1] *Circular to Wesleyan Methodists*, 31 December 1830, p. 93; 30 April 1831, pp. 127–8; 31 December 1831, p. 191.

[2] Gregory, *op. cit.*, p. 98; Baxter, *op. cit.*, p. 439.

[3] Circular of the Rev. John Stephens, London, 7 May 1828; Eckett, *op. cit.*, *passim*; cp. *Remarks on the Resolutions of the Methodist Conference in 1828 and 1829, Relative to the Dissensions in the Society at Leeds, Addressed to the Members of the Methodist Connexion*, London, 1829; and *Defence of the Protestant Methodists against the Calumnious Charges of Mr Daniel Isaac*, London, 1830; Baxter, *op. cit.*, pp. 347–8; *Circular to Wesleyan Methodists*, 31 December 1830, pp. 95–6.

tional independency, was the first and definitive theory of lay demands. Aggressive, self-educated, legalistic, politically liberal but not partisan, Eckett was the greatest lay leader in the divisions of Methodism. His skill, and later his ideas, dominated the first seventy years of the re-unification of Methodism.

But Sigston, Rowland and Eckett still lacked the ministerial leader-ship which Kilham had provided. The need was met in 1834. Dr. Samuel Warren, a leading younger minister, opposed Bunting's scheme for a Theological Institution. Some claimed Warren attacked it because 'others were nominated to be governors and teachers'. But the Institution could also be attacked as a scheme to give Buntingites jobs, which it did, and to indoctrinate ministerial candidates with Buntingite views, which it did less successfully. The Institute was 'anti-Methodistical', said Warren; and he claimed, 'This movement has not originated with our People but with some principal Preachers.'[1] Warren suddenly and unenthusiastically became the new Kilham.

The Lancashire laymen put up Warren as plaintiff in two un-successful Chancery suits against his exclusion from the Manchester pulpit. On 7 November 1834, they launched the Grand Central Association. Despite the Lancashire group's talk of the reform bill and the rights of Englishmen, they cared little for reform of their legislature, the Conference. They wanted the Institute stopped, the Organ Case disavowed, more lay power in the chapels and lay spectators in Conference–a large public gallery not adult manhood suffrage. The laymen freely conceded that 'Dr. Warren's case is not immediately connected with the principal objects of the Association.'[2] That body held public meetings and advocated withholding supplies from the ministers. As the Buntingites started a newspaper against the Association, the *Watchman*, the Association replied with a paper of their own, *The Watchman's Lantern*, edited by Picton. While the *Lantern* probably had a larger readership than the *Circular*, it was mainly confined to the north west and to Yorkshire, and its dis-tribution network was feeble.

But the Association did not remain long in the hands of the Lancashire laymen. Eckett appeared at its first Delegate Meeting, in Manchester, in April 1835, to advocate circuit independence. He was 'regarded as a Conference spy rather than as a hearty friend of

[1] Gregory, *op. cit.*, pp. 170–1.
[2] *At a Meeting Held This Day in Manchester of Trustees, Leaders, Local Preachers and Stewards of the Four Circuits; William Smith, Esq., of Reddish House in the Chair*, Manchester, 1834; *The Watchman's Lantern*, 8 April 1835, p. 179.

Reform, by many of the Delegates'. But he was soon expelled from Wesleyanism and began to accompany Warren on his speaking tours. With the assistance of the Protestant Methodists who soon joined the Association, and with that of other minority groups who joined later, such as the Independent Primitive Methodists of Scarborough, Eckett seized power in the Association. He stopped an attempt to unite with the New Connexion and drafted a circuit independence constitution for what was eventually known as the Wesleyan Methodist Association. Picton and Warren soon left; Eckett dominated the new denomination; and after fifteen years' struggle, Rowland followed his colleagues.[1]

The Association, like the New Connexion, took about 6 per cent of Wesleyan members. Methodist historiography persistently underestimates the extent of this secession, claiming it to number 'about a thousand'.[2] This figure simply represents net loss of membership during the period of the secession. In 1837, the Association numbered 21,000, and well over a thousand Wesleyans probably joined the New Connexion. But Wesleyanism was able to cover all but a fraction of these losses by vigorous recruiting, and the controversy stimulated nothing inside Wesleyanism but reaction in the Buntingite party, which now required a test or declaration of loyalty from the ministers.

The deficiencies of the reform movement during 1827–35 were largely met by the Rev. James Everett (1784–1872). Everett was 'superstitiously attached' to Wesley, regarding Buntingism as 'a manifest departure from his spirit'. He was virtually the first Methodist antiquarian, a bibliophile and a successful author of biographies. Like Sigston, Everett was greatly influenced by Bramwell. But Everett combined evangelistic zeal with an unusual gift for anonymous satire. He was deeply and increasingly contemptuous of the Buntingite regime; and his attitude to Conference, which he rarely attended, was expressed by a typical gesture in 1841. Charged with publishing satires on Bunting and many other ministers, he sent a letter to Conference, refusing to answer general and unsubstantiated charges, and bearing the seal of the Anti-Slavery Society, 'a negro in chains, with one knee upon the ground, the hands clasped, and the eyes imploringly turned to heaven, saying, "Am not I a Man and a Brother?"'[3]

[1] Picton, *op. cit.*, p. 133.
[2] Frank Baker, *A Charge to Keep*, London, 1954, p. 51; cp. J. Robinson Gregory, *A History of Methodism*, London, 1911, vol. 1, p. 267.
[3] Richard Chew, *James Everett: A Biography*, London, 1875, pp. 14, 15, 60–2, 191–4, 206, 220 ff, 328–33.

Most reformers feared the social pretensions of the Buntingites, their claims to education, their wealth and dress, their association with the lay aristocracy of Wesleyanism, their ecclesiastical claims. But Everett and his circle despised the hierarchy as vulgar and ignorant parvenus: they 'were all men raised from the lowest strata of society', who lacked 'early training and mixing in good society'. Everett was an even less promising leader for lay reformers than the superior Dr. Warren. Indeed as late as 1840, he described Kilham as a 'horsefly, which invariably passes over the sound part of the animal, and instinctively finds its way to a sore spot, upon which it feeds'.[1]

But a term of office in the Book Room, in 1822–3, hardened Everett's hostility to Bunting. Proximity to the Buntingite machine, bad pay and conditions, and probably the feeling that he was slighted by the Buntingites, led him to withdraw. Through poor health he became a supernumerary. This provided him with a small pension, and, far more important, enabled him to remain a minister outside circuit routine and circuit discipline. By 1831 Everett was complaining of Bunting's 'prejudices' against him. These prejudices were justified. Everett was already busily working against Bunting. The Wesleyan leader was very wary of Everett. In 1838, he persuaded Everett to accompany him on a holiday in the Lakes, presumably hoping to reconcile him, and perhaps even to offer him a leading position. The most notable incident the contemptuous Everett recorded of this curious expedition was that Bunting fell through a chair.[2]

After a short period as a bookseller in Sheffield, Everett wisely moved to Lancashire, then the centre of the reform movement. He set up his book shop and publishing firm in Manchester in 1825, the year of Rowland's first expulsion, and remained in business for nine years. When at last Everett appeared in Conference in 1834 to attend Warren's trial, Bunting seized the opportunity to get him out of Manchester and into circuit work by ending his supernumeraryship. Everett accepted this without much objection. Fear of a Warren–Everett–Rowland alliance in Lancashire was exaggerated. Everett, a publicist not a man of action, was not interested in playing a promi-

[1] Thomas Stanley, *Memoirs of Mr Robert Swan Stanley, Late Collector of Inland Revenue, Liverpool, the Alnwick Stanley Family, and a Few of Their Contemporaries*, London, 1878, p. 9; *Wesleyan Takings, Or Centenary Sketches of Ministerial Character; as Exhibited in the Wesleyan Connexion during the First Hundred Years of Its Existence*, London, 1840, p. 328.

[2] Chew, *op. cit.*, pp. 172–4, 191, 220–6; James Everett, *Notes and Memoranda of What Has Been Thought, Felt, Said, Sung and Done; and of Who and What Has Been Seen and Heard; Intermingled with Narratives, Descriptions, Criticisms*, vol. 3, p. 606 (Hartley Victoria College, Manchester); Chew, *op. cit.*, pp. 308–9.

nent part in the Theological Institution controversy. Later in 1834, he had a secret meeting with Warren but nothing came of this. Instead Everett wrote a pamphlet on the controversy, criticizing both sides, in secret even from 'those of my own views'. About the same time he began writing and publishing the *Wesleyan Takings*, a series of satires on Wesleyan ministers, later collected into one volume for the Wesleyan centenary in 1839. The 1841 Conference censured Everett for the *Takings*.[1]

The following year he became a supernumerary again, claiming that his health was too poor for circuit work. He did not re-open his business but began a great campaign against Bunting. Despite his alleged ill-health, he made extensive preaching tours. Between 1843 and 1848 he travelled 8,000 miles annually, twice as far as Wesley travelled in a year. No reformer was as well known or as respected by Wesleyans as Everett was by 1849. Mr. Joseph Swinburne of South Shields, declaring allegiance to Everett in September 1849, said he had heard Mr. Everett preach, and the sermon 'had brought tears to many cheeks as well as his'.[2] Like the abortive holiday in the Lakes, Bunting's failure to stop the farce of Everett's supernumeraryship indicates the Wesleyan leader's reluctance to force open conflict with his opponent.

The next stage in the campaign was to establish a reform newspaper. By the 1840s the reformers had learnt the lesson of the failure of the *Circular* and the *Lantern*. Unlike the flourishing *Watchman*, they were propaganda sheets rather than newspapers, containing only reform news and studies of ecclesiastical polity, undiluted by crimes, curiosities, market prices, and parliamentary intelligence. Two attempts at new style reform papers were made in the 1840s, the short-lived *Wesleyan Chronicle*, and the less specifically Liberal *Wesleyan and Christian Record*, with which the former amalgamated at the end of 1844. The *Wesleyan*, allegedly £1,000 in debt, ceased publication in December 1848, but restarted as the *Wesleyan Times* in January 1849. By 1852 it sold twice as many copies as the *Watchman*.[3]

[1] Chew, *op. cit.*, pp. 266–7; James Everett, '*Methodism As It Is*', *With Some of Its Antecedents, Its Branches and Disruptions; Including a Diary of the Campaign of 1849, Protracted during a Period of Seven Years; With a Special Reference to the Character, Power, Policy and Administration of the 'Master Mind' of John Wesley's Legislative Successor*, London, 1863, vol. 1, p. 135; Everett, *Notes and Memoranda*, vol. 3, pp. 635, 670, 675; Chew, *op. cit.*, pp. 332–3.

[2] Chew, *op. cit.*, pp. 350 ff; *Wesleyan Times*, 24 September 1849, p. 634.

[3] *Wesleyan and Christian Record*, 21 January 1846, p. 31; 26 October 1848, p. 4; 9 November 1848, p. 4; Everett, *Notes and Memoranda*, vol. 6, p. 1042; *W.T.*, 10 May 1852, p. 296.

Everett's part in this is obscure. His disingenuous diary states that he was engaged by 'Mr. Healey, proprietor of the *Wesleyan Record*' to write for the paper, on 23 December 1844. But Everett's own marked copy of the paper shows that he had been writing for it some time by then.[1] Despite the enigmatic vicissitudes of editorship and publication that the *Wesleyan* and the *Wesleyan Times* suffered, Everett was evidently central to the two papers. Both provided the facilities of a normal religious weekly and a fairly cautious critique of the hierarchy; as time went on, attacking their 'extravagant pretensions, claims and measures', with increasing force.[2]

But detailed and savage attack on the hierarchy was left to the *Fly Sheets*. The first appeared in 1844; it was reprinted in 1846, when a second appeared; a third followed in 1847, and a fourth in 1848. They were anonymous apart from the notice, 'By Order of the CORRESPONDING COMMITTEE for detecting, exposing and correcting Abuses. London, Manchester, Bristol, Birmingham, Leeds, Hull and Glasgow.' At first posted to ministers only, they were later reprinted and sold publicly. They were written either by Everett and his closest allies, or more probably by Everett alone. He refused to state whether he had written them or not, and it has not yet been established that he did. But there is no plausible alternative author; anonymity was virtually Everett's trademark; the style and approach is his; the *Fly Sheets* contain passages justifying Everett's career, highly unlikely to have been written by anyone else; and the section in Everett's diary on the *Fly Sheets* consists of pasted-over sheets and a short passage full of painstaking innuendoes.[3]

Secrecy and anonymity fascinated Everett: it demonstrated his own superiority; he gained a paradoxical notoriety; and he delighted in the confusion and uncertainty of the vulgar uninitiated. Anonymity also had a practical purpose. To the rank and file Everett was the zealous evangelist. Many who heard his sermons no doubt also read his anti-Conference editorials of the forties. But it assisted his reputation for piety that they should not immediately associate the two. It was even more important to separate the image of Everett the evangelist and Everett the author of the *Fly Sheets*.

The strength of the *Fly Sheets* is their remarkably skilful analysis of the Buntingite system, much of which was taken from the published

[1] Everett, *op. cit.*, vol. 4, p. 934; *Wesleyan*, 19 December 1844, pp. 264–5 (Hartley Victoria College copy).

[2] *Wesleyan*, 15 January 1845, p. 40.

[3] Everett, *op. cit.*, vol. 6, pp. 984–6.

*Minutes*, and was unexceptionable to anyone but Buntingites. But a great deal of the pamphlets consisted of well-authenticated but scandalous accusations against Bunting and his followers.[1] All this was very useful in arousing lay feelings against the hierarchy, but it did little for Everett's reputation for holiness. It was useful, and remained useful for years, for Everett's followers to be able to take refuge in doubt as to the authorship of the *Fly Sheets*.

By 1846 the *Fly Sheets* terrified Bunting and his followers. The ageing Wesleyan leader had other problems. The New Connexion pamphlet, *Wesley's Ghost*, encouraged a spate of imitations, particularly in the West Riding. Congregationalists, who had long disliked the more dynamic, centralized, and condescending Wesleyans, added their contribution. In 1847, the Congregational *Christian World* published an article strongly attacking Buntingism. This piece, later discovered to be the work of a Wesleyan layman, Bailey Hillyard, caused great dismay and necessitated a flow of defensive Buntingite pamphleteering.[2]

The temperance movement also assisted. James Buckle exposed to the readers of the *London Temperance Intelligencer* the fact that the newly built Centenary Hall, home of Bunting's Missionary Society, headquarters of his party, monument to the piety and generosity of Wesleyan laymen, and symbol, to opponents, of Buntingite extravagance and ostentation, let out its cellars as a wine and spirits vault. The Rev. Elijah Hoole, a junior Missionary Society official, attempted to denounce Buckle's impudence; he prayed, he said, 'that God may give you repentance of this sin'. But the scandal, publicized by the *Wesleyan*, severely damaged the Buntingite reputation, especially since Wesley condemned 'all who sell' 'spirituous liquors' as 'poisoners general' who drive men 'to hell, like sheep'.[3]

What Bunting called 'the annoyances arising from teetotalism' multiplied. A group of teetotal Wesleyans in West Cornwall seceded

[1] *All the Numbers of the 'Fly Sheets', Now First Reprinted in One Pamphlet*, London, 1849, pp. 8, 27–8, 33, 50.

[2] Gregory, *op. cit.*, pp. 394–5; Scrutator, *Wesley's Ghost and Whitfield's Apparition*, London, 1846; new or pirated edition, London, 1847; Scrutator, *The Third Appearance of Wesley's Ghost*, London, 1849; Adelphos, *Wesley!! Or the Midnight Visitor. A Tract for All Methodists*, London, 1847; Bailey Hillyard, *Numerical Statistics of Wesleyan Methodism for the United Kingdom of Great Britain and Ireland for the Last Eighty Years*, London, 1849, p. 3.

[3] James Buckle, *The Wesleyan Centenary Hall Spirit Vaults Exposed, and the Temperance Principles of John Wesley Defended against the Practical Opposition of the Methodist Conference and Missionary Committee*, London, n.d., p. 11; John Wesley, *Sermons on Several Occasions*, London, 1956, p. 581; *Wesleyan*, 29 October, 1845, p. 704.

to form a separate body which later united with the Association. A prolonged controversy on teetotalism in Bristol in 1841–2 coincided with another in south Lincolnshire. The latter was perhaps less obvious, for Lincolnshire and Cambridgeshire were now in open revolt against the hierarchy.[1]

The evangelistic campaigns of James Caughey, the American Evangelist caused a further crisis. The Buntingites deeply distrusted Caughey and finally excluded him from Wesleyan chapels. His many lay supporters 'looked at the blow struck against him as levelled against revivalism as much as against irregularity and encroachment'. Four sermons by Caughey sold 11,000 copies among Methodists.[2]

Finally, the forties saw the long delayed organization of a local preachers' benevolent society. In 1833, a Buntingite minister commented of one such scheme, 'Fair on the face but designed to effect a powerful organization of the Local Preachers for other and different purposes.' The *Wesleyan*, and later the *Wesleyan Times*, strongly advocated organization. The Local Preachers' Mutual Aid Association was established in October 1849. Despite close personal connections, reformers never took over the L.P.M.A.A. But this possibility dismayed Buntingites in the forties.[3]

Bunting's regime was toppling. Bunting himself was now 'haunted by an almost morbid feeling' that his powers were declining. At the Conference of 1844, the year of the *Wesleyan*, the *Wesleyan Chronicle*, and the first *Fly Sheet*, 'the tide perceptibly began to turn'. Bunting though President found Conference so troublesome that at one point he tried to leave the chair and bring proceedings to a premature close. Bunting had thrown tantrums before, but not in despair. In 1845,

[1] Gregory, *op. cit.*, pp. 318–19; *A Vindication of the Case of the Tee-Total Wesleyan Methodists of St Ives, Cornwall; with an Incidental Exposure of the Domination of the Wesleyan Priesthood*, Penzance, 1842; *Teetotalism Defended, and Freed From the Misrepresentations of Its Opponents in a Letter to the Rev. Jacob Stanley. By a Member of the Bristol North Circuit*, Bristol, 1841; John Field Smyth, *op. cit.*, pp. 5–6; William Wright, *The Practice of Wesleyan Priests a Violation of Christ's Precepts; or, a Few Words of Explication Relative to the Unscriptural Treatment of Messrs Wright and Christian of Stamford, from Mr B. Gartside, Wesleyan Superintendent*, London, 1842, p. 6; T. E. Howell, *Odd Fellowship and Wesleyan Methodism*, London, 1841.

[2] William B. Carter, *The Case Tested: Being an Inquiry into the Character and Labours of the Rev. James Caughey; and the Action of the British Wesleyan Conference Thereon*, London, 1847, p. 36; *A Voice from America, or, Four Sermons, Preached by the Rev. J. Caughey, the Great American Revivalist, by a Manchester Minister*, Manchester, 1848.

[3] *Rules of the Wesleyan Methodist Local Preachers' Friendly Society*, Manchester, 1853, cover (Methodist Archives copy); *Wesleyan*, 3 October 1844, p. 87; *Wesleyan Times*, 19 June 1849; p. 371; 8 October 1849, pp. 677–8.

Conference elected Jacob Stanley, a 'liberal' minister as President. Reformers suddenly began to think of ousting the Buntingites by electing anti-Buntingite presidents who would reconstruct the committees and thus destroy the Buntingite machine from within. In 1846, the *Wesleyan* advocated William Atherton as presidential candidate. Atherton, not a partisan Buntingite, but scarcely a reformer, easily defeated the 'official' Buntingite candidate, Thomas Jackson. The *Wesleyan* proclaimed the end of the 'cycle in which the Presidential office moved amongst a few'.[1]

Samuel Jackson, the 'anti-Buntingite' candidate in 1847, was a very right-wing minister whose virtue in the eyes of his supporters was to be hated by Bunting. The *Wesleyan* was delighted at Jackson's success. But he was not the man to dismantle Bunting's system. He was separated from the Buntingites by personalities, not policy. As President he did nothing to stop the introduction by George Osborn, a leading younger Buntingite, of a test on the *Fly Sheets*. During Conference 650 ministers signed the test, condemning the pamphlets and denying any share in their production. This development should have disturbed reformers: in 1834–5 such enquiries had accompanied mass expulsions. But their mood was expressed by the Rev. William Griffith when he declared, 'the Bunting party is losing its power– they . . . are very sore about it'.[2]

Reformers optimistically ran Joseph Fowler for president in 1848. Fowler was a liberal suspect enough for Bunting to charge him with writing the *Fly Sheets*. Had Fowler been elected, it would have been a triumph second only to electing Everett. Buntingites rallied and Fowler was defeated. Reformers remained sanguine. 'Struggle . . . as they may, the men who have ruled the Conference . . . must finally yield,' the *Wesleyan* announced.[3]

But the Buntingites could still command majorities in Conference and they were now desperate to recover their former power. Everett, openly accused of writing the *Fly Sheets*, still refused to sign Osborn's test. Although Bunting remained markedly reluctant to clash with Everett, Bunting's followers were eager for this final confrontation. Evidently, by July 1849, 'the Cabinet' had determined to force a crisis. In the words of a minor Buntingite, 'I think the "Fly Sheet" business will be ended this Conference . . . it is intended to summon

[1] Gregory, *op. cit.*, pp. 281, 375–6, 405–6, 409–10, 420; *Wesleyan*, 15 July 1846, p. 338; 26 August 1846, p. 410.
[2] *Wesleyan*, 4 August 1847, p. 4; Richard Chew, *William Griffith: Memorials and Letters*, London, 1885, p. 28.
[3] *Wesleyan*, 29 June 1848, p. 4; 17 August 1848, p. 4.

the suspected offenders to Conference'. They would be asked to sign the test, 'and if they refuse they will have discipline inflicted upon them for contumacy of our Church Court'. The *Wesleyan Times* was still mainly concerned with promoting Fowler: reformers probably thought an attack on Everett would scarcely be anything more serious than the censure he received for the *Takings* in 1841.[1]

But Fowler suddenly fell ill and withdrew. Thomas Jackson was at last elected President, and 'the dominant party' were 'literally delirious with their unexpected triumph'. Any doubts about the expediency of forcing Everett to take the test were now dispelled. He was summoned to Conference. The Secretary said, 'Mr. Everett was strongly suspected of being the author of the *Fly Sheets*.' Everett replied, 'If I am the most suspected, then there must be the most evidence against me; produce it.' There was no evidence. Everett refused the test. Samuel Jackson moved and John Rattenbury seconded his expulsion. There were two dissentients only, presumably Samuel Dunn and William Griffith, who were subsequently expelled, for contributing to the anti-Buntingite press. The *Wesleyan Times* proclaimed,

'The Conference is the most finished form of *absoluteism* [sic] upon earth. It *crushes*, it annihilates everything like opposition; it exults in its own giant strength; it is regardless of the feeling and character of all who *attempt* resistance–I say who attempt resistance–for successful resistance there is none! God only know the end.'[2]

The expulsion of the three was the declaration of the last and greatest war in Methodism. The violence of these wars was the cause of their participants' hilarity. The search for perfection was postponed. It was no longer necessary to suffer priestly tyranny in Christian silence. When David Rowland spoke in Sheffield he

'entertained the audience with an account of his expulsion from the Society, and concluded by calling on the Rev. Samuel Jackson, to come forward, if he was present, and confront him. This was responded to by a large portion of the assembly, with cries of bravo, bravo; others bawled out–Jackson is not here, but Anderson is; when immediately a furious cry broke forth from different parts of the chapel–'Down with him!' 'Out with him!' and similar significant expressions.'[3]

[1] Samuel Dunn, *Recollections of Thomas Jackson and His Acts*, London, 1873, p. 21; Chew, *Griffith*, p. 61.
[2] Gregory, *op. cit.*, pp. 394–5, 437, 451–2, 456; *Wesleyan Times*, 1 August 1849, p. 491; 8 August 1849, p. 517.
[3] *Watchman*, 12 August 1835, p. 253.

Reform meetings had the same spirit and served the same ends in the 1830s and the 1850s. Narratives of trials and expulsions, with their interminable debates on the nuances of Methodist law, their revelation of ministerial atrocities, their demonstration of the courage and wits of the solitary layman fighting for his Methodist life, fascinated the reformers. In 1849, the secular press joined in. *The Times* attacked the Conference at length; its proceedings were 'a gross outrage on all our old English principles of fair play'. The persistent disgruntled anticlericalism in English life could be expressed at length and without restraint.[1]

Thus while the reform movement needed an alliance of laymen and ministers, the outbreak of 'agitation' necessarily destroyed this alliance. Just as the evangelistic 'offshoots' rejected the hierarchy and established a new, highly informal ministry of their own, the constitutionalist 'secessions' soon dismissed or lost their ministerial leaders. Warren had lasted a mere three years as leader of the Associationists, and became a clergyman of the Church of England. Everett survived a good deal longer, but his relationship with the Reformers was one of pure convenience. Everett would not lead the mass movement his propaganda had inspired. Leadership passed almost immediately after the Conference of 1849 into the hands of laymen, notably Joseph Chipchase, Hildreth Kay, and William Cozens-Hardy.

When the Reformers met at Albion Street Chapel, London, in March 1850, said Everett, in a revealing phrase, 'the lay Delegates enunciated their principles and opinions'. He demonstrated his dissociation from the delegates by publishing a series of satirical sketches of them. Lay leaders recognized their detachment from their ministerial figureheads. 'Dr. Warren's case is not immediately connected with the principal objects of the Association,' the Liverpool group had announced. When Chipchase discussed the three in 1851, he observed,

'The reform movement owed much to the fact of their expulsion—not that the principles which had led to recent developments of Christian feeling did not exist before, but because the expulsion of those three men had afforded the opportunity of manifesting, in a striking and effectual manner, the sentiments and opinions of the whole Connexion.'

The internal conflicts of the hierarchy, which have dominated historians of the divisions of Methodism as much as Wesley has

[1] Chew, *Everett*, p. 408.

dominated historians of eighteenth-century Methodism, were mere handles to the laymen.[1]

When Chipchase and his fellow laymen came to express their beliefs they largely reiterated Eckett's teachings. As Chipchase put it in 1852, the first principle of the reformers was

> 'the independency of each separate Church. Each church has the management of its own affairs and . . . elects its own officers, and exercises its own discipline.'

Another reformer wrote,

> '*The Conference is not to make the local societies, as on the present system, but they must make it to be and do just what they like.* . . . The absolute finality, as far as authority goes, of the local courts must be secured, and at no price surrendered.'

What the reformers wanted was 'a "cheap Gospel"' and the right to do what they liked in their own chapels. Larger reform issues were comparatively secondary. A reform leader complained in 1853, 'Heart and soul are enlisted in some petty circuit broil, but there seems an utter inability to take large and comprehensive views of the great principles of the movement.'[2]

The lay Reformers' policy was simple and consistent. Pamphleteering, newspaper propaganda, and, above all, the mass meeting, articulated hostility to the hierarchy and consolidated the attack on it. Stopping the supplies cut off the most irksome necessity of supporting the hierarchy, and if successful, would overwhelm the Buntingites. Many who were not reformers believed that 'the Conference would be compelled to take a lower tone by pecuniary difficulties'.[3]

To laymen 'agitation' was a permanent Guy Fawkes night. To ministers it provided the opportunity for a salutary bloodletting. Trouble makers of long standing could at last be expelled. The chapel could be purged of dissidents and a fresh start made. The hierarchy dismissed and excluded members with a macabre zest. The Rev. Isaac Keeling wrote to Bunting from Leeds in the middle of the Organ Case, 'We have had, and are expecting, some very desirable resignations.' The *Watchman's Lantern* declared in June 1835, ' "*There is a division,*

---

[1] Everett, *Notes and Memoranda*, vol. 7, p. 2011a; *Wesleyan Delegate Takings, passim*; *W.T.*, 14 March 1851, p. 162.

[2] *Wesleyan Reformer*, September–October 1852, p. 133; *Wesleyan Methodist Association Magazine*, October 1853, p. 473; *Wesleyan Methodist Penny Magazine*, February 1853, p. 29.

[3] Benjamin Gregory, *Autobiographical Recollections*, London, 1903, p. 392.

*there must be a division, there shall be a division*" so say ... some of the preachers, particularly that wholesale and *"con amore"* ex-communicator, the Rev. Samuel Jackson.'[1]

Thomas Jackson, as President, attended the Norwich district meeting of 1850. He was reported to have said,

> ' "Every person taking part in agitative meetings must be expelled. *Every delegate*, without exception, must be cut off." On one of the ministers saying that to carry out such measures in his circuit would ruin it, the President said firmly, "You must do your duty, Sir, every agitator must be expelled. . . . Expulsion must be carried on through the land–to the extent if necessary of *every member*, and then . . . *we shall have* the chapels, and we can begin again, as Wesley did, and shall soon have Methodism more glorious than ever." '

Wesleyanism took Jackson's advice. Over 100,000 members were expelled or forced into 'resignations'.[2] The Norwich district took Jackson particularly seriously, by 1855 the number of Wesleyans in Norfolk had been more than halved. But Jackson's characteristic Methodist belief in the efficacy of the chapel deceived him. In eighty years, Norfolk never began to recover its losses. Wesleyanism as a whole regained its membership total of 1850 only in 1876. It never recovered its position relative to population.

Expulsion was too easy. The minister was the source of membership. He could get rid of a member simply by withholding his class ticket. Dismissal of officials was only slightly more difficult. If, as rarely happened, members or officials obtained a trial, the minister could treat any item of their conduct as a crime, require the leaders' meeting to pronounce as to the facts, and himself pass what sentence he chose. Benjamin Gregory, a moderate critic of Buntingism, commented,

> 'But too many Superintendents in 1849 did not trouble themselves at all with such trivial technicalities as trial by leaders' meeting or special district meeting. They simply drew their pen across a "sympathizer's" name in a Class Book, or if a Leader had contributed to the fund for the expelled ministers, his Class Book was just pocketed and his members left ticketless and thunderstruck. . . .

---

[1] Gregory, *Sidelights*, p. 480; *The Resolutions of a Special District Meeting*, Leeds, 1827, pp. 14–15 (Methodist Archives copy); *Watchman's Lantern*, 3 June 1835, p. 249.

[2] *W.T.*, 21 January 1850, p. 39.

Most of these exploiters of expulsion . . . were already "famous in the congregation" for . . . "an intemperate use of authority".[1]

Gregory blamed the system and doctrine of Buntingism. But Buntingism itself was little more than a development of Wesley's own autocracy, an autocracy essential to his system. The inquisition into the *Fly Sheets* was the descendant of those inquisitions in band and class which invigorated eighteenth-century Methodism. The first 'wholesale and *"con amore"* ex-communicator' was Wesley himself, who could and did purge his societies as ruthlessly as the Jacksons purged nineteenth-century Methodism.[2] Methodism was a pioneer mass movement. From 1739 to 1849 it exhibited traces of the totalitarian dedication and rigour which many later mass movements developed.

The thoroughness of the purge of 1849 demonstrated the bankruptcy of Buntingite Methodism. A new reformed Methodism was ready to take its place. It already existed in varying forms, New Connexion, Bible Christian, Primitive Methodist, Associationist. Eighteen forty-nine led first, in 1857, to the establishment of the most determined exponent of reformed Methodism, the United Methodist Free Churches (which amalgamated the Association and reformers of the fifties), and later to the reform of Wesleyanism itself.

*The Doctrine of Methodist Reform*

Political themes have often been noted in the doctrine of reform.[3] But they were really popular only with a section of reformers. 'This is the age of Reform . . .,' declared David Rowland in 1835. 'Every institution, civil or ecclesiastical is feeling its renovating power . . . and I ask what reason is there why Reform should not penetrate even the Weslyean Methodist Conference?' Rowland, Picton, and the Lancashire laymen were fond of making the point. But the reformers of Liverpool and Rochdale did not constitute or even dominate the reform movement. Other reformers used politics quite cynically. The *Fly Sheets* attack the Buntingite *Watchman* by alleging that hundreds of pounds from the Centenary Fund had been spent on it. 'Would the Whigs of the Wesleyan body, if they had known it . . . have given their vote to support a tory paper?' the *Fly Sheets* asked. Less astute Wesleyans were rather confused on the political questions now

[1] Gregory, *Sidelights*, p. 471.
[2] e.g., John Wesley, *Journal*, London, 1930, vol. 1, p. 418.
[3] e.g., E. R. Taylor, *Methodism and Politics, 1791–1851*, Cambridge, 1935, *passim*.

regarded as central to the division of Methodism: *in 1815*, one zealous reformer contrasted 'the excellent civil constitution which we enjoy as Englishmen and the extremely arbitrary and unequitable ecclesiastical government under which we labour as Methodists.'[1]

Democracy was more generalized in reformed Methodist thought than in liberal or radical politics, and it acquired a religious character. William Griffith, the republican reform leader, burnt in effigy by a Derby mob in 1863 for disrespect to the Prince of Wales, confidently held that *'Christianity recognizes the natural equality of men'*. But he regarded Tom Paine as an 'enemy of truth,' and his concern with equality must be seen in a religious context. Associationists in the 1830s and Reformers in the 1850s agreed in supporting a *religious* democracy; 'We have no MASTERS but Christ,' the Association declared of ministers and laymen, 'and they and we, from the President of Conference down to the poorest among us, are BRETHREN.' The Reformers reiterated the point: 'the LORD JESUS CHRIST . . . is . . . the sole RULER, the sole LEGISLATOR, the only one GREAT HEAD of the CHURCH'.[2]

This religious democracy approximated to congregationalism. John Pyer, the Tent Methodist leader – who may have been responsible for the importation of a mass of Congregationalist terminology into Tent Methodism – eventually became a Congregationalist minister. Everett took the congregational view of primitive Christianity, arguing that in the early church 'the laity', that is 'all who were accredited members', took 'a very prominent part in all its affairs, both legislative and disciplinary'. Eckett adopted the congregational principle that the church is the community of Christians in a particular locality. The elaborate and centralized organization of Wesleyanism, with its powerful hierarchy, was to give way to a simple democracy of brother Christians in every neighbourhood, a peculiarly efficacious doctrine in support of lay control in the chapel.[3]

[1] *Report of a Meeting . . . at the Tabernacle, Hull*, p. 15; *Fly Sheets*, p. 28; *Exposition . . .*, Manchester, 1815, p. 8.

[2] Chew, *Griffith*, pp. 126, 190–3; *An Affectionate Address of the United Wesleyan Methodist Association to the Private Members of the Methodist Societies; Wherein the Dangerous Policy Adopted by the Conference is Briefly Exposed, as Being the Foundation of the Present Grievances of the People; and the Principles of the Association, Set Forth, as the Means of Securing and Perpetuating a Better State of Things; with an Appeal to the Societies on Their Behalf; to Which Is Added an Earnest Appeal to Those Members of Conference Who Have Been Unwilling Parties to Its Offensive Measures*, Liverpool, 1834, p. 12; *Wesleyan Delegate Takings*, pp. 165–6.

[3] Russell, *op. cit.*, pp. 132 ff; *Wesleyan Delegate Takings*, pp. 165, 169; Everett, *Methodism As It Is*, vol. 1, p. 163; Baxter, *op. cit.*, pp. 434 ff.

Wesley regarded the connexion as a means of binding together the mortal and the imperfect in one centralized body, which, by the exercise of his leadership, would be directed towards scriptural holiness. Eckett merely saw the connexion as an administrative machine to promote recruitment, by providing a consultative national assembly of elected delegates to advise the autonomous localities, and by enabling strong chapels to assist the weak with money, prayers, and preachers.

Eckett associated circuit independence with free representation. Separate allotment of representation and other constitutional facilities to laity and ministers, whether on the New Connexion principle of parity or the Primitive Methodist principle of lay dominance, clashed with the thorough democracy of fully developed Methodist reform. Church power should be in the hands of the equal, elected delegates of a sovereign congregation, free to choose whom it would. It became a commonplace in later years that Free Methodists 'glory in two great principles, Free Representation and Circuit Independence'. Later still, when circuit independence was criticized for leading to 'circuit selfishness', the democratic notions underlying both the 'two great principles' were emphasized more strongly in connection with free representation. Mr Frederick Ogden of Rochdale declared in 1905, 'to me . . . the principle of equal rights for all men, whether ministers or laymen, is a matter that cannot easily be set aside. Nay, sir, to me the spirit of democracy is the distinctive feature of Free Methodism . . . it is a crime against God to compromise such a principle.'[1]

The reformers' religious egalitarianism challenged Buntingite reliance on wealth, education and power. Liberal Methodists were confident that religious democracy was itself evangelistic. A democratic church spoke to the democratic heart of the people. 'A wave of democracy' had 'passed over the land,' and the church which did not come into 'harmony with the new times' would find her 'influence . . . weakened, her usefulness . . . crippled, her very existence . . . endangered.'[2]

But evangelism needed simplicity, and freedom from wealth and education, as well as constitutional democracy. In 1834, the Association contrasted the 'showy chapels, pealing organs, and other formal appendages' with the 'lively services' and 'holy fervour' of the old-time religion. 'Have you not published through the land', Buntingites

---

[1] *Ibid.*, pp. 261, 434, 460–1, 466–7; *U.M.F.Cs. Magazine*, August 1863, p. 554; *Free Methodist*, 21 June 1888, p. 389; 27 July 1905, p. 481.

[2] *F.M.*, 13 June 1889, p. 371.

were asked in 1846, that, 'the Centenary Hall is your glory, and that ages yet unborn shall see in it the emblem of your greatness? Is not this Hall a temple erected to Mammon? The mahogany, the mirrors, the carpets, the curtains, with other costly decorations, are they not offerings made to the god of this world? O foolish men!' Robert Winfield, in turn Wesleyan, Primitive Methodist, Revivalist, and New Connexionist, claimed that 'pride, respectability, human learning, etc.' prevented Wesleyans from evangelizing.[1]

Buntingites were committed to theological distinctions between ministers and laymen; reformers rejected them. 'It is vain to assert,' wrote one,

'that a man, who but an hour ago was a local preacher . . . has, no sooner than the hands of certain doctors have been laid on his head (who by-the-by have had no hands laid on their heads), than he . . . at once . . . is able to administer the sacraments, to expel members by the hundreds, has superior wisdom to ten, or twenty, or even a hundred local preachers and leaders; can sit in the Conference, is no more a layman, but is converted into one of a *higher order*, from a plain *Mr* So-and-so to the REV. Mr So-and-so. It is a mere fiction, a mere creation, and has no countenance anywhere but among the ambitious priests of Rome.'

In 1835, Eckett and others stated the positive side of the case, the reform doctrine of the co-pastorate of ministers and laymen: 'In some Christian Churches the whole or nearly the whole of the work of teaching and overseeing the Church devolves upon a Ministry wholly devoted to the duties of the sacred office. In Methodism, it is not so: the duties of teaching and overseeing are largely shared . . . by the Local Preachers and leaders.' Here is a purely theological analogy to the concept of democracy.[2]

Spiritual equality acted against the idea of the church. 'God gave

---

[1] *The Second Affectionate Address of the United Wesleyan Methodist Association to the Officers and Members of the Methodist Societies; Wherein the Dangerous Policy Adopted by the Conference Is further Exposed, and the Principles of the Association Set Forth and Explained, and Objections Answered; with a Variety of Facts, Comprising Notices of the Introduction of the Organ into New Brunswick Chapel, Leeds, the Liturgy into Grosvenor Street Chapel, Manchester, etc., etc., also Proofs Relating to the Present Controversy*, Manchester, 1834, p. 12; Vetus, *Wesley's Ghost*, pp. 6–8; Robert Winfield, *Sketches on Important Subjects Connected with the System of Christianity; with a Representation of the Blessed Trinity, in a Figure, Executing Their Important Offices, from One Eternal Fountain, or Divine Essence. Also, the Author's Conversion, with Seven Manifestations from the Lord, etc.*, Derby, 1845, p. 46.

[2] *W.R.*, December 1852, p. 185; Baxter, *op. cit.*, p. 285.

me commission to preach. The Conference has no power to annul
that commission. I regard myself as much a minister of Christ as ever
I was,' wrote William Griffith. If the church had no power to take
away this commission, it had no power to give it. It was reduced to
impotence. Theological opinion received the same drastic treatment.
Associationists and Free Methodists illustrated their position on the
question by affixing the motto 'The Right of Private Judgment in the
Reading of the Sacred Volume' to their denominational magazine.
Mr. William Wright of Stamford strongly condemned any infringe-
ment of private judgement:

> 'The greater part of the noble army of Martyrs, whose heroism is
> celebrated in our synagogues every sabbath day *were persecuted to
> death for preaching Christ in opposition to the constituted authorities.*
> Our holding up these worthies to general admiration shows that we
> approve of an independent spirit in our ancestors; and when we
> condemn this in the moderns, we are only acting over again the
> farce of the Jews who, in the days of our Lord, built the sepulchres
> of the ancient Prophets, and murdered their contemporaries.'[1]

Office, orders, commission, ecclesiastical authority, had little if any
place in the doctrine of reform. Reformers rejected 'the drowzy
Methodism of Britain', and called for 'an active spiritual ministry'.
Whether circuit independence, or private judgement, or an active
spiritual ministry, worked, could only be determined by their fruits.
This inherent radicalism in reformed Methodism was closely connected with the reformers' concern for revivalism. Perhaps Hugh
Bourne was the true Methodist reformer, when, for a brief period
only, he demanded that a seat in the Primitive Methodist Conference
should depend on whether a minister succeeded in getting an increase
in his circuit during the previous year; and that ministers who did get
such an increase should also be paid a bonus. This short-lived and
impracticable vision of *la religion ouverte aux talents*, in which distinctions, offices, organization, wealth and education were nullified,
inspired Methodist reform.[2]

*The Division of Methodism*

In the century following Wesley's conversion, two great ideas
dominated Methodism: Wesley's search for Christian Perfection or

[1] Chew, *Griffith*, p. 78; William Wright, *op. cit.*, p 34.
[2] William B. Carter, *The Case Tested*, p. 36; *Small Minutes of the Conversations and Decisions of the Delegates Assembled at Sunderland in the Sixth
Annual Meeting or Conference of the Primitive Methodist Connexion*, Bemersley,
1825, p. 6.

Scriptural Holiness, and the Methodist people's search for a religious democracy. Christian Perfection was born of an authoritarian personality. It vitalized a severe and demanding ethic. It was imposed by a drastic system of authority and control. It sought to create on earth a heaven of saints. The ideal of a religious democracy emerged in the conflict between the interests of local communities created almost incidentally in the search for perfection, and the demands of a disciplinarian hierarchy. This ideal required a religion of liberty, community and personal responsibility. It sought to create on earth a heaven of brothers.

The conflict of the two ideas arose from an organizational conflict of chapel and connexion. This conflict was sharpened in Methodism by the development of a local lay officialdom, essential to the expansion and survival of the movement, taxed but not represented, indispensable but unrecognized; opposed to an omnipotent hierarchy, divorced through itinerancy from any permanent share in chapel society, invested with absolute power over persons and property, and committed to the rigorous quest for perfection. The inherent cleavage in Christianity between priest and people, between those who control and direct the religious system and prescribe its goals, and those who support and submit to this system, was exacerbated to the point of prolonged and disastrous conflict in a few decades by the velocity of the Methodist movement. Tetzel's pence symbolize the Reformation. The symbols of conflict in Methodism are an organ forced upon laymen, and a theological college laymen refused to support. Both tested the hierarchy's power to rule against lay wishes.

The organizational merges into the social. An educated aspirant hierarchy presented the dictates of perfection to its poor and ignorant followers. This indoctrination may have been useful to industrialization. But industrialization and its concomitants were very dangerous to Methodism. Rapid economic and social change ended the acceptance by lay members of their leaders' directives. Laymen developed their own aspirations. They resented the cost of the hierarchy, and its monopoly of denominational power and theological opinion. But divisions among laymen still remained. At denominational level, the hierarchy recruited the new Methodist lay aristocracy to a small share in power, and were rewarded with their loyalty in the struggle with the local laymen. At the local level, while friction still arose between them, the minister and the 'business' officials, trustees and stewards, themselves a *local* lay aristocracy, clashed with the private members and their lay ministers, the class leaders and local preachers.

The dividing line between Conference men and reformers repeatedly runs between different levels of education, wealth and fame. During sixty years a mere handful of Wesleyan ministers and Conference laymen supported movements which, by 1857, had the allegiance of 45 per cent of Methodists. The threat of vertical divisions in Wesleyanism – say, within the hierarchy – came to little. Instead the movement was divided horizontally on social and organizational lines. Reform propaganda, said Thomas Jackson, won 'many religious people, particularly among the poor'. Reformers' leaders were unknown laymen. The more educated of these were dismayed by the 'vulgarity, ignorance, narrow mindedness and cant' of their humble followers. Of course the reformers preserved and then supplemented their own elites: without some wealthy men they could not have survived. In Bristol, for example, the lay leaders of reform were producers of boots, coal, oil and creosote. But this is a long way from the ministerial 'London dons' and the 'Hundred rich men' who saved them in the 1850s.[1]

The division of Methodism was a small reformation. Theological, social and organizational conflicts created, on the one side, the Wesleyan Methodist Connexion, a massive ecclesiastical organization which friend and foe, Protestant and Catholic alike, have often compared to Roman Catholicism; and on the other, a dozen or more denominations more or less in opposition to Wesleyanism. Wesleyan catholicity – its doctrines of ministry and sacrament, its stress on order, its hierarchical rule – suggest many Roman analogies; reformed Methodism's doctrine of spiritual equality, its stress on evangelism, its system of representative government, have obvious parallels in Protestantism as a whole. The two cardinal ideas of the Reformation, justification by faith, and the priesthood of all believers, could find far more unqualified acceptance in reformed Methodism than among Wesleyans.

On both sides, great ideas faded into organizational realities. Methodism, reformed and Wesleyan, was to decline into the comfortable chapel life Hugh Price Hughes cruelly called 'shopocracy'. At Conference, the great ideas were still paraded to vindicate the divisions of Methodism. But these divisions themselves, and later indifference to the great ideas that sustained them, were to bring Methodism into its ecumenical age.

[1] Thomas Jackson, *Life of the Rev. Robert Newton*, London, 1855, p. 147; Picton, *op. cit.*, pp. 143–4; Eayrs, *op. cit.*, pp. 232, 241 ff, 251 ff, 255; Everett, *op. cit.*, vol. 1, p. 216; Thomas Nightingale, *Some of the Reminiscences and Experiences of My Life*, London, 1891, p. 20.

# Part Two

# Aspects of Ecumenicalism

# CHAPTER THREE

# The Dynamics of Ecumenicalism

The decline of Christianity is a major characteristic of British society in the present century. Since 1900, the membership of all the largest indigenous denominations has decreased. The Church of England has lost 7 per cent of its membership since 1925. In the last thirty years, Methodism has decreased about 15 per cent. Since the beginning of the century, the Congregationalists and Baptists have been nearly halved in number. Many subtleties of the religious scene present intractable problems to the statistician. But as Article XIX informs us, 'The visible Church of Christ is a congregation of faithful men'; and their heads can be counted. While the heavenly realm may rejoice more over one than over ninety-nine, the visible Church displays more interest in the latter than in the former. Christianity is a converting religion, and Christians are rightly concerned today by their failure to make, and indeed to retain, active professing believers. Statistics are therefore of great importance. Few other measures of religious growth and change arouse the interest created by membership figures.

*Ecumenicalism and Statistics*

During the period of Christianity's numerical decline, ecumenicalism has rapidly grown in importance and popularity, and ecumenical activity has been interpreted as an effect of numerical decrease. On this interpretation, united churches result from organizational response to adverse conditions. The united church is a new phenomenon, complicating the sociological schema of a sect-denomination-church transition. The development of denominations contains an ecumenical option, amalgamation in a 'superdenominational' organization consciously constructed from religious groups of sufficient standing to have acquired their own forms, constitution, outlook and loyalties. These amalgamations are *super*-denominational because they stand above and are composed of separate denominations, and because they are envisaged and sought as an advance on existing organizations.

Although ecumenicalism minimizes religious conflict, the existence of the ecumenical movement presupposes a situation of conflict. Religious organizations, like other institutions, engage in various conflicts: to suppress or alter rivals, or to usurp the privileges and powers possessed by rivals, for example. These organizations also come into conflict with society itself in attempting to convert members of society from secular to religious allegiances. Religious organizations tend to measure success, in general, and in these conflicts, by their own size and growth. When *frontal* growth, i.e. the acquisition of new members by the normal processes of recruitment and enrolment, fails, the organization seeks to achieve its goals by *lateral* growth, i.e. amalgamation with other organizations in possession of membership and resources of their own. The superdenomination is a weapon in a conflict. It first develops in the context of the struggle for power within the religious world, and later gains particular prominence as a means to offset adverse changes in the relation of religious organizations and society.

The ecumenical phase of Methodism offers various examples of superdenominational organization. The Wesleyan Methodist Association (1836), the United Methodist Free Churches (1857), and even the United Methodist Church (1907), are partly or wholly attempts to construct a superdenomination as an instrument in religious conflict inside Methodism. The unions projected by the leaders of the Wesleyan Forward Movement, culminating in the Methodist Church of 1932, were designed as weapons in a conflict with the Church of England. The United Methodist Church and the Methodist Church are also the best English illustrations of the superdenomination as an attempt to regain lost power in an increasingly recalcitrant society. In this respect study of Methodism may elucidate current religious developments, notably the attempt to form an Anglican-Methodist superdenomination; and the future progress of the incipient movement for Anglican-Roman Catholic unification.

Methodism is peculiarly rich in ecumenical forms. It also offers the possibility of constructing very simple 'statics' and 'dynamics' of ecumenicalism. The crucial index of success and failure in religious organizations is membership. This and many other aspects of change in these organizations can be quantified. Methodist statistics are unusually reliable. Membership of a Methodist denomination is temporary and subject to quarterly scrutiny. In other denominations membership is permanent and even irrevocable, and current real strength correspondingly more difficult to assess. Methodists have kept membership statistics for 200 years without a break–probably longer than any other religious group. They have kept them with some care, and during the last 100 years they have supplemented simple membership data with various other kinds of statistical records.[1]

Static quantities of membership greatly influence interdenominational relations, and each separate organization's attitudes and policies. Table One lists membership of the major Methodist denominations. The total membership of these denominations was

TABLE ONE. *Membership of Major Methodist Denominations by Census Years, 1801–1931.*

|      | BCs    | MNC    | PMC     | UMFC   | UMC     | WMA    | WMC     |
|------|--------|--------|---------|--------|---------|--------|---------|
| 1801 |        | 4,851  |         |        |         |        | 89,529  |
| 1811 |        | 7,448  |         |        |         |        | 145,614 |
| 1821 |        | 10,404 | 16,394  |        |         |        | 200,074 |
| 1831 | 6,650  | 11,433 | 37,216  |        |         |        | 249,119 |
| 1841 | 11,353 | 20,506 | 75,967  |        |         | 22,074 | 328,792 |
| 1851 | 13,324 | 16,962 | 106,074 | *45,000* |       | 20,557 | 302,209 |
| 1861 | 16,866 | 22,732 | 127,772 | 52,970 |         |        | 319,782 |
| 1871 | 18,050 | 22,870 | 148,597 | 61,924 |         |        | 347,090 |
| 1881 | 21,209 | 25,797 | 169,422 | 65,067 |         |        | 380,956 |
| 1891 | 25,608 | 28,756 | 181,167 | 67,200 |         |        | 424,220 |
| 1901 | 28,315 | 32,324 | 188,683 | 72,568 |         |        | 454,982 |
| 1911 |        |        | 205,086 |        | 144,888 |        | 485,535 |
| 1921 |        |        | 198,806 |        | 138,110 |        | 464,945 |
| 1931 |        |        | 200,816 |        | 140,458 |        | 500,010 |

*Note:* 1. The figure in italics indicates approximate membership of the 'Wesleyan Reformers'.

2. Abbreviations: BCs: Bible Christians; MNC: Methodist New Connexion; PMC: Primitive Methodist Church; UMFC: United Methodist Free Churches; UMC: United Methodist Church; WMA: Wesleyan Methodist Association; WMC: Wesleyan Methodist Church.

*Source: Minutes.*

94,000 in 1801, 841,000 in 1931. But by 1931 Methodism has divided into a series of denominations, notably Primitive, Free and, later, United Methodists. The pattern is complicated by the fact that the Wesleyan Methodist Association and some of the 'Wesleyan Reformers' united to form the United Methodist Free Churches in 1857; while, in 1907, this denomination joined with the Bible Christians and the New Connexion to form the United Methodist Church.

Union begins among the smaller Methodist groups. A considerable gap exists between the size of the groups involved in the unions of 1857 and 1907 and the two largest denominations, which were not

[1] Unless otherwise stated, statistical data in this chapter is taken from the respective denominational *Minutes.*

seriously involved in the union movement until well into the twentieth century. These smaller bodies are shorter-lived and less stable than the larger. The fact that they are absolutely small in size creates problems: small organizations may be viable, but they also require more effort from their members than large organizations do. The small *relative* size of these groups is important too. The complete series of denominations created a common frame of reference for each individual group. The smallest of these felt the pressure of larger units who opposed the doctrines and practices of the smaller units and continuously demonstrated the wider opportunities of a bigger organization.

Methodists themselves frequently associated size and ecumenicalism. A Free Methodist commented in 1887 that, if churches did not unite, another solution to the problem of competing units would emerge and 'In all probability it will be on the principle of *"The weakest goes to the wall"*. Churches cannot for ever maintain a feeble, languishing existence; there must come a time when they become "either mended or ended".' Another Free Methodist writer asked in 1900, 'When shall we realize that in these days small Denominations are worked at a great disadvantage, and . . . at a heavy cost?' A New Connexion minister observed in 1889 that

'Modern conditions make advancement more and more difficult for the smaller Denominations. It must be remembered . . . how the power of propagation has relatively declined, or has come to be more and more dependent on large material resources. . . . The social forces are against small Denominations, and their struggles will be greater.'[1]

Methodists also contrasted relative size of denomination, as well as absolute number of members. Speaking of the imminent union of 1907, a New Connexion minister said in 1905, 'There was a time in business life when a man turned a corner and his future success was assured. The Wesleyans had turned that corner; the Primitives had nearly, and the new Church, when Union was accomplished, will have turned it.' It was generally agreed that the larger churches did not need union. H. P. Hughes, the Wesleyan leader, observed in 1886 that the Primitive Methodists 'have so extensive and vigorous a life of their own that they have probably not yet realized the need and advantage of reunion'. They were 'too strong'. A Primitive Methodist

[1] *Free Methodist*, 8 September 1887, p. 285; 22 March 1900, p. 197; *Methodist New Connexion Magazine*, May 1889, p. 284.

minister commented modestly in 1903, 'Without laying ourselves open to any accusation of . . . "swelled head" . . . our numbers and success do not predispose us to make haste for union.'[1]

This discussion assumed a critical size for the organization. The concept was relative. Most Methodist denominations operated in a frame of reference provided by the Methodist world. They understood critical size as a level below which the organization could not survive losses from migration, have an adequately paid and trained ministry, mobilize capital for expansion, publish denominational literature, and carry out other functions of Methodist denominations. In Methodist eyes, only Primitive and Wesleyan Methodists had passed the critical size. Both denominations were highly successful – by the standards of Methodism alone – and their need of union was reduced. Hughes recognized this when he said that the Primitive Methodists were 'too strong' to be interested in union. His paradoxical claim that his own denomination, twice the size of the Primitive Methodist Connexion, was not strong enough, was due to the fact that, alone of Methodist denominations, the Wesleyans were strong and large enough to have standards *outside* Methodism. The Wesleyans, in particular that section of Wesleyans headed by Hughes, aspired to appear on a larger stage than Methodism, and to assume the role of the Church of England. Since the Church of England was several times larger than the Wesleyans, this bid had to be achieved through union. The Wesleyan frame of reference was larger than that of the Free Methodists. But the leaders of both denominations were turned towards union by the concept of critical size.

Other dynamic factors are involved in the ecumenical process. Table One provides an overall picture of advance. The average decennial growth rate of the total membership of the denominations listed is 19·3 per cent. If this explained the whole situation, the super-denomination would probably appear simply as an instrument in interdenominational conflicts. But this largely deceptive picture of advance must be supplemented by consideration of membership–population ratios (M.P.Rs). The M.P.R. – here indicated by expressing membership as a percentage of the relevant population – is the crucial index of strength of a religious organization. Simply to state absolute membership figures without reference to the population from which it might be drawn, as many writers do, has limited value. The data of Table Two and Graph One illustrates what from the historical point

[1] *F.M.*, 12 October 1905, p. 650; *Methodist Times*, 18 November 1886, p. 765; 24 December 1903, p. 920.

of view is probably the most interesting aspect of the membership of religious organizations.

TABLE TWO. *Membership of Methodist Denominations as a Percentage of Population by Census Years, 1801–1931.*

| | BCs | MNC | PMC | UMC | UMFC | WMA | WMC |
|---|---|---|---|---|---|---|---|
| | | | (a) *total Great Britain Population* | | | | |
| 1801 | | 0·05 | | | | | 0·85 |
| 1811 | | 0·06 | | | | | 1·22 |
| 1821 | | 0·09 | 0·12 | | | | 1·42 |
| 1831 | 0·04 | 0·07 | 0·23 | | | | 1·53 |
| 1841 | 0·06 | 0·11 | 0·41 | | | 0·12 | 1·77 |
| 1851 | 0·06 | 0·08 | 0·51 | | | 0·10 | 1·45 |
| 1861 | 0·07 | 0·10 | 0·55 | | 0·23 | | 1·38 |
| 1871 | 0·07 | 0·09 | 0·57 | | 0·24 | | 1·33 |
| 1881 | 0·09 | 0·09 | 0·58 | | 0·22 | | 1·31 |
| 1891 | 0·08 | 0·09 | 0·55 | | 0·20 | | 1·28 |
| 1901 | 0·08 | 0·11 | 0·51 | | 0·20 | | 1·23 |
| 1911 | | | 0·50 | 0·36 | | | 1·19 |
| 1921 | | | 0·46 | 0·32 | | | 1·09 |
| 1931 | | | 0·45 | 0·31 | | | 1·12 |
| | | | (b) *Great Britain Population, age 15 and over* | | | | |
| 1841 | 0·10 | 0·17 | 0·64 | | | 0·19 | 2·79 |
| 1851 | 0·10 | 0·13 | 0·79 | | | 0·15 | 2·25 |
| 1861 | 0·11 | 0·15 | 0·86 | | 0·36 | | 2·08 |
| 1871 | 0·11 | 0·14 | 0·90 | | 0·37 | | 2·09 |
| 1881 | 0·11 | 0·12 | 0·90 | | 0·35 | | 2·02 |
| 1891 | 0·12 | 0·13 | 0·85 | | 0·31 | | 1·98 |
| 1901 | 0·11 | 0·13 | 0·76 | | 0·29 | | 1·83 |
| 1911 | | | 0·73 | 0·50 | | | 1·72 |
| 1921 | | | 0·64 | 0·45 | | | 1·51 |
| 1931 | | | 0·59 | 0·41 | | | 1·47 |

*Note*: For abbreviations see Table One
*Source: Minutes*; Censuses.

These organizations are committed to expansion. Unless membership is already coextensive with society as a whole, an increasing M.P.R. is essential. A stable M.P.R. is just healthy. It means that net change in membership is equal to the increase that would take place over a period if no members were recruited from outside, but no members were lost, and parents were replaced on death by their children. The organization would be literally 'holding its own'. But, whatever the actual increase of membership, a falling M.P.R. is pathological: neither the replacement of parents by their children nor the recruitment of new members is sufficient to offset the losses of membership from deaths and withdrawals.

Examination of M.P.Rs seriously challenges the generally accepted picture of a 'religious boom'[1] between 1850 and 1900, or of '*fifty years*

[1] E. R. Wickham, *Church and People in an Industrial City*, London, 1957, pp. 107 ff. Bishop Wickham's own attendance figures show the churches actually losing ground in his 'boom' period, though this is not clarified in the text. Cp. pp. 108–9, 148.

GRAPH ONE. *Membership of the Major Methodist Denominations as a Percentage of Total Great Britain Population by Census Years, 1801–1931 (Semi-log Scale).*
*Source:* Table Two

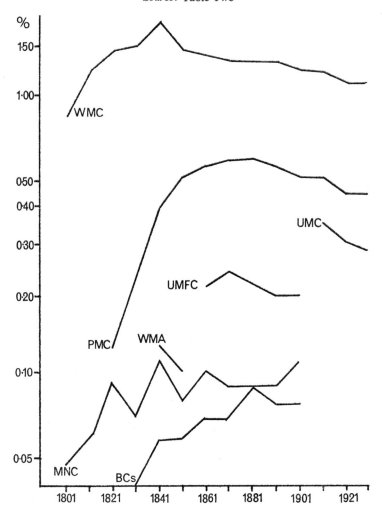

of church expansion'.[1] In the most dynamic section of British religion in the nineteenth century, the boom years, as far as the crucial M.P.R. is concerned, were 1800–50. If the rapid advance of 1801–41 had been maintained, between one in four and one in five persons in Great

[1] J. Edwin Orr, *The Second Evangelical Awakening in Britain*, London, 1949, p. 9.

Britain would have been Methodist by 1931. In fact the figure was less than one in fifty. Methodism received its severest setback in the decade 1841–51. At the beginning of the decade, the Methodist New Connexion suffered serious losses through the Barkerite controversy. But this schism was insignificant in the total picture. The great disaster was the *Fly Sheets* controversy which reduced Wesleyan membership by about 100,000 between 1850 and 1855. Thereafter Methodism never recovered its M.P.R. Its worst decade after 1861 was 1911–21: in twelve years Methodism was united.

But the *Fly Sheets* controversy conceals another pattern. Neither Wesleyanism nor the New Connexion recovered from major secession. But Primitive Methodists suffered only slight reduction in the rate of increase of their M.P.R. in the 1840s. Marked deceleration in M.P.R. only occurred in the 1850s. In 1861–81, Primitive Methodism approached stability. There is some evidence to suggest that if the *Fly Sheets* had not divided Wesleyanism, that denomination would have had a similar experience. Using total population figures, Wesleyan M.P.R. began to stabilize in 1871–81; adopting the more useful fifteen-plus age group base, the Wesleyans slightly *improved* their position in 1861–71. Eliminating the effect of schism, it seems that M.P.R. only enters a really critical phase after 1881.

With one exception only, the various unions occurred after that date. The exception is the formation of the United Methodist Free Churches in 1857. As that denomination was composed of the Wesleyan Methodist Association, which had decreased in membership, and consistently lost ground in M.P.R. terms, since its inception; and the Wesleyan Reformers, whose membership was already declining, the U.M.F.Cs can hardly be used as evidence against the view that ecumenicalism thrives on a falling M.P.R. The United Methodist Church was formed in 1907 from two denominations with a falling M.P.R., the Free Methodists and the Bible Christians, and one, the New Connexion, which was only just recovering some of the ground it had continuously lost since the middle of the previous century. All three denominations forming the Methodist Church in 1932 had suffered prolonged fall in M.P.R., despite the 1920s revival.

A falling M.P.R. means general organizational decline. But it is also a factor in the consciousness of denominational leaders. The editor of the *Free Methodist* commented gloomily in 1888, 'The probability is that Free Methodism has now reached . . . its full growth, and that all it will be able to accomplish will be to maintain an increase in fair proportion to the increase in population.' The more sophisticated

New Connexionists had understood since the 1870s that 'At the present rate of progress . . . the Christian Churches would never permeate the entire population, inasmuch as the population increased more rapidly than the churches multiplied among them.' The *Methodist Recorder* remarked in 1895, 'If Wesleyan Methodism were to increase regularly by 5,000 members a year it would be but holding its own. Nay, it could hardly be said to hold its own, in view of the steady increase in population.' H. P. Hughes persistently complained that 'Taking a larger view of Methodism, and remembering the great increase of the population, they would see that for the last forty years they were practically stationary.'[1] Aware of decrease in M.P.R., Methodist leaders looked to the ecumenical option to provide both an access of membership in some sense and a concentration and rationalization of resources adequate to accelerate the recruitment of new members.

But secular change in M.P.R. was less apparent to the organization, and possibly less effective in altering the conscious policies of its leaders, than fluctuations in growth rate. The best measure of growth rate available, that used by the denominations themselves, that used in this study is *net change in full membership*. In other words, the increase or decrease in the total number of full members during any given period is taken as an index of organizational growth. This is a very good index, especially since Methodist membership was temporary.

But it is important to be clear what growth is not. It is not, for example, the rate at which new members are made, data on which is not available before the 1870s. The same recruitment rate may accompany altogether different growth rates. In Wesleyanism a recruitment rate of 9–10 per cent accompanied a *decrease* of 0·9 per cent in 1878-9, but an *increase* of 2·8 per cent in 1905-6. The growth rate is simply a quantitative summary of *all* the processes of loss and gain of membership within the organization: the difference between the total number of new full members added in a year, and the total number of full members lost in a year, from whatever causes, gives net change in that year. Growth rate for any given year is obtained by expressing net change in that year as a percentage of the total full membership figure for the previous year. By definition a monocausal explanation of growth rate is worthless, since the same growth rate can obviously be caused by many different combinations of organiza-

[1] *F.M.*, 28 June 1888, p. 401; *M.N.C. Mag.*, July 1871, p. 436; *Methodist Recorder*, 25 April 1895, p. 265; 30 April 1896, p. 293.

tional changes, even if the wide range of social factors that might promote these internal changes is ignored.

The extreme uncertainty of the causes of a particular growth rate makes this a subject peculiarly adapted to tendentiousness. While most historians regard Hughes' 'Forward Movement' as an attempt to break down barriers between church and people that led to a renaissance of Wesleyanism, Sir George Hayter Chubb, a stout Wesleyan Tory, attributed the decrease of Wesleyan membership in 1895–6 to 'Endeavour Societies; Wesley Guilds; Armenian agitations and the like', but especially to 'the unwise speeches and writings' of 'a leader of Radical Methodism', i.e. Hughes.[1]

Other examples of the ideological use of growth rates, less evident, and hence more dangerous, could be cited. The favourite Wesleyan explanation of adverse changes in growth, reflecting the hostility of the leadership to political activity, was that 'times of great public excitement have not been helpful to the growth of the Church'.[2] Yet during the period of the reform bill agitation, 1831–2 was a good year for Wesleyans (growth rate +2·9 per cent), and 1832–3 an outstanding year (+9·3 per cent). In the twentieth century, the Wesleyans' two best years were 1904–5 (+2·3 per cent), and 1905–6 (+2·8 per cent), a period of considerable political agitation, particularly among Nonconformists. The Primitive Methodist view, reflecting the denomination's claim to be the church of the people, that economic conditions affect membership, especially that depressions reduce growth because their humble supporters are too poor to keep up membership, is also questionable. In the very serious depression of the early 1840s, 1841–2 was a good year for Primitive Methodism (+3·8 per cent), 1842–3 a very good year (+7·4 per cent). Economic factors may sometimes be important, the depression of the 1870s is probably a relevant example. But most economic analysis of Methodist growth is casual and uninformed.

The evidence, so far as it is available, is summarized in Table Three and Graph Two.[3] The data shows close similarity between movements of the growth rate for each denomination, suggesting perhaps that certain external factors, felt in common by all Methodist denominations, greatly influence their development, while *internal* changes have relatively little effect. The general pattern is one of marked oscillation, often from fairly high growth to absolute decrease.

[1] *M.R.*, 7 May 1896, p. 319.

[2] *Ibid.*, 5 April 1900, p. 10.

[3] Annual averages for triennial periods have been used to provide a slightly more generalized picture than that offered by figures for separate years.

**TABLE THREE.** *Average Annual Growth Rate of Methodist Denominations by Triennial Periods, 1767–1932.*

| | BCs | MNC | PMC | UMC | UMFC | WMA | WMC |
|---|---|---|---|---|---|---|---|
| 1767–1769 | | | | | | | 8·5 |
| 1770–1772 | | | | | | | 3·3 |
| 1773–1775 | | | | | | | 3·6 |
| 1776–1778 | | | | | | | 4·1 |
| 1779–1781 | | | | | | | 3·3 |
| 1782–1784 | | | | | | | 3·8 |
| 1785–1787 | | | | | | | 5·9 |
| 1788–1790 | | | | | | | 4·3 |
| 1791–1793 | | | | | | | 1·9 |
| 1794–1796 | | | | | | | 9·1 |
| 1797–1799 | | | | | | | 5·0 |
| 1800–1802 | | | | | | | 0·6 |
| 1803–1805 | | 1·4 | | | | | 3·1 |
| 1806–1808 | | 10·6 | | | | | 7·5 |
| 1809–1811 | | 3·7 | | | | | 4·8 |
| 1812–1814 | | 1·5 | | | | | 5·7 |
| 1815–1817 | | 4·1 | | | | | 3·9 |
| 1818–1820 | | 2·4 | | | | | − 0·4 |
| 1821–1823 | | 3·6 | 60·0 | | | | 4·7 |
| 1824–1826 | | − 0·4 | *4·6* | | | | 1·7 |
| 1827–1829 | 6·5 | 4·8 | *6·2* | | | | 2·4 |
| 1830–1832 | − 4·3 | 0·2 | 7·0 | | | | 1·2 |
| 1833–1835 | 6·1 | 12·4 | 11·2 | | | | 4·4 |
| 1836–1838 | 8·5 | 7·5 | 6·2 | | | *9·9* | 0·7 |
| 1839–1841 | 6·0 | − 0·4 | 4·0 | | | − 1·8 | 3·5 |
| 1842–1844 | 4·2 | − 7·9 | 4·8 | | | − 2·3 | 0·9 |
| 1845–1847 | − 3·1 | − 1·2 | *− 0·9* | | | − 2·8 | 0·2 |
| 1848–1850 | 5·8 | 5·5 | *6·4* | | | 3·9 | 1·9 |
| 1851–1853 | − 1·2 | − 3·2 | *1·1* | | | − 4·8 | − 8·4 |
| 1854–1856 | 1·9 | 4·7 | − 0·5 | | | − 0·2 | − 0·9 |
| 1857–1859 | 7·6 | 5·1 | 4·3 | | *8·5* | | 3·6 |
| 1860–1862 | 1·9 | 2·1 | 4·0 | | 7·8 | | 3·7 |
| 1863–1865 | 0·6 | 0·0 | 2·0 | | 2·3 | | 0·6 |
| 1866–1868 | 1·0 | 0·6 | 1·4 | | 1·2 | | 1·2 |
| 1869–1871 | − 2·1 | − 2·6 | 0·4 | | − 0·6 | | 0·5 |
| 1872–1874 | − 0·3 | 0·1 | 0·6 | | − 1·0 | | 0·4 |
| 1875–1877 | 5·7 | 1·7 | 2·9 | | 1·3 | | 2·8 |
| 1878–1880 | − 0·3 | 1·6 | 0·1 | | − 0·7 | | − 0·5 |
| 1881–1883 | 4·7 | 2·5 | 2·2 | | 1·4 | | 2·6 |
| 1884–1886 | − 0·1 | 0·6 | 0·4 | | − 0·3 | | 0·4 |
| 1887–1889 | 2·1 | 1·3 | 0·4 | | 0·2 | | 0·7 |
| 1890–1892 | 0·3 | 0·4 | − 0·3 | | 0·2 | | 0·3 |
| 1893–1895 | 1·7 | 0·8 | 0·4 | | 0·6 | | 0·1 |
| 1896–1898 | 0·8 | 1·2 | 0·4 | | 1·1 | | 0·3 |
| 1899–1901 | 1·3 | 1·6 | 0·7 | | 0·7 | | 1·0 |
| 1902–1904 | 1·9 | 2·6 | 1·4 | | 2·1 | | 1·4 |
| 1905–1907 | 2·6 | 1·9 | 1·6 | | 0·8 | | 1·6 |
| 1908–1910 | | | − 0·1 | − 0·5 | | | − 0·5 |
| 1911–1913 | | | − 0·3 | − 0·8 | | | − 0·4 |
| 1914–1916 | | | − 0·4 | − 0·4 | | | − 0·6 |
| 1917–1919 | | | − 0·2 | − 0·5 | | | − 0·6 |
| 1920–1922 | | | − 0·3 | − 0·1 | | | 0·6 |
| 1923–1925 | | | 0·6 | 0·7 | | | 1·5 |
| 1926–1928 | | | 0·1 | 0·1 | | | 0·6 |
| 1929–1931 | | | − 0·3 | − 0·4 | | | 0·0 |
| 1932 | | | − 0·6 | − 1·0 | | | 0·0 |

*Note*: 1. Figures in italics denote use of incomplete data.
2. For abbreviations see Table One. *Source: Minutes.*

GRAPH TWO. *Average Annual Growth Rates of the Major Methodist Denominations, by Triennial Periods, 1767–1932.*
Source: Table Three

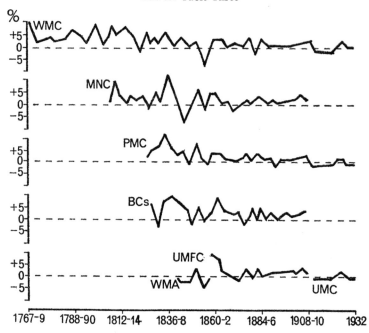

Only during four periods does any denomination improve its growth rate more than two triennia in succession.

Above all, sudden and rapid changes in growth rate, especially noticeable in the nineteenth century, give way first to a brief period of steady, low growth, then to absolute decline. Historians who concern themselves particularly with the industrial revolution period, probably over-emphasize the degree to which this period was particularly congenial to Methodism. From an eighteenth-century situation of great success, Methodism does progressively worse in the nineteenth and twentieth centuries: the eighteenth century saw continued growth; the nineteenth, periodic 'revival'; the twentieth, decline.

About the period of the downturn in Methodist M.P.Rs, i.e. in the 1880s and 1890s, the characteristics of the growth rate change also. The last revival phase of the period 1790–1890 occurs in 1875–86. The growth rates of these years indicate sudden and rapid accession of membership, followed by loss of members and/or failure to recruit. The growth rates of the next period of considerable increase of membership, 1893–1907, provide a much more gradual curve. The

96

rapid turnover of membership, associated in the nineteenth century with high growth rates, is *reduced*; but the steadier advance of the post-1890 situation means lower growth rates. The denominations are labourers sent to the harvest. In the early nineteenth century they worked fast, dropping or spoiling a lot of the crop, but gathering a very great deal. Even after 1890, the harvest is still, at least occasionally, ripe. But the labourers' muscles are feebler and their reflexes slower. They lose and spoil less. But they gather far less.

Decline in growth rates concerned denominational leaders more than failure to surpass critical size and to maintain M.P.R. Membership returns were consulted as assiduously as politicians consult other data. 'In no other Denomination', wrote a Methodist in 1900, 'do statistics occupy a higher place, nor discharge a more responsible duty. They are the criteria of our corporate strength, and our spiritual condition. We allow them to exercise considerable dominion over us, and are elated or depressed according as they are favourable or otherwise.'[1] The message of these all-important returns was one of decreasing success, and then of failure and decline. In 1854 a New Connexion minister lamented, 'We are dishonoured before the world; our Lord and Master is dishonoured by the non-advancement of his Church'. A Primitive Methodist wrote in 1892,

> 'It is a most humiliating fact that, notwithstanding our almost desperate efforts to get up a "Forward Movement" . . . *we have to-day in the Home Districts some hundreds of members fewer than we had eight years ago.* Eight years of stagnation and worse! Only think of it, that for eight years we have made no perceptible headway as a connexion against the Kingdom of Darkness in the British Isles!'

A Wesleyan commented in 1903, 'that the net result in members of a year's work should be only 1·04 per cent cannot be regarded with complacency. . . . What is the Methodism that halts and crawls at this poor dying rate?'[2]

It was argued, not surprisingly, that deficiencies in growth rate were due to the divisions of Methodism. The incoming Wesleyan President of 1895 observed, 'Nothing has more effectually hindered the progress of Christianity than the absence of that oneness for which the Saviour prayed.' 'There could be no doubt', said a tutor of a

[1] *F.M.*, 26 April 1900, p. 289.
[2] *M.N.C. Mag.*, July 1854, p. 397; *Primitive Methodist World*, 28 April 1892, p. 324; *M.T.*, 23 April 1903, p. 269.

Wesleyan college in 1903, 'that it was this state of division that was an enormous weakness to them in their religious work.' Above all it was Hughes' claim that 'Division . . . was the curse of Methodism.'[1]

Union would save Methodism. A Wesleyan commented in 1897, 'Perhaps recent decreases in the various Methodist bodies point to the desirability of Methodist reunion.'[2] Individual denominations regarded union as 'an addition to membership', a way 'to increase our numbers'. In a more general phrase, union was said to be 'for the conversion of the world to Christ'.[3] Everything the denomination stood for could be sacrificed to this great aim. The *Free Methodist*, in a vigorous ecumenical editorial of 1890, wrote, 'It is all very well to boast of our Free Methodism, and to crack up our principles; but if our churches are dying out in various parts . . . in God's name what matters our constitution! Something else is wanted beside a polity and that something is LIFE.'[4]

But the ecumenical movement is probably not simply a matter of denominational leadership's conscious response to evident failure of growth. The organization as a whole exhibits certain characteristic changes in this period, changes that suggest the shift from frontal to lateral growth was an organizational imperative. These changes can be seen in the patterns of recruitment, loss and leakage during 1866–1932, figures for which are given in Table Four. 'Leakage' is decrease of membership from the failure of migrant members to re-register as members on removal. 'Loss' is decrease of membership from all causes other than leakage, emigration and death. All three figures are expressed as a percentage of the *total* membership of the previous year, the most relevant figure.

The figures show certain interesting contrasts. The Wesleyans, having virtually nation-wide coverage, suffer far less from leakage among their migrant membership, than do the more localized sects, especially the Bible Christians who were largely confined to Devon and Cornwall. Even the United Methodist Church which amalgamated the smaller groups failed to reduce its leakage rate to the Wesleyan level. On the other hand, Wesleyan Methodism, approxi-

---

[1] *M.R.*, 1 August 1895, p. 515; 23 August 1903, p. 10; D. P. Hughes, *Life of Hugh Price Hughes*, London, 1904, p. 147.

[2] *M.R.*, 14 January 1897, p. 30.

[3] *F.M.*, 8 January 1903, p. 26; *M.N.C. Mag.*, July 1855, p. 373; *Proceedings of the Second Ecumenical Methodist Conference Held in the Metropolitan Methodist Episcopal Church, Washington, October, 1891*, London, 1892, pp. 128–9.

[4] *F.M.*, 30 October 1890, p. 9.

TABLE FOUR. *Average Annual Leakage, Loss and Recruitment of Methodist Denominations by Triennial Periods, 1866–1932.*

| | Leakage | | | | | Loss | | | | | Recruitment | |
|---|---|---|---|---|---|---|---|---|---|---|---|---|
| | BCs | MNC | UMC | UMFC | WMC | BCs | MNC | UMC | UMFC | WMC | BCs | WMC |
| 1866–1868 | | | | 5·6 | | | | | 4·4 | | | |
| 1869–1871 | | 5·9 | | 5·6 | | | | | 5·2 | | | |
| 1872–1874 | | 5·2 | | 5·6 | | | 5·2 | | 4·5 | | | 12·8 |
| 1875–1877 | | 4·8 | | 5·3 | | | 5·7 | | 4·2 | | | 10·3 |
| 1878–1880 | 7·3 | 5·3 | | 5·6 | | | 6·7 | | 4·3 | | | 12·5 |
| 1881–1883 | 6·2 | 4·8 | | 5·2 | 3·2 | | 6·6 | | 4·5 | 5·9 | *14·6* | 12·5 |
| 1884–1886 | 6·1 | 4·5 | | 4·6 | 2·8 | | 5·8 | | 4·5 | 5·8 | *11·8* | 10·1 |
| 1887–1889 | 6·0 | 4·3 | | 4·5 | 2·5 | | 4·9 | | 3·9 | 5·2 | *15·0* | 9·5 |
| 1890–1892 | 4·9 | 3·8 | | 4·2 | 2·5 | 5·0 | 4·3 | | 3·6 | 4·6 | *11·9* | 8·7 |
| 1893–1895 | 4·7 | 3·4 | | 3·9 | 2·3 | 4·7 | 3·4 | | 3·3 | 4·5 | *12·4* | 8·8 |
| 1896–1898 | 4·7 | 3·3 | | 3·6 | 2·2 | 4·8 | 3·0 | | 2·9 | 4·3 | *10·7* | 8·0 |
| 1899–1901 | 4·6 | 3·3 | | 3·6 | 2·0 | 3·7 | 2·9 | | 2·8 | 3·7 | *10·8* | 7·7 |
| 1902–1904 | 4·7 | 3·4 | | 3·7 | 2·1 | 3·9 | 2·9 | | 2·4 | 3·6 | *10·2* | 7·9 |
| 1905–1907 | | 3·6 | | 3·8 | 2·0 | | | | 2·2 | 3·7 | *11·7* | 8·0 |
| 1908–1910 | | | 3·4 | | 1·6 | | | 2·7 | | 3·5 | | 6·1 |
| 1911–1913 | | | 3·6 | | 1·5 | | | 2·7 | | 3·1 | | 5·8 |
| 1914–1916 | | | 3·0 | | 1·3 | | | 2·1 | | 2·8 | | 5·1 |
| 1917–1919 | | | 1·9 | | 0·9 | | | 1·6 | | 2·1 | | 4·0 |
| 1920–1922 | | | 2·2 | | 1·0 | | | 2·0 | | 2·5 | | 5·1 |
| 1923–1925 | | | 2·0 | | 0·8 | | | 1·9 | | 2·1 | | 5·5 |
| 1926–1928 | | | 1·9 | | 0·8 | | | 1·7 | | 2·1 | | 4·9 |
| 1929–1931 | | | 1·9 | | 0·7 | | | 1·7 | | 2·0 | | 4·3 |
| 1932 | | | 1·7 | | 0·7 | | | 2·0 | | 1·9 | | 4·1 |

*Note:* 1. The tables show leakage, loss and recruitment as a percentage of the total membership of the previous year.
2. Figures in italics denote use of incomplete data.
3. For abbreviations see Table One.

*Source: Minutes.*

mating much more to the Church of England than to the sectarian Methodist groups, suffered more from loss than other groups except the Bible Christians. This probably indicates a higher degree of indifference or alienation among its members. But despite these differences, all these organizations undergo rather similar changes in 1866–1932. Each column of figures shows a slow if irregular decrease over the period. Whether the absolute size of the organization is *growing*, as is the case with the Wesleyans, or *decreasing*, as with the United Methodists, all exhibit a decrease in the rates of recruitment, loss and leakage.

A high level of turnover, hinted at by changes in growth rates, is giving way to a lower. The Wesleyan loss rate throughout is roughly half the Wesleyan recruitment rate. Both rates decrease rapidly during the period. The organization changes in such a way that it *recruits* less new members, but *loses* less existing members. The hard core of the denomination is being reached. This hard core is more loyal, but proselytizes less, and secures less frontal growth. The slowing up of organizational processes accompanies a shift of emphasis from frontal to lateral growth, and increases organizational pressure for the transition to the superdenomination.

TABLE FIVE. *Death Rates of Methodist Denominations Compared with Great Britain Death Rate (age group 15 and over), 1871–1931 (per cent).*

|      | GB  | BCS | MNC | PMC | UMC | UMFC | WMC |
|------|-----|-----|-----|-----|-----|------|-----|
| 1871 | 1·9 |     | 1·8 | 1·7 |     | 1·5  | 1·6 |
| 1881 | 1·7 | 1·5 | 1·4 | 1·6 |     | 1·4  | 1·4 |
| 1891 | 1·8 | 1·4 | 1·4 | 1·7 |     | 1·5  | 1·1 |
| 1901 | 1·5 | 1·2 | 1·3 | 1·4 |     | 1·3  | 1·0 |
| 1911 | 1·4 |     |     | 1·4 | 1·1 |      | 0·9 |
| 1921 | 1·3 |     |     | 1·5 | 1·1 |      | 1·1 |
| 1931 | 1·4 |     |     | 1·6 | 1·4 |      | 1·2 |

*Note*: 1. Methodist death rates calculated by expressing deaths as a percentage of total membership of the previous year.
2. GB: Great Britain. For other abbreviations see Table One.
*Sources: Minutes*; B. R. Mitchell and P. Deane, *Abstract of British Historical Statistics*, Cambridge, 1962.

The labourers are getting tired. They are also getting old. Denominational death rates, the number of deaths in a given year expressed as a percentage of the *total* membership of the previous year, are given in Table Five to which Great Britain death rate for the appropriate age groups (age fifteen and over) is appended. The Wesleyans, much the richest Methodists, had the lowest death rates.

Primitive Methodists, particularly strong in the north and north-east where death rates are high, had the highest Methodist death-rate.

The overall pattern of the figures shows a steep fall in all death rates after 1880. This is partly due to the recruitment of young people at the end of the nineteenth century. The Wesleyans, for example, developed a category of junior membership in the third quarter of the century. Junior membership grew 6·9 per cent per annum in 1881–1906, at a time when full membership was growing 1·1 per cent per annum. Not surprisingly, while Great Britain death rate stood at 1·4–1·5 per cent, Wesleyan death rate fell to 0·9 per cent in 1902–10. The denomination was being rejuvenated through recruitment of new young members.

But this rejuvenation was limited; it made no impression on the Wesleyan M.P.R., for example. It was also temporary. While full membership rose 0·078 per cent per annum in the period 1906–32, junior membership fell 1·10 per cent per annum. The death rate consequently shows a sharp upturn. The current death rate of the Methodist Church is just under 2 per cent, while Great Britain death rate (age group fifteen-plus) is under 1·5 per cent. The ageing of the members follows organizational decline, again suggesting a hard core membership and a less vigorous and aggressive organization seeking to replace lost frontal growth with lateral growth.

The organization's general response to all these changes is indicated by a series of organizational decisions over the forty-year period from 1886. At various times in this period, votes were taken at the local level on the unification of one Methodist denomination with one or more others. These votes were taken in the circuit quarterly meetings, composed of representative and *ex officio* local lay leaders under the chairmanship of the superintendent minister of the circuit. They provide a detailed insight into various aspects of the attitudes and expectations of Methodism in the late nineteenth and early twentieth centuries.

The Primitive Methodist votes on union of 1900 and 1924 illustrate organizational reaction to denominational decline in this period. In 1900, the Primitive Methodists had 186,466 full members. They had undergone a decline in M.P.R. for two decades amounting to a drop of about 16 per cent. They had not had an annual increase of more than 1 per cent per annum since 1884. On the other hand they were still very close to their earlier and remarkable successes, and they were in the middle of a definite if short revival of their fortunes. By 1924 the situation had deteriorated markedly. The denomination still had only 200,986 members. Its M.P.R. had fallen by 29 per cent since 1881. It had suffered thirteen annual decreases of membership. The damage done by this prolonged absolute loss of membership was increased by the fact that it began and coincided with the denomination's lengthy centenary celebrations of its early prowess. Conference declared in 1909 that 'there was a deep sense of humiliation and shame, that, in the very midst of our Centenary celebrations we were confronted by figures that told of spiritual decline in every department of our home-work'.[1]

In 1900 the denomination voted on union with the Bible Christians, a group less than one-fifth the size of the Primitive Methodist Connexion, concentrated in two counties the Primitive Methodists had scarcely penetrated; while in 1924, the Primitive Methodists were faced with absorption into a new denomination of which they would form less than one quarter. The change in attitudes between these two dates is all the more remarkable therefore. In 1900 the Primitive Methodist quarterly meetings rejected union; in fact only 18·5 per cent of the voters supported the project. But in the changed circumstances of 1924, the Primitive Methodists were no longer willing to maintain their separate denominational existence, and they voted 71·2 per cent in favour.

A similar change of attitude took place in Wesleyanism. In 1886, the Wesleyans were 412,384 strong. Their M.P.R. had fallen 3 per cent since 1861. While 1884–6 were bad years for the Wesleyans, they had had very good years in the 1870s and 1880s. In fact their increase of 3·4 per cent per annum two years in succession, in 1883–4, was something they never again improved on. By 1924 however, their M.P.R. had fallen 27 per cent since 1861. In 1907–20 they had had fourteen consecutive years of absolute loss, a net decrease of 22,000 members.

In 1886–7, Wesleyans considered Hughes's scheme of union with the New Connexion, a body whose total membership slightly exceeded that of the Wesleyans in the one county of Cornwall. 140 quarterly meetings, 18·1 per cent of the total, voted in favour of this scheme. In 1924, the union proposals involved amalgamation with the Primitive and United Methodists, many of whom were strongly hostile to the Wesleyans. On this occasion, 85·2 per cent of Wesleyan quarterly meetings voted in favour.

The United Methodist figures are somewhat more complex. In 1904

[1] Quoted in H. B. Kendall, *History of the Primitive Methodist Church*, London, 1919, p. 159.

the Bible Christians, the New Connexion, and the Free Methodists, voted to unite with each other. Various combinations of these bodies had been proposed unsuccessfully for the past seventy years. By 1904, the Free Methodists had suffered a drop of 22 per cent in their M.P.R. since 1871; the New Connexion M.P.R. had fallen 10 per cent since 1871 while the Bible Christians' M.P.R. had fallen 8 per cent since 1891. From comparative indifference, and in some cases open hostility to each other, the three denominations reached near unanimity in 1904, each voting over 90 per cent in favour of union.

By 1914, the United Methodist M.P.R. was 15 per cent lower than the combined M.P.R. of the three denominations in 1901. The new church had been peculiarly unfortunate. In 1924, it had 8,048 less members than it started with in 1907, a drop of 5·4 per cent. Only 66·1 per cent of United Methodist voters were in favour of union, compared with the 90-plus per cent votes of 1904. But in 1904, the three denominations were to a large extent uniting *against* the Wesleyans: the 1905 New Connexion Conference voted 86 per cent against union with that denomination. In 1924 the United Methodists, despite persistent strong grievances, accepted union with the Wesleyans, a significant abandonment under the pressure of decline of positions regarded as vital in 1904.

*The Geography of Methodism*

A definite deterioration can be seen in most aspects of denominational life from the late nineteenth century onwards. In the 1870s and 1880s, M.P.R. begins to fall sharply. Growth rates slacken about 1890, and growth becomes absolute decline in 1907–20. By the 1920s, the entire process of membership turnover is markedly reduced in scale, and the organization shows signs of ageing, and an increasing preference for lateral as opposed to frontal growth.

But these adverse changes do not occur uniformly throughout the organization and this is of some importance in ecumenical developments. Changes in growth, recruitment, loss and leakage are accompanied by a geographical shift of Methodism from north to south. Two different aspects of this shift can be seen. One is a long term change in the distribution of denominational membership; i.e. in the proportion of total full membership in any one area; the other is a short term acceleration of north to south movements about 1880, causing a high growth rate in certain 'new' areas and a lower growth rate, or even decreases, in certain 'old' areas.

Long-term change in distribution of membership can best be illus-trated from Wesleyanism.[1] In 1801 Wesleyanism was dominated by the West Riding, which provided 17·3 per cent of the total member-ship. The other major areas were Lancashire (10·4 per cent), Cornwall (9·6 per cent), and the North Riding (5·1 per cent). The strongest concentration of Methodism was in the north, north-east, midlands, and south-west. Middlesex and London provided 4·1 per cent of the total membership in 1801. Elsewhere in the south were very few Wesleyans indeed.

By 1901 the overwhelming pre-eminence of the West Riding had gone. It was challenged by Lancashire (12·0 per cent in 1901, com-pared with the West Riding's 12·9 per cent) and by Middlesex and London (7·7 per cent). Within the various regions the most midland or metropolitan counties showed the most vigour by 1901: in the south-west, Gloucestershire and Bristol; in East Anglia, Essex; in the midlands, Warwickshire. The importance of Birmingham, Bristol, Manchester, and London, indicates a new phase in Wesleyanism. These areas, now containing a larger proportion of the total number of Wesleyans, were often quite weak, on the M.P.R. index. Lanca-shire Wesleyanism, for example, had a M.P.R. of 1·3 per cent in 1901, compared with the North Riding (3·9 per cent) and Cornwall (6·6 per cent). In other words, although, owing to large concentrations of population, there were many large chapels in Lancashire, the true strength of Wesleyanism in that county was less than in Oxfordshire (1·7 per cent), Wiltshire (1·5 per cent), or Northamptonshire (1·4 per cent).

About 1880, these long-term changes in Methodism were accelerating (see Figure Two). The 'new' methodist areas began to grow at disproportionately high rates compared with the 'old' areas. The short-term change in the growth pattern of Methodism can best be seen in Primitive Methodism. In 1861–81, the picture is dominated by the growth of Lancashire and Cheshire, Yorkshire, Lincolnshire,

[1] Distribution by regions: Scotland; North West (Cumberland, Westmorland, Isle of Man; Lancashire and Cheshire; North East (Northumberland, Durham, North Riding); West Riding; West Midlands (Shropshire, Worcestershire, Herefordshire); Midlands (Staffordshire, Derbyshire, Nottinghamshire, War-wickshire, Leicestershire, Rutland); East Coast (East Riding and Lincolnshire); Wales and Monmouthshire; South West (Cornwall, Devon, Somerset, Gloucestershire); Thames Valley and South Midlands (Berkshire, Oxfordshire, Buckinghamshire, Northamptonshire, Bedfordshire, Hertfordshire); East Anglia (Huntingdonshire, Cambridgeshire, Norfolk, Suffolk, Essex); Mid South (Dorset, Wiltshire, Hampshire); and London and the South East (Middlesex and London, Surrey, Sussex and Kent).

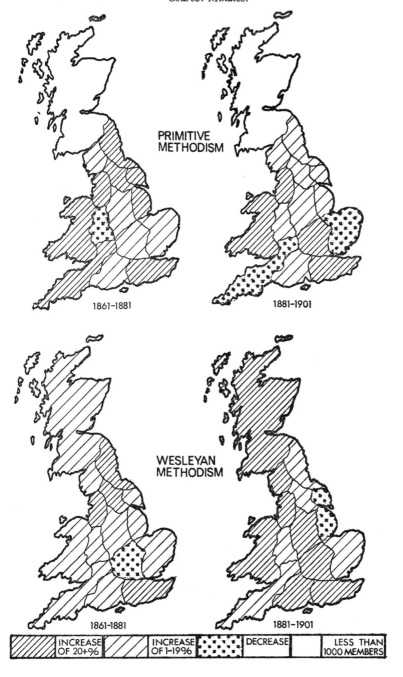

FIGURE TWO. *Growth of Primitive and Wesleyan Methodism by Regions, 1861–1881 and 1881–1901.*
Source: Minutes.

PRIMITIVE METHODISM

1861–1881

1881–1901

WESLEYAN METHODISM

1861–1881

1881–1901

INCREASE OF 20+% | INCREASE OF 1–19% | DECREASE | LESS THAN 1000 MEMBERS

Northumberland and Durham, the denomination's traditional areas. In 1881–1901, the north-east, the east coast and the West Riding no longer contribute as strongly as before to the growth of the denomination. Instead London and the south-east, and the Thames valley and south midlands region, are of new importance. This change can be seen in detail in Table Six. But in London and Middlesex, the centre

TABLE SIX. *Primitive Methodist Growth Rates in Selected Areas, 1881–1901 (per cent).*

|  | 1861–1881 | 1881–1901 |
|---|---|---|
| Essex | 15 | 44 |
| Middlesex and London | 131 | 45 |
| Durham | 98 | 9 |
| West Riding | 72 | 18 |
| Great Britain | 33 | 11 |

Source: *Minutes.*

of the area where the denomination was growing fastest, the Primitive Methodists formed only 0·1 per cent of the population. This change is largely due to migration from 'old' areas into 'new'.

The denomination needed large-scale readjustment to meet the changed situation in which growth was taking place in the areas where it had been traditionally weak. The individual member faced new problems: to be a Primitive Methodist in Kilburn or Tottenham was altogether different from being one in Crook or Ossett. The denomination was weak in the new areas, and the attractions of Wesleyanism and Anglicanism, or of abandoning religion altogether, much stronger. In particular the migrant members of these new southern chapels were likely to desire the social mobility implicit in membership of the Wesleyan or Anglican churches, and to be alienated from their own comparatively outlandish and obscure denomination.

Free Methodism underwent this change relatively slowly, but Wesleyanism changed almost as quickly as Primitive Methodism (see Figure Two). In 1861–81, Wesleyan growth is concentrated in the oldest and strongest areas of the denomination: the West Riding and the north-east; and in two other areas, Lancashire and Cheshire, and London and the south-east. The two old regions fall away after 1881, and give place to a large new block of high growth regions stretching from the midlands to the south-east and the mid-south, while Wesleyanism like other denominations began to grow rapidly in Wales and Scotland in this period. Wesleyanism especially grew in London. This was due not to the evangelical vigour of the Forward Movement but to migration. As a Wesleyan told Charles Booth, 'the great source of growth' for Methodism in London was 'immigration from the country'.[1]

Wesleyan recruitment rates were also particularly high in these 'new' areas. While Cornwall, Yorkshire and Durham were recruiting comparatively slowly, the London districts were recruiting very fast, and the Lancashire and Scotland districts only a little slower. Following this concentration of growth in the south came a wave of new building. Of the 612 new chapels built by the Wesleyans in 1912–32, forty-three were built in the London area alone. Twelve new chapels were constructed in Birmingham, seven in the Portsmouth conurbation, three each in Dover, Bournemouth and Southampton, and seven in Bristol, but only three in Sheffield and two in Leeds.[2]

This new activity, illustrated by reference to specific areas in Table Seven, strained Wesleyan resources. In London and the home counties

TABLE SEVEN. *Decennial Average Wesleyan Methodist Growth Rate in Selected Areas, 1881–1911 (per cent).*

| | |
|---|---|
| Hertfordshire | 38 |
| Kent | 11 |
| Middlesex and London | 25 |
| Surrey | 30 |
| Sussex | 23 |
| Cornwall | – 3 |
| Lancashire | 9 |
| West Riding | 3 |
| Great Britain | 8 |

*Source: Minutes.*

Wesleyanism was nowhere more than 1 per cent of the population in 1901, and Wesleyanism was incomparably stronger in these areas than the other denominations. On these small congregations fell the considerable burden of chapel building. In 1925–31, the Wesleyan 1st London District built one new chapel per 770 members: the Halifax and Bradford District built one per 20,725 members.[3] Obviously more was demanded of London members. But in no denominations were these migrant members hardy pioneers on a religious frontier, eager to make the extra effort and sacrifice necessary to establish their

[1] Charles Booth, *Life and Labour of the People in London*, London, 1902. *Third Series, Religious Influences*, vol. 3, p. 215.

[2] Figures from *Returns of Accommodation Provided in Wesleyan Methodist Chapels and Other Preaching Places (For the Year 1931) Obtained by the Wesleyan Chapel Committee in Pursuance of a Minute of the Conference of 1931*, London, 1932.

[3] Figures based on William Humphrey–E. Aldom French, 14 December 1931, in French Papers (Methodist Archives).

denomination in these new areas. They wanted 'that fashionable suburban church . . . whose groined roof echoed each sabbath morning to the sweet voices of the choir chanting the everglorious Te Deum'. If it was lacking they were offended. Migrants and new suburbanites often found, amid the villas, a 'comfortless' chapel in a 'wretched' situation, occupied by a bucolic rural society. As the *Recorder* observed in 1908, 'The typical village chapel does not attract the city man; it is a poor little place, and the pulpit supply is of necessity chiefly from . . . local preachers . . . the local preacher is an offence, the dingy chapel is "impossible", and the family once living and active members in the Church, slip away to go elsewhere or nowhere.' The effort involved in replacing the village chapel engulfed by suburbia with a more appropriate edifice was frequently beyond the migrants.[1]

Many of them were uncertain whether to preserve their denominational allegiances at all, let alone promote denominational advance. The Rev. Samuel Horton observed in 1920 that 'there is a new generation of Primitive Methodists growing up who care little or nothing for the denominational label'. A United Methodist minister, the Rev. E. E. Redman, declared, 'Methodism without a prefix would give us a standing we do not possess today.' Union offered such Methodists both the promise of more financial assistance for the new areas, and the opportunity to shed outlandish denominational labels for progressively more anonymous and respectable titles, United Methodist Church, Methodist Church. Failing some drastic advance such as union, the Methodists of the new growth areas remained unreliable. Richard Pyke commented of the Bible Christians' recruits in Forest Hill about 1900, 'If anything displeased them they left without any great distress.' Not surprisingly, Wesleyan figures of leakage and loss were particularly high in the new growth areas after 1880.[2]

Changes in the geography of Methodism shed more light on the union voting figures. The new growth areas, which are largely the most dynamic regions of the denomination, and where the denominational traditions are weak, and the resources of the denomination few, particularly favour the move to the superdenomination. In 1900, 1904 and 1924, areas where Methodism was old and strong in M.P.R. terms, but either growing slowly or actually declining – such as Corn-

---

[1] W. Hargreaves Cooper, *In Methodist Byways*, London, 1904, pp. 174-5; *Wesleyan Methodist Magazine*, January 1868, p. 83; *M.R.*, 20 February 1908, p. 12.

[2] *United Methodist*, 11 March 1920, p. 124; 5 August 1920, p. 384; Richard Pyke, *Men and Memories*, London, 1948, p. 72.

wall, East Anglia, Lincolnshire, Yorkshire and Durham – supported union comparatively weakly; while the new growth areas generally supported union strongly.

In 1900 the only Primitive Methodist district actually to vote in favour of union was the sparse but rapidly growing Scottish district. The other areas sympathetic to union were in Lancashire and southern England, both new growth areas. In 1904, Free Methodists in Lancashire and the south were much more enthusiastic about union than those in East Anglia or Yorkshire. Both in 1904 and 1924, Wales and Scotland were high growth, pro-union areas where Methodism was not particularly dense. In 1924, while Lancashire did not support union strongly (although there was much more support in the county than there was in the West Riding), the midlands, Thames valley, London and the south-east were the heart of the union movement, while Cornwall, Yorkshire and Durham were much more critical.

*The Dynamics of Ecumenicalism*

These studies in Methodist statistics suggest a possible outline theory of 'ecumenical dynamics'. With one very important qualification, ecumenicalism in an advanced industrialised society is a function of the decline of religion. This is very obvious at the level of conscious policy making. Methodist leaders, who were particularly conscious of statistics, and who viewed the vicissitudes of their denominations in stark terms, were evidently influenced in making decisions about ecumenical policies by such concepts as critical size and growth rate. As Table One shows, after 1851 the denominations formed very stable percentages of the Methodist population. More weight in the Methodist world could only be obtained by 'lateral' growth. The eventual result was the United Methodist Church. Similarly, as Table Three and Graph Two illustrate, growth rate fell disastrously after 1850, and the denominations steadily decreased in size after 1906. The result was the Methodist Church.

But fundamental changes were taking place in the organization as a whole, as changing patterns of growth rate might suggest, which made the ecumenical option more attractive. A chronic fall in membership-population ratio meant that members were lapsing and not being replaced by new recruits; and that parents could not persuade children to take their place. The factors causing this situation are discussed in the next chapter. Deceleration of growth rate emphasizes the organization's failure to recruit: the absolute number of members, irrespective of population, halted and then fell. Reduction of turnover accompanied this phenomenon. The denomination was failing to recruit, but it still kept a similar percentage of the recruits it made, roughly 50 per cent. The total stock of members changed less from year to year, and members were more loyal to the denomination. This loyalty is also seen in the reduction in scale of leakage of members on removal.

In the late nineteenth- and early twentieth-century situation, the reliance of the denomination on a smaller number of more committed members – less but better, some might say – was paradoxically pathological. It arose from the denomination's failure to attract in any large quantity new recruits, who would have introduced, if only temporarily, fresh influences in the denomination; and who on lapsing would have left a larger area of potential re-recruiting round the denomination. The faithful members' characteristics are most clearly shown by the fact that, after 1910, they were steadily ageing. Obviously the organization needed staid and elderly hard-core membership. But unleavened by new and young recruits, they formed an unadventurous and unbalanced community, involved in a vicious circle: less new recruits left the society less balanced, and the less balanced it became the less willing it was to recruit and the less able it was to attract new members. A denomination with a falling M.P.R., reduced turnover, ageing membership, and dwindling frontal growth, is ready for the lateral growth opportunities available in the ecumenical option.

Not all can seize these opportunities however. The staid and elderly are unenthusiastic. So are all who hanker for the better days of the past, and who are deeply committed to the denomination. So too are the older, stronger areas of the organization where denominational feeling is stronger, where the past and its conflicts are nearer, and where chronic decline of the severest kind creates pessimism and defeatism. These sections of the denomination have no hope for the future, and consequently find ecumenicalism irrelevant; they feel great loyalty to the denomination and would rather be members of a dwindling band of the faithful, than part of a vast anonymous ecumenical crowd.

Enthusiasm for the ecumenical option comes from such younger members as the denomination possesses, all who are indifferent to the past and to denominational tradition, and those who inhabit 'new', socially expansive regions where denominational tradition is feeble and social aspiration and rejection of the past predisposes members to an interest in a wider future. Despite denominational difficulties, of which they are aware, these sections of the organization are optimistic, alive to new ideas, confident the corner can be turned, eager for large solutions to large problems, and impatient of petty denominational loyalties which obstruct the coming of the one Great Church. Ecumenicalism is not simply born of adversity, but of hope in adversity.

# CHAPTER FOUR

# Social Change and Secularization

Wesley's Methodism demanded entire loyalty of its followers. But even in the eighteenth century, the emergence of chapel society restricted the possibility of complete dedication to the doctrines of Methodism and the directives of the hierarchy. As the nineteenth century progressed, it brought a series of new challenges to religious commitment. Members ceased to dispute with ministers but, as Methodists became more educated, prosperous and respectable, they began to question their religion itself. In the long run, this development was more dangerous than schism. The Methodist reformers rejected the hierarchy, but remained zealous Methodists. The new Methodists accepted the hierarchy but revolutionized Methodism.

*Biblical Criticism and the Theory of Evolution*

Sanction, control and a perfectionist ethic characterized the old Methodism. These presupposed a highly personalized relationship between God and man. If God is an all-powerful person, punishing those he accuses, rewarding those he favours, any morality based on teachings of the Bible, his book, has a certain urgency. But if God is understood in more general, and theoretical terms, then morality becomes more permissive. Similarly, if the Bible is verbally inspired, accurate in every word, and describes without exception real events, real people, a real personal God, then morality of the strictest kind can be demanded. But if the Bible is only inspired in a rather general sense, obviously inaccurate at least in parts, and composed of poetry, myth, etc., then morality is at once far less clearly defined and less urgent. A Methodist commented in 1888, 'If the Bible merely *contains* a revelation, less or more, its practical authority is loosened if not lost.' In 1932 the present Methodist Church based its doctrines on 'the Divine revelation recorded in the Holy Scriptures', the very position rejected by this writer. Nineteenth-century biblical criticism was the necessary prelude to general Methodist reunion.[1]

As the century progressed, Methodists became more prosperous, and more educated. They modified their attitude to the Bible in the light of new ideas, and consequently amended various beliefs based upon their reading of the Bible. But even at the end of the nineteenth century some Methodists were hostile towards biblical criticism, and maintained the verbal inerrancy and divine inspiration of the scriptures.

A Wesleyan writer answered *Essays and Reviews* with an argument curiously inconsistent with the Protestant belief in private judgement. He rejected the view

> 'that *the conscience of each man is to be the ultimate authority*–the ultimate standard of truth and rule of conduct;–that if conscience and the Bible appear to differ our first impression must be that we have mistaken the Bible; but if on further inquiry, we are convinced that this is not the case, then we must conclude that the views against which our conscience revolts are human imperfections or mistakes, and not part of the Divine message.'

The writer condemned this fallacy because he wished to preserve the Bible as the inerrant authority of a perfectionist ethic: 'such a theory' of the Bible 'utterly destroys the regulating and governing power of Holy Scripture'.[2]

But confidence in the scriptures was already being undermined. Some Methodists feared in the 1870s that 'many orthodox believers . . . have a great aversion to the doctrine of verbal inspiration. They think the theory mechanical and degrading.'[3] The establishment of theological colleges threatened the old ideas. Ministers acquired closer acquaintance with biblical texts in their original languages and manuscripts. By the 1860s men closely in touch with modern German scholarship, and fairly critical of traditional views of scripture, were being appointed to the staff of theological colleges. By the 1880s and 1890s, a large number of Methodist ministers had been trained in modern types of biblical criticism. This change required a continual rewriting of official positions on the 'Higher Criticism'.

The situation was confused. On the one hand some denounced 'the muddy, mystic and pedantic commentaries which have been flooding this country from Germany' and condemned the 'so-called "findings"

[1] *Methodist New Connexion Magazine*, October 1888, p. 582; cp. Appendix 2.
[2] *Wesleyan Methodist Magazine*, November 1861, p. 1003.
[3] *M.N.C. Mag.*, March 1870, p. 163.

of "Higher" Critics of the Old Testament'.[1] On the other hand, even Bible Christians had to concede that 'for the most part' there could be no quarrel with biblical criticism. In 1889 Wesleyans were told that 'The attitude of the Christian towards scientific and historic criticism is not necessarily hostile. . . . If criticism can assist us to apprehend the human element in the Bible, we welcome it with thankfulness,' although they had been warned in 1856 against 'the perilous experiment of "distinguishing the human and the Divine" in the Bible'.[2]

The Methodist dilemma was clear. Private judgement on the teachings of 'Higher Criticism', however much suppressed, had to be accepted as part of the Protestant tradition in the long run. A Primitive Methodist pointed out that

'Protestantism has given the right to think, which is the right of manhood. The Saxon nations have revolted from the iron despotism of a priesthood that demanded that men should accept dogmas without investigation and without intellectual conviction. This same Protestantism must not try to impose the old yoke on the behalf of a new set of opinions.'

Indeed, however painful this might be, the believer must reject any error that came to light in the Bible, in order to guard the purity of its revelation.[3] Contradiction abounded. Some Methodists held the biblical critic, Cheyne, to be a 'deadly assailant of the truthfulness and trustworthiness of a very large portion of the Holy Writ', others that he 'was full of fine spiritual teaching'. Methodists were bewildered by the whole problem that

'they are God-fearing men, they are scholars deeply versed in the letter of the Word of God; they are men whose amiable "charity" it were an offence to call in question; nay, they are recognized and influential ministers of religion who are the foremost to add to or take from the oracles of God: some questioning the very possibility of inspiration.'[4]

These Methodist reactions to ideas which reached English nonconformity in the mid-nineteenth century, were complicated by contemporary scientific ideas. The Mosaic authorship and scientific

---

[1] *M.N.C. Mag.*, March 1859, p. 184; *Primitive Methodist Magazine*, March 1893, p. 140.
[2] *B.C. Mag.*, June 1894, p. 337; *W.M. Mag.*, December 1856, p. 1116; April 1889, p. 314.
[3] *P.M. Mag.*, February 1884, p. 149; *M.N.C. Mag.*, January 1892, pp. 7–8.
[4] *W.M. Mag.*, January 1866, p. 1; October 1889, p. 796; *Methodist Monthly*, August 1892, pp. 254–5.

accuracy of Genesis had been under attack since the work of eighteenth-century critics. If this authorship was disproved or put in serious doubt, the authority of the work was weakened if not gone. If this happened then certain key passages and consequently the morality based upon them were discredited; while the reduction of the Pentateuch to the level of mythology destroyed belief in the ominiscience (and hence the divinity) of Jesus, who apparently regarded it as a historically accurate work.[1] Geological discoveries and the theory of evolution began to challenge the veracity of the work at a crucial point, its narrative of the origin of life, and of human life in particular.

Methodists upheld the accuracy of the cosmogony and chronology of Genesis well after 1850. 'Senex' (a significant pseudonym) assured the New Connexion in 1883 that Whiston's chronology of Genesis was now upheld by astronomy; and William Cooke, in his inaugural address at the opening of Ranmoor College, in August of that year, told candidates for the New Connexion ministry 'that the human period is that, and that only, which the Holy Bible records'.[2]

But although formal acceptance of Mosaic *authorship* probably lasted well into the twentieth century, the scientific accuracy of the Pentateuch was surreptitiously abandoned. The *Wesleyan Methodist Magazine* ran a routine denunciation of Darwinism in March 1867. The following October it warned that, in biblical matters, 'old views upon several points may yet yield to scientific objections, which as yet remain in suspense'. In December 1868 it became more explicit, remarking, casually enough, that 'It may be assumed that man has been much longer a resident of this world than the commonly received chronology admits.' By August 1873, the date of creation was regarded as an open question.[3]

Yet the theory of evolution could not always be so discreetly accepted, as the crisis over the Rev. W. H. Dallinger's Fernley lecture showed. For seven years Dallinger was prevented from giving this lecture, regarded as an occasion for exposition and defence of Methodist orthodoxy. He rejected arguments for a 'final cause' but held the principle of 'CONCURRENT ADAPTATION' in nature, as evidence for the divine.[4] When finally given, in 1887, the lecture created great

---

[1] Cp. *United Methodist Free Churches Magazine*, June 1861, pp. 339–40.

[2] *M.N.C. Mag.*, January 1883, pp. 8–15; October 1883, p. 585.

[3] *W.M. Mag.*, March 1867, pp. 263–5; October 1867, p. 902; December 1868, p. 1070; August 1873, p. 692.

[4] J. Scott Lidgett, *Reminiscences*, London, 1928, p. 18; W. H. Dallinger, *The Creator and What We May Know of the Method of Creation*, London, 1887, pp. 72 ff.

controversy. The *Bible Christian Magazine* noted that the 'epoch-making book' of this 'ardent Evolutionist' marked a new departure in what had been 'amongst all Protestant churches . . . hitherto . . . the most conservative of what has been commonly accepted as Evangelical truth'. It added, 'That any believer in Revelation can be an Evolutionist, must be, to all simple unscientific believers utterly inexplicable.' A Free Methodist writer felt that 'The Connexional sanction of the Wesleyan Methodist body has been given to the theory of evolution.' The lecture was praised as 'a valuable contribution to the battle against unbelief', which indeed it was, in the sense that it accepted evolutionary ideas but retained a theistic position.[1] Yet the work marked the irrevocable rejection of the Genesis creation narrative. The effect of this on the status of Genesis, and of the Bible as a whole, was far more important than the abstract debate about final causes.

Reactions to the conflict between evolutionary ideas and Genesis changed significantly. Simple rejection of evolution was still possible. 'The miserable theories which would lay man lower than the dust and trace his "dim original and prime" among the crudest and lowest forms of organic things' indicated that 'science . . . had gone mad in the climax of its pride'.[2] But as this attack became more difficult to sustain, some held that, even if true, evolution could not affect the central verities of religion just as biblical criticism would leave the true riches of the Bible untouched. The *Methodist New Connexion Magazine* argued that, 'Were the descent of man from a primordial speck of living jelly to be demonstrated with mathematical precision, it would leave unaffected the question of the existence of a supreme Deity.'[3]

Others simply denied that science and religion clashed. 'Moses and geologic science shake hands' Bible Christians were told. By a disarming process of reasoning, Samuel Hulme discovered that 'As both Nature and Revelation are divine works, they cannot contradict each other.' Thus, 'The books of nature and revelation beautifully harmonize. There may be *seeming* discrepancies, but they exist not in the books, but in the human comprehension.'[4] Those who found this impossible to believe nevertheless expected a reconciliation of religion

[1] *B.C. Mag.*, April 1888, pp. 189–90; *U.M.F.Cs. Mag.*, February 1888, p. 88; *P.M. Mag.*, January 1888, p. 57.
[2] *W.M. Mag.*, September 1863, p. 816.
[3] *M.N.C. Mag.*, February 1882, p. 107.
[4] *B.C. Mag.*, July 1863, p. 270; *M.N.C. Mag.*, October 1870, p. 603; *P.M. Mag.*, April 1858, p. 159.

and science in an imminent utopian future. 'We are nearing a Religio–
Scientific age', a Free Methodist claimed in 1894, 'an age in which the
so long judged antagonistic things of the scientist will be built into the
great temple of revealed truth.'[1]

When this theological micawberism ran out, some urged respect for
evolutionary ideas, pointing out that 'To throw mud is one thing, to
overturn hard facts is another and different matter'.[2] A perhaps more
acceptable retreat was found in a trivial natural theology, in which a
'sunny wander in the green fields with eyes opened by science' provided evidence for the existence of God from the 'wonders of nature'.[3]
Denominational magazines' 'Scientific Notes' always tended to be
mere recitation of natural curiosities. By the 1890s, when the evolution controversy was largely settled and lost, the magazines engaged
more lavishly than ever in such misleading exercises, while flatly
rejecting the position of an earlier age. A Primitive Methodist wrote,

'The old contention that the Bible is an infallible teacher of science–
that in the childhood of the race there were anticipated the results
of ages of vast research including the data secured by the trained
skill of scientific men of today–is heard no more. The wonder is
that reflecting men could ever have conceived anything so contrary
to reason.'[4]

*The Obsolescence of Theology*

New Methodists dismissed the biblical theories of old. This change
accompanied and assisted rejection of older Methodist ideas about
hell as a divinely appointed place of unspeakable and interminable
torture reserved for the wicked on their death.

'There endless crowds of sinners lie,
And darkness makes their chains!
Tortured with keen despair they cry,
Yet wait for fiercer pains'

the Bible Christians discovered. Discussing the unrighteous, a Primitive Methodist pointed out that 'As soon as the dread sentence is
pronounced, hell from beneath will move to meet them, while amidst
the shrieks and groans of their despairing souls, demons will drag

[1] *M.M.*, August 1894, p. 225.
[2] *W.M. Mag.*, March 1888, pp. 220–5; *M.N.C. Mag.*, April 1898, p. 151.
[3] Frank Ballard, *The Mission of Christianity, or, What Are Churches for?
A Modern Religious Inquiry*, London, 1891, p. iv.
[4] *P.M. Mag.*, May 1891, p. 294.

them down to the doleful regions of woe'. As late as 1872, Wesleyans were directed to 'the brink of the "lake"' and to 'the everlasting smoke of its "fire and brimstone"'. The whole Methodist world was agreed on hell. Bunting loved to shake the sinner 'over the burning billows of the bottomless pit'. Everett gained the nickname of 'the hell-fire lad'.[1]

This happy agreement on doctrinal matters did not preserve the unity of the brethren. Christianity, in general, is a system of rewards and punishments, in which hell is an essential element. If there is no hell, there is nothing to be saved from. Hell is the basis of a coercive system of compliance. Thomas Jackson noted, 'No man who duly considers what it is to be guilty in the sight of an Almighty Lawgiver and Judge, can ever be happy either in life or in death, while he remains uncertain as to whether or not his sin may be forgiven'.[2] This fear had an important role in all Methodist groups. Evangelism meant proclaiming the God who 'reserves inevitable and terrific punishment for . . . sin in eternity'.[3] Further, the fear of hell was used and commended as a means of securing moral conformity, a policy exemplified in the vivid declaration of the *Bible Christian Magazine*, 'Young men, an impure thought . . . has in it all the elements of a DAMNATION *that burneth for ever*.' A Primitive Methodist noted,

'The theology of our fathers, in its sterner features, often filtered down through the fingers of a closed hand, or the application of the toe of a boot. They believed in both Law and Grace, but with a powerful predilection for the law, especially when the sinner was a refractory boy.'[4]

The Wesleyan, S. R. Hall, feared that the non-attenders at the class meeting were 'going to hell gospel-hardened'; while the Primitive Methodist, Joseph Gibson, warned such that they faced 'the pit of blackness and darkness'. Those who seceded or were expelled were consigned to hell: reformers accused Wesleyan ministers of believing 'That when a superintendent cooly [*sic*] draws his pen through an individual's name, that act is immediately ratified above, and a pen drawn through the name as it stands . . . in the Book of Life.' The

[1] *B.C. Mag.*, May 1850, p. 182; *P.M. Mag.*, April 1855, pp. 205–9; *W.M. Mag.*, February 1872, p. 140; *U.M.F.Cs. Mag.*, September 1886, p. 499; Richard Chew, *James Everett: A Biography*, London, 1875, p. 72.

[2] Thomas Jackson, *Recollections of My Own Life and Times*, London, 1873, p. 326.

[3] *W.M. Mag.*, July 1858, p. 620.

[4] *Ibid.*, June 1867, p. 547; *B.C. Mag.*, October 1889, p. 469; James Flanagan, *Scenes from My Life*, London, 1907, p. 25.

accusation had some strength: Buntingites believed they could 'pronounce a decision on the career of the departed', especially if they were opponents.[1] Hell was a weapon in ecclesiastical conflict, used to secure conformity to different sets of doctrines. Within an organization it had an integrative effect. Between one organization and another, its function was divisive; and belief in hell was associated with rigorous doctrines, with a strong penal content, which themselves promoted division.

But after 1875, the concept of hell was increasingly modified. Primitive Methodists noted the concealment of hell in 'soft and dainty phrases'. In 1900, Joseph Ritson noted,

> 'At the opening of the century the doctrine of eternal punishment was held almost universally and in its most literal and absolute form. . . . It is still in the creeds, and in some form it is still held by many in all the churches; but it cannot be denied that comparatively little is heard of it in the pulpit.'[2]

By 1878, the New Connexion rejected the idea of *eternal* punishment. In 1884 its *Magazine* described death as 'peace and sleep', and in 1889 it adopted a common reinterpretation of hell, the estrangement of the believer from God, in this life. The *Wesleyan Methodist Magazine* of 1878 wanted a more 'positive' approach to hell, and less emphasis on 'the *poena damni* of the old theology'. In 1885, the Wesleyan J. R. Gregory called for a 'more charitable' attitude on this question. M. G. Pearse, the leading Wesleyan novelist, and H. P. Hughes, the most popular Wesleyan minister of the end of the century, both agreed that sin was a medical, not a legal concept, and if the sinner was merely sick, the torments of hell could scarcely be appropriate.[3]

The Wesleyan, G. W. Olver, rejected both the eternal duration and the bodily torment associated with hell in his Fernley Lecture for 1878. The trustees refused to publish the lecture, and he was given a quasi-official answer and condemnation. The Rev. J. A. Beet was

---

[1] T. Nightingale, *Life of the Rev. Samuel Romilly Hall*, London, 1879, p. 53; *P.M. Mag.*, July 1865, p. 396; *Wesleyan Delegate Takings: or Short Sketches of Personal and Intellectual Character, as Exhibited in the Wesleyan Delegate Meeting, Held in Albion Street Chapel, London, on the 12th, 13th, 14th and 15th March, 1850, by Some of Them. Together with an Exposition and Defence of the Resolutions, Passed at That Meeting*, Manchester, 1850, pp. 162–3; Benjamin Gregory, *Autobiographical Recollections*, London, 1903, pp. 404–5.
[2] *P.M. Mag.*, June 1875, p. 341; December 1900, pp. 823–4.
[3] *M.N.C. Mag.*, December 1878, p. 680; August 1884, p. 496; February 1889, p. 94; *W.M. Mag.*, May 1878, p. 396; March 1885, p. 211; *The City Road Magazine*, August 1874, p. 375; D. P. Hughes, *The Life of Hugh Price Hughes*, London, 1904, p. 249.

condemned by the Wesleyan Conference in 1898, and again in 1902, for denying the eternal duration of punishment. The official Wesleyan position on hell was still peculiarly stringent. Beet merely wrote,

'The writers of the New Testament agree to describe, with more or less definiteness, the punishment to be inflicted in the day of Christ's return as actual suffering. . . . They give no ground for hope that the agony of the lost will ever cease; but they do not plainly and categorically assert its endless continuance.'[1]

Yet, on the popular level, the battle against hell was already largely won by the writings of Frank Ballard, a Wesleyan Minister. In a vigorous attack on hell-fire preaching, he rejected the picture of 'God our Father' as 'a merciless Shylock, exacting the last throb of agony from an innocent and helpless victim'. Ballard was denounced. The *Wesleyan Methodist Magazine* condemned his 'off-hand, incidental, jaunty, jerky style' and his 'wanton and injurious imputations'. The *Bible Christian Magazine* rejected his 'absurd caricature' and found him 'a little too smart'. The *Primitive Methodist Magazine* announced, 'Mr Ballard has committed a grave mistake in publishing this pamphlet', and asked 'Did not Jesus preach about unquenchable fire? Can we improve on His Method?'[2] Despite this, Ballard's great popularity suggests that he had succeeded in disarming the Methodist hierarchy of its strongest weapon against dissident members and external enemies.

The abolition of hell released Methodism from the coercive element in the Methodist ethic, and from meticulous observances which it had inherited from Wesley, and from the Christian tradition of a millennium. The 'three-storey universe' had been blurred. The wealthier and more educated Methodists of the late nineteenth century wanted a more discreet and respectable creed than the boorish old-time religion. The *Stamford Mercury* expressed this point of view in 1883 when it asked, 'When will religious revivalists . . . recognize the fact that no field for their exertions exists amongst the uniformly intelligent and highly virtuous inhabitants of this place? "They that be whole need not a physician." '[3] If they were whole in Stamford, they were whole

---

[1] G. W. Olver, *Life and Death, the Sanctions of the Law of Love*, London, 1878; J. L. Posnett, *Notes on the Rev. G. W. Olver's Fernley Lecture*, London, 1878; Hughes, *op. cit.*, pp. 600–3; J. A. Beet, *The Last Things*, London, 1898, p. 193.

[2] Frank Ballard, *Is Amusement Devilish?*, London, 1889, p. 8; *W.M. Mag.*, June 1890, p. 465; *B.C. Mag.*, March 1890, pp. 145–9; *P.M. Mag.*, September 1889, p. 570; February 1890, p. 123.

[3] Quoted in Eileen Mumby, *Methodism in Caistor*, Caistor, 1961, p. 18.

in Birmingham, Bristol and London. The new Methodists sat loose to all that might suggest they were not.

Hard-line Methodism gave way to soft. Denominational opinion became uneasy about the rigid doctrinal system Methodism had inherited, with its stark emphasis on hell and its severe notions of rewards and punishments. The denomination solved the problem this inheritance presented to its new respectability by abandoning the inheritance. A New Connexion writer of 1897 lamented, 'Our theology, the chief articles of which are so rational, and temperate, we have been ignobly afraid to teach.' The *Wesleyan Methodist Magazine* commented in 1881 that a 'sentimental and irrational clamour . . . has recently been raised against dogmas and creeds'.[1]

Faced with this process optimists claimed that 'the things which cannot be shaken will remain', and that 'In the sifting of creeds only the chaff will be blown away.' Pessimists and conservatives condemned these changes as 'the present fashionable "down-grade" in theological teaching'. But Ballard destroyed doctrine with the devastating thesis that 'There is absolutely no such thing as "orthodoxy". It is, at most, only a relative term adopted with wise complacency by a section of the religious community.'[2] Benjamin Gregory condemned the new ideas of the nineties as 'a crude and puffy product of the time', and insisted that abandonment of doctrine meant the decline of the organization. Yet his position 'gave great offence to several of the leaders and to a considerable number of the rank and file of Methodism'. Optimists and progressives were in the ascendant.[3]

The new Methodists, prosperous and respectable, gladly adopted the concept of progress as the basis of Christian belief. But although optimistic elements are scarcely lacking from Christianity, the concepts of the fall, sin and judgement, concentrated attention on human depravity and incapacity. The theory of evolution reinterpreted human history as an upward not downward trend. Reinforced by the general sympathy for the idea of progress in nineteenth-century England, the theory proved irresistible. In 1864 the *Wesleyan Methodist Magazine* declared, 'We strongly object . . . to the representation of the Fall of Man as a "step in the development of the race".' Yet by 1890, its readers learned that 'Progress is the law of life and of

[1] *M.N.C. Mag.*, May 1897, p. 141; *W.M. Mag.*, January 1881, p. 66.
[2] *B.C. Mag.*, January 1890, p. 64; *P.M. Mag.*, February 1884, p. 149; *M.N.C. Mag.*, December 1890, p. 754; Frank Ballard, *What Are Churches for? Part 1. The Home*, London, 1890, p. 14.
[3] Benjamin Gregory, *Sidelights on the Conflicts of Methodism*, pp. 574 ff; Gregory, *Autobiographical Recollections*, p. 439.

health. . . . The Bible speaks much of this law of Progress,' and indeed that 'The Methodist Church is, in spirit, progressive.'[1]

The theological implications of progress were made clear by a Bible Christian who wrote in 1855 that 'Theology, in its domestic sense, as an *objective* study, is not progressive, but *subjectively*– referring to the possibility of our minds getting a deeper insight into the latent meanings of a revealed system of truth–it is progressive.' Acceptance of the historical relativity of perceptions of an *'objective'* truth brought Methodism very near Ballard's dictum. This idea of progress meant elimination of dogma and creed. A Free Methodist declared,

'We cannot help feeling that it would be better for the rising life of our churches if we had fewer creeds. We would not have our young men feel that they have to be held down and cramped by the thinking of a past, and possibly a dead age. . . . Rather let the truth come in all the freshness and force of new life; let it come in the garb of modern science if it will. It is all the same truth, and must lead up to the same great God.'[2]

In particular, progress led Methodism to reconstruct its concept of the deity. A Primitive Methodist writing in 1900 saw the most significant change in nineteenth-century theology as that from 'the Divine Sovereignty' to 'the Fatherhood of God'. Older ministers were dissatisfied. Lidgett, the leading Wesleyan exponent of this new concept, was accused of heresy in 1897, and his Fernley Lecture for that year was held up by Randles, the current president, because 'the lecture did not take sufficient account of Divine Justice'. But so fast were attitudes changing that, five years later, Randles proposed Lidgett for a post at one of the Wesleyan theological colleges.[3]

The all-loving father figure disposed of hell. It did not however deal with the challenge of science to the whole anthropomorphic scheme. Here idealist philosophy came to the rescue. Christians welcomed this philosophy as an apparently complete rejection of materialism, interpreting the world in terms of mind, idea, 'force' and 'immanence'. Of course it tended to produce, in conjunction with theology, a generalized pantheism, unacceptable to Christians who wished to preserve some of their traditional theology and organizations but quite attractive to others.

[1] *W.M. Mag.*, July 1864, p. 645; January 1888, p. 1; May 1890, p. 342.

[2] *B.C. Mag.*, October 1855, p. 380; *U.M.F.Cs. Mag.*, June 1888, p. 285.

[3] *P.M. Mag.*, December 1900, pp. 822–3; Lidgett, *op. cit.*, pp. 22–3.

Pantheism was condemned but idealist theology was extensively used. 'B.Sc.', in his 'Chats on Contemporary Science', assured the New Connexion that one of 'the general principles on which the doctrines of modern physics rest' was that 'Force is a manifestation of the divine will'. The *Methodist Monthly* talked fashionably about 'The Immanence of God'. H. P. Hughes, symbol of the Wesleyan 'Forward Movement' had great 'sympathy with the neo-Hegelian exposition of Christianity, which T. H. Green . . . had taught him'. The *necessity* of idealist theology in a world in which a Wesleyan could casually speak of man as 'the end of the evolutionary process', was clear: 'Unless God is immanent in the universe, energizing in all its forces, and controlling all its processes, it would be impossible in these days to believe in the reality of Providence.'[1]

While idealistic philosophy refurbished the idea of God, *kenosis* mitigated the problem of incarnation. Ministers began to emphasize fellowship and service rather than authority and control. They wanted to teach an incarnate God who was not a supernatural ruler and judge but a charming friend and servant of all. They were disturbed by biblical critical evidence of limitations on Jesus's knowledge; and they were no longer confident, in the new, scientific age, that they even knew what incarnation was. *Kenosis*, emptying, was claimed to be the process by which God surrendered omnipotence and omniscience to become incarnate in Jesus Christ. The humanity of the saviour was confirmed, his divinity discreetly minimized: thus presenting Jesus as friend rather than ruler while explaining his apparent shortcomings; and all this was done by using for the old-fashioned 'incarnation' the new, scientific Greek word *kenosis*.

Methodists enthused over *kenosis*, despite official caution. Wesleyan writers claimed that 'Christ came to supply . . . the immanence of God in man'. They emphasized in true kenotic manner 'the intense and thorough-going humanness' of Christ, i.e. his elimination of the divine. Others confidently declared that 'Man has been taken up into the person of God's son', and that 'In the perfect man God most fully realized himself'; and they preached kenotic sermons on 'The Son of God under Human Limitations' and 'God's Impoverishment Man's Enrichment'.[2]

These changes replaced Methodist commitment to traditional

---

[1] *M.N.C. Mag.*, February 1898, p. 46; January 1888, pp. 50–1; *M.M.*, February 1900, pp. 33–35; R. M. Pope, *The Life of Henry J. Pope*, London, 1913, p. 211; Hughes, *op. cit.*, pp. 134–5; *W.M. Mag.*, February 1898, pp. 97–8.

[2] *W.M. Mag.*, May 1896, p. 235; June 1896, p. 403; *P.M. Mag.*, December 1893, pp. 721–3; December 1895, pp. 895–7; December 1896, pp. 901–4.

doctrines by commitment to the personality of Christ. A Primitive Methodist, discussing the authority of the creeds, asked, 'What is the mind of Christ? That is the central thing–the highest in authority– the last in appeal. Historical traditions and ecclesiastical documents are shell and husk.' A Free Methodist praised the new 'Christo-centric' faith, which had all the superiority of 'real *spiritual* religion' over 'creeds' and 'theology', and disparaged older Christianity in which 'Christ is almost lost in . . . reasonings and pleadings of creeds'.[1] The personality of Christ, read in the flexible terms of the late nineteenth-century bourgeoisie, replaced older and stiffer doctrines of the divine majesty, of sin, death and hell.

Bible Christians preached on 'The Heroism of Christ' and stressed his 'completeness of character and generosity of disposition'. A New Connexion writer declared, 'We delight to hold up the character of our Master–Christ as the highest and noblest of all history.' Among the achievements of the century's theology, the *Primitive Methodist Magazine* listed, 'the clearer apprehension of Christ's true humanity', one of the most important aspects of which was that 'Jesus sat at the Social Board'. Wesleyans also praised 'The Feasting Christ'; spoke of his 'intensely magnetic' personality and 'matchless mental power'; glorified 'The homeliness of Jesus', and 'his loving, sunny, sympathetic life'. Not surprisingly, a Free Methodist noted that 'the Cross is preached more in its spirit than in its outward horror and bloody shame'.[2]

Themes of violence, death and destruction, common to traditional Christian theology and art were being replaced by the 'loving, sunny, sympathetic life' of Jesus. This travesty of the New Testament signi-fied the complete recasting of Christianity according to the wishes of the religious bourgeoisie of the late nineteenth century. Social change had rendered traditional Christianity obsolete. Educated believers found the fundamentalist attitude to the Bible old-fashioned and undignified. They wanted to see it not as a book of crude folk-lore, whose veracity though dubious could never be questioned, but as a repository of great spiritual truths. The aged and uncouth idea of hell now seemed as barbaric as certain sections of the Old Testament. Believers refused to be party to the reputed happenings in hell; and

[1] *P.M. Mag.*, May 1884, p. 23; *M.M.*, August 1894, p. 231.
[2] *B.C. Mag.*, January 1873, pp. 4–12; January 1875, p. 6; *M.N.C. Mag.*, August 1895, p. 269; *P.M. Mag.*, December 1900, p. 823; March 1891, pp. 138–42; *W.M. Mag.*, June 1896, pp. 403–5; March 1896, p. 210; February 1880, pp. 145 ff; June 1883, pp. 401–6; *M.M.*, August 1894, p. 231; August 1895, p. 226.

they rejected the belief that their settled and comfortable lives could be expected to end in the dreadful violence of eternal punishment.

Gradually they extricated themselves from traditional doctrines and creeds. They began to construct a much looser, vaguer and more palatable Christianity. God was not ruler and judge but loving father. The universe was progressive and dynamic, informed by a divine evolutionary benevolence. Christ was no longer the immediate and overwhelming demonstration of divine omnipotence and justice in human life. He was, instead, rather like a popular minister of religion, smiling but grave, enormously learned, wise and experienced, but full of help, understanding, generosity, and fun. He was still infinitely superior to ordinary men, but he showed that he was one of us, for he 'sat at the Social Board'. Religion was a permanent Sunday School Anniversary, Christ the affable minister, the universe a tidy church hall full of happy faces. Traditional Christianity was dead.

*The Decline of the Class Meeting and the Rise of 'Worship'*

Such doctrinal change demanded organizational change. The older structure of Methodist life was too rigid and severe to express the new theology of friendly religion. In particular, new ideas conflicted with the aims of the class meeting. Even in the 1870s, ministers agreed that class was 'the inmost institution of Methodism . . . the matrix within which every element characteristic of Methodism is nurtured'; and that 'If ever the day should come when the Class Meeting is either actually or virtually abolished, Methodism will lose its identity and be merged into something else, widely, if not essentially, different.'[1]

Methodism existed to evangelize, i.e. to recruit members. Its characteristic 'emphases' were on 'perfection' or 'entire sanctification', i.e. on conformity to Methodist values. Its characteristic institution was the class, which served to secure this conformity. 'The primary object of class-meetings was to mark disorderly walkers', a Wesleyan apologist noted.[2] The system of Methodist 'fellowship' could promote a profound camaraderie, but the class was also the means of directing and controlling members. In Wesley's system, doctrine and organization were intimately connected. A Wesleyan lady, Mrs. Mary Lomas, recognized this clearly when 'she most cordially believed in the doctrines . . . of the society but regarded the discipline as not less calculated to promote holy living'. Even among the most liberal

---

[1] *U.M.F.Cs. Mag.*, January 1866, p. 42; *W.M. Mag.*, April 1865, p. 335.

[2] Humphrey Sandwith, *A Reply to Lord John Russell's Animadversions on Wesleyan Methodism, in His 'Memoirs of the Affairs of Europe from the Peace of Utrecht'*, London, 1830, p. 61.

Methodists of the 1850s, 'To be absent from class meeting for any length of time was to run serious risk of dismissal.'[1]

But from an early period, superior members were hostile to the class. A New Connexion writer in the 1860s feared that 'In recent years, ministers, members, and non-members have been innoculated with an Anti-Class-Meeting virus.' A Wesleyan writer of 1864 noted that '*a dislike to class-meetings* is spreading among the families of our more wealthy people'. Methodists began to resent the threat to their respectability of guidance by fervent but poor leaders who they regarded as inferior to themselves: 'Class-leaders now consist mostly of poor, illiterate men; how unseemly for a person of respectability and education to be taught by a humble artizan.'[2]

Methodists objected, however, not merely to being governed by poor saints but to being governed at all. They disliked being interrogated as to their behaviour and 'experience' and preferred not to give 'testimony' on such subjects. The rebellion was particularly associated with those who were 'educated amid greater refinement', and were 'presumed to be somewhat superior to many of their neighbours in Taste'. Such people found the class monotonous and stereotyped. E. E. Kellett cited the nonsense choruses sung by the faithful: 'And take a pill, and take a pill, and take a pilgrim to the skies'. A Free Methodist in 1873 commented, 'Many persons assign the formality of our class-meetings, as a reason for not attending; they say it is the same old thing repeated over and over again.' Of course, the purpose of the class was conformity: it strove towards perfect monotony. As long as this monotony was vitalized by the zeal, or fear, of the members, it was acceptable. As soon as the emotions behind the class faded, what was left was irksome and irrelevant duty, a feast of jargon.[3]

Alienation from the class may be explained as mere surfeit. Dr. Eric Baker wrote in 1959,

'The class meeting has disappeared . . . because the letter killed the spirit. I can remember as a boy sitting in such a meeting while one after another . . . described what God had done for him, usually

---

[1] Alexander Bell, *Memorials of Mrs Mary Knowles Lomas*, London, 1844, p. 49; Thomas Pointon Dale, *History of Brunswick Church, Bury*, Bury, 1896, p. 82.

[2] *M.N.C. Mag.*, February 1867, p. 125; April 1873, p. 210; *W.M. Mag.*, September 1864, p. 881.

[3] *M.N.C. Mag.*, October 1874, p. 593; *W.M. Mag.*, April 1865, p. 336; E. E. Kellett, *As I Remember*, London, 1936, p. 135; *U.M.F.Cs Mag.*, January 1873, p. 8.

forty years before. As they appeared to be unaware that he had done anything since, it is not surprising that people soon got tired of that.'

But alienation from the class meeting came not 'soon' but late in Methodist history, and it coincided with rising respectability. Benjamin Gregory, himself a conservative in religious matters, agreed that 'such spiritual reunions' as the class 'must be dreary and dismal to all who do not feel the necessity of intense personal earnestness in religion'. He recognized that religious testimony particularly offended the respectable. 'A certain monotonousness is inseparable from a . . . record of the alternations and recurrences of Christian life,' he wrote. 'Besides, there seems to many . . . a certain provincial tone about the simplest utterances of earnest godliness.'[1]

The predicament of many was summed up by the Wesleyan 'Anxious' when he wrote in 1892,

'For three generations my family have been earnest supporters of Methodism, and their love is equally shared by me, but I have never been able to join a class. There is something which makes it impossible for me to reveal my hopes, my fears, my joys, my sorrows, and to lay bare my innermost thoughts.'

Many of the 'children of fathers and mothers who played a great part in the formation of our denomination', a Free Methodist noted in 1903, were now not members but merely seat-holders.[2]

Despite resistance from older and more conservative leaders, the victory went to new liberal ideas. A committee appointed by the New Connexion in 1875 advocated reduction of the class to an *optional* membership test, although this was finally rejected at the 1882 Conference. The 1895 Free Methodist Assembly recognized, in its 'Circuit Rules and Regulations', 'Class Meeting' and 'sacramental' members, tested by attendance at class or the sacrament respectively. A Wesleyan committee, appointed in 1904, came to similar conclusions. Its proposals were shelved indefinitely: the force of events rendered implementation unnecessary.[3]

By the end of the nineteenth century, members could absent them-

[1] Eric W. Baker, *Fathers and Brethren*, London, 1959, p. 12; Benjamin Gregory, *The Thorough Business Man, Memoirs of Walter Powell, Merchant, Melbourne and London*, London, 1871, pp. 70, 99–100.
[2] *Methodist Recorder*, 30 June 1892, p. 451; *Free Methodist*, 10 September 1903, p. 606.
[3] *M.N.C. Mag.*, July 1876, p. 390; July 1882, p. 395; J. Robinson Gregory, *A History of Methodism*, London, 1911, vol. 2, pp. 110–12.

selves from class with impunity, not least because their absence would scarcely be noticed. Wesley's classes contained approximately a dozen members. After his death the class meeting remained small. At Probus, in Cornwall, classes apparently averaged eighteen members in 1816. The median size of the forty-one classes of the Mansfield Circuit in 1814 was thirteen. But the median size of a famous 'model' class at Spring Head chapel, Wednesbury, during 1886–1905, was seventy-three members. In 1904, W. Hargreaves Cooper described a model class leader who ran two classes totalling 170 members.[1]

This drastic increase in size indicates the transition from small, closely-knit, disciplined groups to a large, optional weekly gathering probably indistinguishable from a week-night service. Evidence of attendance levels is sparse. But about 1900, apparently only 40 per cent of members attended class. Not surprisingly, with the declining popularity of the class, leaders were difficult to recruit, and especially in urban areas such as Manchester and London, female class leaders were widely appointed. Such leaders probably exercised little control over members and confined themselves – on the modern Methodist pattern – to the quarterly distribution of tickets.[2]

By 1900 the class meeting had partly disappeared or been altered out of recognition, even though it remained in theory at least the test of membership. The changes it underwent indicate the nature of changes taking place in Methodism as a whole. Discipline was no longer acceptable. In 1884, Joseph Bush asked class leaders, in words which would have been treason for a Wesleyan minister thirty years before, 'Are we not verily guilty before God if we exclude members hastily?' Twelve years later a Wesleyan writer commented, 'It is wonderful . . . with what lightness we dispatch people – Methodistically, I mean – when any of our methods and usages is irksome to them. . . . The Church chariot may easily become a Juggernaut.'[3] Failure of nerve characterizes the contrast between this attitude and the beliefs and behaviour of traditional Methodism.

The class was converted from the organ of discipline and control to the organ of 'fellowship', sociability, entertainment. Bible Christians wanted the class to be 'more social – more like a family circle'. A New Connexion writer pictured the modern class with 'no stiffness, no

[1] Thomas Shaw, *Methodism in Probus, 1781–1961*, Probus, 1961; J. E. Alcock, *Notes on the Progress of Wesleyan Methodism in the Mansfield Circuit*, Mansfield, 1900; *Methodist Times*, 25 January 1905, p. 50; W. Hargreaves Cooper, *In Methodist Byways*, London, 1904, p. 57.

[2] *M.R.*, 4 June 1891, p. 424; 7 March 1907, p. 25.

[3] *W.M. Mag.*, May 1884, p. 394; May 1896, p. 327.

formality, no making of speeches, no use of hackneyed expressions', conducted, with great blessings for all, in a 'bright, cheery apartment'.[1] The new class is seen at its most characteristic in *Daniel Quorm and His Religious Notions*, M. G. Pearse's best seller. The studied provincialism of the book, its ideal of homely commonsense, and its cult of cheerfulness, apparently struck just the right note for late nineteenth-century Methodism. Daniel gave the class a deadly blow. The doleful, sin-obsessed class leader of his youth was 'enough to kill any class meetin'', he observes. 'We leaders must keep the place bright and cheerful and attractive if we want to keep the members. Why, I should everybid as soon . . . think o' goin' with my apron on and in my shirt sleeves as think o' takin' all my cares an' worries to the class.' The class leader should in fact be 'a kind o' doctor, that can give each one the prescription he needs – the blessed promise that suits his case'.[2] The idea of sin has disappeared, as has the disciplinary function of the class; and the new emphasis of the class, on comfort, friendship and entertainment, demands removal of alienating religious boundaries.

While the Class Meeting declined, Methodists became more interested in worship. Toward the end of the nineteenth century great emphasis was laid on respectable and orderly services whose value was measured by their influence on the spiritual susceptibilities of Methodists. Primitive Methodists became sensitive about such behaviour as 'coming late to the house of God, stumping up the aisle with a heavy tread, or with squeaky boots'. A New Connexion condemned the efforts of 'rough pulpit comedians'.[3]

By 1878, Wesleyans were presumed to prefer 'the devout and the orderly' and to find impassioned gospel services 'more than unpleasant'. The modern Wesleyan preacher of 1896 was 'more sympathetic and human', having extensive 'acquaintance with modern literature . . . contact with life', and 'a hopeful breadth of vision and a sweet reasonableness of tone'. M. G. Pearse 'was brought up among people who felt that a good sermon was an enjoyment, an entertainment'. Pearse's preaching was ' "full of vivid illustrations and especially of exquisite dramatic vignettes, revealing a tender and pitiful insight into the pathos and frailty of our common life"'. His role in the economy of Hughes' West London Mission was to ' "edify the saints"'.[4]

[1] *B.C. Mag.*, June 1888, p. 290; *M.N.C. Mag.*, January 1885, pp. 20–7.
[2] M. G. Pearse, *Daniel Quorm and His Religious Notions*, 1st Series, London 1905, pp. 61 ff.
[3] *P.M. Mag.*, February 1888, p. 78; *M.N.C. Mag.*, May 1897, p. 140.
[4] *W.M. Mag.*, June 1878, p. 463; January 1898, pp. 39–41; G. Unwin and J. Telford, *Mark Guy Pearse*, London, 1930, pp. 33, 43, 147.

Emphasis on worship as a spiritual experience or, in more secular terms, an entertainment, did not signify a greater Methodist awareness of the Christian tradition of ritual. Commenting in 1917 on his travels as President of the Primitive Methodist Conference, the Rev. Arthur Guttery said,

> 'Especially among the young I found a craving for an orderly and beautiful service that should provide a worthy channel of expression for the sincerities and sanctities of worship. At more than one Sacramental service the choir led the praise with great reverence, and an anthem did not detract from the devotional quality of the hour.'

But the members who wanted a choral anthem did not necessarily want a greater emphasis on sacramental traditions. The Rev. James Lockhart spoke in 1915 of the 'debased . . . significance' of baptism in Primitive Methodism, and observed, 'There is evident lack of conviction in the general attitude towards it, and an interrogatory note as to its value and obligation.'[1] Worship meant decorous behaviour in chapel, trained choirs, respectable and edifying sermons. It had relatively little to do with Christianity.

The most colourful Wesleyan innovation in the field of ritual was the love-feast, in which members ate cake or biscuits and drank water from a loving-cup before proceeding to testimonies and hymns. Towards 1900, the idea of sharing a common cup seemed unhygienic and disreputable, and the service as a whole was regarded as outlandish and undignified. Methodists viewed love-feasts 'as somewhat quaint survivals', of a not very amusing kind. They lingered only in two or three remote areas.[2]

When specifically Methodist rituals were under attack, more general Christian traditions of worship could scarcely hope to flourish. By 1908 Wesleyans were disturbed by 'neglect and slovenliness over the Holy Communion'. A Wesleyan claimed that 'Many places were vacant at this New Testament festival'. Those who attended were met by a curious hotch-potch of surviving Anglican forms and new extempore additions and curtailments. The Rev. J. E. Rattenbury complained, 'The mutilation of our Communion Service is a deplorable fact of our Church life.'[3]

[1] *Primitive Methodist Leader*, 23 April 1917, p. 237; 16 September 1915, p. 613.
[2] Cooper, *op. cit.*, pp. 110 ff; Frank Baker, *Methodism and the Love-Feast*, London, 1957, pp. 56 ff, 61.
[3] *M.R.*, January 1908, p. 3; 19 November 1908, p. 14.

The sacrament was attacked in other ways. At the end of the nineteenth century, under the influence of teetotalism, Methodists made their communion with a preparation known as unfermented wine. After 1900 they adopted from America the practice of using, instead of a single chalice from which all communicants drank, individual cups of glass, china or aluminium. The 1904 Wesleyan Conference made this practice optional at the discretion of the superintendent.[1] The 'germ'-conscious movement to replace the chalice with cups indicates the growing sensitivity of Methodists to social differences among themselves. Despite the development of friendly religion, there were co-religionists with whom contact seemed undesirable, either verbally in the class meeting or orally in the Holy Communion. Charles Kelly, President of the Wesleyan Conference, observed that he was not 'anxious to live in the same house with some of our Methodistic relatives'.[2]

Traditional forms of Methodism were fast losing their appeal. The brutal young openly expressed indifference. The Rev. J. Taylor Binns, related in 1890, how when a mother reproached her daughter for falling away, the girl said, 'Mother, tell me pray, what has your Methodism or your religion ever done for you?' Less alienated Methodists preserved their denominational loyalties in spite of, rather than because of, denominational traditions. A Free Methodist declared in 1904 that 'the sheer indifference to questions of Church government displayed by church-going city people is amazing'. Mr. William J. Davey, a Wandsworth Wesleyan, observed in 1909, 'The connexional spirit . . . is weaker in London than anywhere else. . . . I know Methodism from the Tyne to the Tamar, and nowhere do I find people more ignorant of Connexional ideals than in the metropolis. Our suburban congregations are apt to settle down to semi-Congregationalism.'[3] Pressure towards a looser and vaguer theology was accompanied by pressure towards a looser and vaguer church life. Methodists demanded choirs not sacraments; 'worship' not class meetings. In denominational life, the specific was giving way to the general, the significant to the uplifting, the disciplined to the cheerful. All these changes pointed toward ecumenicalism.

*Methodism and Culture*

With these changes, the older ethic disappeared. In early Methodism,

[1] *M.R.*, 4 August 1904, p. 9.
[2] *Ibid.*, 7 July 1904, p. 15.
[3] *Ibid.*, 11 September 1890, p. 683; 8 April 1909, p. 4; *F.M.*, 25 February 1904, p. 116.

chapel life provided its own relaxations and amusements. In the 1800s, the Rev. William Myles, a Wesleyan travelling preacher could describe the love-feast as 'a religious entertainment'.[1] But the rigorous perfectionist ethic severely restricted the culture and leisure activities of Methodists. From his customary vantage point of superiority, Everett accused Methodists of only reading and writing books of 'a devotional rather than a literary character', lacking in 'originality or genius'.[2] The tradition of Wesley the self-styled *homo unius libri* had grown to outweigh the tradition of Wesley the scholar; Hugh Bourne dismissed biblical studies with the cry, 'O Lord, direct my soul into the plain Bible!'; the Bible Christians condemned those who 'like the Corinthians, are puffed up with a knowledge of science–history, geography, astronomy and various others'. Even in the comparatively intellectual New Connexion, a writer under the title 'Spoiled by Philosophy' can contrast intellectual activity, 'stiff and cold', with the more desirable state of feeling.[3]

Methodists rejected many leisure cultural activities, high and low. A Bible Christian catalogue of sins in 1850 consisted of 'the ballroom, the card-table, the village wake, the race-course, the bowling-green, the cricket ground, the gin-palace, or the ale-house'. A comparatively moderate New Connexion article on dangers of the Christian life listed, among other items, '*Undue fondness of dress, fashionable evening parties . . . and games of amusement*'.[4] A Primitive Methodist, now fighting a losing battle, announced in 1894 that,

'The associations of the football field . . . are impure and degrading. . . . Let us take the advice of the Word of God, "And come out from among the ungodly, and be separate from sinners". . . . As Primitive Methodists, let us take the lead in this matter and renounce this great evil.'[5]

Dancing was as wicked as football. The most grievous threat to the

---

[1] Quoted in Baker, *op. cit.*, p. 37.
[2] J. Everett, '*Methodism As It Is*'. *With Some of Its Antecedents, Its Branches and Disruptions; Including a Diary of the Campaign of 1849, Protracted during a Period of Seven Years; with a Special Reference to the Character, Power, Policy and Administration of the 'Master Mind' of John Wesley's Legislative Successor*, London, 1863, vol. 1, p. 181.
[3] H. B. Kendall, *The Origin and History of the Primitive Methodist Church*, London, 1909, vol. 1, p. 140; *B.C. Mag.*, September 1881, p. 345; *M.N.C. Mag.*, May 1871, pp. 257–68.
[4] *B.C. Mag.*, May 1850, p. 182; *M.N.C. Mag.*, April 1869, pp. 201–8.
[5] *P.M. Mag.*, May 1894, pp. 359–60.

class meeting according to a Wesleyan was the 'midnight dancing party', if 'thoroughly enjoyed', that is.[1]

Novel reading led to profligacy, Wesleyans learnt in the 1850s. The New Connexion was informed that novel reading 'enfeebles the intellectual powers; vitiates and corrupts the taste; unsettles and mis-leads the judgement; feeds the passions and pollutes the heart'.[2] Wesleyans and Free Methodists were agreed upon the sinfulness of concert-going, and all Methodists concurred in rejecting the abomina-tions of the theatre. This was hardly surprising since 'the theatre caters for the lowest passions of human nature', actors and actresses are 'almost without exception, most vicious and profligate', and one could not see anything in a theatre but 'young women . . . in the appearance of semi-nudity . . . performing immodest gestures'.[3]

The basic sin of these activities was two-fold: firstly, they might arouse interests in directions other than religious, above all they might stimulate sexual interests; secondly, they appealed to the young and tended to '*loosen the bonds of family life, or weaken its moral discipline*'.[4] Discipline and authority are the essential elements of the classic Methodist ethic. The most serious breaches of this ethic are sexual–dress, dancing, novels, theatre, concerts, impure thoughts–and are regarded by Methodist moralists as special province of the young. But in a world of rising prosperity and education, some Methodists felt dissatisfied with the rigidity of this ethic, and demanded removal of various restrictions. Pressure for change seems to come from one direction. Just as the ethic was largely directed against the young, so it was the young who caused the purveyors of the ethic to falter. 'The fact is', wrote a Methodist in 1886, 'our young people must have amusement. If the Church will not provide it, the Devil will.'[5]

The organization needed to preserve the allegiance of members and members' children; and as a Wesleyan writer commented, 'the young people, especially, of Methodist families . . . are rapidly acquiring a taste for . . . social and public amusements'. Newer church organiza-tions such as the Bands of Hope offered 'entertainments'. It was important that these should be '*lively . . . instructive . . . elevating*'.

[1] *W.M. Mag.*, April 1867, pp. 319–20.
[2] *Ibid.*, December 1855, pp. 932–4; *M.N.C. Mag.*, April 1867, p. 218.
[3] *W.M. Mag.*, August 1859, pp. 693–4; *U.M.F.Cs Mag.*, September 1872 pp. 513–19; *M.N.C. Mag.*, February 1868, p. 108; July 1873, p. 404; April 1886, p. 235.
[4] *W.M. Mag.*, February 1877, p. 69.
[5] *M.N.C. Mag.*, April 1886, p. 234.

Unfortunately the improving tone of these occasions was continually diluted by 'dressing up' and 'scenic displays', not to speak of 'vulgar' dialect recitations.[1]

Yet what was to be done? The churches had to move with the times. That they did can be illustrated by the rise of the 'Conversazione'. For many years the New Connexion Conference had been accompanied by a sober 'Tea Meeting' at which edifying denominational speeches were made. In 1881, the Conversazione was launched–with a string band, an exhibition of 'curiosities', and a positively sensational lecture on electricity. At the next Conference, the Conversazione attracted more visitors than the Tea Meeting. By 1893, at least twice as many visitors attended the former as attended the latter.[2] Evidently popular support for the organization *had* been secured, but the organization to which loyalty was demanded had itself changed.

At the same time, games and dancing were accepted. A few Wesleyans played cricket in the 1840s. In the 1860s games were introduced into Richmond Theological College, although the Governor 'was blamed by a section for his leniency to athletics'. Some Methodists remained opposed to outdoor games till the end of the century, but most had been won over before then. Football and cricket 'within certain limits . . . may prove positive blessings', one writer claimed. Up to a point, such activities provided 'a healthy recreation'. In fact the biographer of Freddie Cleminson 'wisely tells the young people into whose hands Freddie's history may fall' that 'his religion . . . did not prevent him from joining in the sports at playtime'.[3] Desire to impress the 'young people' with the sporting qualities of the saints was a new departure in Methodism.

Another departure was slightly less acceptable. But by the 1890s, an occasional dance in the privacy of your own home was even condoned by Primitive Methodists, and Free Methodists were told that such a practice could be left to 'individual conscience and judgement'. A Wesleyan writer felt dancing was 'unwise for Christians, as an amusement', but agreed that 'the mere *act* of dancing cannot be wrong'.[4] The shift is outwardly slight but highly significant.

A similar process can be seen in the case of the ban on novels. If the

---

[1] *W.M. Mag.*, April 1867, pp. 319–20; July 1873, p. 638.
[2] *M.N.C. Mag.*, July 1893, pp. 389–91.
[3] W. Fiddian Moulton, *William F. Moulton*, London, 1899, p. 25; D P. Hughes, *op. cit.*, p. 44; *M.N.C. Mag.*, January 1884, p. 16; *U.M.F.Cs Mag.*, June 1890, p. 351; *W.M. Mag.*, January 1875, p. 77.
[4] *P.M. Mag.*, March 1891, p. 141; *U.M.F.Cs Mag.*, June 1890, pp. 350–1; *W.M. Mag.*, April 1890, p. 265.

young Methodist had one great craving, it was to read fiction. Of course fiction was available–the *Pilgrim's Progress* for example–or more recent edifying tales, some from the pen of Methodists.[1] But these were a little staid, and a strong pent up demand for modern religious fiction persisted inside Methodism. Silas Hocking's venture into print dissatisfied the 'elderly people' of Burnley Free Methodism, but delighted the young. The young carried the day, even though a Wesleyan writer commented in 1866 that 'The so-called "religious" novel is the most offensive to correct taste.'[2]

But by the end of the century liberal views had triumphed. The severe *Wesleyan Methodist Magazine* admitted illustrated advertisements for ladies' underwear in the 1880s. The actress Mrs Langtry appeared, in colour, to advise Wesleyans to use Pears Soap. In the 1890s Wesleyans were being offered 'Merlin's Book of Charms and Epitome of Palmistry', with its 'Charms against Witchcraft . . . For Love, Marriage, the Cure of Diseases'. Secular pleasures were in the ascendant. The Rev. Frank Ballard answered the question, 'Is amusement devilish?' with a very firm 'No'. The aged Benjamin Gregory commented sourly, 'We must begin a series of sweeping changes with a drastic revision of our Hymn Book. The section *For Believers Praying* must make room for one *For Believers Playing*; and that *For the Society at Prayer* for one *For the Society at Football*.'[3] In this new liberal atmosphere the novel was finally accepted.

At first Methodists closed their eyes to their own actions. The new Editor of the *Methodist New Connexion Magazine* told his readers in 1871, 'We cannot have "stories". . . . All the proprieties would be shocked.' Yet a 'story' had appeared in the *Magazine* nine years before. The alternative to self-deception was defiant gesturing on the brink. In 1873, the *Wesleyan Methodist Magazine* announced proudly that 'every trace of the pen of the novelist' was excluded from its pages. Four years later it began publishing *The Deformed Duchess of Ferrara: An Episode in the History of the Reformation*.[4]

Within a comparatively short time, the religious novel, formerly so offensive to correct taste, won general acclaim. Publication of *Nestleton Magna: A Story of Yorkshire Methodism* brought interesting

[1] e.g., Alfred Barrett, *The Boatman's Daughter: A Narrative for the Learned and Unlearned*, London, 1847.

[2] Silas K. Hocking, *My Book of Memories*, London, 1923, p. 71; *W.M. Mag.*, January 1866, p. 2.

[3] Frank Ballard, *Is Amusement Devilish?*, *passim*; *W.M. Mag.*, November 1891, p. 716; August 1893 (insert in copy in Bodleian Library).

[4] *M.N.C. Mag.*, January 1871, p. 28; *W.M Mag.*, January 1873, p. 1.

reactions. The *Bible Christian Magazine*, which did not publish its first serial, *The Hope of the Forresters*, till 1884, commented sourly, 'The sensational element is not "conspicuous by its absence"; many a reader, we dare say, will conclude that there is enough of it and to spare.' But the equally zealous *Primitive Methodist Magazine*, which launched *Up and Down: A Tale of Religious Experience* the same year, liked the book, declaring 'Fiction is here used as our Lord Himself used it, to bring out in clear and striking relief the charms of truth.' The *Methodist New Connexion Magazine* provided a significant comment. 'A Methodist novel'; it cried in mock dismay, 'Alas! and have we not fallen on degenerate times? Would our fathers and founders have written such a book?' The answer was that 'The Founders of Methodism did not altogether ignore our aesthetical nature. . . . The new phase which Methodism is putting on with regard to its recognition of the claims of general literature, and its appreciation of some of its more attractive forms, we contemplate without disapproval and without alarm.' The trend, so shocking to the proprieties six years before, meant in fact that 'Methodism is going to add beauty to strength, not substitute ornament for stability'.[1]

Official publications for general reading showed an apparent intellectual decline at the end of the century, as they adopted a new, popular, format. Denominational magazines rapidly increased in size in the 1880s and 1890s, replacing theology with a profusion of photographs, drawings and novels. In vigour and intellectual quality the new magazines were all inferior to the old. In tone they echoed the new style class meeting, comfortable, cheerful, uncritical.

The new denominational magazines symbolized the new Methodist doctrine that amusement, leisure and recreation were to be accepted, if cautiously. A Bible Christian writer pointed out that the modern cry for 'occasional leisure and relaxation' was 'an element in the robuster manhood of the time' and that recreation was 'a holy necessity'. A Primitive Methodist, explaining incidentally that 'Jesus sat at the Social Board', insisted that 'Consecration and cheerfulness are not foes but friends and companions in the Christian pilgrimage. We gratefully recognize the fact that a change has come over the church in its attitude towards many of the pleasures of life.'[2] Perhaps there was some resistance to this change for although Free Methodist young men were told in 1890 that *'Amusements in themselves are*

---

[1] *B.C. Mag*, September. 1877, p. 428; *P.M. Mag.*, June 1878, p. 380; *M.N.C. Mag*, May 1877, pp. 243–4.
[2] *B C. Mag.*, June 1881, pp. 241–2; *P.M. Mag.*, March 1878, p. 139.

*right*', though not of course 'amusements which lead to sin', doubt still remained and in 1897 the denomination as a whole was informed that 'CHRISTIANITY APPROVES OF AMUSEMENTS IN THEM-SELVES'.[1]

Communal entertainments were now available to Methodists. Grand Oriental Bazaars, Old English Fayres, Grand Shakespearian Bazaars, Orient Missionary Exhibitions, and humble imitations, were repeated in chapel after chapel.[2] These, like other chapel entertainments were novel in various ways. New technologies, made available partly by rising standard of living, provided sources of amusement. Electrical devices, displayed at bazaars and exhibitions, fascinated Methodists. Games and parades on Sunday School Anniversary were replaced by Sunday School outings as railway transport became available.[3]

The projection of photographs and pictures opened a new era in Methodist entertainment. The 'magic lantern', judiciously used, was a source of great blessing. Magic lantern demonstrations were held to have great evangelistic effect: the twisting bishop of modern times could hardly expect a greater impact. But evangelism was now re-interpreted as entertainment, a reinterpretation seen also in the new emphasis on 'worship'. An enthusiastic operator of magic lantern services urged fellow Wesleyans that such occasions required careful preparation and a high degree of efficiency. 'I think', he wrote, 'this is only fair to the people who are invited to come out during the winter evenings, often in inclement weather, so that they may not be sent home disappointed or vexed'. These are the criteria of entertainment rather than evangelism.[4]

Methodist entertainments in the 1900s were also new in the sense that they relied more on secular culture than older chapel life did. Mr. Arthur Bates of Luton recalled,

'About 1904 or 1906, Mr. S. Bennett started a Junior Choir. . . . We were trained to sing such pieces as "Pretty Village Maiden" and "The Huntsman's Chorus". I well remember one concert given in the Large Hall, when among the items were tableaux illustrating different songs, and one in particular, "Daddy", with Mr. Bennett

[1] *U.M.F.Cs Mag.*, June 1890, pp. 349–50; *M.M.*, October 1897, p. 304.
[2] Dale, *op. cit.*, p. 137; Brian le Messurier, *History of the Mint Methodist Church, Exeter*, Exeter, 1962, p. 29; J. Douglas Tearle, *Our Heritage. Chapel Street Methodist Church, Luton, Centenary, 1852–1952*, Luton, 1952, p. 21.
[3] e.g., Shaw, *op. cit.*, pp. 34 ff.
[4] *M.R.*, 29 January 1891, p. 83.

sitting with a girl member on his knee dressed in a white nightdress holding a candle while the song was sung.'[1]

While chapel celebrations began to display a surprising if bewildered worldliness, and entertainment criteria were introduced into chapel life alongside new entertainment technologies, acts of worship were themselves increasingly interpreted as entertainments. A religious service bestowed a 'blessing', perhaps little different from the 'enjoyment' of those who went to the music hall. Just as music hall performances varied, so did services: some were 'a good time', others were not. A Birmingham Wesleyan, writing of a visit to Newland Chapel, Hull, in 1921, commented,

'I received a most courteous welcome from the official in the porch and was conducted to a seat and provided with a hymnbook. Soon after the organist entered and commenced a prelude. . . . The choir then filed reverently and quietly into their seats on the rostrum, and when the minister rose and gave out the first hymn one felt himself to be surrounded by a quiet reverential atmosphere, and after the first line or two of the hymn I felt . . . I was in for a "good time". . . . One felt that each worshipper was part of the whole family. . . . A Hull friend . . . to whom I mentioned my experience confirmed it by saying, "You can't help but sing when you go there." '[2]

The metamorphosis of religious act into entertainment seems near complete.

## The Ethic of Community

The new Methodists of the late nineteenth century evolved a new 'Christian Perfection' for their entertainment-oriented chapel life. The theology which supported this new ethic was comfortable and hopeful. God the Father spread benevolence throughout the world. 'I can't abide to hear folks . . . puttin' everything that is sad, and bad, and miserable to be the Lord's will,' declared Daniel Quorm. Instead the divine is seen in 'a five-pound note' sent for a poor old couple by 'our boy in Australia'; and in the 'hillside', with 'all the air sweet . . . furze-blossoms and flowers; and then up in the clear blue sky a lark . . . singing.' Christians, said Daniel, are 'Under His wing. . . . And in there we don't mind the dark a bit. It's so safe, an' so warm; so snug. We can take His hand and then go 'long our way rejoicing.' Thus the religious life is 'trust, simple trust, that feels so

[1] Tearle, *op. cit.*, p. 35.
[2] Frank Baker, *The Story of Methodism in Newland*, Hull, 1958, pp. 51–2.

safe that it never thinks about it'. If life is snug, the after-life is snugger. Heaven is 'home', it is where 'old friends' meet.[1]

Christianity means conformity to the 'simple, normal but complete manhood' of Jesus. Cheerfulness must accompany normality. 'The highest duty of a Christian is to be a *happy person*,' Pearse believed. The Christian must also be 'genuine'.[2] He must shun extremes. A Wesleyan writer denounced 'the *theatrical* view of life . . . big, garish, exciting and romantic'. Daniel Quorm condemned all finery and display, for 'it vexes and worrits all the grace out o' folks'. 'Cynical and despairing' attitudes are just as reprehensible; 'pessimism' was caused by 'a bad psychology and a jaundiced mind'. Education was a doubtful asset. Daniel Quorm said that the virtue of the fathers of Methodism was that 'They were mighty learned in the Scriptures and didn't trouble their heads much about any other kind o' learnin'.'[3]

Shunning extremes, the Christian seeks to be contented. The 'religious view of life', Wesleyans were told, was expressed in Jesus's words, 'Learn of me; for I am meek and lowly in heart'. Methodists should not be ambitious. They must know that '*It is noble to rejoice in another's success*', and to '*be content with a lower place when God has clearly marked out another for a higher*'. Methodists should not be carping and critical. They must belong to 'the usual run of reasonable, kindly, contented people'.[4] Methodists never strive after the brilliant, the remarkable, or the outstanding. 'The truly great and solemn things of life,' wrote a Wesleyan minister in 1900, 'are its pure simple duties and pleasures. The unpretending flower of the ivy is said to be specially rich in nectar, and the bees haunt it far more eagerly than they do many of the brilliant blooms which seem such favourites of the sun.' Pearse insisted that what the church wants is not 'strength and beauty' but 'homeliness and heart'. The ideal President of the ideal Conference was, said the evangelistic Harold Murray, one who could say, 'We peg away and do our best, and trust in God, and that's about all there is to it.'[5]

Wesley's Christian Perfection was an ethic appropriate to the attempt to improve the unregenerate and ignorant through direction

[1] Pearse, *op. cit.*, 1st Series, pp. 34, 52, 57; 2nd Series, pp. 3, 20–2.

[2] *W.M. Mag.*, May 1896, pp. 323–4; Unwin and Telford, *op. cit.*, p. 29; *M.R.*, 6 December 1928, pp. 13–14.

[3] *W.M. Mag.*, December 1894, pp. 795, 797–8; February 1898, p. 98; Pearse, *op. cit.*, 1st Series, pp. 25, 68.

[4] *W.M. Mag.*, December 1894, pp. 707–8; July 1895, pp. 515–17; *M.R.*, 11 January 1923, p. 8.

[5] *W.M. Mag.*, December 1900, p. 905; Pearse, *op. cit.*, 1st Series, pp. 48–9; *M.R.*, 6 December 1928, pp. 13–14.

and control by an alien force: theologically, God; organizationally, the Methodist hierarchy. This ethic was accompanied by the complex structure of Christian doctrine and ritual. The promotion of perfection created the chapel community. During the nineteenth century, when ethic doctrine and ritual were largely destroyed, the chapel community survived, though not unchanged. As the higher things Wesley offered to his followers were progressively eliminated from the Methodist horizon, the chapel community bulked larger and larger, not because it was expanding but because all else was contracting. A Methodist writer observed in 1892, 'The Methodist people love to gossip and shake hands, and the bigger the crush around the tea urn the more enjoyment they seem to extract from the cheerful cup.'[1] This desire was not new. But it had been obscured by the higher ambitions of Wesley and his preachers. When secularization eroded ethic, doctrine and ritual, the chapel, the indestructible nucleus and residuum of the movement, remained.

Chapel itself was a demonstration of respectability. As the nineteenth century progressed, the search for respectability increasingly affected Methodists. They demanded better chapels; abandonment of biblical and doctrinal crudities; nice singing; 'a good time'; modest pleasures; and a cheerful, happy, unambitious society. They eschewed everything drastic and extreme; they sought to avoid all conflicts; they held up the ideal of respectability and moderation in religion and life. This was the stuff of which ecumenicalism was made.

Rising prosperity had weakened denominational commitments. The decline of hell marked the supersession of rigid denominational boundaries and a reduction of the severity of religious conflict. A modestly aspirant Methodism sat loosely to its beliefs and practices. It valued most what Methodist chapels, whatever their denomination, had in common. In formulating its own ethic, the ethic of an organization seeking modest entertainments and community, it adopted attitudes inimical to conflict and disagreement; which laid great stress on reconciliation, unity and 'fellowship'; which, to achieve these ends, were ready for accommodation with virtually every religious position; and which instilled the optimism that, in the face of disasters, could believe in the solutions to denominational problems offered by the ecumenical option. The unreality and self-deception of this ethic was exceeded only by that of the ecumenical solutions adopted.

[1] *M.R.*, 5 May 1892, p. 299.

# CHAPTER FIVE

# Church and Ministry in Theory and Practice

*The Structure of Reformed Methodism*

The struggle to reduce hierarchical power posed fundamental questions about Christian life and community. Wesley's Methodism was organized as a connexion, in an attempt to replace the inefficiency, divided control, and vested interests of contemporary Anglicanism, by a united and dedicated movement committed to individual and corporate self-sacrifice for the Gospel's sake. Wesley's ideal was a new model army of saints living under the strictest martial law. This was a total theory of Christianity, in which the Christian is nothing but a religious man; and it was a priestly theory of Christianity, since priests are nearer to this state of total Christianity than their followers are. But this ideal system foundered on reality. Methodist laymen had their own interests and their own beliefs, and these were formulated in the reform movement.

Being Methodists, the reformers adopted the principle of *connexionalism*, co-ordination of effort and centralization of control and direction through a series of courts culminating in one supreme authority. Even the groups which approximated closest to congregational independency, preserved vestiges of the connexional system. Reformers also advocated the right of the people to *representation* in connexional government. All non-Wesleyan Methodists shared the fundamental principle of the New Connexion, '*that the church itself is entitled, either collectively in the persons of its members, or representatively, by persons chosen out of and by itself, to a voice and influence in all the acts of legislation and government*'.[1] Nominated and self-perpetuating organs of government, in particular a ministerial conference, appointed by ministers to have supreme control in ministerial and lay affairs alike, were theoretically rejected.

But within thirty years of the formation of the New Connexion,

[1] *The Jubilee of the Methodist New Connexion*, London, 1848, p. 143.

laymen wanted more than the franchise. They challenged the connexional system as such. 'Connexionalism and despotism are synonymous terms,' said one reformer.[1] Robert Eckett expressed the protest of these later reformers. 'I know no scriptural precept or example,' he declared, 'which will justify any Conference, however it may be constituted, in making laws as to what shall qualify for Church-membership, or in exercising appellant jurisdiction, to annul, reverse, or alter the decisions of the Churches, or of other local Courts, as to the discipline to be exercised in Churches.'[2] This belief was embodied in the principle of *independence* of local courts. Several variations of this principle were possible. Eckett advocated 'circuit independence', in which the autonomous unit was the circuit and its quarterly meeting.

Apart from O'Bryan's brief General Superintendency of the Bible Christians, consciously modelled on Wesley's autocracy, reformed connexionalism vested central authority in a Conference, or 'Assembly', 'Yearly', 'Annual' or 'General Meeting'. Beside abandoning the name 'Conference', reformers abandoned its exclusively ministerial and non-representative character. But once reformers had adopted a system of representation, however feeble, idiosyncratic or inequitable, they clung to it with great conviction.

The conservative New Connexion adopted 'parity' of laymen and ministers in Conference, i.e. the few ministers and the many members had the same number of delegates. The even more conservative Bible Christians allowed a dozen or so lay delegates, each representing one district of eight circuits, in every four conferences; and relied on parity of the New Connexion type in every fifth or 'Great Conference' to 'prevent priestly domination'.[3]

To Primitive Methodists the problem of 'priestly domination' meant the possibility that ministers might decide their own salaries. To prevent this, they constituted their Conference on the 'Two to One' principle, two lay delegates to every ministerial delegate.[4] Equality of representation had not yet been reached: even in 1820, Primitive Methodist laymen outnumbered ministers not two to one

[1] *Wesleyan Times*, 18 October 1852, p. 693.

[2] *W.T.*, 29 January 1855, p. 67.

[3] *Life of the Reverend Alexander Kilham*, London, 1838, pp. 366–7; *A Digest of the Rules, Regulations and Usages of the People Denominated Bible Christians*, London, 1872, p. 114; F. W. Bourne, *The Bible Christians: Their Origin and History, 1815–1900*, London, 1905, pp. 206–7.

[4] *General Minutes of a Meeting Held at Nottingham, in August, 1819, and of the First Annual Meeting held at Hull, in May, 1820, by the Delegates of the Society of People Called Primitive Methodists*, Burslem, 1820, pp. 2–3.

but 163 to one. But a further step had been taken towards reform. The Associationist and Free Methodist system that local courts should 'freely elect' representatives to the denomination's Annual Assembly, without consideration of whether they were ministers or laymen, was, in theory, even more radical than the Primitive Methodist.[1] But free representation was an abstract concept, and ministers, elected in preference to laymen, dominated the Assembly.[2] This did not prevent Free Methodists clinging to free representation as proof that they were the most reformed Methodists of all.

With the exception of the Arminian Methodists, perhaps the most characteristic 'offshoot' from Wesleyanism, lay officials in reformed Methodism rejected election of delegates to Conference by the society of private members for election by circuit officials. But the New Connexion, Independent Methodists, Association, Free Methodists, and Wesleyan Reform Union at least elected delegates by circuits rather than by districts, itself a mark of considerable radicalism.[3] Such a system was indispensable to circuit independence, while district representation was a mark of conservatism among non-Wesleyans.[4] Under this system, the democracy of direct election by all church members was displaced, not merely by indirect representation of the members through circuit officials and circuit representatives, but by double indirect representation: the officials and circuit representatives elected *their* representatives to the district meeting, which in turn elected its representatives to conference. Thus, despite the 'democratic' elements in Methodist reform, reformed conferences vastly over-represented ministers, and gave them, as circuit or district officials, a direct *ex officio* vote in the appointment of delegates; although these conferences gave no direct representation to the private members.

The basic function of the conference, whatever called, and however constituted, was to direct the connexion. Like Wesleyans, most non-Wesleyans recognized their conference as the 'highest' and 'only

[1] *Foundation Deed of the United Methodist Free Churches*, London, 1864, p. 6.

[2] e.g., *Free Methodist*, 2 August 1888, p. 489.

[3] Primitive Methodist *Minutes*, 1820, p. 2; *General Rules for the Government of the New Connexion of Methodists*, Leeds, 1803, pp. 20–1; James Vickers, *History of the Independent Methodists*, Bolton, 1920, p. 201; *Foundation Deed of the U.M.F.Cs*, p. 6; *The Origin and History of the Wesleyan Reform Union*, Sheffield, 1896, p. 83.

[4] *Rules of the Tent Methodist Society, Adopted at the First General Meeting of Representatives Held in Bristol, May the 27th and 28th, 1822*, Bristol, 1822, p. 9; *Digest of the Rules . . . of the . . . Bible Christians*, p. 109; *The General Consolidated Minutes of the Primitive Methodist Connexion*, London, 1849, p. 102.

legislative court'. Even the Assembly of the Association and the United Methodist Free Churches could, at fixed intervals, introduce constitutional alterations, subject to scrutiny by the circuits and churches.[1] Reformed Conferences also stationed ministers although the churches of the Association and Free Methodist denominations could reject the ministers stationed with them, under certain minor penalties. The Primitive Methodist Conference further reduced its own powers of stationing, merely exchanging a limited number of ministers between districts, on the floor of the Conference rather than in committee, and left the bulk of the stationing to the districts themselves.[2] The Wesleyan Reform Union Annual Meeting simply kept a register of ministers.[3]

Even in reformed Methodism, ministers were paid full-time agents of the denomination, the conference its supreme authority. Ministers were therefore in a sense its employees, just as they were in Wesleyanism, even though as in Wesleyanism, *the quarterly meeting not the conference paid these employees*. Most reformed conferences could examine, appoint, veto and expel ministers. Even the Wesleyan Reform Union offered the denomination's ministers a voluntary examination. Conference jurisdiction over ministers tended to grow into appellate jurisdiction over cases involving members and lay officials, even in reformed Methodism.[4] But circuit independence rejected such jurisdiction, Free Methodist *local* courts alone having 'the exclusive power of suspending and expelling' members and lay officials.[5]

Non-Wesleyan conferences could also levy the denomination for connexional funds. But connexional funds of polities based on circuit independence were purely optional.[6] The option was real. In 1904, Free Methodist per capita income from circuits for different connexional funds varied between 30 per cent and 70 per cent of that raised by the New Connexion and Bible Christians, which did not accept circuit independence.[7] Non-Wesleyan polities were similarly

---

[1] *Foundation Deed of the U.M.F.Cs*, p. 14.
[2] *Ibid.* pp. 7–8; Primitive Methodist *Minutes*, 1821, p. 4; 1828, p. 15.
[3] *Origin and History of the W.R.U.*, p. 84.
[4] *Digest of the Rules . . . of the . . . Bible Christians*, p. 21; *Rules . . . of the New Connexion*, pp. 6, 12–15, 22; Primitive Methodist *Minutes*, 1821, p. 4; *Foundation Deed of the U.M.F.Cs*, p. 13; *Origin and History of the W.R.U.*, p. 84; *Conversations between the Preachers and Representatives of the Arminian Methodist Connexion*, p. 11; Primitive Methodist *Minutes*, 1828, p. 17; *The General Rules of the Primitive Methodist Church*, London, 1922, pp. 198, 199.
[5] *Foundation Deed of the U.M.F.Cs*, p. 14.     [6] *Ibid.*, pp. 7, 13.
[7] *Methodist New Connexion Magazine*, April, 1904, pp. 124–5.

divided on the question of conference control over local affairs. The Bible Christian, New Connexion and Primitive Methodist Conferences retained general surveillance of circuit affairs, and could veto such matters as division or alteration of circuits. Association and Free Methodist polities severely restricted such powers. Each society in the denomination had 'Liberty to have such particular rules as to Church Government, and as to its ministry, as each may think proper to adopt; provided that there be nothing in the rules so adopted clearly repugnant to the Word of God'. The Assembly could not interfere with such rules, except to expel any church or circuit which became 'in the judgement of the . . . Assembly corrupt in doctrine or neglect or refuse to submit, or to enforce the morality enjoined by the Holy Scriptures, with reference to the conduct of any of its preachers, officers, or members' [sic].[1] By these provisions Eckett attempted to ensure circuit independence. The local church or circuit was a voluntary member of the denomination, with right of secession. The central authority could not oblige it to do anything. It could merely expel it.

While reducing conference power over the localities, reformers happily accepted an executive, at denominational level, somewhat stronger than the Wesleyans. This executive was the continuation committee. Boyden and Askew's comment on the Free Methodist Connexional Committee, that it was 'to a large extent the executive of the Annual Assembly', was true of all continuation committees.[2] During conference the committee had a role somewhat similar to the Wesleyan memorials committee, channelling connexional opinion and initiating resolutions. But the continuation committee could initiate denominational business between conferences, and it seems to have provided a more specific and identifiable executive than in Wesleyanism, where personal leadership was diffused among departments, colleges, and London committee members. Strong leadership was acceptable in conference, and at denominational level, in reformed polities, so long as it could not encroach on local affairs.

The district was the largest local unit. It was usually a compara-

[1] *General Rules . . . of the New Connexion*, pp. 15–22; Primitive Methodist *Minutes*, 1820, pp. 5, 9; *Consolidated Minutes*, 1849, p. 27; Wesleyan Association *Minutes*, 1836, pp. 16–17; *Foundation Deed of the U.M.F.Cs*, p. 15.

[2] William Baggaly, *A Digest of the Minutes, Institutions, Polity, Doctrines, Ordinances and Literature of the Methodist New Connexion*, London, 1862, pp. 181, 191–2; Primitive Methodist *Minutes*, 1828, p. 30; *Consolidated Minutes*, 1849, p. 100; William Boyden and Edwin Askew, *Handbook of the United Methodist Free Churches*, London, 1887, p. 147.

tively late innovation. Like conference, the district meeting contained a small number of *ex officio* members, but it was basically composed of lay and ministerial circuit representatives, in the same proportion as conference.[1] The district meeting relieved conference of business by dealing with purely district affairs. It also shared in denominational business, such as examining candidates for the ministry.[2]

But while most district meetings served merely 'to shorten the duration of Conference',[3] those of Primitive Methodism had much wider powers. Like the Bible Christians, the Primitive Methodists were an alliance of different individuals and groups of evangelistic laymen. But although these groups were shortlived among the Bible Christians, they persisted in Primitive Methodism, where extensive geographical coverage enabled different leaders to form extensive local fiefs. These conditions encouraged the growth of what was called 'Districtism', i.e. *district* independence.

Under this system the district meeting was more than the conference for it stationed the majority of ministers within its boundaries,[4] and control of the itinerancy is perhaps the main character of the executive in Methodism. In the middle of the nineteenth century, too, district meetings had greater 'popularity and influence' than conference, which was 'little known by the rank and file and indeed wrapped in obscurity and mystery'. District meetings provided a basis for attacks on Conference, especially in the 1840s, and blocks of district delegates could greatly influence conference business.[5] 'Districtism', like circuit independence, sought to counterbalance ministerial power in the denomination with lay power in the localities.

But the most important local unit was the circuit of chapels, governed by the circuit quarterly meeting. The quarterly meeting was usually composed of the circuit ministers; the circuit stewards, appointees of the meeting itself, who were responsible for the business of the circuit; local preachers; class leaders; and other representative or semi-representative members, often co-opted by the meeting rather than elected by the members. The meeting was, in the Arminians'

---

[1] Bible Christian *Minutes*, 1824, pp. 7–8; Baggaly, *op. cit.*, pp. 202–4; Primitive Methodist *Minutes*, 1821, p. 2; Boyden and Askew, *op. cit.*, pp. 137–8.

[2] e.g., *Digest of the Rules . . . of the . . . Bible Christians*, pp. 18–21; *Rules of the Tent Methodist Society*, p. 9; Primitive Methodist *Minutes*, p. 4; *Jubilee of the Methodist New Connexion*, p. 144.

[3] *Ibid.*, p. 145.

[4] Primitive Methodist *Minutes*, 1821, p. 4.

[5] H. B. Kendall, *The Origin and History of the Primitive Methodist Church*, London, 1909, vol. 2, p. 366; H. B. Kendall, *The History of the Primitive Methodist Church*, London, 1919, pp. 74, 108.

words, a gathering of 'The whole of the Male official characters of the circuit'.[1] Representation of the members of society was provided by a small number of persons elected by the society.

Association and Free Methodist polities added an element on which Eckett insisted. This was the *ex officio* presence of local preachers, a logical consequence of the doctrine of reformed Methodism; for if local preachers were co-pastors with ministers they had as much right as ministers to *ex officio* privileges. The arrangement also made organizational sense. The other members of the quarterly meeting were ministers, officials who were mainly business men, and lay representatives. In such a situation, spiritual leadership, and hence general direction, would come from the minister, whose prestige and education gave him the central position. The presence of local preachers, specifically spiritual lay leaders, educated in religious matters, could offset this.[2]

The quarterly meeting had considerable power over circuit ministers. It invited them to the circuit, subject to the stationing decisions of higher courts. Within the limits of tenure provided by connexional regulations the meeting had complete discretion over the length of a minister's stay in a circuit. While he was in the circuit the meeting paid him. It could dismiss him, at least between conferences in the New Connexion, and at any time in Free Methodism. When he left the circuit, both among the Bible Christians and New Connexionists, the quarterly meeting gave him a certificate of good conduct, one of the earliest concessions demanded by reformers after Wesley's death.[3] Despite the power of Conference, in non-Wesleyan polities the quarterly meeting had practical control of the running of the ministry.

The quarterly meeting also possessed rights amounting virtually to sole power of initiation and veto on all matters of circuit boundaries in Free Methodism, and to a lesser degree in other non-Wesleyan polities. It had appellate jurisdiction over cases involving members only. In the New Connexion the quarterly meeting also had the

[1] *Conversations Between the Preachers and Representatives of the Armenian Methodist Connexion*, p. 7.

[2] Bible Christian *Minutes*, 1825, p. 11; *Digest of the Rules . . . of the . . . Bible Christians*, pp. 40–1; *Conversations Between the Preachers and Representatives of the Arminian Methodist Connexion*, p. 7; *Protestant Methodist Magazine*, October 1830, p. 312; *General Rules . . . of the New Connexion*, p. 10.

[3] Bible Christian *Minutes*, 1819, p. 9; *Conversations between The Preachers and Representatives of the Arminian Methodist Connexion*, p. 7; Vickers, *op. cit.*, p. 20; *Origin and History of the W.R.U.*, p. 84; Baggaly, *op. cit.*, p. 189; *General Rules . . . of the New Connexion*, pp. 10–11, 15; Edwin Askew, *Free Methodist Manual*, London, 1899, pp. 22–3.

theoretically important right to send such cases to conference. The quarterly meeting *as a whole*, unlike that of Wesleyanism, appointed circuit stewards who had general supervision over and responsibility for circuit business.

The quarterly meeting normally constituted the electoral college which sent representatives to the district meeting and/or conference. It was the basic unit of denominational government in reformed Methodist polity. Reformers demanded a voice for quarterly meetings on acceptance of new legislation. This right remained vague in Free Methodism, but in the New Connexion by the end of the nineteenth century quarterly meetings considered any 'fundamental laws affecting the whole body'. Free Methodist quarterly meetings had sole judicial powers over members and officials, and were protected from any decision of a higher court, except expulsion.[1]

Separate churches in the circuit had their own court, the leaders' meeting, which, like the quarterly meeting, was an official rather than a representative body. It consisted of chapel officials, society stewards, leaders, local preachers, trustees, and occasionally a small co-opted or elected representation of the private membership.[2] The leaders' meeting admitted and disciplined members, subject only to review by the quarterly meeting. It appointed class leaders; though in the Wesleyan Reform Union it could only nominate. Usually, it could also appoint the society steward, who was to the chapel what the circuit steward was to the circuit.[3]

---

[1] Bible Christian *Minutes*, 1830, p. 11; *Digest of the Rules . . . of the . . . Bible Christians*, pp. 17, 40–2; *Prot. Meth. Mag.*, October 1833, pp. 307, 313; *Origin and History of the W.R.U.*, p. 84; Baggaly, *op. cit.*, p. 192; *General Rules . . . of the New Connexion*, pp. 8–12, 20–1; *General Rules of the Methodist New Connexion*, London, 1890, p. 74; Primitive Methodist *General Rules*, 1822, p. 15; *Minutes*, 1820, p. 10; 1821, p. 2; *General Consolidated Minutes*, 1849, pp. 32, 173; *General Rules*, 1922, pp. 57–8; Askew, *op. cit.*, pp. 23 ff; *Foundation Deed of the U.M.F.Cs*, p. 14; M. Baxter, *Methodism: Memorials of the United Methodist Free Churches, with Recollections of the Rev. Robert Eckett and Some of His Contemporaries*, London, 1865, p. 430; Oliver A. Beckerlegge, *The United Methodist Free Churches. A Study in Freedom*, London, 1957, pp. 71–2.

[2] Bible Christian *Minutes*, 1825, pp. 10–11; *Rules of the Tent Methodist Society*, p. 6; *Prot. Meth. Mag.*, October 1830, p. 310; Baggaly, *op. cit.*, p. 184; Primitive Methodist *Minutes*, 1820, p. 12.

[3] *Digest of the Rules . . . of the . . . Bible Christians*, pp. 13, 15–16, 18–21; *Conversations between the Preachers and Representatives of the Arminian Methodist Connexion*, pp. 9–10; *Rules of the Tent Methodist Society*, pp. 6, 9; *Prot. Meth. Mag.*, October 1830, p. 310; *Origin and History of the W.R.U.*, pp. 86–7; Baggaly, *op. cit.*, p. 183; *General Rules . . . of the New Connexion*, pp. 6, 8–9, 12; Primitive Methodist *Minutes*, 1820, pp. 11–15; Askew, *op. cit.*, p. 19; *Foundation Deed of the U.M.F.Cs*, p. 14.

But no reformed polities, except the Independent Methodists and Wesleyan Reform Union, provided anything but a limited role for members, in the church or society meeting. *Local* government in non-Wesleyan denominations meant government by meetings of officials, especially by the quarterly meeting. 'Representation' in non-Wesleyan constitutional practice meant representation of the quarterly meeting in higher courts; 'independence' meant protection of the quarterly meeting from these higher courts. Direct democratic representation of the members was exceedingly limited. The reform movement in Methodism, which largely derived its leadership from lay officials, was concerned with extending the power of lay officialdom.

The same concern explains the cornerstone of reformed local church government, the demotion of the minister in local affairs. He had some powers. The Bible Christians and New Connexion constitutions allowed *ex officio* ministerial chairmanship of local meetings. As the New Connexion *Jubilee Volume* put it, ministers 'have the honour of presiding in the respective meetings, and a corresponding power of salutary control over their proceedings'.[1]

Otherwise the position of the minister in relation to the local officials was weak. *Ex officio* ministerial chairmanship in local meetings was rejected by Free and Primitive Methodism. If no minister was present at a *bona fide* official meeting in the New Connexion, the meeting could elect its own chairman. In all reformed polities, with the possible exception of the New Connexion, if the chairman, whether minister or layman, refused to put a properly proposed and seconded resolution, he had to vacate the chair so that the meeting could elect its own chairman. The meeting's rights were taken seriously. When the young Richard Chew went as an Associationist minister to Stratton in 1848, he began his first church meeting with the question, 'What is the business of this meeting?' One of the members abruptly replied, 'It is your business first to give out a hymn, and then pray, after which we will elect a chairman to preside over the meeting.'[2]

The minister was further demoted. It was fundamental to the hierarchical Wesleyan polity that the minister nominated, the local meeting elected, the various lay officials. But in reformed polities, which were basically self-perpetuating lay oligarchies, lay officials

[1] *Jubilee of the Methodist New Connexion*, p. 146; *Digest of the Rules . . . of the . . . Bible Christians*, pp. 13–15.

[2] Primitive Methodist *Consolidated Minutes*, 1849, p. 6; *Digest of the Rules . . . of the . . . Bible Christians*, p. 50; Edward Boaden, *Memoir of the Rev. Richard Chew*, London, 1896, pp. 28–9.

were invariably appointed by the meeting as a whole. All could nominate, all could vote.

### Changes in Reformed Methodism

Towards 1900, Bible Christians and Primitive Methodists took steps to democratize their constitutions. In 1877, the year the Wesleyans finally allowed laymen into their Conference, the Bible Christians extended the parity of the fifth or Great Conference to the other four. In 1889, Bible Christians went further and allowed the society meeting to elect representatives to the elders', i.e. leaders', meeting.[1] In 1903, five years before the Wesleyans, Primitive Methodists granted the society meeting the right to elect representatives to the leaders' and quarterly meetings. In 1916, a Primitive Methodist committee recommended, though this was never enacted, that lay members of seven years standing, and not merely officials, should be eligible for election to conference.[2]

These democratizing changes in non-Wesleyan polity paralleled changes in Wesleyanism itself. But the latter years of the non-Wesleyan denominations were notable for changes in the other direction. While the Wesleyan Conference was making belated concessions to demands for reform, its counterparts were reasserting connexionalism. Minor but significant changes, fairly early in the nineteenth century, pointed in this direction.

Hugh Bourne's Deed Poll of 1830 created twelve 'permanent members' of the Primitive Methodist conference, roughly paralleling the Legal Hundred. In twenty years their status had so grown that they were spoken of as the 'twelve *Deed Poll* members'. A belated attempt, in 1889, to destroy the view that these members formed a special and pre-eminent class in Conference, failed.[3] In 1846, the New Connexion introduced its Deed Poll, which appointed twenty-four Guardian Representatives, 'with whom the property and interests of the Connexion' were 'legally invested'.[4] Like Primitive Methodist Deed Poll members, the Guardian Representatives were not a 'legal' conference in the manner of the Legal Hundred but a special and superior status group.

While reformed Methodism was inventing new types of senior

[1] Bible Christian *Minutes*, 1876, p. 32; 1877, pp. 39–40; 1889, p. 37.
[2] Primitive Methodist *Minutes*, 1903, p. 214; 1916, p. 194.
[3] Primitive Methodist *General Consolidated Minutes*, 1849, p. 2; William Goodman, *A Popular Handbook to the Deed Poll of the Primitive Methodist Connexion*, London, 1889, pp. 12, 18–19.
[4] Baggaly, *op. cit.*, pp. 114, 124.

statesmen, or senators, it also strengthened the position of 'the ministry'. Despite much resentment, the New Connexion abolished preachers' certificates in 1838. The Bible Christians followed suit in 1867. In the New Connexion, the Rev. George Wall protested that the connexional polity 'rests greatly on the pillars – *lay representation*, and *annual certificates of preachers*'.[1]

But the major changes that increased connexional and ministerial power, and brought non-Wesleyans nearer to the Wesleyans in polity, took place in the two largest reformed denominations, the Primitive Methodists and the Free Methodists. The size and geographical spread of these two organizations hindered the attempt to combine central direction with local autonomy. A conference or assembly was duly and solemnly constituted. It was expected to give denominational leadership. But it found itself thwarted by local independence, and alienated by local indifference to denominational issues. The obvious solution, as denominational leaders saw it, was to improve on reformed polity by giving additional power to the most educated and enlightened sections of the denomination, the ministers and the conference.

Primitive Methodist leaders sought to do this by shifting, in certain areas of denominational life, from 'Two to One' to parity. The General Committee, executive of the denomination, was constituted on the basis of parity. When the Stationing Committee was set up in 1886, it adopted parity. In 1916, reconstitution of Deed Poll membership of Conference on the basis of parity was proposed.[2] At the same time 'Districtism' was superseded and conference authority strengthened. In 1883, a committee was appointed to inquire into 'the readjustment of the Home Districts, with a view to an approximate equalization of membership'. Despite resistance, the Sunderland District, the Leeds District and, later, the Tunstall and Bristol Districts were divided. These changes destroyed the dominant blocks of district representatives in Conference, and also extended the range of Conference stationing, by increasing the number of districts, and consequently the number of inter-district transfers.

Up to 1885 Conference still did its stationing on the floor of the house. In 1886, however, a stationing committee was at last formed to

[1] George Wall, *An Address to the Members of the Methodist New Connexion on the Subject of Preachers' Certificates, Interspersed with General Remarks on the Working of Their System of Church Government*, Manchester, 1838, p. 17; Bourne, *op. cit.*, p. 394.
[2] Primitive Methodist *Minutes*, 1886, pp. 118–19; 1916, p. 193; *The General Rules of the Primitive Methodist Church*, London, 1922, p. 14.

provide a draft of proposed stations of preachers as a basis for Conference discussion. In 1901, the district stationing committees were required to supply the conference with what was carefully called 'a suggested first draft of the Stations'.[1] While district stationing continued, both these measures extended connexionalism in Primitive Methodism.

A similar attack took place on circuit independence in the last thirty years of the separate existence of Free Methodism. This attack was above all the work of Richard Chew (1827–95), a protégé of Eckett's[2] who nevertheless came to modify his system. In 1872, Cleckheaton chapel applied to the Assembly for permission to secede from the Heckmondwike Circuit and form a separate Free Methodist circuit. The chapel, the wealthiest in the circuit, wanted to escape the burden of paying for weaker chapels, an essential financial aspect of the circuit understood in a connexional sense. It also wanted to contract out of the itinerancy altogether, by having a full-time minister of its own, on the congregational model, instead of sharing him with the other chapels of the circuit, on the Methodist model. The Cleckheaton case was comparatively novel, but the chapel, believing that the Assembly was obliged, under circuit independence, to ratify its actions automatically, had made advanced preparations for life as a one chapel circuit by the time the Assembly heard the case.

This was, a speaker informed the Assembly, 'really and truly a conflict between *congregational* and *connexional* principles'. Although the Assembly was largely critical of Cleckheaton, Chew supported the separation because it was already so far advanced, and so much bad feeling had been caused, that Heckmondwike Circuit could no longer be worked as a unit. But he and the Rev. S. S. Barton moved two resolutions to deal with future cases. These advised the Assembly against consenting 'to the separation of single Churches from circuits, except in such special cases as shall not be prejudicial to the evangelistic character of Methodism, or to the harmonious and efficient working out of our Connexional principles', and stressed 'the importance and necessity' of consultation with the Assembly before 'local action' was taken to divide circuits.[3]

[1] Primitive Methodist *Minutes*, 1883, p. 97; 1885, p. 115; 1886, pp. 118–19; 1894, p. 174; 1898, p. 167; 1901, p. 198; *Primitive Methodist World*, 25 June 1885, p. 420.

[2] Boaden, *op. cit.*, pp. 127–9.

[3] *Ibid.*, p. 203; Free Methodist *Minutes*, 1872, pp. 71–2; *United Methodist Free Churches Magazine*, September 1872, pp. 551–3.

The following year another case came before the Assembly. Shrewsbury Road and Brunswick Road Chapels, Sheffield, wished to separate from the Mount Tabor Circuit and form a new Free Methodist circuit of their own. Mr. Beckerlegge believes the Assembly's acceptance of this request indicates the reality of circuit independence. But the criticism of the two chapels' conduct was simply that they had consulted the Connexional Committee not the Assembly. Contemporaries did not criticize the two chapels for flagrantly asserting circuit independence, but for assuming that the Connexional Committee was as competent to *control* circuit affairs as the Assembly now was under the Chew–Barton resolutions. Since the Committee's approval of the scheme was endorsed by the Assembly, the case demonstrates not the impotence of connexional authority, but the working of the Chew–Barton resolutions and the Assembly's recognition of the Connexional Committee as the denominational 'executive'.[1]

Circuit independence was modified again by the amendment of the Foundation Deed in 1890. Under Chew's guidance, two amendments were adopted. The first provided that if any circuit in which there was 'any Chapel, or other property, settled on Connexional Trusts', failed to apply for, or to accept, a minister stationed by the Assembly 'in the usual manner', the President or his appointee should, for the time being, take over the superintendency of the circuit. This provision, while scarcely reverting to Thomas Jackson's doctrine of 1849, 'The Chapels are ours, the Debts are yours', gave greater force to the provisions of the connexional model deed on which much of the denomination's property was established, and gave compulsory force to the Assembly's stationing in the many circuits possessing such property.

The second amendment widened the Assembly's powers of expulsion. Hitherto the Assembly could only expel for doctrinal errors, or breaches of 'the morality enjoined by the Holy Scriptures'. Now it could also expel a circuit, society or church, 'if in any other manner or matter it should so act as in the judgement of the Assembly to be unfit for, or unworthy of, continued union with the . . . United Methodist Free Churches'. This broad new formula gave the Assembly much greater power in dealing with the localities.[2]

Though the second amendment was much less provocative it shortly proved much more important. After the 1891 Assembly, a dispute

---

[1] Beckerlegge, *op. cit.*, p. 69; *U.M.F.Cs Mag.*, September 1873, p. 512.
[2] Free Methodist *Minutes*, 1890, pp. 183–5.

arose in Bristol North Circuit. The Connexional Committee sent the circuit a deputation, which held an inquiry, and proposed a basis of settlement which the Connexional Committee upheld. The circuit claimed that its independence had been infringed. The 1892 Assembly seemed to favour this view, but at the end of the debate Chew made a very important speech.

' "In this discussion," he said, "we have not heard anything, so far, about our Connexionalism, though we have heard enough of our Circuit Independence. . . . A stranger in the gallery, listening to this debate, would think we were a gathering of the representatives of Congregational Churches, met for friendly counsel and mutual help. But we are a *Connexion*; we are based upon a Connexional principle, with Connexional authority. . . . Our fathers instituted a complex system, combining the Connexional principle with Circuit Independence. . . . The danger is that we push this local independence so far as to paralyse our Connexional authority . . . Free Methodism is on its trial. Its future will much depend on our discussions here to-day. If we come to the conclusion that each circuit can do as it likes, as sure as I am here we cannot work our Connexion; we shall introduce a principle of disintegration and as a Connexion we shall gradually cease to be." '

Chew then claimed that the second amendment of 1890 meant that the 'Assembly has a right to see that the good reputation of the several parts of the denomination shall be maintained. But if the Assembly is responsible for the maintenance of the character of every part of the Connexion, it must have the right of inquiry and investigation.' Circuit discipline must be administered by the circuit. But the Assembly had the right to advise on circuit matters, and if its advice was refused, to expel a circuit. Chew carried the rejection of Bristol North Circuit's complaint, and a resolution that stated 'that Circuit Independence is not absolute, as in our constitution it is limited by the Connexional principle'.[1]

Chew's opinion was the most important event in the history of reformed Methodism after Eckett. Free Methodism was 'on its trial' and the verdict was adverse. But Chew sought only to improve, not to destroy, circuit independence. In 1890, he contributed to a draft scheme to unite the Free Methodists and the New Connexion. This scheme preserved much of the circuit's freedom from financial levy, a freedom characteristic of Free Methodism but unknown in the New

[1] Boaden, *op. cit.*, pp. 337–40; Free Methodist *Minutes*, 1892, pp. 201–2.

Connexion.[1] Even the cause of ecumenicalism could not persuade Chew to desert the principle of circuit independence.

### The United Methodist Church

But Chew's constitutional ideas prepared the way for the United Methodist Church of 1907. The constitution of this body was the work of three of the four largest reformed Methodist denominations. Since leaders of the fourth, the Primitive Methodist Church, freely praised this constitution, it may be regarded as the liberal Methodist ideal of the Church in the twentieth century.

The United Methodist constitution was a compromise between those of the New Connexion and the United Methodist Free Churches, following, with one very important exception, the lines of the abortive New Connexion-Free Methodist union scheme of 1890, but including one major concession to Bible Christian polity. The United Methodist *Conference* (and the acceptance of the name by the Free Methodists is instructive) was constituted on the basis of parity. It contained various *ex officio* members, including Guardian Representatives; and delegates of the district meetings. Parity was a theoretical Free Methodist concession to the other two denominations, although in practice it meant that the United Methodist Conference had more laymen than the Free Methodist Assembly. Guardian Representatives were a Free Methodist and Bible Christian concession to the New Connexion; and district rather than circuit representation, a Free Methodist and New Connexion concession to the Bible Christians. These concessions, especially abolition of direct circuit representation in Conference, moved rightwards, i.e. towards the Wesleyan end of the Methodist spectrum. But Free Methodists and New Connexion both agreed that the efficient working of the new, 150,000 strong, denomination demanded district representation.

Free Methodists made their most striking concession on the powers of Conference. At a very late stage in negotiations, and without notice to the Free Methodist public, the proposals of 1890 were abandoned in one major particular. Clauses 5 (e) and (f) of the scheme of 1890 allowed the element of optional contribution to connexional funds characteristic of Free Methodist polity. Clause 5 (e) made support of the ministry and 'the obligations of the Connexion' compulsory. But 5 (f) merely gave Conference the right to 'appeal to the Circuits for the loyal fulfilment of their obligations to sustain other institutions and funds of a distinctly Connexional nature'.

[1] *Methodist New Connexion Magazine*, July 1890, p. 447.

The United Methodist constitution, as finally published, preserved Clause 5 (e), but replaced 5 (f) with the provision that the Conference may 'take such action as it may deem necessary or expedient to induce the circuits loyally to fulfil in any manner which the Conference may think desirable their obligation to sustain all institutions and funds of a Connexional character'. The Conference need not stop at 'appeal' as the Free Methodist Assembly had to, it could 'act'.

In local affairs also the United Methodist constitution was rather less 'reformed' than that of Free Methodism. The most notable concession to Free Methodism was the admission of local preachers to *ex officio* membership of the local meetings, an arrangement resisted by the New Connexion as far back as 1836. A compromise was struck on church meeting representation in the leaders' meeting, universal in Free Methodism, but probably still quite rare in the New Connexion. The church meeting was to elect its representatives, but the leaders' meeting was to nominate them. Again, this was a step backward from reform. Finally the Free Methodists conceded *ex officio* ministerial chairmanship of local meetings, although, following the Bible Christian constitution, if the ministerial chairman refused to put a properly proposed and seconded resolution, he was required to vacate the chair and allow the meeting to elect a successor.[1]

The United Methodist constitution was closer to Wesleyanism than either Chew's Free Methodist constitution or that of contemporary Primitive Methodism. A Wesleyan unionist justly observed that 'the curious and hopeful thing is that in the union which brought into being the United Methodist Church, the Methodist New Connexion set its stamp upon' the Free Methodists, 'and lifted them to its own level'.[2] That the Free Methodists accepted the United Methodist constitution, while Primitive Methodists professed willingness to do so, indicates the degree to which both denominations were drawing nearer to Wesleyanism in the early twentieth century. Non-Wesleyan laymen were willing to allow greater power to their own weaker and more modest ministers than their ancestors had been willing to allow to the Wesleyan hierarchy. At the same time, in common with Wesleyan laymen, non-Wesleyans lost interest in denominational affairs as the nineteenth century progressed. Both developments brought ecumenicalism nearer.

[1] *Minutes of the First Conference of the United Methodist Church*, London, 1907, pp. 41–66.

[2] W. H. Heap–J. Ernest Rattenbury, 1 March 1922, in Rattenbury Papers.

*The Reform of Wesleyanism*

Six years of civil war in Methodism during 1849–55 produced the United Methodist Free Churches, a large new denomination based on circuit independence, with James Everett as its first President, and Robert Eckett as its first Secretary; the Wesleyan Reform Union, a small denomination with a congregational polity similar to that of Independent Methodism; and a depleted but reformed Wesleyanism. The third effect of the *Fly Sheets* controversy, though scarcely the most striking in reformers' eyes, was not negligible.

Very soon after the expulsions, the Buntingites made some concessions. The 1852 Conference rejected any suggestion that 'the responsibility of the *sentence* in disciplinary cases' should be taken from the minister; but it allowed the quarterly meeting to appoint a mixed lay and ministerial special circuit meeting which could give judgement not merely on the facts of a case, but 'whether, in their opinion, those facts are violations "of the Laws of God, or of our own Body" '.[1] The lay officials still only constituted a jury, but a jury of a more powerful kind which could pronounce not merely on facts, but, in theory at least, on whether they constituted a breach of Wesleyan law.

The hierarchy made another, but unofficial, retreat before agitation. Faced with the financial difficulties created by the policy of 'No Supplies', the President summoned a large and elaborately prepared mixed financial meeting in 1853,[2] a move that demonstrated the hierarchy's dependence on the lay aristocracy of Wesleyanism. As Everett dramatically put it, 'some 100 rich men . . . by their wealth, and by their liberal issue of it, became the ruling power that ruled the Clique, that ruled the Conference, that ruled the People'.[3] Bunting's mixed committees gained power. At the end of the 1850s, Henry Fowler, the Liberal politician, and son of Joseph Fowler, the reformers' presidential candidate of 1848–9, observed complacently that the mixed committees, or committees of review, as they were now called, gave 'a due amount of lay influence . . . upon all connexional proceedings'.[4]

[1] Wesleyan Methodist *Minutes*, 1852, pp. 156 ff.

[2] T. P. Bunting and G. Stringer Rowe, *The Life of Jabez Bunting, D.D.*, vol. 2, London, 1887, p. 366.

[3] James Everett, '*Methodism As It Is*'. *With Some of Its Antecedents, Its Branches and Disruptions; Including a Diary of the Campaign of 1849, Protracted during a Period of Seven Years; With a Special Reference to the Character, Power, Policy and Administration of the 'Master Mind' of John Wesley's Legislative Successor*, London, 1863, vol. 1, p. 216.

[4] Henry Hartley Fowler, *A Lecture on the Institutions of Wesleyan Methodism*, London, n.d., p. 13.

Many Buntingites of 1849 recanted over the next quarter of a century. T. P. Bunting, who in 1835 pledged himself to 'prevent the introduction of Lay Delegation into the Methodist Conference', advocated this very measure in 1871.[1] When William Griffith, expelled with Everett in 1849, went to the first Methodist Ecumenical Conference in 1881, some Wesleyans, he said, 'even thanked me for the part taken by us in 1849'. Joseph Hargreaves, one of the three ministers who administered the *Fly Sheets* test, insisted on shaking Griffith's hand.[2]

While this recantation was in progress the balance of power in Wesleyanism shifted in favour of more liberal views. When J. Gilchrist Wilson inaugurated his six years term at the Book Room in 1857 with a speech attacking Book Room methods, 'Veterans like Osborn, Rattenbury, Scott and Prest, and other gods of the mountain, realized that they would no longer be able to hush voices, and that their word would not be taken for law'. George Osborn pleaded in vain 'with tears in his eyes' in 1868 for two years' demotion in ministerial status for the radical and troublesome young Hugh Price Hughes.[3] Applause greeted this defeat. By 1870, younger and more liberal ministers had replaced retiring Buntingites in the theological colleges, the Book Room, and the Chapel Committee, and virtually controlled Bunting's old stronghold, Foreign Missions.

In 1861, a group of these, alienated by the addled reaction of the *Watchman*, started a new paper for 'younger Methodism', under the leadership of G. T. Perks and W. M. Punshon. The pale liberalism of this paper, the *Methodist Recorder*, was very popular indeed. Despite its caution, as early as 1867, the *Recorder* could speak darkly of the mixed committees of review as 'the House of Commons of Methodism', whose 'action and influence seem to foreshadow a time when other functions, additional to those now possessed, will be exercised by the combined ministry and laity of our Church'.[4]

In the 1860s efforts were made at mild reform of the committees of review. But their very existence was an argument for lay representation. Their composition was haphazard and confusing. The appointment of *one* lay delegate per district to bring a breath of representation

[1] Wesleyan Methodist *Minutes*, 1831–35, London, 1838, pp. 563–5; T. Percival Bunting, *Laymen in Conference?* London, 1871, *passim*.
[2] Richard Chew, *William Griffith: Memorials and Letters*, London, 1885, pp. 225, 227.
[3] Charles H. Kelly, *Memories*, London, 1940, p. 172; D. P. Hughes, *The life of Hugh Price Hughes*, London, 1904, pp. 58–60.
[4] *M.R.*, 18 December 1861, p. 447; 19 July 1867, p. 236; 18 August 1871, p. 474; 19 August 1873, p. 472.

to each committee in turn, illustrated both the absurd ingenuity and the prodigious futility of Wesleyan gradualism. Since the committees met simply to review the business of each department during the previous year, they were precluded from discussing any large question of policy. In any event, their decisions were mere recommendations to Conference which could and did reject them.[1] The committees of review, originally planned to prevent lay delegation, simply established the *principle* of lay participation in connexional affairs, and demonstrated the inadequacy of non-representative lay participation.

Open discussion of lay representation began in 1871 with T. P. Bunting's pamphlet *Laymen in Conference?* Despite Bunting's drastic change of front, he was hardly the man to agitate the connexion. Indeed the traumatic experience of 1849 made Wesleyans fearful even of discussing his appeal to 'Throw open the doors of Conference to duly selected representatives.' A few pamphlets appeared, one of which called the quarterly meetings to memorialize Conference for lay representation. After three years, 7 per cent of them did.[2]

Towards the end of the movement for lay representation, hints were made of the necessity of conceding lay demands to avoid open conflict. As one spokesman put it, 'Up to this time there had not been any strong expression of feeling; but there was a deep under-current throughout the whole Connexion in reference to this matter and unless laymen were admitted into the Conference agitation would be sure to arise.'[3] But agitation remained a threat. The Wesleyan public was quiescent; and the only overt pressure was that of converted Buntingites such as William Arthur, W. M. Punshon, and J. H. Rigg, liberal ministers like T. B. Stephenson, and lay dignitaries such as Bunting and Fowler, who had changed his mind on the committees of review.

Negotiations began in 1870 with a discreet Conference Committee 'To Consider Various Suggestions', one of which happened to be reform of the mixed committees of review. The published *Minutes* made no reference to this committee. Few ministers yet agreed on lay representation in Conference, but some very important leaders had apparently concluded that some measure of change was necessary.

[1] Bunting, *op. cit.*, pp. 3, 7, 9–10; *M.R.*, 12 February 1875, p. 88; 19 February 1875, p. 99.

[2] Bunting, *op. cit.*, p. 22; Henry Arthur Smith, *Essays on Wesleyan Methodism*, Truro, 1874, *passim*; Peter Prescott, *Two Questions Discussed: 1. Does Methodism Need Lay Representation? 2. Does it Need a Sustentation Fund?*, South Molton, 1875, pp. 16–17; *Lay Representation in the Wesleyan Conference*, London, 1871, pp. 51–3; *M.R.*, 7 August 1874, p. 450.

[3] *M.R.*, 16 June 1876, p. 340.

A series of Conference debates and committees at various levels followed. Many ministers urged mere enlargement and improvement of the mixed committees of review, perhaps unified in one Consolidated Committee of Review, or 'Mixed Diet', subordinate to and excluded from Conference. Bunting wanted a two session conference, one session with 'something like parity of numbers between ministers and laymen', dealing with general affairs, and another all-ministerial session with control over ministerial affairs.

Broadly speaking, this was what the Connexion got, despite the bitter resistance of die-hard Buntingites. 'For himself', said George Osborn in 1875, 'he was not going to build again that which it had been his aim through life to keep down or pull down. In resisting any attempt to alter the principles of Methodism he would spend his last sixpence and breathe his last breath.' A year later, 88·3 per cent of Conference voted for the lay representation it had rejected since Wesley's death eighty-five years before, at the cost of devastating the denomination. It was, said the *Recorder*, 'the supreme critical moment'.[1]

The year after, in 1877, the new constitution of Wesleyan Methodism was adopted. Conference was divided in two sessions. The first was the Pastoral Session, consisting of 240 ministerial representatives elected by the ministers of the district synod, and of such other ministers as Conference should determine. This session had a number of 'reserved subjects' allotted to it: the constitution of Conference itself, all questions of denominational literature, public worship, division and alteration of circuits, and all matters affecting ministers.

The Representative Session, which followed the Pastoral, was composed of the 240 ministerial representatives who had already sat in the Pastoral Session, and 240 lay representatives, of whom 210 were elected by the lay officials in the district synod, and thirty by the Representative Session of Conference itself. This session could deal with all but the 'reserved subjects', i.e. with the business and financial affairs of the denomination. The district synods or district meetings were likewise divided into two sessions. Circuit representation, which T. P. Bunting had advocated, was rejected, and so was any concept of direct representation of the laity; the non-Wesleyan precedent of double indirect representation based on the quarterly meeting being followed. But, since the Wesleyan lay officials were all ministerial nominees, genuine lay representation was still excluded. Non-

[1] *M.R.*, 19 August 1873, p. 471; 15 August 1875, p. 486; 18 August 1876, p. 480.

Wesleyan reaction was expressed by the Free Methodist who wrote, 'Never before in our time have we seen a mountain in so much labour, and bringing forth so small a mouse.'[1]

The system continued unaltered for twelve years. In this period Wesleyan opinion began to polarize. The *Watchman* was finally wound up in 1883–it never recovered from the shock of lay representation. Two years later Hugh Price Hughes launched the *Methodist Times*. The *Recorder* was now on the right of the denomination, and the Forward Movement provided a new radical left with new constitutional demands. Since the Pastoral Session had priority, ministers met first and discussed what they chose, including items on the Representative Session's agenda. Many of these ministers then had a second vote in the second session, in which laymen as a whole never commanded an absolute majority. This situation could be partly improved, from the lay point of view, if the Representative Session met first and could vote free from the pressure of previous Pastoral Session decisions.

But before pressure could build up, J. H. Rigg led Conference, in 1889, into a new, and extraordinary, compromise. The Pastoral Session would still meet first, but it would only meet for a few days to consider 'reserved subjects'. The Representative Session would then meet, while the ministers of the Pastoral Session who were not representatives–at least 200 to 300 in number–went sightseeing in the Conference town, or entertained themselves in some other way. When the Representative Session ended, the Pastoral Session reconvened, and deliberated on such of the Representative Session's business as it chose.

The so-called Rigg Sandwich soon created dissatisfaction. Hughes described it as 'unnatural, costly and cumbrous'. Another radical, the Rev. T. E. Westerdale, claimed that 'the present arrangement gives satisfaction to no one except those who are anxious to keep alive the doctrine of pastoral supremacy'. In 1896, the Pastoral Session appointed a committee on the order of sessions. It proposed that the Representative Session should convene first, but failed to solve the major problem of such an arrangement, the election of the President. In Wesleyan constitutional law, he was *nominated* by the 'illegal' Pastoral Session members, and *elected* by the Legal Hundred, still the only legal Wesleyan Conference. In practice the Legal Hundred merely ratified the Pastoral Session's nomination. Since the President pre-

---

[1] Wesleyan Methodist *Minutes*, 1877, pp. 213 ff; *U.M.F.Cs Mag.*, August 1877, p. 512.

sided over both sessions, reversal of their order might mean 'nomination' by the representatives.[1]

The Pastoral Session, led by Rigg, who had now exhausted his radicalism, opposed the priority of the Representative Session on this issue alone. The President, said Rigg, was 'the chief pastoral officer' of the Connexion, a kind of temporary archbishop. Lay votes should not secularize his office. Rigg was supported by the *Recorder*, now under the editorship of the conservative Rev. Nehemiah Curnock. Curnock replaced the timid liberalism of Perks and Punshon with a sort of neo-Buntingism. The ministers were the 'most real representatives of the Churches', and should therefore have the greatest 'honour and authority', the *Recorder* declared. Two principles, 'the pastoral initiative and the distinctive responsibility of the ministers in the Churches of Methodism', i.e. pastoral supremacy and itinerancy, demanded priority of the Pastoral Session. Presented with the argument that priority of the Representative Session was inevitable, the *Recorder* grandly pronounced, that 'Nothing is inevitable until the ministers are persuaded of its justice and utility.'[2]

The Pastoral Session's resistance was met by the nearest approach to a mass movement in Wesleyanism since 1855. The newly formed and only semi-official Methodist Councils in the large towns provided a useful and highly publicized outlet for radical feelings silenced in the district synods. The *Methodist Times* actively canvassed for priority of the Representative Session, and polled ministers on the question. This bold course, described by the *Recorder* as 'nothing less than indecent', elicited 1,074 replies, from just over half the ministers. Sixty-five per cent of respondents favoured election of the President by the Representative Session.[3]

The connexion was divided. At the 1897 Conference, Hughes proposed a compromise; priority for the Representative Session, election of the President for the Pastoral. This formed the basis of the final settlement. The Representative Session was to be increased to 300 ministers and 300 laymen, although the proportion of Conference nominees was also to be increased. The reserved subjects were to go

[1] David J. Waller, *The Constitution and Polity of the Wesleyan Methodist Church*, London, 1898, p. 45; *M.R.*, 22 May 1890, p. 357; 18 February 1897, p. 115; 29 July 1897, p. 569; *Methodist Times*, 3 July 1890, p. 660; 30 July 1896, p. 520.

[2] *M.R.*, 29 July 1897, p. 571; 4 February 1897, p. 80; 18 February 1897, p. 111; 25 February 1897, p. 137.

[3] *Ibid.*, 4 February 1897, p. 80; 18 February 1897, p. 111; 8 April 1897, p. 243; *M.T.*, 7 January 1897, p. 9.

on being reserved. The Pastoral Session was to nominate the President a year in advance, and the Legal Hundred would elect him at the beginning of the next Conference, i.e. in the Representative Session. The system was adopted in 1900 and survived till the demise of Wesleyanism as a separate denomination in 1932. The reform aroused bitter feelings. One minister said, with some justice, that it was part of a movement 'to make their old Methodism for which their fathers had suffered like the other branches of Methodism'.[1]

In practice lay representation in conference meant at some points less, at some points more, than it did on paper. Analysis of attendance lists for the first thirty years of the Representative Session showed that ministers outnumbered laymen, despite theoretical parity, and since most lay delegates came to Conference only once, ministers had experience as well as numbers on their side. But if laymen were even weaker in the Representative Session in practice than they were in theory, that Session as a whole was stronger than was generally believed. After their disturbing confrontation with J. H. Rigg in December 1903, the New Connexionists, Bible Christians, and Free Methodists, recorded their conclusion

'that with the Wesleyans the *Pastoral Conference* is regarded as an essential; and that notwithstanding all the changes which have been introduced into the Wesleyan system, *the sole and exclusive authority of the ministers in regard to doctrine, discipline, and stations, is untouched.*'[2]

The picture was overdrawn. The Representative Session was powerless over many areas of government, notably stationing. But in its own sphere it was almost unlimited by the Pastoral Session, and a definition of the proper sphere of the Representative Session proved difficult to find. In theory, for example, the Representative Session had no voice on doctrinal matters. In practice, lengthy debates on the appointment to theological college tutorships of J. A. Beet (1898 and 1902) and George Jackson (1913), showed that the Session could and would handle doctrinal questions. E. Aldom French claimed in 1920 that 'the Representative Session . . . is the more important session–it meets first, it speaks for the whole Church, it deals with the most vital

[1] *M.R.*, 6 May 1897, p. 316; 29 July 1897, p. 590; Wesleyan Methodist *Minutes*, 1899, p. 349; *M.R.*, 27 July 1899, p. 23; 28 July 1898, pp. 26, 38; 4 August 1898, p. 39.
[2] *Ibid.*, 12 June 1890, p. 404; 19 June 1890, p. 432; 23 January 1908, p. 5; *Methodist Union. Minute Book, December 18th, 1902, to September 18th, 1907*, p. 20.

matters, and there has never been a conflict between the two sessions'.[1] Such a conflict–which was just beginning–was largely prevented by the Pastoral Session's recognition of its weakness.

But the system as a whole remained profoundly undemocratic. Not till 1892 did the quarterly meeting, still composed entirely of ministerial nominees, get the power to send elected delegates to synod in addition to the circuit stewards who had seats *ex officio*. The most significant aspect of the reform–the first real crack in ministerial rule since 1791–was that these delegates were not to be ministerial nominees.[2] No progress was ever made in enfranchising the members with a vote for a conference representative. Instead the members got a vote for representatives to the leaders' and quarterly meetings. Rigg, with his usual clarity, warned that it affected 'a definite and essential principle of Wesleyan Methodism', for 'The leaders' meeting could not be better described than as an extension of pastoral superintendence,' and now it was to be turned into a democracy. But in 1908 Conference empowered the members of society to nominate and elect up to eight representatives for the leaders' and quarterly meetings. The New Connexion historian, George Eayrs, said that, in the whole history of Wesleyanism, this was 'the most significant act in making the bounds of orderly freedom wider'.[3] The minister's power was still overwhelming, but it was limited. Theoretically, a member could be elected a representative to the quarterly meeting, and thence to Synod and Conference, against ministerial opposition.

By 1908 Wesleyan, United and Primitive Methodism had drawn closer together. Their disagreements turned round the question of the relation of minister to laity. The most obvious difference was in Conference and District Meeting, where non-Wesleyans had one omnicompetent representative session; while the Wesleyans had two sessions, one with its all-ministerial composition and 'reserved subjects'. At the same time Wesleyan laymen only shared in stationing by voting with ministers at district synod to elect one *ministerial* representative on the all-ministerial stationing committee. In reformed polities, laymen shared fully in stationing.

Outside Conference, the denominations diverged most on the power of the minister in the leaders' and quarterly meetings. In Wesleyanism the minister was *ex officio* chairman of the local meetings. In United Methodism, he had this right, but could be expelled from the chair for

---

[1] *Aldersgate Primitive Methodist Magazine*, September 1920, p. 613.

[2] Wesleyan *Minutes*, 1912, pp. 618–20; Waller, *op. cit.*, pp. 127–9; Wesleyan *Minutes*, 1902, p. 111; *M.T.*, 6 March 1890, pp. 221–2; 13 March 1890, p. 252.

[3] Wesleyan *Minutes*, 1908, pp. 108–9; *United Methodist*, 25 April 1918, p. 194.

delinquency. In Primitive Methodism the minister, theoretically, had no such right at all, although in practice he probably chaired virtually all meetings by 1900. But in United and Primitive Methodism, whatever the personal ascendancy of particular ministers in particular situations, acts of the local meeting were acts of the whole meeting, and all powers of speaking and voting were open to all. In Wesleyanism, the minister continued to nominate all officials, the meeting simply to elect. In any disciplinary case heard by Wesleyan local meetings, the minister was the judge, the officials merely the jury.

This system and the doctrine of the ministry on which it was based, constituted the 'pastoral supremacy' in Wesleyan Methodism, which, claimed a New Connexion leader, was 'unparalleled in any Nonconformist community' and 'in many respects . . . unequalled by the authority possessed by the clergy of the Established Church'.[1] Despite Wesleyan reforms, even in 1932, the 'pastoral supremacy' however residual, was still 'unparalleled in any Nonconformist community', including United and Primitive Methodism.

## Convergence in the Doctrine of the Ministry

It is a commonplace of Methodist history that Methodists have never been divided by doctrine. The Rev. John Scott Lidgett announced in 1909 that, 'The theology of all branches is identical.'[2] The Wesleyan Conference itself did not subscribe to this view. Replying to proposals for a Methodist Ecumenical Conference, it declared that Methodists 'do not acknowledge the same standard of doctrine and characteristic differences are found in their exposition even of doctrines which are nominally held in common'.[3]

Conference was right. Even Lidgett agreed that in the past Methodists had been divided 'in regard to the general position of the ministry and the laity'; although he claimed that 'the Wesleyan Methodist practice has now come so entirely into line both on principle and practice that I see no difference'.[4] Between a fifth and a quarter of the Methodists of 1929 saw differences which Lidgett did not; and a

---

[1] G. Packer (ed.), *Centenary of the Methodist New Connexion*, London, 1898, p. 196.

[2] W. J. Townsend, H. B. Workman and George Eayrs (eds.), *A New History of Methodism*, London, 1909, p. 421.

[3] *Proceedings of the Oecumenical Methodist Conference Held in City Road Chapel, London, September, 1881*, London, 1881, p. xiv.

[4] *Minutes of Proceedings Taken before the Select Committee of the House of Commons on the Methodist Church Union Bill. Methodist Church Union Bill (Scotland)*, p. 72.

recent Methodist historian claims that the 'major difficulty' over union in the 1920s was created by 'doctrinal factors'.[1]

The pastoral supremacy written into the Wesleyan constitution was supported by a doctrine of the ministry in many ways closer to those of Anglicanism or even Roman Catholicism than to those of Primitive and United Methodism. These doctrinal differences were fundamental to the division and reunification of Methodism, as they are to the division and reunification of Christianity. As Lidgett rightly said, the different sections of Methodism were converging in their doctrine of the ministry by 1932, as they were converging in organization. But although doctrines of the ministry in Methodism converged more quickly than organizational practice, Methodists were still divided on this crucial question right up to their reunification in 1932.

After 1849, the most striking feature of Wesleyan teaching was its refusal to give ground to ideas favoured by reformers. This conservatism was symbolized by the Rev. William Burt Pope, whose *Compendium* introduced many generations of Wesleyan students to theology. Pope was a rigorous Buntingite in his views on polity and doctrine. His discussion of the ministry begins quietly enough. The Christian ministry, Pope claims, appears in the New Testament as 'a Presbyterial body'. It consists of 'men called to this function by the Holy Ghost, approved of by the Church by its representatives, and ordained to office by their brethren in the same order'.[2] The two elements, the divine call, and the church's commission, fit well into the Protestant tradition. So does Pope's claim that 'The universal priesthood of Christianity' teaches 'the true dignity and essential equality of individual Christians, and the corporate sanctity of the Church whose inalienable prerogatives are represented by its ministry'.[3]

But Pope claims more than this. The ministry has important functions: 'dispensing the Word of doctrine, watching over the flock, and ruling in the congregation'. The third function means, 'governing the Church by maintaining and guarding the doctrines and laws of Christianity . . . exercising discipline as to receiving and excluding the members of its fellowship, and by the general regulation of its affairs'. Pope justifies this situation by claiming that the ministers' authority is 'committed to them by the Chief Shepherd, to whom alone they are

[1] J. H. S. Kent, 'The Methodist Union in England, 1932', in Nils Ehrenstrom and Walter Muelder, *Institutionalism and Church Unity*, London, 1963, pp. 218–19.
[2] William Burt Pope, *A Compendium of Christian Theology*, London, 1879, vol. 3, p. 335.
[3] *Ibid.*, p. 336.

finally responsible. .... Such rule as they have is ordained of Christ, and the solemn sanctions of their responsibility are connected with the great day when they must give account to Him.' This is pure Buntingism. The pastor is accountable for the flock on the Day of Judgement. His power over the flock must be as awful in its completeness as it is awful in its responsibility.

Pope also claims that the ministers' 'jurisdiction may be said also to be representative of that of the congregation itself', i.e. that the ministry has great power because the church has given it this power, as its representative. But Church and ministry cannot disagree, for 'all that the Church has received as a corporate body from its Head it lodges again in a certain sense with its ministers: all, literally, and without deduction'. The 'representation' of the Church by the ministry is a legal fiction. So is the Church's commission, which can only be administered by the ministry itself and not by the Church as such, for it has given all its divinely appointed powers to the ministry, 'all, literally, and without deduction'. Pope necessarily condemns as 'excesses' any attempt to give the laity 'a voice in matters which affect the ministerial jurisdiction as such', since

> 'The Methodist doctrine is that our Lord left the Keys – the general government of His body, the special binding and loosing of authoritative decrees, the reception and expulsion of members – to the Church itself, as represented, however, by the men whom the spirit would raise up with the concurrence of the congregation to represent its authority.'[1]

Pope's views were well summarized by the minister who in 1878 opposed lay representation in the Wesleyan Conference because

> 'It seems to me that many passages of Scripture render it abundantly clear that the governing power in the Church . . . belongs exclusively to the clergy . . . and that to the laity . . . it belongs only to obey. I am sorry to seem to put it so harshly, but I cannot tone down the language of Holy Scripture. To the clergy it is said, "feed", "rule", "govern", "watch"; to the laity, "remember", "know", "obey", "submit". '[2]

The Wesleyan hierarchy still claimed to rule the Church, and to impose their teachings, without restriction.

Such views as these remained strong in Wesleyanism twenty years later. G. Stringer Rowe, Bunting's biographer, informed ministerial

[1] *Ibid.* pp. 344–5, 358–9.
[2] *M.R.*, 21 July 1876, p. 405.

students at Headingly College in 1895, that 'There is no room for a separate and specialized priesthood', which 'would invade . . . the common office and privilege of the people of God'. But the minister was 'the Lord's herald and representative', sent 'to treat with' men 'on His behalf'. And if the minister was 'the Church's minister–the Church's servant', he possessed delegated powers which his constitutional sovereign did not. 'The flock,' said Rowe,

> 'will acknowledge you as its pastors. . . . They will assign to you a certain presidency, in virtue of which you are to be their accepted guides and instructors in the things of God . . . and, as a matter of sacred order, there will be committed to you, on behalf of the Church, the administration of the Sacraments.'[1]

The 'harshness' is largely gone, but the doctrine is the same. The minister is a servant with 'a certain presidency'; he is the 'guide'; he will 'treat with men'; 'sacred order' determines that he should administer the sacraments. There may be, in theory, 'no room for a separate and specialized priesthood', but a lay assertion of the priesthood of all believers would at once invade 'sacred order'.

Contemporary non-Wesleyan ministerial doctrine is quite different. J. Robinson Gregory did no great injustice to the Primitive Methodist doctrine of the ministry when he stated that 'The Primitive Methodist minister possesses no pastoral authority whatever. There is no function which a layman cannot, in theory and practice, discharge just as well as a minister.'[2] The details of such a view were developed by William Cooke, the New Connexion leader, whose *Christian Theology*, has the distinction of being the sole non-Wesleyan counterpart to Pope's *Compendium*.

While Pope begins quietly and reaches a crescendo, Cooke begins loudly only to fade at the end. 'The Christian ministry', he declares, 'is an institution of Divine appointment.' It

> 'is undoubtedly the most important office which God has assigned to man, embracing duties the most sacred and spiritual, and responsibilities the most solemn and weighty. A minister is the steward of the mysteries of God. . . . He is an ambassador for God, and has to negotiate with men in reference to their eternal interests, and beseech them to be reconciled to God.'[3]

[1] G. Stringer Rowe, *The Christian Priest*, London, n.d., pp. 13, 24–6.
[2] J. Robinson Gregory, *A History of Methodism*, London, 1911, vol. 1, p. 230.
[3] William Cooke, *Christian Theology*, London, 1863, p. 642.

Pope and Rowe could only concur in these sentiments.

But Cooke divides ministerial functions between 'men exclusively set apart to the work', *and* 'men who connect with it a secular calling'. Here we see the Buntingite bogey, and reform doctrine, of the co-pastorate of ministers and laymen, a genuinely operative priesthood of all believers. Cooke bases this division of labour not on scripture or Divine command, but on 'The voice of reason', and grounds the very existence of a separate 'ministry' in reason alone. The system of men 'set apart' confers 'certain advantages', says Cooke, and compares it to the fact that 'To the medical art men are exclusively devoted'. 'Indeed', he goes on,

> 'the experience of mankind has found that every institution of any importance and magnitude must have its agents, whose time and labour must be wholly devoted to its particular interests. . . . It is plain that the great demands of the ministry are such as men involved in secular pursuits are not in a position to perform.'[1]

A minister is in fact a professional, comparable to a doctor. Cooke devotes the bulk of his study of the ministry to an essential characteristic of the professional, his salary. Not only is the minister a professional, he is and ought to be paid by the Church, whose paid 'agent' he is.[2]

Wesleyan and non-Wesleyan doctrines of the ministry have different purposes. Wesleyan writers such as Pope and Rowe sought to establish, as older Buntingites did before them, the claim of the ministry to the most prominent place in the church: powers and responsibilities divinely laid upon them entitle them to 'all, literally, and without deduction'. But a non-Wesleyan writer such as Cooke seeks merely to justify the *existence* of a separate ministry, and its claim as the Church's agent to the Church's money. After the high-flown language of Cooke's exordium, there is nothing in his case for a separated ministry that will not justify a separated caretaker. This is of as much importance for the subsequent history of Methodism as Rowe's concept of 'sacred order'.

These two doctrines of the ministry, the Wesleyan, emphasizing the 'delegation' of the ministry from above and the minister's character as 'ambassador' of a higher authority, conference or God; and the non-Wesleyan, emphasizing the 'commission' of the ministry from below and the minister's character as agent or 'representative' of the Church,

---

[1] *Ibid.*, pp. 643–4.
[2] *Ibid.*, pp. 650–62.

began to converge at the end of the nineteenth century. Even in his heyday Pope failed to convince all Wesleyans. The *Yorkshireman* remarked in 1878, that, 'His position on questions of ecclesiastical polity is undoubtedly higher than suits the tastes of many Methodist folk'.[1] By that time his teachings did not suit the realities of Methodist life either, for the laity had invaded ministerial jurisdiction, even if they merely succeeded in holding beach-heads. In the years that followed, as the laity in Conference assumed ever greater powers, organizational factors rendered Pope's doctrines more obsolete. The very rationale of these doctrines was gone. The greatest effect of 1849 was to make another 1849 impossible. Never again could the hierarchy contemptuously shake the keys in the laity's face. What then was the purpose of proving at length their right to do so?

Younger generations of Wesleyan writers began to see the minister less as a man called by God, whose call was ratified by an autonomous and supreme hierarchy, more as a servant commissioned by the Church through its existing commissioned servants or representatives, the ministers. By so doing they recognized changes in the structure of Wesleyanism after 1877, and came more into line with the ideas of community implicit in late nineteenth-century Methodism: the minister was less a ruler in the congregation, more an elder brother in a happy family. They also came closer to non-Wesleyan teaching.

The most conservative of these new Wesleyan theologians, J. Robinson Gregory, was emphatic that 'The Christian ministry is not a separated priesthood. The Christian minister is a priest in no sense than that in which all believers are priests. . . . The minister is the authorized representative of the congregation, or church; he has been separated for his work.' Here are two new notes. The identification of 'congregation' and 'church' is hardly in the tradition of the highest connexionalism; while the view that the minister is 'separated for his *work*' comes close to Cooke. But Gregory still retains traces of older thinking, however muted. He claims, for example, that 'considerations of something higher than propriety, expediency, or ecclesiastical order place certain functions, such as the administration of the Sacraments' in ministerial hands.[2]

In this higher 'something' we can see the incipient vagueness of the last generation of Wesleyan theologians, of whom Dr. Kent says that they 'lacked a completely coherent position'.[3] But the vagueness

[1] R. W. Moss, *The Rev. W. B. Pope, D.D.*, London, 1910, pp. 70–1.

[2] J. Robinson Gregory, *The Theological Student. A Handbook of Elementary Theology*, 1892, p. 208.

[3] Ehrenstrom and Muelder (eds.), *op. cit.*, p. 208.

meant slightly more than that. For Rowe, 'order' was intrinsically sacred and unquestionable. It was the outward form of that ministerial jurisdiction appointed by God, and summed up in the phrase 'pastoral supremacy'. A writer more sensitive to prevailing attitudes towards 'order', was more defensive. He bolstered up order with the 'something higher', and as later Wesleyans became more defensive they also became vaguer about the concept.

The year after Gregory wrote, a younger man, George G. Findlay, published a book on the church. Findlay was aware of the new ideas of Church as community in a way in which Gregory never was. 'To us', wrote Findlay, 'the Church is not the priesthood, the ritual, the form of sacrament or government; it is *the society of Jesus*. We find its germ cell in the little company of brother disciples gathered round the Master in common talk and at a common table.'[1] Here the theme of 'Jesus sat at the Social Board' is translated explicitly into terms of Church and ministry. The minister is indeed brother not ruler: 'We disavow sacerdotalism. . . . The apostles were disciples first, and brethren first, before they were apostles.' Consequently Findlay emphasizes that 'The ministry exists for the sake of the Church, and arises out of the Church, and not vice versa.' Every member of the Church 'has spiritual qualities and spiritual duties'. The egalitarian note is struck with greater confidence by Findlay than by any of his Wesleyan predecessors.

If a separate ministry is necessary, it is simply to provide specialized agents: 'In the various functions of her ministry the Church does but specialize and concentrate in particular organs the powers which exist diffused throughout her whole membership.' The minister is, so to speak, the liver or kidneys of the Church. He is certainly not the head. It is not even entirely clear that Findlay would have put it as strongly as that. Christ entrusted administration of sacraments to no 'definite order of men', he wrote. It was 'a matter of obvious fitness, and belongs to the doing of things decently and in order' that the sacraments should be administered by ministers. But 'It concerns the well-being, not the very being of the Church.'[2] In an emergency, or in other special circumstances, Findlay hints, particular organs can be supplanted by others without jeopardizing 'the very being of the Church'.

The year Findlay published his book, E. Aldom French, later

[1] George G. Findlay, *The Church of Christ as Set Forth in the New Testament*, London, 1893, p. 75.
[2] *Ibid.*, pp. 35–6.

convenor of the committee that united Methodism, left college. Findlay looked to this future event. He would be, he said, 'Thankful ... if any word of his should in the smallest measure serve to knit more closely the children of Methodism to the mother Church.' Twenty-eight years after his book appeared it was cited by A. S. Peake as evidence of the essential identity of Primitive and Wesleyan Methodist views on Church and ministry, and hence of the propriety of these two denominations uniting.[1] The evidence was good even if the case was limited. Findlay advanced the Wesleyan transition from the concept of the minister as delegate from above to that of the minister as representative from below. Many Wesleyans still held aloof from these new-fangled ideas. Many non-Wesleyans held the representation theory of the ministry in a form extreme enough to have surprised Findlay. But as the denominations began to converge in organizational form, they converged also in the theories of Church and ministry which underlay these forms.

[1] George G. Findlay, *The Church of Christ as Set Forth in the New Testament*, London, 1893, p. 5; *Primitive Methodist Leader*, 7 July 1921, p. 425.

# CHAPTER SIX

# Aims and Conflicts in the Ecumenical Phase

## *The Struggle with Wesleyanism*

Modern ecumenicalists justify Christian unity in general terms. But the history of ecumenicalism is particular and specific. Not only does union presuppose disunion, but particular unions presuppose particular disunions. Methodist ecumenicalism begins among the secessionist bodies of Methodists, all of whom had greater or lesser grievances against Wesleyanism, illustrated in previous chapters. 'Offshoot' Methodist denominations, recruited almost entirely outside Wesleyanism, had comparatively little tradition of conflict with Wesleyanism, but had grievances nevertheless. Primitive Methodists believed Wesleyans to be 'more than half-Anglican'. They were obsessed with the Book of Common Prayer, 'that medieval production'. They stood 'in the way of the realization of reforms and ideals that most other Free Churchmen regard as of the very essence of Free Churchism'. They did their best to seduce the youth of Primitive Methodism.[1]

Non-Wesleyan ecumenicalism developed in a context of conflict. Reformers divided Wesleyanism to win, for themselves at least, the changes they demanded; to further their cause they would even unite with each other. As secession followed secession, the possibility of uniting secessionists on their common principles became apparent to many. A union of reformed or liberal Methodists would further the struggle for reform of Wesleyanism. Under Eckett's influence the Wesleyan Association, which was to provide the nucleus of Free Methodism, in turn the nucleus of United Methodism, adopted in 1836, the resolution,

'That it is desirable that some plan should be devised by which the different Societies, who are separated from the Wesleyan Conference, may be brought so to unite, as that they may regard each

[1] *Aldersgate Primitive Methodist Magazine*, 1901, pp. 239, 398; *Methodist Recorder*, 1 August 1901, p. 13; 15 August 1901, p. 7.

other as members of one common family, professing one common faith, cultivating friendship towards each other, adopting a common token of membership, and uniting as far as may be practicable in promoting plans for general usefulness.'[1]

The outlook is ecumenical but polemical. Many others shared Eckett's dream. 'Fraternus' declared in 1853 that 'To unite the whole of the liberal members of Methodism into one great Church seems to be the greatest *desideratum*, as, it is to be feared, it would be the greatest task, of the age.' Mr. William Ellis of Scarborough made the purpose of this union explicit. 'Methodist Reformers,' he said, should unite to form a 'powerful and effectual . . . check' to the 'Ecclesiastical corruption and Priestly intolerance' of Wesleyanism.[2]

By the 1850s the theory of union as a weapon against Wesleyan resistance to reform was a commonplace. The details of the theory remained vague. If, for example, all non-Wesleyan Methodists had united in 1860, a prospect which seemed as unlikely then as it does in retrospect, they would have formed a denomination two-thirds the size of Wesleyanism. But how this would have promoted reform of the Wesleyan constitution is unclear. The united resources of the denomination might have produced more pamphlets and more speeches. These resources might have been used to confront Wesleyan chapel with a rival 'free' chapel on the other side of the road.

The separated denominations provided pamphlets, speeches and chapels in profusion. Their effect on the Wesleyan constitution was gradual, indirect, and small; and there is no reason to suppose that a united liberal Methodism would have provided more of these weapons, or that the surplus would have been more effective. But problems such as these did not deter unionists, who could always fall back on the argument that union itself had a moral force in the battle against obscurantism. Samuel Hulme told a union meeting at Leeds in 1867 that the separation of reformers 'has weakened the practical influence of liberal principles before the world, and has presented to the religious public the idea that liberal principles are divisive in their tendency'.[3]

The argument for union as a stroke of anti-Wesleyan policy, though weak, got stronger as the nineteenth century progressed. Richard Chew hinted at a new perspective when he said, 'It would be good to

[1] Wesleyan Association *Minutes*, 1836, pp. 16–17.
[2] *Wesleyan Times*, 27 June 1853, p. 403; *United Methodist Free Churches Magazine*, February 1858, p. 83.
[3] *U.M.F.Cs Mag.*, August 1888, p. 476.

have a union of all liberal Methodists. That union would tend to prepare the way for a still grander union in times to come.'[1] In 1878, Wesleyans admitted laymen to Conference. In 1881, Wesleyans joined Methodists from all over the world in the first Methodist Ecumenical Conference. Reunification of British Methodism suddenly became a larger and more exciting possibility. But these Wesleyan concessions made a union of non-Wesleyans, which would be basically an anti-Wesleyan union, paradoxically the more desirable. As the Rev. John Walls put it: if the small non-Wesleyan denominations each separately united with the Wesleyans, as each deemed the Wesleyans had made sufficient concessions, 'the terms would be Wesleyan in each case'. But 'if we begin at the other end and bring the liberal Methodist churches together first, then in after-years the amalgamated Church will be in a position to demand a liberal church polity for the great Methodist Church of the future'.[2]

Walls' theory was a refinement of Eckett's policy of securing reform through union. Eckett thought in terms of war and sought unified command. Walls looked to the peace terms which would end the conflict and proposed to negotiate from strength. The greatest practical exponent of Eckett's and Walls' ideas was a Free Methodist, Rev. William Redfern, who followed his anti-Wesleyan interpretation of Methodist history in 1906 with the achievement of an anti-Wesleyan union in 1907. In the preface to his *Modern Developments in Methodism*, Redfern hoped that he had 'made some contribution, however slight, to the cause of Methodist reunion'. The hope was genuine. Redfern sincerely looked to the reunion of all Methodism, on liberal Methodist terms. As he put it, 'That fascinating dream, "Methodist union", can never be realized by the forgetting or ignoring of history.' He clarified the point. 'The clerical ideal . . . the supremacy of the pastoral office', beloved of Wesleyans, had to be supplanted by 'the Scriptural ideal', of 'the brotherhood of the Church'. 'Pastoral supremacy', he said, 'is an insurmountable barrier to union. Liberal Methodism will never go back on its own history.' But pastoral supremacy would not last for ever: 'Some day it will be disowned; and then there will be Methodist reunion.' Before that date, Redfern argued, liberal Methodists must 'stick together' and form 'a strong democratic Methodist Church'.[3] Where the reformers of the 1850s

[1] *Free Methodist*, 14 July 1887, p. 230.
[2] *F.M.*, 8 November 1888, p. 707.
[3] *Ibid.*, 21 July 1904, p. 466; William Redfern, *Modern Developments in Methodism*, London, 1906, pp. vii, 151, 163–4.

AIMS AND CONFLICTS

used the pamphlet and the mass meeting, Redfern used the negotiating table. But the policy was still the same, the creation of a new Methodism purged of Wesleyan obscurantism.

## The Struggle with the Church of England

While some Methodists saw union as a means of reforming Methodism, others saw it as the means to advance Methodism in English society. For a long time Wesleyans regarded Methodism as a subordinate agency of the Church of England. Bunting was a zealous champion of church rates. Even Samuel Warren, Bunting's first great ministerial opponent, ended his life as a clergyman of the Church of England. But the persistent aggressiveness of the Church of England, and the increasing sensitivity of an expanding Methodism, forced a reappraisal of Methodist relations with the Church.

Tractarianism and ritualism alienated many Methodists. As late as 1919, a Wesleyan advocated union to fight the 'knotted whip . . . idolatory of crucifixes . . . priestly auricular confession and its invasion of the sanctities and privacies of the family'.[1] The continual polemic which sought to prove that Wesley's true heirs were Anglo-Catholics, not the Wesleyans 'who . . . dared to take his name and reject his principles', convinced few Methodists and offended many.[2] 'Anglican clergy', wrote a Wesleyan minister, 'never will meet us on equal terms . . . we are interlopers in their parishes.'[3]

But if Anglicans were believed to despise Methodism, they were also believed to prey upon it. Dr. Joseph Baylee, Principal of St. Aidan's College, allegedly boasted, with amazing ineptitude, 'I am a constant poacher on our Wesleyan brethren, and on the raw material I find among them, to a very considerable extent, of earnest-minded and devoted young men fit for Church of England Missionaries.'[4] 'Servant girls . . . and other young persons'; 'children from our Sunday Schools'; Methodist undergraduates; 'wealthy friends' who 'receive favourably the advances of fashionable curates', were all seduced, Methodists believed, into the Anglican fold.[5]

The vicar of Owston Ferry, Lincolnshire, who refused the Wesleyan

[1] *M.R.*, 11 September 1919, p. 5.
[2] G. W. Taylor, *John Wesley and the Anglo-Catholic Revival*, London, 1905, p. 31; cp. H. M. Luckock, *Who Are Wesley's Heirs?*, London, 1891; A. J. Mason, *John Wesley*, London, 1898, etc.
[3] *M.R.*, 1 May 1919, p. 13.
[4] *Ibid.*, 17 June 1863, p. 229.
[5] William Hudson, *An Answer to Bishop Wordsworth's Pastoral*, Lincoln, n.d., p. 8; *M.R.*, 1 May 1919, p. 13; *Wesleyan Methodist Magazine*, April 1871, p. 347; October 1871, p. 884.

176

Henry Keet the prefix 'Rev.' on his daughter's gravestone, and Bishop Christopher Wordsworth, who applauded the vicar's stand against the 'deadly sin' of schism, created a national *cause célèbre*.[1] But more serious in the long run were continual petty insults of the sort offered by the Staffordshire clergyman who told a Wesleyan that 'the ministers she heard were only a lot of cobblers and tailors, that they had no right to preach, that there was only *one* Church, and that by going to chapel she was in danger of losing her soul.'[2]

As Methodism grew it became increasingly sensitive to such attacks. 'A Layman' put the point nicely in a pamphlet to Wordsworth,

> 'Wesleyans constitute a powerful, wealthy and intelligent body, and therefore are not in a position to submit quietly to insult and condemnation. . . . Pause! My Lord, before you advance further in opposition to them. . . . A century's snubbing by the Church of England has made them Heroes; and they will guard . . . their doctrines, sanctuaries and altars against Episcopal edicts and sacerdotal assumption.'[3]

The *Methodist Recorder* observed with some regret in 1890 that, 'Within the memory of men now living it would have been impossible to recruit Methodists to any considerable extent for the battle in favour of disestablishment. That day is gone by–thanks to the intolerance and hauteur of Anglican priests and deacons.'[4]

The Anglican attack was a powerful stimulus to Hugh Price Hughes' Wesleyan Forward Movement which had Methodist union as a major aim. Mr. K. S. Inglis has recently treated the Forward Movement as part of a massive and self-effacing social service operation by the churches at the end of the nineteenth century. On this view the Forward Movement–an attempt 'to think out Christianity freshly in the light of new secular knowledge . . . and to grapple with a changing society'–had for its ultimate aim ' "meeting the needs of . . . social groups" '. Mr. Inglis cites Hughes' statement in 1885, 'Methodism has reached the parting of the ways. We must either go back into the obscurity of a class religion, and the impotence of a moribund sect, or we must go forward to the blessed opportunities and far

---

[1] Christopher Wordsworth, *A Pastoral to Wesleyan Methodists in the Diocese of Lincoln*, Lincoln and London, n.d., pp. iv, 4.
[2] *M.R.*, 26 June 1874, p. 353.
[3] A Layman, *The Wesleyans and the Church. A Friendly Appeal to the Bishop of Lincoln*, London, 1876, p. 6.
[4] *M.R.*, 19 February 1890, p. 135.

reaching beneficence of a national religion, which preaches the Gospel to the poor.'[1] Mr. Inglis' interpretation lays stress on 'blessed', 'beneficence', 'Gospel', and 'poor', in this programme. Hughes probably laid stress on 'obscurity', 'sect', 'opportunities', and 'national religion'. The context of the Forward Movement is the crisis in Methodism caused by resurgent Anglicanism, rather than the overlapping crisis caused by awareness of a vast urban population alienated from Christianity.

The Forward Movement merges into the Wesleyan unionist movement of the 1910s and 1920s. The leaders of both were deeply hostile to 'the Anglican sect', as Hughes called it, or 'the Anglo-Catholic Church', as R. W. Perks preferred to describe it. Comparing Methodism and Anglicanism, Perks, Hughes' most important supporter and the leading lay Wesleyan unionist, said of the former, that 'Her pastorates are not "livings", and her preachers are not hirelings; they do not mutter ancient shibboleths; they have not to rely for the effect of the preaching of the Gospel on sensuous externals.'[2] John Bond, prominent Forward Movement man, and the most active Wesleyan unionist of the 1890s, was also an active disestablishmentarian. George Jackson, theorist of the younger generation of the Forward Movement, observed that 'Anglican intolerance' had created a 'gulf between the Anglican Church and Methodism'. 'Now', he declared, 'we are Methodists, and we are Dissenters.'[3] The Rev. E. Aldom French, secretary of the Wesleyan and United Union Committees, who had worked under Jackson at Edinburgh, largely based the case for union on 'the growth of Anglo-Catholicism'. The Anglo-Catholics were determined 'to carry the Gospel of Catholicism into every village in the country'. French declared, 'So far as possible, Evangelicals are closing their ranks.'[4]

Methodist union was the Forward Movement's grand design. It appealed to the Methodist longing for expansion. Methodism, fascinated by statistics, and aware of itself as a very recent and dynamic phenomenon in English Christianity, expressed its arrivism in a cult of size. Methodists contemplated their membership returns

[1] K. S. Inglis, *Churches and the Working Classes in Victorian England*, London, 1963, pp. vii, 70.

[2] *M.T.*, 20 February 1896, p. 120; R. W. Perks, *The Re-union of British Methodism*, London, 1920, pp. 11 ff; Denis Crane, *Sir Robert W. Perks: The Story of His Life*, London, 1909, p. 109.

[3] *M.R.*, 9 March 1905, p. 6; George Jackson, *The Old Methodism and the New*, London, 1903, pp. 17–20.

[4] *M.R.*, 20 July 1922, p. 4; 26 July 1928, p. 4.

with the pleasure a successful businessman might derive from his sales graph. A Primitive Methodist wrote frankly, 'It is very pleasant to regard gratefully the position and power of our Connexion–"our first ten members", and "our latest statistics".'[1] The Methodist Ecumenical Conferences tended to degenerate into panegyrics of the size, progress and power of Methodism.[2] Hughes, and Perks to a lesser degree, were fascinated by Methodist size, which Hughes notoriously exaggerated.

The 1890s saw a new emphasis. 'Let us all become liberal "Christian Imperialists",' Methodists were urged. Hughes was the greatest exponent of this 'Christian Imperialism'. The sway of Christ the King was his favourite day-dream. A 'British Imperialist to his fingertips', as his daughter described him, he saw himself as the Cecil Rhodes of the Wesleyans, pursuing policies of 'aggressiveness' and 'spiritual audacity'.[3] French told the Wesleyan Conference of 1920 that 'Anglicanism was a world-wide force, but let them not forget that Methodism was more so, and held the future well-being of the whole world in its keeping as no other Church did.'[4] Leaders who thought in this way regarded union as a necessary element of denominational expansion.

They also thought of it in more complex terms. Bunting, despite his subservience to the political and ecclesiastical establishment, expressed a deep-seated Methodist desire for political and social influence. Hughes' dream of a 'national religion' articulated not merely a Wesleyan but a common Methodist ambition. The *Primitive Methodist Magazine* confidently predicted in 1906 that in thirty years time the denomination would be 300,000 strong. 'In writing this way,' it assured its readers, 'we are not thinking of the glory of our denomination as an ultimate end, but rather what it might do with this constantly increasing weight and force.' The historian of Primitive Methodism wrote in 1919, in tones reminiscent of Hughes' 'national religion' programme of 1885,

'The War has helped to make our Church more national than, a few years ago, she could even have dreamed of becoming. For four years we have been in the full tide of the nation's life, and never

[1] *M.R.*, 16 April 1896, p. 257; *Primitive Methodist World*, 13 March 1890, p. 205.
[2] *Proceedings of the Oecumenical Methodist Conference Held in City Road Chapel, London, September, 1881*, London, 1881, pp. 1–40, etc.
[3] *M.R.*, 13 December 1900, p. 23; D. P. Hughes, *The Life of Hugh Price Hughes*, London, 1904, pp. 111, 182, 551, etc.
[4] *M.R.*, 22 July 1920, p. 8.

again, it is to be hoped, shall we subside into its shallows. Even if we should be called upon to oppose, we shall still be a recognized part of "His Majesty's Opposition".'

Free Methodists, reassured in 1902 that, 'ours is a great church. . . . There is no doubt upon that matter now,' had been told the previous year, 'Governments must be subject to the influence and follow the lead of the church on spiritual and moral matters. . . . Governments will have to defer to the will of the churches on these matters instead of ignoring us as in the past.'[1] An old Methodist minister wrote to the Rev. W. E. Sangster in April 1943, that 'The big thing is the revival of Methodism and the rallying of the young men who are really keen, to the making of Methodism into a thing that statesmen *must* notice, and Cabinet ministers must respect. That was what Hughes did and nobody has done it since.'[2]

Hughes was dismayed by Methodism's 'present impotence in national life'. His nightmare was that 'British Methodism would cease to count in the England of the Twentieth Century'.[3] His political ambition was a predominant Methodist influence in the Liberal Party. He became very indignant when 'the wire-pullers', a shadowy but malevolent group within the party, secured adoption of policies unacceptable to Hughes. Such wire-pullers, Hughes warned, would not succeed at elections if they were going to alienate 'the ministers and people of the free and democratic churches.'[4]

Hughes uttered his *fiat* with the greatest fervour over Parnell: unless the Liberals dissociated themselves from this 'adulterer . . . traitor . . . liar of the most shameless type', he announced, 'Mr. Gladstone will never return to power, the Liberal Party will be pulverised'. Hughes had, he claimed with evident pleasure, created an 'extraordinary and almost unprecedented crisis' by wielding the gigantic and almost irresistible influence of the Evangelical churches'.[5] How much greater would this influence be if Methodism was united.

In this mood, Methodists stopped thinking of themselves as a subordinate agency of a benevolent Anglicanism, and began to think of themselves overthrowing a hostile Anglicanism. The Wesleyan Home Mission Department's report of 1886 observed, 'Whatever Church

[1] *A.P.M. Mag.*, 1906, p. 660; H. B. Kendall, *History of the Primitive Methodist Church*, London, 1919, p. 172; *Methodist Monthly*, 1901, p. 437; 1902, p. 21.

[2] Paul Sangster, *Dr Sangster*, London, 1962, p. 293.

[3] D. P. Hughes, *op. cit.*, p. 147; *M.T.*, 17 April 1890, p. 365.

[4] *M.T.*, 10 December 1891, p. 1305; 10 March 1892, p. 241.

[5] *Ibid.*, 27 November 1890, p. 1211; 11 December 1890, p. 1253; 18 December 1890, p. 1276.

can succeed in winning for Christ the non-worshipping multitudes who are unfortunately at present a distinct majority of the English people, both in town and country, will inevitably become in the hour of its victory *the* Church of England.' Since Methodism was believed to be growing faster than any other denomination, it was clear to whom the victory 'inevitably' belonged. 'In the twentieth century we shall be the Church of the English people,' Hughes confidently predicted. The victory, when it came, would be a victory over crypto-Romanism. 'The virtual suppression of Evangelicalism as a governing force in the Church of England', remarked H. B. Workman in 1912, 'has made Methodism more conscious of itself as the representative Evangelical Church of the country.'[1]

The Forward Movement party did not stop at wishful thinking. A persistent Wesleyan ambition, from the 1860s, was the million pound fund. By 1890 such a fund had aroused Perks' interest. It took him eight years to launch it. The million guineas, as it had now become, of the Twentieth Century Fund, were to be devoted to two great objects: the provision of 'village elementary schools', to protect the children of Nonconformity from 'Anglo-Romanism', and, above all, 'a building in London', as the headquarters of twentieth-century Methodism. 'It must be large', said Perks, 'it must be central, it must be monumental.' Since, though this was not always explicit, the 'building' was also to house Hughes' West London Mission, it was a project analogous to Bunting's Centenary Hall half-a-century earlier. Wesleyanism, whose present headquarters were in east central obscurity, would have a magnificent building in west London to rival the Anglicans' Church House, the Roman Catholics' new Westminster Cathedral and, above all, Westminster Abbey. Over these headquarters Hughes would preside, *de facto* archbishop of Methodism. Sir Henry Lunn justly described the project as a 'challenge to the Church of England'.[2] Hughes did not live to see the new building begun, directly opposite Westminster Abbey. But the atmosphere of the first service held on the site was worthy of Hughes himself: 'One may imagine an awe-stricken whisper running round the grim gargoyles of the Abbey, "The Methodists have come!"'[3]

[1] Quoted in Perks, *op. cit.*, p. 7; *Proceedings of the Second Ecumenical Methodist Conference Held in the Metropolitan Methodist Episcopal Church, Washington, October, 1891*, London, 1892, p. 75; H. B. Workman, *Methodism*, Cambridge, 1912, p. 105.

[2] *M.R.*, 23 October 1863, p. 373; 11 November 1897, p. 887; 28 July 1898, p. 32; *M.T.*, 16 October 1890, p. 1052; Henry S. Lunn, *Chapters from My Life*, London, 1918, p. 256.

[3] *M.T.*, 5 February 1903, p. 91.

The Westminster Central Hall, built appropriately by the firm of architects who expressed the aspirations of Welsh nationalism in Cardiff Civic Centre, remains the architectural monument to Methodist ambitions at the beginning of the twentieth century. The ecclesiastical monument is the Methodist Church itself, for Methodist Union was throughout crucial to Forward Movement thinking. If the idea of a great anti-Wesleyan church fascinated the liberal Methodists, the concept of a united Methodism fascinated the Forward Movement.

The Rev. J. E. Matthews summed up these ambitions when he wrote, in 1922,

'Methodism for years has been suffering from megalomania and pride. We like to do things in a big way, e.g. the Twentieth Century Fund and the Central Hall, we boasted more than any other Church of our Roll of Honour in the war. We like to "show off" our titled lay men. At the root of this agitation for Union of the Methodist Churches I believe the same spirit is to be found.'[1]

To Matthews the drive for union was contemptible. But to those who struggled to build a greater Methodism, in reaction to years of Anglican scorn and of exclusion from national life, union was the key to victory.

Perks told Penzance Wesleyans in 1899 that 'Methodists were not going to play the part of poor relation to the Anglican Church any longer. Within twenty-five years he expected they would find Methodism was the premier church of the country. But, first, Methodism must be reunited, and, second, the State church must . . . split into its natural fragments.' There was nothing new about Perks' scheme, except perhaps the expectation that the Anglicans would decently disintegrate into two divided but honest parts, the Protestant – a client of Methodism – and the Papist – an appendage of Rome. Twenty-five years before, the *Recorder*, with which Perks' father was closely connected, observed that Wesleyanism 'taken alone, is a pigmy . . . compared with the Church of England. . . . But if the forces of Methodism, instead of being cut up into half-a-dozen self-acting and independent battalions were united in one compact army, how different would be the proportions.' United Methodism could 'be brought into comparison with the Establishment', and 'compel the attention of the legislature'.[2]

---

[1] J. E. Matthews–J. Ernest Rattenbury, 4 March 1922, in Rattenbury Papers.
[2] *M.T.* 16 November 1899, p. 798; *M.R.*, 2 January 1874, p. 7.

When Hughes claimed that among 'the terrible results' of Methodist disunion was 'the Romeward movement' of the Church of England,[1] he carried most Methodists with him. But like liberal Methodists earlier in the century, Methodist anti-Anglicans were vague about the possible effects of united Methodism.

Bruce Rose, a minister of the United Methodist Church, suggested that union of Methodism would give Methodist thinking more moral influence over the Church of England. 'Think of the impact of our evangelical and united mind on the Anglican Church,' he urged. Hughes seemed to lay much emphasis on the converting virtues of 'Connexional Unity'. By extending the connexional principle throughout a united Methodism, maximum converting power would be assured. Methodism would win for Christ 'the non-worshipping multitudes' and, as the Home Missions Report put it, 'would inevitably become in the hour of its victory, *the* Church of England', i.e. by sheer size.[2] The argument was a strong one: the Church of Ireland had long been disestablished on the grounds that it was manifestly an alien and minority church; Hughes, the Welshman, must have been particularly conscious of the displacement by Welsh non-conformity of the Church of Wales, shortly to be disestablished. What could happen in Ireland and Wales could happen in England.

But the most popular theory centred on the villages. Village Methodism was often overshadowed by the Church of England. At Owston Ferry, the Wesleyans made a brave show with their Centenary Chapel. But even here, four miles from Wesley's birthplace, the lantern of the church school and the perpendicular tower of the parish church showed where power in the village lay. In many villages, Methodism did not even possess a chapel. A united Methodism could establish Methodism in many places, consolidate its strength in others. As a Wesleyan put it, union would bring together 'small congregations and struggling causes' in the villages, in one strong chapel, 'a bulwark of strength . . . to oppose the forces of evil and the arrogance of Roman and Anglican priesthood'.[3]

Perks saw union as bringing 'a new Methodist church in at least 2,000 more English villages'. For

'One of the most powerful arguments in favour of Methodist Union is the immense service which can be so rendered to the village population of England and Wales. Nearly ten millions of the total

[1] *M.T.*, 24 October 1901, p. 770.
[2] *U.M. Mag.*, August 1921, p. 230; *M.T.*, 5 September 1901, p. 641.
[3] *M.T.*, 28 April 1904, p. 296.

population of England and Wales live in villages. . . . There are 14,000 of such villages in England, and in 4,300 of them there is no Nonconformist chapel at all. The villagers must go to the parish church or worship in some neighbouring village or town. Many of the parish churches are practically deserted. Thousands of them are hardly distinguishable from a Roman Catholic church.'[1]

Union might also assist in the struggle against the establishment by increasing Methodist influence over the Liberal Party, and hence secure political changes which Methodists desired, and bring pressure to bear on the Church of England through Parliament. In 1874, the *Recorder* looked to a united Methodism which would 'compel the attention of the legislature'. Thirty years later it was a commonplace among Methodists that a united Methodism would be 'a greater power in the State'; it would 'occupy a position of power and influence in these realms such as it has never approached before'; it would 'mould and transfigure the life of the nation'.[2] French explained to the Wesleyan Conference of 1919 what this transfiguration meant. 'What was needed', he said, 'was that this nation should be lifted, the Gospel of Christ was the only power that could do this. In spite of all protests, the Government of our country had given way to the publicans and brewers.'[3]

Once more, the precise mechanism by which union would work, eluded Methodists. They hoped, like Hughes, that the volume of their united voice and vote would overwhelm the politicians, at least of the Liberal Party. But the hoped for political effects of Methodist Union were not so much a subject of reason as of emotion, among those who were desperate for national recognition of their denomination. The *Recorder* put the alternatives as unionists saw them in 1919. Was Methodism to be united, 'a society and an association that "counts" ', that 'is "somebody" ', so that 'the average man may not ignore its power, and even the statesman must consider its prestige'; or was divided Methodism to be a 'society . . . "very amusing" to the ordinary person, and to the statesman a negligible quantity'.[4]

The strident Methodist demand for recognition may displease. But the word 'Nonconformity' summed up a whole world of inferiority and exclusion from 'the full tide of the nation's life'. Some may prefer the 'wine' of Puritanism in the fullness of state power to the 'vinegar'

[1] Perks, *op. cit.*, p. 22.
[2] *F.M.*, 4 August 1904, p. 489; *A.P.M. Mag.*, 1901, p. 855; *M.T.*, 6 September 1894, p. 610.
[3] *M.R.*, 24 July 1919, p. 8.
[4] *Ibid.*, 20 March 1919, p. 10.

of the generations of proscription and proletarianization that followed
the Clarendon Code. But soured though their protestantism might
have been, to Methodists it remained precious. They continued to
believe in their importance to the nation, which they had, when the
hated Church of England was decadent and effete, 'alone saved . . .
from a revolution similar to that of the French', an opinion in which
historians have been eager to concur. They also preserved the belief
that the nation would give them recognition. After the Liberal victory
of 1906, a Free Methodist declared, 'The turn of the Nonconformists
has come. They have waited long, and they have waited patiently, but,
as events show, they have not waited in vain.'[1] As events showed, they
had waited, and were to go on waiting, in vain. But in the years after
1906, Methodist Union offered to a generation the prospect of 'The
turn of the Nonconformists' at last.

## The Ecumenicalism of Mission

Both reform and vindication of Methodism seem small in the
twentieth-century perspective, when the Christian religion itself is in
decline. But Methodist leaders were aware, especially after 1880, that
the very existence of their denomination was in danger. Long before
the theology of crisis was invented, Methodism had reached its crisis
and in that crisis looked to ecumenicalism.

Liberal Methodists justified their schemes of union with the doctrine of reform, Forward Movement Methodists, by the appeal to
Protestantism and denominational chauvinism. But in the crisis of the
whole Methodist world, union needed justification in loftier and more
general terms, close to the ideology of modern ecumenicalism. The
use of proof texts from scripture marks this third phase of the unionist
movement. One such text was Jesus's prayer that those who believed
in him 'may all be one; even as thou, Father, art in me, and I in thee,
that they may also be in us, so that the world may believe that thou
hast sent me'. Another text, favoured by A. S. Peake, proclaimed that
Christ 'is our peace who has made us both one, and has broken down
the dividing wall of hostility'.[2] That these two passages constituted
the whole of a meagre harvest did not reduce the conviction that
union was in the will of God. The Wesleyan evangelist, Gipsy Smith,
told the 1920 Conference that

'They would never settle Methodist Union as they ought until they

[1] *A.P.M. Mag.*, 1902, p. 657; *M.M.*, 1906, p. 72; Christopher Hill, *Puritanism and Revolution*, London, 1958, p. vii.
[2] Jn. 17.21; Eph. 3.14: *Revised Standard Version*.

began to pray. They would never discuss themselves into it–never! They must pause to consider the mind of the Lord. If they had a theory keeping them from the Prims and the Prims had a theory keeping them from us–it was not the mind of the Lord. His mind was that they should be one.'

Since this was so, unionists were fond of pointing out, 'those who oppose Union are fighting against God'.[1]

The moral imperative of union could be expressed in other ways. Many held that union conformed to world trends. 'The moral and spiritual forces of the universe are on the side of those who are striving towards the goal of a reunited Methodism,' claimed R. Wilberforce Allen. The Rev. W. Russell Maltby, a fellow Wesleyan, warned of 'almost unanimous condemnation' if 'we should isolate ourselves from the general world-wide movement towards Union'.[2] The Primitive Methodist leader, Sir William Hartley, claimed in 1904 that 'There was a unanimous feeling that in the future the Primitive Methodists would be bound to come into a Methodist Union of some kind or other or they would be discredited in the eyes of the nation.' Union was 'in the air, it is in all the trend of things'. Indeed it was 'the next step forward in the progressive evolution of the Spirit of God'. 'We may claim', wrote a member of the denomination in 1904, 'that hitherto, we have kept abreast of the spirit of the age. Should the other churches unite and we remain alone, we shall suffer in *morale* through lagging behind the spirit of the age.'[3]

World War One assisted the argument. French wrote in 1916,

'The special disasters that have ruined the world of our time are due to disunion, to the fact that class is set against class, nation against nation. . . . The essential mission for the Church today is to set an example of union and love. . . . It appears as if the Spirit of God Himself were now manifestly leading the Churches to closer union, and as if to resist the tendency were to "quench the Spirit", and therefore a deadly sin.'

Perks concurred in this view. 'The world is yearning for Unity', he wrote in 1920. 'It is tired and weary of strife.'[4]

[1] *M.R.*, 18 May 1920, p. 14; 22 July 1920, p. 9.

[2] R. Wilberforce Allen, *Methodism and Modern World Problems*, London, 1926, p. 198; *M.R.*, 2 August 1928, p. 8.

[3] Arthur S. Peake, *The Life of Sir William Hartley*, London, 1926, pp. 103–4; *A.P.M. Mag.*, 1901, p. 157; *Primitive Methodist Leader*, 9 June 1921, p. 361; *A.P.M. Mag.*, November 1904, p. 917.

[4] *M.R.*, 13 April 1916, p. 4; Perks, *op. cit.*, p. 5.

The League of Nations naturally came to mind. The *Recorder* observed in 1919,

> 'That which moves in the world is moving in the Churches. . . . But the Churches do not appear to have the same courageous leadership granted to them. The goal is as clear for the Churches as for the nations. . . . Christian unity is their definite charge from God, as the League of Nations is the definite charge for the nations.'[1]

Another moral standard impelling the churches toward union at the end of World War I was current popular veneration of 'our boys' at the front. 'Our soldier lads do not understand our differences,' said Perks. 'They see only too clearly the wasted forces of Methodism in our villages.'[2]

In the crisis of Methodism many looked to a divinely appointed, morally imperative, ecumenical salvation of the churches. It was necessary, said French, 'to wrestle with God'. Since union was so appointed, it was natural that it should seem both costly and urgent. French urged the need 'at all costs', of 'almost headlong haste' to stop the 'drifting from the churches and apparently from religion, amongst the masses especially who are now coming to power in England'.[3] His fellow Wesleyan, Ensor Walters, declared in prophetic tones, 'All over this country men know in their hearts that all is not well. Empty Churches–depleted Societies–the Lord's Day sweeping away, gambling increasing! All is well!–Keep your little settled communities–All is well! It is not well. I thank God I have for the first time in my life the chance to vote for a union of this kind.'[4]

Union meant evangelism, or, in more modern terms, ecumenicalism meant mission. As H. J. Pope believed, Methodism 'must be a church that will convert, otherwise its distinctive genius will vanish'.[5] When Methodism failed to convert, it looked to union. French told a parliamentary committee that the union movement in Methodism was 'a spiritual movement actually intended to secure the more effective service of the age and evangelization of the world'.[6] Lidgett declared, 'Only a re-united Church can evangelize the world. . . . We

[1] *M.R.*, 2 January 1919, p. 3.
[2] Perks, *op. cit.*, p. 5.
[3] *M.R.*, 4 April 1912, p. 5; E. Aldom French (ed.), *Evangelism. A Reinterpretation*, London, 1921, p. 11.
[4] *M.R.*, 21 July 1927, p. 6.
[5] R. M. Pope, *The Life of Henry J. Pope*, London, 1913, pp. 249–50.
[6] E. Aldom French, *Evidence re Uniting Act*, p. 7: French Papers (The Rev. Cyril A. French).

cannot afford in these days the narrowness of outlook, the friction, or the isolation which weakens the influence of the Christian Churches.'[1]

Improved evangelism was linked with a stronger moral campaign. Peake 'was certain that the evangelization of England would receive a new impetus if the Methodist Churches lead a united attack against the forces of evil'.[2] Even the Rev. J. E. Rattenbury, the leading opponent of union, conceded that 'One powerful Church might make the forces of evil tremble, where now they are unmoved by the thin piping of contending sects.' Mr. William Evans, a London Primitive Methodist, confessed

> 'he would not willingly give up all his associations unless he had seen a vision of something greater and more wonderful. If they knew as he knew the evils that were being wrought by the Sunday cinemas, the flaming gin palaces, the bookmaker and the immorality in London, they would realize the need of a powerful and united Church that would stand for righteousness. One Methodist Church could face up to the vested interest of the drink traffic.'[3]

Union meant more preaching and more prophecy. It also meant more members. Evangelism means recruitment, to one denomination or another. When French said, 'Our business is to capture the democracy for Jesus Christ,' he meant, to recruit more Methodists. This was the underlying hope of ecumenicalism. The Rev. Robert Brewin informed his fellow Free Methodists in 1907, 'Union will have the effect of rapidly increasing the number of our church-members'. With union, the *Primitive Methodist Leader* announced in 1924, 'The whole Methodist Church will enter upon a new era of extension which will rival the early days.'[4]

'Revivalism' seemed to cling to unionists, many of whom, especially in the 1920s, were closely connected with evangelism. J. E. Matthews complained of unionists 'singing old Methodist hymns and promising Revival'. The united Church began to appear as a promised land into which the converts would pour in their thousands. 'There is every reason,' wrote a Wesleyan in 1929, 'to hope and believe that . . . a Revival will coincide with the coming of Methodist union . . . with the consummation of union a great forward movement on quite un-

[1] *M.T.*, 21 October 1909, p. 2.

[2] Leslie S. Peake, *Arthur Samuel Peake, A Memoir*, London, 1930, p. 165.

[3] J. Ernest Rattenbury, *Christian Union and Methodist Fusion*, London, n.d., p. 8; *Methodist Leader*, 23 June 1927, p. 394.

[4] *M.R.*, 27 July 1922, p. 4; *M.M.*, November 1907, p. 327; *P.M.L.*, 27 November 1924, p. 776.

precedented lines is anticipated; is indeed, inevitable. . . . The Methodist Revival is coming. There is a new feeling of optimism in the air.'[1]
The cruel disappointments which followed both the union of 1907 and
that of 1932, and the greater sophistication which the disasters of the
last thirty years have bred in ecumenicalists, may make these hopes
seem ridiculous. But the zeal with which union was sought cannot be
understood without knowledge of the faith in its converting efficacy;
and even the ecumenicalists of today may share in some form this
early hope that union *would* advance the cause of Christianity.

The decreases of Christianity made Methodist Union 'a solemn
necessity', for 'a United Methodism would be more efficient for the
evangelization of the world'.[2] But the precise operation of this process
also was obscure. Some suggested that union would bring greater
*moral* efficiency, that 'A great Christian Reconciliation would arrest
the man in the street.'[3] Once arrested, unionists suggested, he would
be unable to resist the spectacle of Christians practising towards each
other, if not towards anyone else, the love they preached. This was a
weak argument: unionists could not demonstrate that the man in the
street knew of the divisions of Christianity, would know when they
were ended, or would care.

Arguments based on the effect of union on the churches themselves
had more force. Here a basic disagreement about the character of the
Church arose. Was the Church primarily an organization, subject to
the pressures felt by organizations, and amenable to organizational
reforms; or was it a spiritual institution which could only be weakened
or strengthened by spiritual forces? E. Aldom French strongly emphasized the former view. Methodism had to 'organize' in the face of
decreases. 'The machinery of Methodism is out of gear', he claimed:
'Methodism is clearly neglecting the essential principles of successful
organization'.[4] Rattenbury inclined to the other view. In the face of
the Methodist crisis, Rattenbury called for 'greater devoutness and
consecration'.[5]

French carried the day. But a policy of organizational improvement must be appropriate to the type of organization concerned. The
advocates of such a policy were confident that they knew what sort of
organization Methodism was. Some held that Methodism was a

---

[1] J. E. Matthews–J. Ernest Rattenbury, 4 March 1922, in Rattenbury Papers;
*M.R.*, 17 January 1929, p. 5.
[2] *M.R.*, 14 June 1917, p. 5; 15 April 1920, p. 5.
[3] *Ibid.*, 12 December 1918, p. 4.
[4] *Ibid.*, 22 April 1915, p. 10; 1 June 1916, p. 4.
[5] *Ibid.*, 21 October 1915, p. 10.

*business*, dealing in evangelism, supplying salvation, manufacturing saints: an especially attractive notion when the persuasive idea of rationalization was in the air. 'We are told', said the Rev. Joseph Kirsop in 1901, 'that things in the twentieth century have to be done on a great scale. Small businesses, small churches ... will be an anachronism in the age on which we have entered.' Nineteen years later, French told the Wesleyan Conference that 'He did not believe that a small Church could live today, any more than a small business or a small Army.' Even opponents of union adopted this terminology. 'This business', complained Mr. T. Bolam of Willington Quay, 'savours too much of company promoting and watered stock, with the interest of the small shareholder at a discount.'[1]

The *Recorder* had hinted at a second interpretation in 1874, with its talk of 'battalions' and 'one compact army'. Christians are always fond of military metaphors. They were never fonder than during and immediately after the First World War. 'It is significant,' wrote three critics of union,

'that the Scheme began to take practical shape in the war years, when a majority of men were obsessed with the military idea of a united front, and a complex organization centred in one controlling point. Many Methodist people were scared by the feeling that we were losing ground, which they promptly imagined was only to be rewon by combined staff-work.'[2]

But neither the economic nor the military analogy was appropriate, however plausible. Both firms and armies have simple, fairly well defined objectives, which are either shared by the members of the organization or can be compelled upon them by some coercive method. Vested and conflicting interests and viewpoints may exist in both, but they are comparatively weak. In churches, they are comparatively strong; and church members cannot be sacked, jailed or shot for failure to comply with directives. Even if it is assumed that good 'staff-work', or rationalization of plant and labour, *will* be successful in the religious sphere, in the sense of producing more church members, there is little likelihood, even in a highly centralized organization like Methodism, of gaining sufficient control over the members to introduce effective rationalization.

The association of ecumenicalism, rationalization and evangelism

[1] *M.M.*, 1901, p. 89; *M.R.*, 22 July 1920, p. 8; *P.M.L.*, 1 February 1923, p. 71.
[2] T. R. Auty, M. H. Bainton and W. Usher, *Methodist Union. The Case against the Scheme*, London, n.d., p. 8.

had other defects. The major example of union available to Methodist ecumenicalists in the 1920s was the United Methodist Church. Between 1907 and 1921 its membership fell by 7·3 per cent, while that of Wesleyanism fell by 6·3 per cent, and of Primitive Methodism by a mere 3·7 per cent. This was at best a poor demonstration of the dynamism of united churches. Various efforts were made to circumvent this difficulty. One was simply to offer erroneous figures about the progress of the United Methodist Church.[1]

The Rev. Henry Smith, a United Methodist leader, tried another method. In 1927, referring to United Methodist losses since the denomination's inception, he observed that 'They would have been much greater but for our own Union', a proposition difficult to verify.[2]

Others took refuge in equally illogical arguments. French stated that

'The critic of the United Methodist Church is singularly uninformed. That Church came into being at a time when every Church, Established and Free, began to report decreases in members and congregations. Could it be expected that one of the smallest of the Churches could stop that widespread drift? . . . On the other hand the Union undoubtedly saved many of the Churches of the uniting bodies from being crushed out of existence during the war.'

The United Methodist Church's leaders, concluded French, 'unanimously declare that the United Methodist Church is stronger both spiritually and materially for the Union'.[3]

French failed to clarify what sort or size of Church could be assisted by union if the United Methodist Church could not. Had that union been designed merely to save the two smallest parties, the New Connexion and the Bible Christian, while the Free Methodists, 80,000 strong, had no real need of it? Why did the United Methodist Church, 150,000 strong, have double the rate of loss of the Primitive Methodist Church, 200,000 strong? What significance did this fact have for the ecumenicalists' case? Such questions were unanswered. What French did say merely demonstrated the confusion of thought among ecumenicalists when they had to deal with the detailed problems created by their arguments and policies.

But these problems did not prevent unionists sketching rationalization plans which union would facilitate. One of the most emphasized, and indeed most plausible details in these plans, was the reduction in

[1] *M.T.*, 12 February 1920, p. 6; 19 February 1920, p. 6; 26 February 1920, p. 6; 4 March 1920, p. 6.
[2] *M.R.*, 28 April 1927, p. 18.
[3] *M.T.*, 20 January 1921, p. 4.

the number of competing or 'overlapping' chapels. In 1872, the *Recorder* remarked,

> 'It must be admitted . . . that the multiplication of Methodist sects is a great inconvenience, not to say a positive evil. No true Methodist can traverse the county of Lincolnshire for example, especially the villages of that county, without mourning over the loss of power, the waste of money and labour, the perpetuation of rivalry and disunion, which are occasioned by having two or three separate interests in populations where there are barely enough people to maintain one in vigorous efficiency.'[1]

By the 1920s most Methodists expected union to 'settle the problem of overlapping', where all the efforts of the interdenominational Methodist Committee for Concerted Action had failed.[2] 'Local amalgamations' were 'essential' in a united church, French claimed; but a United Methodist minister, the Rev. J. G. Williams, was left to point to 'a serious omission' in the union scheme, the absence of any provision 'for the guidance and, when necessary, the compulsion of local unions or amalgamations by Conference'.[3] Such provisions were impossible, as is shown below. But their absence gravely weakened the case for union as a means of rationalization, especially since as many pointed out, and Henry Smith attempted to disprove, the United Methodist Church, also lacking any such provision, had failed materially to reduce overlapping.[4]

The positive side of rationalization was the co-ordination and consolidation of resources. 'The real genesis and inwardness of the movement for Methodist Union,' said the Rev. William Younger, 'is that it will make for efficiency and co-ordination and national and world unity of policy and action.'[5] Again the details were a little vague, but certain proposals stood out. The leadership of a united church could be drawn from a larger area; ministerial training could be managed better and more economically in the larger units union would provide; the new denomination would have a larger market for its literature; and, by being able to draw on a larger membership, could raise funds more easily.[6]

[1] *M.R.*, 1 March 1872, p. 102.
[2] *Holborn Review*, July 1920, p. 373.
[3] *M.R.*, 21 July 1932, p. 4; *U.M.*, 24 June 1920, p. 308.
[4] e.g., *M.R.*, 24 June 1920, p. 13; *M.T.*, 2 January 1919, p. 12; 9 January 1919, p. 6; *U.M.*, 13 February 1919, p. 79.
[5] *P.M.L.*, 9 November 1922, p. 715.
[6] e.g., *M.M.*, 1901, pp. 89–90; 1903, pp. 73–5; *Methodist New Connexion Magazine*, June 1904, pp. 206–8; French, *Evidence*, p. 7.

The economies of scale looked for in a united church were many and various. Reduction of overlapping itself would greatly assist. Mr. Percy Stuart, a Bristol Primitive Methodist, wrote in 1916 that

'throughout our Connexion we are spending tens of thousands of pounds yearly that might be saved if we had grace enough to become merged into one great . . . Church. . . . To businessmen it is a serious question as to how far we are justified in subscribing to keep up these competitive churches, the expense of which, by exercising a little business tact and Christian spirit could in a number of cases be avoided.'[1]

Another source of economy would be amalgamation of departments. The whole committee apparatus could be reduced. Here the United Methodist example was encouraging. Proportionately, the Free Methodists used 150 per cent, and the New Connexion and Bible Christians 300 per cent more committee members than the United Methodist Church into which they merged. The provision of one book room publishing one set of denominational literature would also assist; although, if rate of profit on capital is a measure of efficiency, the United Methodist Book Room was less efficient than those of two of its three constituent organizations.[2] Smith claimed that the United Methodist Church saved £12,000 per annum, compared with the three uniting denominations. A colleague raised this estimate to £19,000, and French to £50,000. These sums were not enormous. They represented 1s. 9½d., 3s. 1½d. and 7s. 2¼d., per member per annum.[3]

What was to be done with these liberated resources was unclear. One very popular answer to the question was a sort of 'village charter'. Both Perks and George Eayrs advocated a comprehensive plan for the overlapping chapels in the villages. As Eayrs put it,

'Methodist Church buildings in a village should be used to the highest advantage. The best of them should be made the church, and restricted absolutely to purposes of worship. The next best should be the young people's centre on Sunday and week-days. Another should become the social centre, a village institute and reading room.'

[1] *P.M.L.*, 3 February 1916, p. 71.
[2] French, *op. cit.*, p. 7; *M.M.*, 1903, p. 73; *Methodist Union, Minute Book, December 18th, 1902, to September 18th, 1907*, pp. 62, 111; Meeting of 17 February 1921, in *Minutes of the Wesleyan Methodist Union Committee, etc., 1913–1919*.
[3] *M.R.*, 23 January 1919, p. 4; Wesleyan Committee meeting of 2 May 1918, in *Minutes* . . .; *M.T.*, 20 January 1921, p. 4; *P.M.L.*, 23 August 1917, p. 509.

A radical reform of the village situation seemed urgent. A Wesleyan wrote in March 1920, 'Can any man face the prospect of a Godless Labour running amok without dismay? And what is Methodism doing to stem the torrent? Cycling out ten miles in the slush to preach to three old women.' The simple closure of chapels was unpopular. But in theory the uneconomic use of labour in the village could be reduced by Eayrs' village charter.[1]

The details were characteristically vague. The cost of turning the smallest and most dilapidated chapel into a village institute was never estimated; it hardly could be, for this would involve the question of determining which chapel in the village was the smallest and most dilapidated, scarcely a process likely to appeal to those chapel officials who were expected to vote for union. But as a general idea, especially in the 'back to the land' atmosphere following World War I, the village charter was very popular. It was frequently advocated in a *Recorder* competition on Methodist Union in 1920. The report on the entries commented sarcastically, 'It was an ever-recurrent satisfaction' to the writers that redundant village chapels could be abandoned for worship, and ' "then turned into a village institute where games, lectures," etc, etc, etc.'[2]

The other main use for liberated resources was in building new chapels, in Perks' 2,000 villages or, more usually, in the 'new areas'. It had long been hoped, especially by small and geographically restricted Methodist denominations, that union would reduce 'leakage' of membership through removal to areas where the denomination did not possess a chapel. Under union migrants would be willing to attend another denomination's chapel at present foreign to them. With the large-scale development of new suburban housing areas, usually in areas where Methodism was weak, denominational resources were severely strained. New suburban chapels cost money, which was difficult to raise; but if no chapels were built, membership 'leaked'. In 1929 French claimed that union was essential in view of 'the very great and urgent need in connection with the new populations springing up around the great towns. . . . It is admitted on all sides that we cannot build against one another in these localities and even the strongest anti-unionists have been driven to suggesting the allocation of different areas to the different Churches.'[3]

But ecumenicalists had advanced neither the strategy nor the

[1] *A.P.M. Mag.*, November 1920, p. 758; Perks, *op. cit.*, p. 22; *M.R.*, 18 March 1920, pp. 4–6.
[2] *M.R.*, 18 March 1920, pp. 4–6.
[3] French, *op. cit.*, p. 8.

costing of union beyond a primitive state. Often they merely dismissed such technicalities. In the 1920 Wesleyan Conference, Mr. Harold W. Jackson made a speech against union, analysing the state of Primitive and United Methodist finances, and difficulties which would arise out of limiting clauses of chapel trust deeds. The Rev. John Scott Lidgett, who greatly influenced the union scheme, and who was the first President of the Methodist Church, dismissed these quibbles, 'They were asked to look at their trust-deeds,' he said. 'He was anxious rather to look forward to the Church that was to be.'[1] Ecumenicalism was a vision. Its visionary character can alone explain the confused and delusory bid for rationalization of resources and revitalization of evangelism through union; for this bid was a mere act of faith.

*Ecumenicalism and Commitment to Chapel*

Methodist Union was the dream of uneasy but hopeful leaders. They were uneasy because of adverse circumstances, the weight of Wesleyan reaction, the threat of Anglicanism, or the collapse of their own denomination. But they were hopeful because they believed that through union these circumstances could be permanently overcome. In a world of disaster, ecumenicalism is the creed of the sanguine. But faith is not always easy to communicate. It may even be difficult to justify to oneself. The Rev. Richard Pyke, in turn a minister of the Bible Christian, United Methodist and Methodist Churches, and a President of the latter two churches, spent much of his life working for union. In 1920, he wrote that the alternative to union for 'village Methodism' might be 'leanness, striving, and ultimately death'. But he could hardly convince himself that the United Methodist Church had been more than a necessary evil. 'Here in Devon, for instance,' he wrote, 'we were practically all Bible Christians. We lost much by Union—we found our ministers passing to bigger churches—our leaders did not often come to see us—the old annual family gathering at the Conference ceased . . . and in return for all this, only the far-seeing could appreciate the gain.'[2]

The far-seeing needed to mobilize denominational opinion. 'Don't be anxious as to the "reception" the proposals for Union may have among the "people" . . .' the *Recorder* declared in 1918. 'It is said among our own congregations, "the people are not much interested or concerned".' This was unimportant. 'For the generality there is in most high and spiritual movements little that stirs, or even touches the

---

[1] *M.R.*, 22 July 1920, p. 8.
[2] *U.M. Mag.*, June 1920, p. 184.

imagination. . . . Why are "leaders" desirable save that they are necessary as an offset against the torpor of the average. . . . They ought to be interested, and it is our business to compel their interest.'[1]

But torpor concealed hostility among those who could not 'appreciate the gain', but could envisage the loss. The greatest good of the 'average' member, and indeed the average lay official, was the chapel. The Rev. J. A. Findlay complained in 1919 that 'Church-life has taken the form of intense devotion to one particular building and its associations'. But the truth was rather that the erosive force of secularization, though it might shift all else, could not touch this devotion. A Primitive Methodist layman, Mr. C. G. Hawkins, declared 'There are thousands of little village shrines made holy by sacrifice, prayed for, stitched for, fought for–aye, agonized for!' The union movement with its changes and unsettlements threatened these village shrines. Indeed as the movement became more committed to rationalization, it became a direct attack upon the chapel. 'Unite and where is your tradition?' asked Mr. Hawkins.[2]

The lay member of a denomination, like the citizen of a state, found affairs of government alien. 'To many of our members and officials,' wrote three opponents of union, 'the Conference seems far-removed and relatively unimportant. To them, what matters is the local society, or at most the Circuit.'[3] The union movement though meaningful in the perspective of departmental officials and denominational leaders was meaningless to many chapel members. The movement, wrote a Wesleyan, fell foul of 'Little Bethel', for 'The Methodist, especially the village Methodist', simply wanted to 'run his Chapel in his own way'. He inhabited another world from 'the magnificent ideals of an up-to-date gentleman who sits in an office and manipulates papers', and is impressed with 'the saving grace of bigness, unity of direction, and the inspiration of numbers'. From this perspective unionists could utter their contempt for 'all that is little and snug, comfortable, old and easily-explored', and point to the vastness of the twentieth-century universe. From the perspective of the chapel, union was a 'London-made scheme', the work of 'so-called "leaders"'', chiefly domiciled in the Metropolis.[4]

The views of court and country may diverge. The court often feels, as in this case, that the only answer to its problems is to rearrange the

[1] *M.R.*, 3 July 1919, p. 10.
[2] *Ibid.*, 17 July 1919, p. 4; *P.M.L.*, 7 August 1919, p. 479.
[3] Auty, Bainton and Usher, *op. cit.*, p. 2.
[4] *M.R.*, 2 March 1922, pp. 5–6; *M.R.*, 24 July 1920, p. 9; *P.M.L.*, 22 January 1920, p. 55.

country. In this process, the country feared, all would be lost. Mark Guy Pearse, who probably expressed the feelings of the Methodist rank and file at the turn of the century more accurately than any one else, told a story of Methodist Union. It was concerned with an old Cornishman, who, rightly in Pearse's view, looked at his chapel and said it was 'sacred and I won't have so much as a hand laid upon it'. The same sentiment was uttered, perhaps with less grace, by Mr. J. H. Standeven, a Skipton Primitive Methodist, who had spent £20,000 on Ebenezer Chapel, Halifax. 'I am thoroughly opposed to Methodist Union,' he said, 'and shall do all that I ever can to prevent Ebenezer Chapel, Halifax, which is my gift, being taken over by any union; it is going to remain *Primitive Methodist* as long as I have any influence.'[1]

Chapel meant more than a building however. Sir William Hartley feared in 1904 that 'our officials will want a great deal of educating' in ecumenicalism. The chapel officials' problems were stated, twenty-two years later, by a correspondent to the *Recorder*. He wrote,

'On the one side of our Chapel within a hundred yards is a Free Methodist Chapel; on the other side is a Primitive Methodist Chapel about the same distance away. In each of these chapels are a band of eager, enthusiastic officials who have had a life-long connection with their Chapel, and sphere of work. Supposing, through Union, you close two of these chapels, what is going to become of these various officials?'[2]

These fears greatly influenced the ecumenical programme. The most telling point in anti-unionist propaganda was made by J. E. Rattenbury in 1922. He asked members and officials, '*Are you willing that your Chapel should be closed? . . . Do you think that if your Chapel or one of the other Methodist Churches were closed you would gather under one roof all the people who belonged to the two Chapels?* If you think so experience is quite against your conclusions.'[3] Unionists were caught in a peculiar dilemma. On the one hand, if union was to make Methodism 'a greater evangelistic force through the country', the rationalization consequent upon closure of overlapping chapels was essential. On the other hand, if they advocated closure of chapels as the main plank of their programme, the union movement was doomed. They prevaricated. The virtues of closure were frequently proclaimed. Such schemes as the 'village charter' were advocated to make closure

---

[1] *M.R.*, 30 September 1920, p. 9; *The Wesleyan Methodist*, 27 November 1924, p. 5.
[2] Arthur S. Peake, *op. cit.*, p. 104; *M.R.*, 16 September 1926, p. 4.
[3] *M.R.*, 10 November 1922, p. 7.

seem slightly more palatable. But for over a generation unionists relied for success on liberal promises that the chapels would not be closed.

Before the union of 1907, 'Those who feared that their little chapels would disappear', were reassured that 'it was not contemplated to close any chapel over the heads of the local trustees and authorities'. 'The Conferences have given the most definite guarantees', said French in 1930, 'that local amalgamations of Circuits and Churches will not be forced. They will only take place with local consent.'[1] These promises eliminated the possibility of a rational plan to optimize denominational resources. The purpose of union was to close the chapels; the price of union was to keep them open.

Despite these guarantees, when union was put to the vote in 1924, large blocs of resistance to union appeared in areas of considerable overlap, where the denominations had many overlapping circuits, competing chapels and empty seats.

Durham was a comparatively mild case. Methodism in the county was largely concentrated among the collieries. When Primitive, United and Wesleyan Methodist quarterly meetings came to vote on union in 1924 no less than thirteen circuits in this area rejected it or showed very small majorities in favour.[2] Seating figures are not available for non-Wesleyans here or elsewhere. But Wesleyans had 4·9 seats per member in these circuits, slightly above the national figure of 4·6. Even if the most generous membership–attendance ratio–say that attendance was three times membership–be allowed, there are many empty seats.[3] The average number of members per chapel in

[1] *F.M.*, 10 August 1905, p. 510; *M.R.*, 27 July 1930, p. 3.

[2] *Primitive Methodist:* Barnard Castle; Bishop Auckland; Crook; Thornley; and Willington Circuit. *United Methodist:* Bishop Auckland; Durham; and Seaham Harbour Circuit. *Wesleyan:* Barnard Castle; Bishop Auckland; Crook; Durham; and Spennymoor Circuit. (All voting data from official returns.)

[3] Guesses about membership–attendance ratios are usually deceptively favourable. Despite scarcity of evidence, attendance was probably rarely more than double membership in the nineteenth and early twentieth centuries. When Methodists reported their attendances to Horace Mann in 1851, average attendance at Sunday services (morning, afternoon and evening) exceeded membership by 51–95 per cent; attendance at the best service of the day (evening), by 98–160 per cent. Methodism's ability to attract adherents was almost certainly never higher after 1851. For the 1920s, an approximate membership–attendance ratio of 1:2 has been assumed, and each seat above a seats–membership ratio of 2:1 deemed empty. If Mudie-Smith's figures can be used, the 'average' Methodist congregation in 1900–25 was probably composed of 50 per cent members, 25 per cent children (presumably the members' children) and 25 per cent adult non-members. See: the various *Minutes*; Horace Mann, *Sketches of the Religious Denominations of the Present Day*, London, 1854, p. 110; Richard Mudie-Smith (ed.), *The Religious Life of London*, 1904, *passim*.

these circuits was fifty-three, well below the national average of sixty.[1] Here is a characteristic pre-union situation: thirteen competing circuits, belonging to three denominations, consisting of about 200 rather more than half-empty small chapels inside a square eighteen miles by eighteen miles.

A somewhat more extreme situation existed in the West Riding. A rectangular strip, thirty-two miles long and eighteen miles wide, from Pontefract to Todmorden and from Keighley to Huddersfield, contained twenty-three circuits that rejected union in 1924.[2] The seven Wesleyan circuits among them contained, in all, sixty chapels. On average each chapel had somewhat over 350 seats, and fifty-eight members. In the seven as a whole the ratio of seats to members was 6·1:1 About 14,000 seats were empty. If non-Wesleyans were no worse off, the twenty-three circuits possessed 46,000 empty seats. Here is Methodism in pronounced decay–in sharp contrast to Bristol where the Wesleyans had only 4·4 seats per member, Birmingham where they had 4·1, and Hertfordshire and Middlesex where they had only 3·5.

Cornwall provides the classic case of overlap and excess capacity in the south of England. Nine circuits in a triangle sixty square miles in area, from Camborne to Helston west to Penzance, rejected union,[3] while several other circuits in the area strongly opposed it. The four opposing Wesleyan circuits consisted of forty-eight chapels. These had an average of 330 seats and sixty members, the ratio of seats to members being 5·6:1. The nine circuits probably had 23,000 empty seats between them. In Cornwall as in Durham and the West Riding, the local situation underlying reluctance to support union can be seen clearly.

In all three areas, loyalty to chapel conflicted sharply with ecumenical designs. Unionists could not even seriously argue that short-term sacrifice would bring long-term benefits, that members would lose their beloved chapel but would have the satisfaction of seeing

[1] All data on seats per member and members per chapel taken from Wesleyan *Minutes* and *Returns of Accommodation Provided in Wesleyan Methodist Chapels and Other Preaching Places (For the Year 1931) Obtained by the Wesleyan Chapel Committee in Pursuance of a Minute of the Conference of 1931*, London, 1932.

[2] *Primitive Methodist:* Bingley; Clayton West; Halifax First; Huddersfield; Keighley Second; Leeds First; Normanton; Ossett; Sowerby Bridge; and Wakefield First Circuit. *United Methodist:* Brighouse, Park; Elland, Temperance Street; Greetland; Halifax, Brunswick; Shelf; and Sowerby Bridge Circuit. *Wesleyan:* Cullingworth; Halifax, King Cross; Leeds, Bramley; Leeds, Rothwell; Pontefract; Stainland; and Wakefield Circuit.

[3] *Primitive Methodist:* Camborne; Falmouth; and Penzance Circuit. *United Methodist:* Hicks Mill; and Penzance, Alexandra Road, Circuit. *Wesleyan:* Falmouth; Gwennap; Hayle; and Porthleven Circuit.

local membership, centred in a few selected chapels, increase sharply. Excess capacity and acute overlap characterized areas which had long ceased to be major growth areas. Unionists simply proposed to remove the burden of these half-empty chapels from the thriving suburban Methodism of the south. Members were invited to sacrifice their chapel for the benefit of Methodists hundreds of miles away. They found the scheme implausible.

*Ecumenicalism and Commitment to Denomination*

A larger loyalty than that to chapel created difficulties for ecumenicalism. Members had strong denominational ties. These ties could be highly personalized. A New Connexion layman touched on a sensitive nerve of denominational life, when, criticizing the union movement, he wrote, 'We shall lose the family feeling that belongs to a small denomination. . . . There are many worthy people who pride themselves on knowing either in person or by . . . reputation every man in the Connexion who is worth knowing.' Under the new regime this would hardly be possible. When it came, a whole order would be swept away. The Rev. R. Bevan Shepherd, a Wesleyan opponent of union, said, 'It was as if one stood by and watched preparations being made for dismantling the old home in which one had lived as a child, where one's fathers lived and died, and in which one has passed through the most tender and sacred associations of one's own life.'[1]

Unionists believed such sentiments were mere reaction since denomination had lost or fulfilled its purpose and mission. Anti-unionists disagreed. John Luke told the Bible Christian Conference of 1895 that 'he did not think we had finished our work as a separate people'. When the New Connexion discussed union in 1867, Mr. Firth of Shields 'wanted to know why they should offer themselves to another Church? It appeared as if the concern was worn out, and wanted to be formed into a joint stock company, limited. They had attained a good position standing by themselves, and why should they not continue as a separate church?' J. E. Rattenbury made the same point half a century later. 'I am, personally, strongly opposed', he said, 'to any scheme of Union . . . which destroys the identity of the Wesleyan Methodist Society. I do not believe that our historical mission is exhausted.'[2]

There was a larger disagreement too. Unionists held that God's will

[1] *M.N.C. Mag.*, May 1903, p. 155; November 1905, p. 421; *M.R.*, 17 October 1918, p. 10.
[2] *Bible Christian Magazine*, September 1895, p. 577; *U.M.F.Cs Mag.*, 1867, p. 534; *M.R.*, 16 March 1922, p. 15.

was for all believers to be one. Disunity was sinful. Their opponents frequently held, quite sincerely, not only that their own denomination had a purpose, but that denominations in general did so. Some argued that denominational rivalry was a good comparable to perfect competition. 'The very progress of religion in Protestant countries,' said Mr. Herbert Walker of the New Connexion, in 1903, 'has been due to the fierce competition of ideas, methods and institutions which results from a multiplicity of sects.' Denominations were held to embody the Protestant principle. The Rev. John Higman wrote,

> 'Sects are and have been the very life and salvation of Christianity. . . . They are a providential and divine appointment to get the whole truth of Christ before the world (which one Church never has done and never will do) . . . they are witnesses and safeguards of religious liberty, and . . . they stand for this solemn principle–that every man is bound to think out his religion for himself.'[1]

Such an argument implied that denominations stood for different things, and appealed to different people: every believer had his denomination. The *Methodist Recorder*, in the last days of Nehemiah Curnock's reign, before it became an ecumenical paper under J. B. Watson, had no doubt on the matter. 'It is our growing conviction', it declared, 'that denominationalism is . . . a very real blessing in a country of mixed races and complex historical tradition.'[2]

Those who held such views looked upon union as a mere absorption and loss of all their denomination stood for. A Primitive Methodist minister said in 1892 that,

> 'On sentimental grounds he emphatically rejected the union. The Primitive Methodists had a grand historical name, full of grand historical memories–and he for one was not prepared to drop that name. He hoped he should get to the better land before the names of these sections of Methodism were merged into any meaningless designation.'

A Wesleyan minister warned that union meant 'an unquestionable diminution . . . of the personal and picturesque . . . into an unattractive monochrome'.[3]

---

[1] *F.M.*, 29 January 1903, p. 69; John N. Higman, *Ought We to Accept a Ministerial Session and The Case against Methodist Union on the Proposed Basis*, London, n.d., pp. 9–10.

[2] *M.R.*, 3 March 1904, p. 3.

[3] *Primitive Methodist World*, 23 June 1892, p. 490; *M.R.*, 9 October 1913, p. 23.

Such fears were shared by all parties alike. Higman poured scorn on the idea of churches being 'drawn together into one happy family … will it not result in the wealthiest and most socially powerful denominations eventually wiping the others out?' Critics in the 'wealthiest and most socially powerful denomination' itself, the Wesleyan, also believed that their church would 'cease, and be merged into a huge combine'.[1] More thoughtful opponents of union looked beyond the immediate threat to their denominational values to the future. 'Methodist Union should be considered in its large relations,' wrote Higman. 'The goal which many … have in view is … Reunion of Christendom. It is acknowledged to be a far-off goal, but they are working towards it.' Union with Wesleyanism might mean union with the Church of England; union with the Church of England, union with Rome.[2]

These fears could be discussed and perhaps alleviated. But a good deal of their force was derived from something scarcely open to discussion, and indeed rarely admitted, simple interdenominational hostility. Sometimes this hostility was caused by events of the past. The Rev. J. H. Burkitt wrote, in 1921, of Free Methodist attitudes to 1849. 'I remember how the farmers of Lincolnshire used to speak of it. It had left deep and abiding memories. They never spoke of the "Wesleyans"; it was always "the Conference people".' Miss Eva M. Cape, a London Wesleyan, put the other side of the question. 'I am a Methodist of the third generation,' she wrote,

> 'but, if this so-called Union comes into being, I shall be compelled to leave the Church I love. I do not say that the Prim and other Methodists should not rejoin us, but they left of their own free will, and if they wish to return home, by all means let them do so, but in the spirit of the prodigal son. I see no sufficient reason, however, for the Mother Church to alter her laws or customs to bring about this change.'[3]

Similar sentiments were referred to by the Wesleyan lady who wrote, in 1926, 'I have a daughter who is far better educated than her mother, and she says she "won't stand these outsiders". If they come, she'll go to Church.'[4]

When Arthur Guttery, himself a unionist, was President of the Primitive Methodist Conference, he listened patiently to proposals for

[1] Higman, *op. cit.*, p. 9; *Wesleyan Methodist Gazette*, March 1927, p. 3.
[2] Higman, *op. cit.*, p. 16.
[3] *U.M. Mag.*, July 1921, p. 208; *M.R.*, 16 March 1922, p. 16.
[4] *M.R.*, 9 September 1926, p. 4.

Free Church Federation from the Baptist leader, J. H. Shakespeare. The question of overlapping was raised. 'It was quite true,' said Guttery, 'that some of us would have to go, but who was it? . . . we are not going to clear out of any village for the Baptists, still less for the Wesleyans.' His feelings were reciprocated. A Wesleyan minister suggested to a small chapel in Yorkshire that they should hold week night services with the Primitive Methodists. 'The congregation, to the great surprise of the minister, stoutly refused, one staunch lady member remarking, "I have worshipped here for forty-five years and I am not now going over to the Ranters".'[1]

These commitments, fears, and hostilities had been reduced by the pressures towards union created by decline, by the gradual approximation of the denominations in outlook, polity and belief, and by the new ethic of Methodism which discredited conflict and disagreement. But their presence was strong enough in 1924 to affect the voting for union.

A number of circuits, particularly sensitive to denominational tradition, rejected or were strongly opposed to union in the 1920s. The Wesleyan Epworth Circuit, for example, centred on Wesley's birthplace, voted only 51 per cent in favour of union, a low vote even by Lincolnshire standards. Gwennap Circuit in Cornwall, containing one of the most famous Methodist sites, Gwennap Pit, where Wesley frequently preached to thousands, rejected union. The most interesting Wesleyan example of this kind was Wesley's Chapel in City Road. From the 1880s a definite attempt was made to convert the chapel into a 'Cathedral of Methodism'. Non-Wesleyans donated furnishings at various times, and it served as the venue of both the inaugural Uniting Conference of the United Methodist Church in 1907, and of that denomination's conference of 1920. But in 1924 Wesley's Chapel rejected union.

Leeds, Lady Lane Circuit, perhaps the leading Free and United Methodist West Riding circuit, rejected union. In North Devon, the United Methodist Shebbear Circuit, the birthplace and the first headquarters of the Bible Christian denomination, rejected union. Five Primitive Methodist circuits in Hull rejected union, as did the Primitive Methodists of the East Riding as a whole, whose traditions went back to William Clowes and John Oxtoby. The Primitive Methodist Huddersfield Circuit, where the Northumberland Street chapel had been moved stone by stone to a new site when the old was acquired for the railway, not surprisingly rejected the proposal to end the denomination's separate existence. In Cheshire, the Congleton Circuit

[1] *P.M.L.*, 22 June 1916, p. 399; *M.R.*, 2 December 1920, p. 16.

lying under Mow Cop, in May 1807 the scene of the first Primitive Methodist camp meeting, rejected union. The Primitive Methodist Brinkworth Circuit, in north Wiltshire, the most famous southern circuit within the denomination, voted only 53 per cent for union.

But denominationalism was subject to considerable pressure by 1900. Methodism experienced numerical decline and a north–south shift as the urbanization of British society continued. These developments caused great concern to city Methodists who were willing, often rather reluctantly, to abandon internal conflicts, in order to fight, united, the battle with a hostile world. But in remote and rural areas the old struggles could be pursued in comparative ignorance of these new problems.

The contrast was widely seen. Much hostility survived between Wesleyans and United Methodists in the West Riding in the 1920s. But in the two major urban areas of the Riding, Leeds and Sheffield, comparatively little opposition to union was displayed in 1924, although rural and small town circuits such as the Wesleyan Stainland and Cullingworth Circuits, and the United Elland, Temperance Street, and Shelf Circuits, still pursued conflicts which seemed largely irrelevant in Leeds and Sheffield.

Lancashire Methodism had been foremost since the 1890s in efforts to secure a rapprochement between the divided and conflicting denominations. In Manchester, where the pioneer Methodist Ministers' Fraternal was held, only one circuit of the city's thirty-two rejected union. Even in Rochdale, whose Baillie Street United Methodist Circuit was synonymous with the reform movement, opposition to union was curiously muted. But in outlying areas such as Cadishead, Hopwood and Rawtenstall, religious conflicts were still strong enough for union to be rejected in 1924.

The *Fly Sheets* controversy damaged Wesleyanism in Derbyshire more severely than anywhere else in the country except Norfolk: Derbyshire Wesleyanism lost more than half its members in 1850–5. William Griffith, the most radical of the three expelled Wesleyan ministers of 1849, established himself as pastor of Becket Street Reform Church, Derby. His church rejected union with the Wesleyans in 1924. But opposition to union was largely rural even in Derbyshire. The respective Wesleyan and United circuits of Belper and of Ripley found the grievances of the mid-nineteenth century were too bitter even in 1924 to allow support for union. So, too, the bulk of Primitive Methodist opposition in the county came not from Derby, but from rural industrial circuits such as Chesterfield Second and Staveley.

Probably the most notable area in the south of England where religious conflicts between Methodists persisted into the 1920s was East Anglia. In the Fens–Wash area, from Spalding to Holbeach round the Wash as far as Hunstanton, and inland as far as Downham and Mildenhall, twelve circuits[1] rejected union. Another minor region of conflict appeared in the eastern part of East Anglia, characteristically skirting the area's major urban centre, Ipswich. West and north of Ipswich, Wesleyanism was virtually eliminated in the 1850s. The Framlingham Circuit had petitioned the Wesleyan Conference for reform in *June* 1849, i.e. even before that body began its fateful sitting. In 1924, having been a Free and then a United Methodist circuit, it still rejected Wesleyanism. Farther south in the triangular strip between the rivers Colne and Stowe four circuits rejected union,[2] a striking instance of the survival of religious conflicts in an agricultural area of small towns and villages.

So too in the south west, hostility particularly manifests itself in rural areas, such as the colliery region of Radstock where Wesleyan colliery managers had dismissed miners for attending a reform meeting in 1849, and where both United and Wesleyan Methodists rejected union in 1924; and in the remote strip of Bible Christian country in north Devon, stretching from Okehampton on the edge of Dartmoor to the Kingsbrompton Circuit in the Brendon Hills. A number of other areas, such as north Cornwall, east Cheshire and south-west Shropshire, displayed conflicts largely eliminated by the pressures of urban life.

*Ecumenicalism and Commitment to Class*

But commitment to chapel and commitment to denomination were not simply religious loyalties. Religious commitment often derives strength and significance from its social context. Each Methodist denomination was situated in a carefully graded system, at the top end of which were the Wesleyans, and, towards the bottom, the Primitive Methodists, or 'Ranters'.[3] In Wesleyan eyes all non-

---

[1] *Primitive Methodist:* Mildenhall Circuit. *United Methodist:* Boston, The Square; Downham Market; Holbeach; and Spalding Circuit. *Wesleyan:* Boston; Chatteris; Downham Market; Holbeach; Hunstanton; Lynn; and Wisbech Circuit.

[2] *Primitive Methodist:* Clacton Circuit. *United Methodist:* Walton and Felixstowe Circuit. *Wesleyan:* Great Bentley; and Manningtree and Harwich Circuit.

[3] Thomas Stanley, *Memoirs of Mr Robert Swan Stanley, Late Collector of Inland Revenue, Liverpool, The Alnwick Stanleys, and a Few of Their Contemporaries,* London, 1878, p. 104.

Wesleyans are rather suspect. Only the New Connexion had any particular status. It was, the Buntingite Richard Watson observed, 'a respectable Denomination'.[1] The Wesleyans, for their part, felt they shared in 'the steady prosperity of the country'. They preferred the 'devout and orderly'.[2] If they recognized any social superiors, it was among Anglicans. 'In the metropolis and the large provincial centres,' a Wesleyan layman wrote, 'the members of the Methodist societies are marked by educational culture and refinement of taste quite equal to the scholarly and refined laity of the National Church.'[3]

The New Connexion saw itself as being among Methodists the nearest to the Wesleyans, or occasionally as superior even to the latter. An early nineteenth-century cartoon on Methodist church government, evidently New Connexion inspired, shows both Wesleyan and Primitive Methodist laymen as labouring men. The New Connexion layman however is a gentleman in top-hat and morning coat. The Free Methodists, who were regarded by New Connexionists as socially inferior, regretted that the New Connexion was 'in peril of pushing to an extreme what they conceive to be their Divine vocation—"a mission to the middle classes"'.[4] The New Connexion, of course, also looked down on the Primitive Methodists, 'these noisy Ranters'.[5]

Wesleyan Reformers of the 1850s looked down on the Associationists of the 1830s. The Reformers, who brought 'a large accession . . . of . . . wealth' into the United Methodist Free Churches of 1857, were long uneasy over the proposed union because they felt their ministers to be 'equal to the best and superior to most in other denominations', but that Association ministers were 'seriously inferior in talent and culture'. Once united, the two groups combined to occupy a position of careful superiority to Primitive Methodists and Bible Christians. The former denomination, said a Free Methodist in 1865, with that gentle shudder reserved for successful evangelism, 'seems to have been raised up in the Providence of God to penetrate to a deeper substratum of society than . . . any other denomination'. The Rev. Joseph Kirsop reassured Free Methodists in 1903, 'we need not fear that in

---

[1] Henry Smith, *Sketches of Eminent Methodist New Connexion Ministers*, London, 1893, p. 109.

[2] Inglis, *op. cit.*, p. 85; *W.M. Mag.*, June 1878, p. 463.

[3] A. Layman, *op. cit.*, pp. 6, 10.

[4] *F.M.*, 25 June 1891, p. 4.

[5] William Beckworth, *A Book of Remembrance. Records of Leeds Primitive Methodism*, London, 1910, p. 26.

allying ourselves to the Bible Christian ministry we should demean or degrade ourselves in any way'.[1]

The social tensions between Methodist denominations persisted into the 1920s. But even then, unionists and anti-unionists rarely admitted the existence of such tensions. Walter Runciman faced the issue with determination. 'It was said that Wesleyans and Primitives were not of the same social grade,' he declared. 'It was no use shirking the fact. He longed to see the manager of the colliery sitting in the same pew with the hewer. In Lincolnshire, he did not want to see the farmers in the Wesleyan Church and the labourers in the Primitive Methodist Church'. The same point roused the indignation of the Rev. Samuel Horton, Primitive Methodist union secretary of the 1920s. 'Any Church which stands on social position unchristianizes itself,' he said. 'We are a Church of cottage homes and we are not afraid of the fact.'[2]

Both men were making rare confessions. In 1921, the Wesleyan, Sir Newbold Kay, 'boldly avowed that the only argument against Union was one that could not be stated in public, and that was sheer snobbery'. The *Primitive Methodist Leader* added, 'It was well a Wesleyan should say it.' Arthur Guttery wrote in 1920, 'There is one heresy to which we will give no quarter. It is that which would keep Methodists separate on lines of social or financial distinctiveness. This heresy is afraid of the light of day. It does not even speak in the safety of the committee room. It whispers in suburban afternoon tea-parties.'[3]

But the heresy appeared everywhere in Methodism. When the New Connexion tried, unsuccessfully, to unite with the Bible Christians in the 1860s, there was much 'talk of the difference in social status'. When the Free Methodists entered the United Methodist Church in 1907, the inferiority of the Bible Christians, a collection of 'Devonians and Cornishmen . . . waiting with open mouths' in their 'little anti-quated chapels among the hills', for whatever was given or told them, clearly troubled the denomination.[4] Later still, differences or alleged differences between Wesleyans and Primitive Methodists created similar difficulties. It was insinuated, Horton told Rattenbury, 'that we are wishful to come into Union in order to rid ourselves of intoler-

---

[1] Edward Boaden, *Memoir of the Rev. Richard Chew*, London, 1896, pp. 64, 109; M. Baxter, *Methodism: Memorials of the United Methodist Free Churches, with Recollections of the Rev. Robert Eckett and Some of His Contemporaries*, London, 1865, pp. 170–1; *M.M.*, January, 1903, p. 14.

[2] *M.R.*, 30 September 1920, p. 5; *M.T.*, 11 May 1922, p. 8.

[3] *P.M.L.*, 9 June 1921, p. 355; *U.M.*, 14 October 1920, p. 497.

[4] *M.N.C. Mag.*, June 1870, p. 371; *F.M.*, 13 August 1905, pp. 240–1.

able financial burdens, and that socially, we occupy a grade which makes it difficult for the Wesleyans to associate with us . . . I confess that my blood has been stirred.'[1]

Methodists felt that criticism of each other's social status was incompatible with profession of the Christian religion. Attacks on proposed union schemes on grounds of their financial weakness were more acceptable. The Rev. T. D. Crothers led the New Connexion attack on union with the Bible Christians in the 1860s with the claim that the Bible Christians were too poor a denomination and their ministers too badly paid for union to be anything but a source of friction. His son, the Rev. James Crothers, attacked the scheme of union with the Bible Christians and Free Methodists in the 1900s. He claimed that as £1,000,000 was needed to bring these denominations up to the financial level of the New Connexion, 'Union is "practicable" in the same sense that it is practicable for a man to fling himself over a precipice.'[2] A similar case–against union with the Primitive and United Methodists–was made out by Wesleyans, in the 1920s, notably by Mr. James Rider. Mr. Arthur Holmes, a Primitive Methodist businessman met Wesleyan colleagues at an employers' luncheon, when 'the definite statement was reiterated that *we* only sought' union 'because we were nearly defunct and to save ourselves from bankruptcy'.[3]

Opposition to ecumenicalism on social grounds often came from specific groups. The 'people of social distinction'[4] in the New Connexion who successfully resisted union with the Free Methodists for over thirty years, were led by ministers of high church views centred on the Firths' theological college at Ranmoor, and associated personally with the Firths, and, to a lesser extent, other wealthy New Connexion families. These ministers themselves were closely interrelated: the mantle of T. D. Crothers, a leading figure of the group, fell in the next generation on his son and son-in-law. The laymen in the group, such as the Firths themselves and Mr. Alfred Ramsden, proprietor of the *Halifax Courier*, formed a connexional lay aristocracy.[5]

[1] Samuel Horton–J. Ernest Rattenbury, 25 February 1922, in Rattenbury Papers.

[2] *M.N.C. Mag.*, March 1870, p. 186; February 1904, p. 69; June 1904, p. 219; *F.M.*, 4 February 1904, p. 70.

[3] e.g., *M.R.*, 29 July 1920, p. 8; 3 March 1921, p. 13; *W.M.*, 31 January 1924, p. 9; *P.M.L.*, 14 August 1919, p. 495.

[4] *F.M.*, 25 July 1891, p. 3.

[5] *M.N.C. Mag.*, March 1870, p. 184; June 1870, pp. 391–6; February 1904, p. 69; June 1904, p. 219; George Eayrs, *A Short History and Handbook of the United Methodist Church*, London, 1913, p. 48; J. Stacey, *A Prince in Israel, or, Sketches of the Life of John Ridgway, Esq.*, London, 1862; W. J. Townsend, *James Stacey, D.D., Reminiscences and Memorials*, London, 1891, *passim*.

Another connexional aristocracy led Wesleyan opposition to union in the 1920s. The social division in Wesleyanism on the issue was symbolized by the support given to union by Arthur Henderson, Labour Foreign Secretary, and the opposition of Kingsley Wood, Conservative Chancellor of the Exchequer. When the opposition launched its newspaper, *The Wesleyan Methodist*, in May 1923, it carried a page two article by Kingsley Wood on the plight of the middle classes. A year later it ran another article on the solution to that plight offered by fascism, which would restore 'That priceless treasure, the sense of national duty'.[1] The format of the *Wesleyan Methodist*, which was superior to that of any other Methodist paper, indicates the social position of its readers and proprietors.

In April 1922, the Wesleyan opposition to union produced a manifesto over the signatures of seventy-six ministers. The manifesto caused considerable ill-feeling, especially among Primitive Methodists. Although it made no reference to social differences in Methodism, it was immediately taken to hint at these.[2] This was hardly surprising as the seventy-six signatories, the hard core of Wesleyan opposition, constituted a definite aristocratic element in the Wesleyan ministry. Theoretically the Wesleyan itinerant system created a ministerial democracy. The travelling preachers, like the Jesuits, went where they were sent, and did what they were told, *ad maiorem dei gloriam*. In practice the careers of this group exhibit a definite preference for the superior areas of the denomination.

Twenty-six per cent of the group's appointments fell in London, Middlesex, Surrey, Essex and Kent, where 12 per cent of the denomination's membership lived. But only 23 per cent of their appointments fell in the leading Wesleyan counties, Durham, Yorkshire, Cornwall, Staffordshire and Lincolnshire, where 35 per cent of the membership was to be found. At one extreme, Lincolnshire, containing 4 per cent of the Wesleyan population, but almost entirely lacking the large urban congregations even Durham or Staffordshire could offer, was virtually abandoned by the group; while Surrey, with 1 per cent of the Wesleyan population, but that 1 per cent organized in wealthy and educated suburban congregations, was grossly oversupplied by it.

The group preferred particular circuits even within favoured counties. Twenty-three large circuits, fourteen in London and its suburbs, containing in 1921 about 5 per cent of the Wesleyan popula-

[1] *W.M.*, 10 May 1923, p. 2; 3 April 1924, p. 2.
[2] *M.R.*, 27 April 1922, p. 4; *M.T.*, 11 May 1922, p. 8.

tion,[1] provided the group with 19 per cent of its appointments. A really successful member of this group would spend most of his ministerial life in residential areas of inner London, Finsbury Park, Hampstead and Highgate; and southern suburbs of London such as Croydon and Bromley. This routine might be varied by short periods in the large and prosperous Birmingham circuits, a stay in Sheffield, Carver Street, or Bristol, King Street, capitals of Yorkshire and western Wesleyanism; or a period in the suburban and seaside tour from Birkenhead, through the Liverpool suburbs, to the two Southport circuits. From time to time he would recuperate with a spell in Bournemouth. In all these areas he met with superior educated Wesleyans of considerable prosperity, who shared his high ministerial doctrines, and whose commendation of his acceptability might assist his final promotion to the secretaryship of a committee or the chairmanship of a district.

Some shared his resistance to union; others were perhaps convinced by him. The fifty-nine circuits to which these ministers had been stationed in 1924 were appreciably less favourable to union at the vote of 1924 than Wesleyan circuits in general. But the activities of the ministers in question probably did less than might be supposed to alter the opinions of the circuits. Circuit opinion was a reflection of its own social character (which also no doubt encouraged it to invite the ministers it did), and this character was often clearly defined and unlikely to change quickly. The voting pattern of 1924 illustrates some of these types of circuit.

Leading Wesleyan circuits at this period usually consisted of a fashionable central chapel with some euphonious title, such as Trinity, Brunswick or Victoria, and a hinterland of newer suburban chapels. These circuits, such as Bristol, Clifton; Sheffield, Carver Street; and Birmingham, Belmont Row, combined long Methodist traditions and the new Methodist affluence. Often the central chapels in the circuit used the prayer book services of the Church of England, a fairly clear sign of social superiority. The newer chapels were built in a tasteful and expensive Gothic in the Anglican fashion. A Wesleyan commented of one such chapel, Jesmond, Newcastle, which strongly

[1] Bayswater; Birkenhead; Birmingham, Moseley Road; Birmingham, Wesley; Blackheath; Bournemouth; Bristol, King Street; Brixton; Bromley (Kent); Croydon; Finsbury Park; Highgate; Kilburn and Hampstead; Leicester, Bishop Street; Liverpool, Bootle; Mostyn Road; Richmond (Surrey); Sheffield, Carver Street; Southport, Mornington Road; Sydenham; Wanstead; Wesley's Chapel; and Wandsworth Circuit. Data from the various editions of Hill's 'Arrangements'.

opposed union, that 'Its Gothic architecture and somewhat ornate service' caused a great stir.[1] Some of these circuits, as in Bristol, covered areas which the poorer Methodist denominations never penetrated. They strongly opposed and frequently rejected the scheme to unite them with such denominations. Occasionally opposition from such sources suggests religious overtones; but the religious differences were probably inextricable from the social. In Hull for example, there was considerable antagonism between Primitive and Wesleyan Methodists, and no less than eight circuits rejected union. But Wesleyan opposition was voiced by three circuits possessing all the attributes of fashionability, the central chapel, and the suburban hinterland.

From 1885, Wesleyans added to their fashionable circuits a new category. Mr. Inglis' interpretation of the Central Halls and Mission circuits involves a simplification. Partly these circuits *were* designed as a mission to 'poor people'. But this was not their only, nor perhaps their most important, function. Ministers appointed to them were freed from the restrictions of the three year limit customary in Wesleyanism. In the Central Halls they found very large congregations, waiting for oratory and entertainment. The Central Halls were the cathedrals of Wesleyanism, and to their services came superior Wesleyans who wished to sit under the great men of the denomination. The poor are somewhat lost sight of. Frequently they are physically separated by the attachment to the smart and imposing Central Hall of humble mission halls, on which devolved much of the philanthropic work of the circuit. A Wesleyan with much experience of missions, observed that their poor supporters were generally found in the 'smaller halls associated with the Mission'.[2]

When union was proposed in the 1920s it did not automatically appeal to Wesleyan Mission Circuits as the great instrument for 'the conversion of the world to Christ'. A number of these circuits were very hostile to union. The West London Mission; the Brighton Circuit, dominated by French's Dome Mission; the Westminster Central Hall; the Newcastle Mission and the Albert Hall, Nottingham, were all highly critical of the union scheme. The Bristol and Liverpool Missions rejected it, as did three service missions, the Aldershot Circuit and the Chatham and Portsmouth Garrison Circuits.

[1] *M.R.*, 8 March 1923, p. 10.
[2] Inglis, *op. cit.*, p. 92; E. W. Walters, *Ensor Walters and the London He Loves*, London, 1937, p. 52.

Direct co-operation with United and Primitive Methodists, even for the conversion of the world, also seemed unacceptable to circuits which were in more direct confrontation with them than the Mission circuits usually were. In areas of a mixed residential and industrial character, Wesleyan circuits based on the suburbs of a large town often covered smaller industrial towns forming the head of non-Wesleyan circuits. This contact did not always have happy results. In South Wales, for example, the Wesleyan Cardiff, Roath Road Circuit overlapped the Primitive Methodist Nelson and Caerphilly Circuit. The two circuits rejected each other. A similar situation existed in the West Riding, where the suburban Wesleyan Leeds, Bramley Circuit, and the Primitive Methodist colliery circuit, Normanton, overlapped. Both circuits rejected union.

Even where the confrontation between denominations was not quite so abrupt, residential areas of various types tended to supply much of the opposition to union. Suburban Wesleyan circuits in the north which rejected union, such as Alderley Edge and Knutsford, were however simply a provincial echo of suburban hostilities concentrated in the London area. Here the chapels had comparatively little denominational loyalty, and virtually no concern with the religious issues that divided Methodism. On the whole they welcomed the union movement with considerable enthusiasm, especially in newer suburban areas, where officials may have been more alive to circuit and denominational problems which they believed union would solve. But this enthusiasm was tempered by an uneasiness, especially among Wesleyans, about accepting fellow Methodists. In Bromley, Harrow, Richmond and Croydon, Wesleyans strongly opposed or rejected union. Primitive Methodists, in poorer parts of outer London, such as Kilburn, Tottenham and Walthamstow, followed suit.

The same pattern of opposition was carried into areas which contained the residential districts of migrant Methodism at a later stage in its development. Seaside areas in general, especially those of a residential character, strongly resisted union. The Wesleyan Ulverston Circuit, mainly consisting of Grange-over-Sands, was much more hostile to union than the neighbouring Barrow-in-Furness Circuit. A number of Wesleyan seaside circuits–Whitby, Scarborough, Aberystwyth, Falmouth–rejected union. But this opposition was most concentrated in the south eastern seaside areas, such as Margate, Ramsgate, Eastbourne, Brighton and Worthing, where Methodists from the north retired after a working life in London. Here the older religious conflicts between Methodists could scarcely have been less appropriate. In their place, concern to protect chapel property from those believed to belong to another class, was the major obstacle to the attempt to preserve it in a world which cared little for religion, chapel or Methodism.

# Part Three
# The Unification of Methodism

# CHAPTER SEVEN

# The Origins of United Methodism

## *From the New Connexion to the Association*

The first division of Methodism begins the union movement. In 1796 Kilham and his associates were already planning to unite all reforming Wesleyans in a 'new Itinerancy' purged of the abuses of ministerial power which manifested themselves after Wesley's death.[1] The Wesleyan Conference of 1797 expelled Kilham himself, and the reformers gathered at Ebenezer Chapel, Leeds, on 9 August 1797, to form the new itinerancy or New Connexion, with William Thom as its first president and Alexander Kilham as its first secretary.[2]

But the hope that large numbers of Wesleyans would secede to the new body was disappointed. Kilham soon died and the shadowy Thom, though capable of consolidating the new denomination, was unable or unwilling to lead either in protracted struggle with the Wesleyan Conference, or in an attempt to expand by evangelistic methods. After a bad start the New Connexion grew almost as quickly as Wesleyanism. But this was not enough. In 1827, the New Connexion numbered 10,000, the Wesleyans, 237,000. Two new denominations had now emerged: the Bible Christians, 8,000 strong in 1827; and the Primitive Methodists, already numbering about 30,000.

The New Connexion was now far weaker in the Methodist world than it had been in 1797 when it *was* Methodist reform. The New Connexion always hoped for 'some additions to the body from the Old Connexion'.[3] But such additions were unfortunately small and infrequent. Discontent persisted inside Wesleyanism but the new generation of reformers either did not know or did not like the New Connexion. But only through supplementing lack of native growth by amalgamations with new reformers could the New Connexion deci-

---

[1] *The Life of the Rev. Alexander Kilham*, London, 1838, p. 310.
[2] *Ibid.*, pp. 328–30.
[3] J. T. Barker (ed.), *Life of Joseph Barker, Written by Himself*, London, 1880, p. 109.

sively advance or promote its by now rather formal mission of reforming Wesleyanism.

The Leeds Organ Case of 1827 was the first major constitutional conflict in Wesleyanism for thirty years. But to the disappointment of the New Connexion only a few hundred of the dissidents offended by the case joined that denomination. The rest, under the leadership of two laymen, Matthew Johnson and James Sigston, formed a new denomination, the Protestant Methodists, who were about 3,000 strong. The aggressive radicalism of the Protestant Methodists, who abolished the paid and separate ministry altogether, seemed to suggest that the reform movement had left the New Connexion behind.

The Protestant Methodists' failure to agitate the Wesleyan Connexion for any length of time or to carry off more than the few thousands who joined them was largely due to the lack of a ministerial leader. In 1834 reformers remedied this deficiency. Seizing the opportunity afforded by Samuel Warren's opposition to the Theological Institution, they made him figurehead of a Grand Central Association of reformers. When the Association met at Manchester in April 1835, the Warrenite programme of reforming Conference was already being submerged by the lay demand for control of the chapels which the Association's new recruit, Robert Eckett, interpreted as a demand for 'circuit independence'.

The Associationists remained undecided about their future. Most of them probably preferred to stay Wesleyans if they could. Some thought of forming a new Methodist denomination. Others considered uniting with fellow Methodists. If Wesleyanism was lost, the circle round Warren preferred to unite with the New Connexion. The more radical Associationists, led by Eckett, proclaimed the Protestant Methodists as 'their elder brethren',[1] but were not entirely happy about accepting the Protestant Methodist system as it stood.

Warren was elected President and Matthew Johnson Secretary of the Association's first Assembly, in 1836, but it was dominated by Eckett. The meeting adopted a general statement on church polity: 'Each Society to be at liberty to have such particular rules as to Church Government and as to its ministry, as each may think proper to adopt; provided that there be nothing in the rules so adopted clearly repugnant to the Word of God.' But the virtual Congregationalism of this declaration was modified by the proposal that 'the different Societies . . . separated from the Wesleyan Conference' should be united into 'one common family' to promote 'plans for

[1] *Protestant Methodist Magazine*, May 1835, p. 76.

general usefulness'. This new 'family' would be characterized by the co-operation of its members, by a 'common faith' and a 'common token of membership'. Eckett apparently intended to destroy *Wesleyan* connexionalism altogether and remake the atoms of the system into an entirely 'voluntary' connexion. He may, throughout this period, have assumed that the societies would be associated at circuit as well as at assembly level, but the 1836 resolutions give no guidance on this point.[1]

The Assembly finally appointed a committee to negotiate with 'any section of Methodists with a view to their forming a constituent part of the proposed General Union'.[2] By the 1837 Assembly, the Protestant Methodists, the Arminian or Faith Methodists of Derby and the Independent Primitive Methodists of Scarborough had joined the Association. The following year the Independent Wesleyans of North Wales united with the Association, as did the Scottish United Methodist Churches in 1839.[3] Already, by 1837, the Association, 21,000 strong, was more numerous than the New Connexion, which it replaced as the third largest Methodist denomination.

The New Connexion did profit from the controversy over the Theological Institution. Several thousands of Wesleyans apparently found both Conference and Association intolerable and joined the New Connexion. But this was little consolation when even more joined a new rival denomination. New Connexionist leaders wished to recruit the Association as a whole. For their part, conservative Associationists like Warren preferred the reformed but sober Methodism of the New Connexion to the pseudo-Congregationalism proposed by Eckett for a separate Associationist denomination. The 1836 resolutions gave these conservatives their chance. The union committee approached the New Connexion and negotiations began.

The New Connexionists and Warren wanted to unite the two denominations on the basis of the New Connexion constitution. Eckett wanted to unite them on the basis of the 1836 resolutions. Compromise was impossible. The *Watchman* had earlier drily remarked, 'It may be somewhat doubted whether the association and the Kilhamites are intending to form a union; for not the Kilhamites themselves can be prepared to adopt such a platform of church government as their new friends have . . . laid down.'[4] The paper was right, as the negotiations of October 1836 and January 1837, proved.

[1] Wesleyan Association *Minutes*, 1836, pp. 16–17.
[2] *loc. cit.*
[3] *Ibid.*, 1837, p. 7; 1838, p. 10; 1839, p. 20.
[4] *Watchman*, 11 November 1835, p. 357.

Eckett agreed to abandon free representation and accept the New Connexion system of lay-ministerial parity of representation. The New Connexion offered to abandon the appellate jurisdiction of Conference in circuit affairs. But the New Connexion refused Eckett's main demand, that they should accept the right of local preachers and class leaders to sit in the local church meetings *ex officio*, and the denomination also refused to change its name.

The New Connexion Conference met before the Association Assembly and grandly resolved that, 'The New Connexion having been the first to move in the cause of Methodist Reform . . . the Conference is of opinion that it should not under these circumstances be called upon to make any extensive changes in its system.' Warren, undeterred, proposed to the Assembly of 1837 that the Association should adopt the New Connexion constitution, obviously as a preliminary to reopening negotiations. Eckett and Johnson countered by proposing a constitution based on free representation and circuit independence.[1]

The Eckett–Johnson Constitution was adopted by the Assembly. Warren retired from the Association. Warren's Treasurer, Mr. W. Smith, resigned too, to be replaced by Mr. John Petrie, a supporter of Eckett. The Wesleyan Methodist Association now became the possession of Eckett and his party, who were drawn from the minor groups in the Association, Protestant and Independent Primitive Methodists rather than from leaders of the old Grand Central Association, who always distrusted Eckett. Inside the denomination Eckett behaved not unlike Bunting. He dominated the Assembly debates, usually speaking last, a characteristic trick of Bunting's, and 'sometimes an Upstart was severely handled'. 'His influence in Council was as great as his skill in debate,' while he was said 'to have excelled' Bunting 'in his business ability'. His biographer adds, 'Some persons were wont to point to his ascendancy in our councils as something inconsistent with freedom.'[2]

### The Making of Free Methodism

Like Bunting, Eckett created his own opposition. David Rowland, the first leader of the Grand Central Association, secured the support of

---

[1] *Wesleyan Methodist Association Magazine*, February 1849, pp. 53 ff; *United Methodist Free Churches Magazine*, May 1888, pp. 290 ff; Methodist New Connexion *Minutes*, 1837, p. 46.

[2] M. Baxter, *Methodism: Memorials of the United Methodist Free Churches, with Recollections of the Rev. Robert Eckett and some of his Contemporaries*, London, 1865, pp. 443–4, 474.

James Carveth, an Association minister. Carveth himself was in contact with the leading figure of the new wave of Wesleyan reformers, James Everett, at least by 1851.[1] The struggle to overthrow Bunting paralleled conflict in the ostensibly reformed Association. The *Fly Sheets* might encourage the dissidents of the Association to start a pamphlet war against Eckett. The Rev. Joseph Garside observed, after he had left the Association in 1853,

> 'In that body a rich, restless, ambitious and resolute man has pushed his way into most of the chief offices, and there he sits, year after year, slighting and snubbing such persons as have the audacity earnestly to oppose any of his darling measures, or who, by any other means, happen to displease him.'

David Rowland and his immediate supporters had an additional grievance. The Association had been theirs; and now it was Eckett's. When he left the Association, Rowland said he had been forced 'to turn his back on his own child, for the Association literally was born in his house'.[2]

Eckett showed little affection for his fellow-reformer Everett. He promptly published a pamphlet against anonymous polemics, vindicating the action of the Wesleyan Conference in expelling ministers who refused to answer questions about the *Fly Sheets*. 'I confess', wrote Eckett,

> 'that my sense of propriety strongly revolts against such anonymous charges, as are contained in the "Fly Sheets". . . . If in the Connexion to which I belong, such charges against any of the ministers or other members of the Connexion, were anonymously circulated, and there were strong suspicions that some of its Itinerant ministers were the authors and circulators of such charges, I should not think it improper that inquiry should be instituted for the purpose of discovering the authors; and I think that the circumstances might justify our Annual Assembly in requiring the suspected persons to give categorical answers to inquiries relative to the authorship of such anonymous accusations.'[3]

There were to be no Associationist *Fly Sheets*.

Eckett's advocacy of 'question by penalty' may have pleased Dr. Bunting, but it did not stop Rowland and Carveth from working

[1] *Wesleyan Methodist Penny Magazine*, September 1856, p. 191.
[2] *Wesleyan Times*, 19 September 1853, p. 603; 26 September 1853, p. 614.
[3] *W.M.A. Mag.*, October 1849, p. 469.

against Eckett, nor did it discourage Wesleyans from supporting the 'Three Expelled'. Wesleyan membership fell 56,068 between 1850 and 1851. When Horace Mann took his census in April 1851, the 'Wesleyan Reformers' possessed chapel and other accommodation for 98,813 persons, and their evening congregations numbered 40,655.

This vast fourth wave of Wesleyan dissidents raised the union question once more. The Methodist New Connexion suffered disastrous losses through the Barkerite secession of 1841–2. In 1845 it was only 15,000 strong. During 1848–50, it gained fresh accessions from Wesleyanism, agitated by the *Fly Sheets* controversy. But if the New Connexion could unite the whole body of 'Wesleyan Reformers' to itself, the denomination would be transformed from a tiny, struggling sect, into the restored head of the great reform movement, which now looked nearer to success than ever.

The Association was also in difficulties. It lost members steadily from 1840 to 1847, when it was only 19,000 strong. The Association seemed moribund. An Associationist commented,

> 'In 1847 the re-action had gone so far in the churches of the Association, and the financial difficulties had waxed so great, and the want of organization in many parts of the Connexion was so manifest, as to make it doubtful whether the body could survive. Prophets of evil were not a few, and a feeling of despondency was by no means uncommon.'[1]

Like the New Connexion, the Association needed new blood, received some in the form of Wesleyan dissidents, during 1847–51, but hoped to recruit the 'Wesleyan Reformers' as a whole.

The Reformers themselves were in a weak position. In September 1849, the 'Three Expelled' announced that 'At present we do not intend to join any particular section of the Christian Church.'[2] None of these men was able or willing to lead a mass movement, and the expulsions and secessions of 1850 onwards were probably little to the liking of any of them. In March 1850, a 'Delegate Meeting' of Reformers was held in Albion Street Chapel, London. Since Everett confined himself to writing satirical sketches of the delegates the laymen took over leadership and set up a General Reform Committee. The General Committee 'became the head of the movement; it received and expended funds, employed agents, worked the press, carried out general plans of operation, and entered into communica-

[1] Edward Boaden, *Memoir of the Rev. Richard Chew*, London, 1896, p. 21.
[2] Richard Chew, *James Everett*, London, 1875, p. 419.

tion with Local Committees'.[1] The slogan of the Committee was 'No Secession, No Surrender, No Supplies'. The Reformers would not abandon their claim to be Wesleyans, they would not surrender the struggle to reform Wesleyanism, and they would withhold financial support from the Connexion until it was reformed.

The Reformers wanted to concentrate on disrupting Wesleyanism. Mr. Elliott of Sheffield told the Reformers' Delegate Meeting of 1852 that the movement 'was not to establish separate religious services, but to bring about Wesleyan Reform; not to build new chapels and create societies independent of the old body, but to furnish materials with which to oppose the evils of Methodism'.[2] In 1853, the movement was asked, 'Shall the Reformers now abandon their principles of no *secession*, no *surrender*, by uniting with either the New Connexion or the Association or, by becoming a distinct body, cease to struggle for readmission – on scriptural grounds, into their own church? God forbid!'[3]

But while the refusal to establish a new denomination did not increase the Reformers' ability to hurt Conference, it discouraged many from associating with the General Committee. At their height in 1854 the Reformers had 49,177 members. Yet Wesleyanism had already suffered a net decrease of 94,109, and this figure understated actual loss of members. Thus the movement affiliated to the General Committee accounted for about half the dissidents of the 1850s. The Reformers probably lost ground from 1854 onwards. Many returned from the hectic and confused democracy of the Reformers to the un-reformed but quiet life of the Wesleyans. The Rev. Joseph Posnett claimed in 1899 that, 'in the period immediately following the great secession, 50,000 came back of those that were lost'. This development pushed the Reformers towards a separate denominational life. Mr. Morren of Bradford commented in 1852 that, 'In the Fourth London Circuit to which he formerly belonged, there was a great disinclination to establish separate services; but had they not at length done so, the people would have been scattered.'[4]

Financial difficulties also obliged the General Committee to review its position. In 1852, since only 106 of the 300 circuits connected with it had made any contribution at all, income was only £1,720. In 1853

[1] Richard Chew, *William Griffith: Memorials and Letters*, London, 1885, p. 80.
[2] *Wesleyan Reformer*, September–October 1852, p. 136.
[3] *W.M.P. Mag.*, August 1853, p. 121.
[4] *Methodist Recorder*, 3 August 1899, p. 23; *W.R.*, September–October 1852, p. 140.

it was £1,832.[1] The Committee had extreme difficulty even in publishing a magazine. In March 1855, it had to pay off Everett as agent and speaker, despite his considerable value as a figurehead, because of 'the heavy financial burdens now pressing upon the general fund'.[2] The Committee's appeal for £5,000 per annum in October 1853 altogether failed. These difficulties were partly due to the problems and commitments of the reform circuits, which had to build new chapels, rent preaching places, and provide for ministerial oversight. They were also due to lay reformers' preference for 'petty circuit broils'[3] that made them indifferent to the movement as a whole.

While the Committee was in financial difficulties, its tactics were failing. By January 1853, the policy of annual appeals to the Wesleyan Conference was regarded as 'hopeless'. Not only was Conference dismissing these appeals but, from the end of 1852, Buntingites adopted a new policy of ignoring the polemic and the existence of the Reformers. Wesleyan net loss of membership continued till 1855, but decline was now slackening. The financial strength of Wesleyanism enabled the Buntingites to ignore the Reformers. In the quinquennium 1845–9, the all important Wesleyan contingent fund averaged 7·4 pence per head per year. In 1850, it fell to 7·0 pence per head, lower than it had ever been since 1813. But this was the farthest extent of the success of the 'no supplies' policy. Wesleyans had to struggle for many years with unfilled chapels, and first surplus and then, as a result of restrictive recruitment policies in 1860–80, insufficient ministers. But the denomination never approached financial collapse.

In 1853 the Committee changed its magazine's name from *Reformer* to *Penny Magazine*, and commissioned Everett to draw up a new hymnal in place of the still used Wesleyan book, both developments suggesting the change from a 'movement' to a settled, and seceded, denomination. But formation of a separate denomination would have been explicit confession of failure to reform Wesleyanism. To abandon the movement and rejoin the Wesleyans was unthinkable. The answer seemed to lie in the formation of a united anti-Wesleyan denomination of reformers.

This solution was apparent to the New Connexion, now led by the 'very able, but very sensitive' William Cooke.[4] The initial response of

[1] *W.R.*, September–October 1852, pp. 135–6; *W.M.P. Mag.*, October 1853, p. 152.

[2] Chew, *Everett*, p. 445.

[3] *W.M.P. Mag.*, February 1853, p. 29.

[4] *W.T.*, 4 September 1854, p. 569; *Methodist Monthly*, February 1903, p. 42.

the denomination echoed 1837. In 1851, the New Connexion Conference passed a resolution reminding the world that it 'was the first to
assert and maintain a system of scriptural freedom, in connexion with
the saving doctrines, refreshing ordinances, and peculiar adaptations
of Methodism'.[1]

But as early as 1850, Cooke published his biography of Kilham,
*The First Methodist Reformer*, to demonstrate the virtues of the New
Connexion. The book sold 2,000 copies in the three months following
the Reformers' first Delegate Meeting.[2] The New Connexion had a
further piece of self-advertisement to hand, in the denominational
*Jubilee Volume*, published in 1848. Eckett engaged in 'misrepresentations, buffooneries, personalities, and insults', over the *Jubilee
Volume*'s attacks on the Association,[3] but he had nothing to rival it.
The New Connexion, while piously announcing that it 'would realize
far greater satisfaction in beholding peace restored by the parent
body than in receiving any accessions of numbers from its expelled
members', was busily proselytizing these expelled members. A Reformer observed in 1854, 'The New Connexion . . . have exhibited a
strong inclination to recruit their ranks by draughts from the body of
Methodist Reformers.'[4]

In 1853, the New Connexion Conference called for restoration of
'friendly relations and unity . . . between the parties', and proposed to
promote this laudable end by offering 'the right hand of fellowship to
any who desire to unite with us on the principles and practices of the
Connexion'.[5] Cooke promoted this policy by his Britannia Fields
speech of January 1854,[6] and by more private means.

The Association's public relations amounted to Eckett's controversy
over the *Jubilee Volume* and his public advocacy of question by
penalty, a policy hardly likely to endear him to the Reformers. His
question by penalty pamphlet dismayed the Association. Edward
Boaden, a young Association minister, commented, 'This deliverance
fell like a bomb in the midst of the excited crowd, including many of
our own people; and a great outcry arose against Mr. Eckett. The
fortunes of the Association at that time were low, and not a few

[1] *Minutes of the Methodist New Connexion*, 1851, p. 53.
[2] *Methodist New Connexion Magazine*, May 1850, p. 215; August 1850, pp.
376–7.
[3] *Jubilee of the Methodist New Connexion*, London, 1848; *W.M.A. Mag.*,
September 1850, p. 433.
[4] *M.N.C. Mag.*, July 1851, p. 334; *W.T.*, 4 September 1854, p. 569.
[5] *Minutes of the Methodist New Connexion*, 1853, p. 46.
[6] *M.N.C. Mag.*, February 1854, pp. 83–93.

looked to the Wesleyan Reformers to retrieve them by joining the Association, and this pamphlet gave a fatal blow to that hope'.[1]

But Eckett was cleverer than either Cooke or his own followers took him to be. He had to get rid of his rivals inside the Association, before attempting to deal with the reformers, who had devastated an organization eighteen times as large as the Association. Hence Eckett's advocacy of question by penalty. But at the 1851 Assembly, Eckett's former chief supporter, Matthew Johnson, proposed resolutions condemning question by penalty. A four-day debate followed, in which Eckett triumphantly vindicated himself. Shortly afterwards Rowland and others withdrew from the Association. But James Carveth continued to work against Eckett, and at the 1852 Assembly he was left for one year without an appointment. At the 1853 Assembly he was finally brought to trial, a bizarre echo of the Wesleyan Conference of 1849. Eckett determined to use the trial as a demonstration of the justice and decency of his regime. Carveth was given a public hearing and allowed to speak as long as he liked. But he was dismissed from the Association ministry, and shortly afterwards he joined the Reformers.[2]

The Rowlandites aimed to unite the Association, without Eckett, to the General Reform Committee. As Mr. J. Beynon of Islington put it, in 1852, 'The proximity of the Reformers and Associationists is so close, that there is scarcely a point on which they do not meet and agree.' It was obvious that 'the Association needs an impulse. It wants resuscitation'. Union with the Reformers would provide this. The policy was sound, but for the fatal weakness that Eckett not the Rowlandites controlled the Association. After the 1853 Assembly, the Rowlandites were a tiny divided minority, useful to bait Eckett with, but good for little else.[3]

The New Connexion now had the initiative. They sent a strong delegation to Carveth's testimonial meeting in Liverpool in September 1853. A New Connexionist party emerged among the Reformers. This group dissociated itself from 'ultra-Reformers', who wanted 'every little society' to be 'a law unto itself'.[4] It was led by E. H. Rabbits, a London Wesleyan; a Reform minister at Lynn, the Rev. Charles Bootman, who was in negotiation with Cooke from an early period,[5]

---

[1] *M.M.*, December 1893, p. 379.
[2] *Minutes of the Wesleyan Methodist Association*, 1853, pp. 7–8.
[3] *W.T.*, 14 June 1852, p. 371; 31 October 1853, p. 697; 23 January 1854, p. 53; 3 July 1854, p. 419.
[4] *M.N.C. Mag.*, July 1855, p. 380.
[5] *Ibid.*, November 1854, p. 622.

and William Martin, a layman from Altrincham. In 1853–4, the *Wesleyan Times*, the Reformers' paper, favoured union with the New Connexion. In 1854, one member of the pro-New Connexion group anonymously published *The Wesleyan Methodist Association versus the Wesleyan Reform Movement*, a pamphlet arguing that the Association was jealous of the Reformers, that it had refused to assist them, and that it was committed to the sinister method of question by penalty.[1] Later in 1854, Martin published *Organization of the Reform Societies. Thoughts on Its Immediate Necessity and the Mode of Its Accomplishment*. Martin argued that the Reformers had to organize or perish. But they must maintain the 'connexional principle', and they must not add to the proliferation of Methodist sects. The pamphlet closed with praise of the New Connexion constitution, and urged Reformers to join it.[2]

The situation was not as bad for the Association as the New Connexion and its supporters among the Reformers imagined. Advocacy of the 'connexional principle' was a considerable tactical error. Since the mass movement underlying the reform agitation basically sought power in the chapels, it had comparatively little enthusiasm for the 'connexional principle'. Ministers advocated this principle as the most efficient means of promoting the cause of Christianity and of increasing the numbers of their denomination. But the lay officials who now led the Reformers were comparatively indifferent to the evangelization of the world. They wanted to be masters in their own chapels. To them, connexionalism simply meant ministerial power. They wanted that 'circuit independence' which Eckett had written into the Association constitution.

In July 1853, when the Reformers were beginning to feel the urgency of some change in their situation, Eckett, now completing the rout of his enemies, made his decisive bid to vindicate the Association. Writing in the *Wesleyan Times*, he denied Rabbits' charge that the Assembly of 1851 had established a 'rule' of question by penalty. On the contrary, Eckett insisted, the Assembly, like the General Reform Committee, could only deal in opinions, by its very constitution. Eckett then went on to express his surprise at Rabbits' championship of union between Reformers and New Connexion. Eckett wrote,

'those whom Mr. Rabbits designates "the Reformers", have most decidedly repudiated the authority of any Conference, or any other

[1] *W.M.P. Mag.*, January 1854, pp. 8–9.
[2] *M.N.C. Mag.*, November 1854, pp. 623–4.

meeting, to make laws for the governance of churches, and have strongly professed to have for ever renounced the authority of any Conference, however constituted, to expel local officers, or members, from Church-fellowship; and have stoutly asserted the independence of every society or church, or at least, of every Circuit, in the administration of Church discipline. In these respects they have followed the example of the Association. . . . But, I ask, are these the principles of the New Connexion? Certainly not. They are as wide as the poles asunder. The New Connexion repudiates Circuit independence, and asserts Conference legislation and executive authority.'[1]

This letter dismayed Cooke. He denounced the Association as 'a system of sham liberty and real despotism', castigated Eckett as 'a jealous opponent', and insisted that the New Connexion was not bidding for the Reformers. But Eckett's letter was a very good bid. Even David Rowland's brother Thomas stated that Eckett's letter 'has, in my mind, made up for all the pain and regret he has occasioned me'. Eckett was soon assisted by the New Connexion itself, which shortly provided all the evidence needed that it was, as a Reformer put it, shut up in 'a little sectarian nook'.[2]

Some Reformers shared the views of the Rabbits–Martin–Bootman group. They wanted to solve the problem of the 'Wesleyan Reformers'' future by amalgamating with the New Connexion. Others, more realistically, proposed amalgamation with the Association. Marmaduke Miller, a young Associationist minister, asked, 'Will wise and thoughtful men choose a less liberal system because there happens to be a confessedly talented man, who exercises great influence in the working of the more perfect system?' The *Wesleyan Times* wanted union with the New Connexion or with the Association, without Eckett. But it was difficult to see how to modify the New Connexion's 'less liberal system' to suit the Reformers' demands, or how to remove the 'confessedly talented man' from the Association. By spring 1854, the *Wesleyan Times* was advocating 'the combination' of the ' "Separate Societies" ' of reformed Methodists into 'one League of Methodist Reformers'. In other words, the Reformers would settle down into normal denominational life, but this new denomination would form a 'League' with the Association and the New Connexion to carry on propaganda against unreformed Wesleyanism.[3]

[1] *W.T.*, 18 July 1853, pp. 451–2.
[2] *M.N.C. Mag.*, August 1853, pp. 455–6; July 1854, p. 392; *W.T.*, 25 July 1853, p. 467.
[3] *W.T.*, 4 July 1853, p. 419; 15 May 1854, p. 312; 19 June 1854, p. 393.

But the General Reform Committee did not like the idea of a 'League'. Joseph Chipchase argued that the 'political' and 'religious' aspects of the reform movement should not be separated, presumably fearing that such separation would dilute enthusiasm for reform propaganda while failing to solve the problem of organizing the amorphous reform movement. Lay leaders on the Reform Committee were forced to seek union by the fear that their followers would forestall them. In particular, they were disturbed by Cooke's efforts to annex Reform circuits to the New Connexion.[1]

In August 1854, the Reformers' Delegate Meeting agreed to negotiate with the Association and the New Connexion for union on the basis of the Reformers' Declaration of Principles, drawn up, mainly under Chipchase's influence, in 1852. The vital fifth clause of this Declaration read: 'That while desirous of maintaining the connexional principle, we hold that all local courts should be independent, and their decisions affecting internal economy final.'[2]

Hildreth Kay, Corresponding Secretary to the General Committee, wrote to both denominations, proposing negotiations on the basis of the Declaration. Despite a brief correspondence with the New Connexion, no negotiations followed, for as the New Connexion President, William Mills, assured Kay, in November 1854, 'in our view the union of the two bodies depends simply on the Reformers being satisfied with our system, adopting our laws in their integrity, and partaking of our connexional advantages'.[3]

The Reformers had one possibility left, Eckett and the Association. Despite misgivings even Everett was willing to advocate union with the Association after the rebuff from the New Connexion.[4] In fact only the Association's constitution could accommodate the 'federal union' the Reformers wanted.[5] The New Connexion was left with the few dissentient Reformers who followed the lead of Rabbits and Martin, after their resignation from the General Committee over the fiasco of Mills' letter.[6]

The Association pressed ahead with negotiations as rapidly as possible. In July 1855, the Association and the Reform union com-

[1] *W.T.*, 14 August 1854, p. 517; 25 September 1855, p. 616.
[2] *W.R.*, September–October 1852, pp. 145–6.
[3] *M.N.C. Mag.*, January 1855, pp. 27–31.
[4] Chew, *Griffith*, p. 100; *W.M.P. Mag.*, April 1855, p. 56; September 1855, p. 182.
[5] *W.M.P. Mag.*, September 1855, p. 147.
[6] *M.N.C. Mag.*, October 1855, p. 539; January 1857, p. 39; March 1857, pp. 152–3; August 1859, p. 443; October 1859, pp. 562 ff.

mittees issued a joint circular, embodying decisions of a meeting at Rochdale the previous month. This circular envisaged extreme freedom for local churches and circuits: they were not to be under any obligation to contribute to denominational funds, nor did they have to accept stationed ministers. The Assembly and the Delegate Meeting, sitting respectively in Manchester and Leeds, in July 1855, communicated their sense of urgency to each other and the world by maintaining contact by electric telegraph.[1]

By no means all Reformers were ready to accept union with the Association however. Agreeing on a 66 per cent vote to carry union, the Delegate Meeting failed to secure this by three votes in seventy-three. Not till 1856 did the Reformers finally agree to unite with the Associationists.[2] Of the 46,609 Reformers of 1856, only 19,113 joined the new body in 1857. Probably between 10,000 and 20,000 further members joined in the next few years. A rump of the Reformers established the Wesleyan Reform Union, which has now survived the denomination it proposed to reform by over thirty years. The rest probably drifted into the New Connexion or back into Wesleyan Methodism. The new denomination emphasized its mode of origin, its Methodist claims, its love of freedom, and its commitment to independence, in its name, 'United Methodist Free Churches'. It elected Everett as its first President, Eckett as its first Secretary.

### The Attempted Union of Liberal Methodism

Eckett died suddenly at Clevedon in 1862. His rival, William Cooke, immediately resumed the attempt to annex Methodist reform to the New Connexion, on the New Connexion polity. The 1863 Conference called for the union of 'the several sections of liberal Methodism'. But when the Free Methodist Assembly met shortly afterward, the Rev. William Reed emphasized that the denomination would not surrender its 'two great principles, Free Representation and Circuit Independence', even for the sake of union.[3]

Free Methodist hostility to the New Connexion system had not died with Eckett. But if Cooke wished to make concessions to the Free Methodists, he was hampered by the opposition of a younger minister, the Rev. James Stacey. Stacey, who had just become first principal of the denominational theological college, Ranmoor, was a

---

[1] *W.M.A. Mag.*, July 1855, pp. 306 ff; September 1855, p. 429; *W.M.P. Mag.*, September 1855, p. 188.

[2] *W.M.P. Mag.*, September 1856, p. 141.

[3] M.N.C. *Minutes*, 1863, p. 53; *U.M.F.Cs Mag.*, August 1863, pp. 553–5.

man of high views, anxious to prevent any move further away from Wesleyanism.[1] When, in 1866, Cooke specifically proposed negotiations for union with the Free Methodists, Stacey defeated this move and carried through Conference an appeal for the union of all Methodists.

Since no union could hold both the Wesleyans and the Free Methodists, Stacey's appeal was apparently worthless. But a direct approach to all Methodists meant an approach to the Wesleyans. At the very least this would offend the Free Methodists. Letters were duly sent out, over the name of the current President, Samuel Hulme. The letter to the Wesleyans congratulated them on the state of their connexion and hoped that the New Connexion might soon ' "come again to our Father's house in peace" '. The Wesleyans wrote a brusque reply. For Stacey, this disappointment was tempered by the angry reaction of the Free Methodists when informed of this correspondence.[2]

Cooke organized a meeting of New Connexion and Free Methodist delegates at Leeds for May 1867. But this great triumph, thirty years after the New Connexion-Association discussions, was marred by the Hulme letters. The meeting was held, but the Free Methodists displayed their contempt for the treacherous New Connexion by taking no minutes of the proceedings.[3]

Stacey heightened Cooke's discomfiture by carrying through the 1867 Conference eight 'Bases for Negotiation' with other denominations. The bases precluded union with the Free Methodists by requiring parity of representation, by vesting supreme legislative and executive power in the conference and by demanding *ex officio* ministerial chairmanship in the quarterly meeting. To make matters clear, Stacey included in the bases a statement of the theology underlying these provisions: 'That the Christian ministry is an ordinance of God . . . and has therefore duties and prerogatives of its own, which should be practically recognized in all ecclesiastical meetings.'[4]

The New Connexion could not now unite with the Free Methodists. The Wesleyans would not unite with the New Connexion. But Cooke still hoped for an ecumenical *coup*. Since the Wesleyan Reform Union, the Independent Methodists and the Primitive Methodists were as much opposed to parity and *ex officio* ministerial chairmanship as the

[1] W. J. Townsend, *Methodist Union*, London, 1906, p. 96; *James Stacey, D.D., Reminiscences and Memorials*, London, 1891, pp. 281–3, 310, 363.
[2] *M.N.C. Mag.*, December 1867, pp. 761–2; *U.M.F.Cs Mag.*, 1867, p. 616.
[3] Townsend, *Methodist Union*, pp. 107–8; *U.M.F.Cs Mag.*, 1888, p. 475.
[4] *M.N.C. Mag.*, August 1867, p. 512.

Free Methodists were, only the Bible Christians were left. Union with the Bible Christians had positive advantages. They were about the size of the New Connexion, and hence would not overwhelm or be overwhelmed by their prospective partners; they were virtually confined to areas the New Connexion had never penetrated, thus obviating problems of overlap while providing added geographical coverage; and they were growing much faster than the New Connexion. Cooke persuaded the 1868 Conference to approach the Bible Christians.

The Bible Christian leaders, F. W. Bourne and James Thorne, were flattered by these attentions. The New Connexion was according them recognition as Methodists. It was also offering a solution to the problem of losses from migration out of the south west to the northern industrial districts where the Bible Christians had failed to establish themselves but where the New Connexion was strong. With union, New Connexion chapels would become acceptable to Bible Christians and this 'leakage' would be stopped.

When the Bible Christian and New Connexion delegates met in London, on 3 March 1869, the Bible Christians produced, rather to Cooke's surprise, a 'Document on Union'. This elaborate statement accepted the bases, proposed to raise the stipends of Bible Christian ministers to the New Connexion level, and claimed that the Bible Christian institution of female preachers, embarrassing to the New Connexion, was dying out. 'I cannot conceive', wrote Hulme incredulously, 'that any number of people will ever agree to unite with us on terms more favourable than those the Bible Christians now propose.'[1]

The 1869 New Connexion Conference was nervous about this development. After the Conference, Cooke and Hulme tried to produce a compromise. Complete union was relegated to an indefinite future. But, as stage one in a process of growing together, New Connexion and Bible Christians would enter a 'Federal Union', in which the two denominations would coexist while sharing one name, one Book Room, Ranmoor College, a federal connexional committee and a periodic General Conference.[2]

These proposals were issued as a circular in December 1869. At once the pro-Wesleyan faction met at the house of Stacey's protégé, the Rev. W. J. Townsend. The meeting concluded that, since 'the union committee had forced the pace', they must plan 'opposition

---

[1] *M.N.C. Mag.*, December 1869, pp. 729–41; January 1870, p. 37.
[2] *Ibid.*, July 1869, p. 450; January 1870, pp. 38–9.

procedure'. Stacey kept in the background but Townsend and the Rev. T. D. Crothers, who was to succeed Stacey at Ranmoor, kept up a vigorous attack on the proposed 'Federal Union'. Their main theme was the poverty of the Bible Christians.[1] By May, Cooke had to report that the Townsend group had produced 'much disquiet in various parts of the Connexion'. Conference met in June 1870. Stacey ended the matter with a resolution, carried by seventy-one votes to thirty-five, stating that 'The scheme of federal union with the Bible Christians . . . was, in the present state of Connexional opinion, inexpedient.'[2]

*The Olive Branch and After*

Stacey, Crothers and Townsend now dominated the New Connexion. Their policy was to unite with the Wesleyans, presumably on the basis of lay-ministerial parity of representation. But, as the Hulme correspondence showed, the Wesleyans were indifferent to the New Connexion. Despite the entry of laymen to the Wesleyan Conference in 1878 and the first Methodist Ecumenical Conference in 1881, Wesleyans displayed little interest in solving Stacey's problems. After the Ecumenical Conference, Featherstone Kellett, a Wesleyan minister, discussed union privately with New Connexion ministers, but nothing came of this initiative.[3]

But the rising Wesleyan figure of the 1880s was H. P. Hughes, who was interested in Methodist union as a means of challenging the Church of England. To open the subject in Wesleyanism, he wrote to some ex-Presidents for their opinion on Wesleyan-New Connexion union. At least four replied, the most notable of whom, William Arthur, had no intention of writing for publication.[4] On 18 November 1886, Hughes printed the four letters in his newspaper, the *Methodist Times*, as a 'manifesto' under the heading, *The Olive Branch of Peace*.[5] The letters, though entirely undistinguished, encouraged 140 Wesleyan quarterly meetings to pass general resolutions in favour of Methodist union. Hughes carefully excluded the Free Methodists from his appeal. Methodism, he said, was too near 1849. Instead, he wanted the New Connexion, and possibly the Bible Christians, to join the Wesleyans.

The New Connexion Conference voted strongly in favour of Hughes' scheme. The Free Methodist Assembly, led by Richard

[1] Townsend, *op. cit.*, p. 117; *M.N.C. Mag.*, March 1870, pp. 184, 186.
[2] *M.N.C. Mag.*, May 1870, p. 285; July 1870, pp. 432–4.
[3] *Methodist Times*, 18 November 1886, p. 765.
[4] *M.T.*, 9 August 1888, p. 553.
[5] *Ibid.*, 18 November 1886, pp. 765–6.

Chew, urged a union of liberal Methodists on the defecting New Connexionists.[1] These fears were premature. Soon afterwards, the Wesleyan Conference rejected Hughes' scheme while proposing an interdenominational committee on overlap of chapels.[2] The feelings of the Bible Christian Conference, which met next, were expressed by the Rev. T. P. Oliver, who observed that 'after what had passed in the Wesleyan Conference it was beneath their position to refer to the matter'.[3]

Townsend later claimed that the failure of the Olive Branch finally disillusioned him about Wesleyan-New Connexion union. Perhaps he had acquired Cooke's passion for uniting the New Connexion with whatever denomination was available. In any event, Townsend now took the initiative. With Stacey's reluctant approval, Townsend approached Marmaduke Miller, who now edited the Free Methodist denominational magazine.[4] Although Miller died in April 1889, his successor as editor, J. Swann Withington, favoured talks with the New Connexion, as did Richard Chew. Whatever Stacey felt, both Townsend and the Rev. William Longbottom were anxious to meet the Free Methodists. Despite widespread indifference in both denominations, and strong opposition among Free Methodists in Nottinghamshire and Derbyshire, a joint committee met and published a report in July 1890.[5]

The committee was dominated by Longbottom and Chew, both highly intelligent men who genuinely sought to end the differences between the two denominations. Three major problems could be identified, the chairmanship of the quarterly meeting and the character and power of conference. In Free Methodism, the chairmanship was elective, the assembly was based on free representation and it had little power over circuits. In the New Connexion, the chairmanship belonged to the minister *ex officio*, Conference was based on parity and it had mandatory powers over circuits. These differing systems expressed differing views about the authority of ministers and the character of the Christian community.

The committee produced a finely balanced compromise. The chairmanship was to go to the minister, unless the quarterly meeting protested. Since almost every Free Methodist quarterly meeting

[1] *M.T.*, 23 June 1887, pp. 393–4; *M.N.C. Mag.*, July 1887, p. 392; *Free Methodist*, 14 July 1887, pp. 229–30.
[2] *M.T.*, 28 July 1887, pp. 475–8.
[3] *Ibid.*, 4 August 1887, p. 494.
[4] *F.M.*, 2 April 1903, p. 216.
[5] *Ibid.*, 19 July 1888, p. 460; 30 May 1889, p. 343.

already allowed the minister the chair, such protests were unlikely; but, in the best Free Methodist tradition, the localities were still free to order their life as they chose. Thus both sides were to make concessions on the chairmanship.

They were also to make concessions on Conference. The Free Methodists were to accept parity and abandon free representation, although this would mean that the United Conference had proportionately more laymen than the Free Methodist assembly. In return, the New Connexion were to surrender some of the powers of Conference. Clause 5, sections (e) and (f), of the report proposed that, except in the case of 'funds on which depend the maintenance of the Ministry and the obligations of the Connexion', conference simply had 'the right of appeal' to circuits to support 'institutions and funds'. The United Conference would only be able to compel the circuits to obey it within a defined area.[1]

In this scheme, the New Connexion lost slightly more than the Free Methodists. But as the former was only half as large as the latter, this was reasonable enough. As a whole the scheme was a satisfactory basis on which to unite the two denominations, if union was desired.

Stacey, now ill and dying, was dismayed by the report. He briefly considered as a diversionary measure resuscitating the scheme of union with the Bible Christians, which he had killed twenty years before. But, at the New Connexion Conference of 1890, he confined himself to denouncing, with 'remorseless logic', both the report and, for good measure, a proposal for union with the Wesleyans. After protracted debate, he moved that 'the report fails so to secure the position of the minister as president of circuit and church meetings as to satisfy the convictions of our people', and that this question should be considered by the Free Methodist assembly. The resolution was carried by 106 votes to fifteen.[2]

The *Free Methodist* retorted that, so far from surrendering to Free Methodist views, the report 'concedes to New Connexion circuits the right to remain exactly as they are, and . . . puts the screw upon our own Circuits'. On Chew's advice, the Assembly, invited to adopt Stacey's doctrine of the minister as 'president' of the quarterly meeting, simply returned the matter to the 1891 New Connexion Conference.[3] Though Stacey was now removed from the scene, Townsend

[1] See p. 155 above. *M.N.C. Mag.*, July 1890, pp. 445-50.
[2] F. W. Bourne, *The Centenary Life of James Thorne of Shebbear*, London, 1895, pp. 143-4; *F.M.*, 19 June 1890, p. 1; *M.N.C. Mag.*, July 1890, p. 442.
[3] *F.M.*, 19 June 1890, p. 2; 17 July 1890, p. 9.

had apparently lost his ecumenical enthusiasm of 1888 and the Conference resolved that in view of 'serious differences of opinion' on this subject, 'further action in relation to the proposed union is not at present advisable'.[1]

Free Methodists gave vent to their annoyance. One excited reformer declared, 'the "Union barque" is wrecked! totally wrecked! on the rock of Ministerialism – not to say Priestism!' The Conference decision had been the work of 'occult influences', notably exercised by the superior members of the denomination. Rather prematurely, the *Free Methodist* declared that the New Connexion had ended 'for a generation the question of union between the Methodist New Connexion and our own Churches'. It concluded, 'We are thankful that the Free Churches are not in any degree responsible for the failure of the movement.' It was the New Connexion that had 'given the *coup de grace* to the whole business'.[2]

*Primitive Methodists and Methodist Union*

By the time the Second Methodist Ecumenical Conference met in Washington, not only was the 'Olive Branch' a thing of the past, but the Free Methodist-New Connexion union scheme, stimulated by it, had also been despatched. The situation was now ready for a new development, and it proved a highly unlikely one.

When Samuel Hulme had written his fateful letters in 1866, the President of the Primitive Methodist Conference, the Rev. George Lamb replied,

'I fear, dear Sir, there are insuperable difficulties to the union of the different sections of Methodists into one body, but I must confess that I have thought very little upon the subject; and perhaps more light would enable me to see the possibility of accomplishing the object . . . you have in view.'[3]

In 1891 more light was generally forthcoming among Primitive Methodists. At the Ecumenical Conference, Thomas Mitchell, a leading Primitive Methodist minister, declared,

'It has been thought that in the grand reunion of the coming time our Church would be the last to share in the great fusion of Methodist life. . . . That, I think, is mere assumption. . . . I may venture to prophesy that when the battalions of a united Methodism move on

[1] *M.N.C. Mag.*, 1891, p. 394.
[2] *F.M.*, 26 June 1890, p. 11; 25 June 1891, p. 17.
[3] *M.N.C. Mag.*, December 1866, p. 764.

as a leading force to the conquest of the world for Christ, the stalwarts of the Primitive Methodist contingent will not be found apart or behind.'[1]

Mitchell's speech aroused a definite, though confused, response in the denomination. The Primitive Methodists knew little of the reformed Methodists' hostility to the Wesleyans. But they were aggressively anti-Anglican, and anxious about their growth rate. The 1892 Primitive Methodist Conference insisted that 'it was the fashion nowadays to say that it was not the Primitive Methodists who were anxious about a reunion', while in fact it was only the Primitive Methodists who made 'any practical suggestions with regard to reunion'.[2] What these 'practical suggestions' were, the Primitive Methodists would have had difficulty in saying. The best they could think of in 1892 was to unite with the Bible Christians, of whom they knew virtually nothing, but who were by all accounts a fervent, evangelistic people like themselves.

Under the influence of Mitchell, the Rev. C. C. McKechnie, the denominational editor, and like most such, a strong ecumenicalist, and a layman, William Beckworth, the 1894 Conference finally resolved to confer with the Bible Christians, though the *Primitive Methodist World* impolitely doubted whether it was 'much more than talk'.[3] The denominations held two meetings in London, in January and April 1895. The Bible Christians, still led by F. W. Bourne, were as eager for union as they had been in 1869.

The delegates concentrated on the composition of Conference. Here the two denominations diverged, Primitive Methodists holding 'Two to One', Bible Christians advocating parity of ministers and laymen. Delegates agreed that the united church should adopt parity; but that the two denominations were so close together 'that neither would be required, in the event of union, to make any perceptible change'.[4]

This opinion was naïve. If, in a united church, ministers advanced to parity, there would be less seats for laymen. To Primitive Methodist laymen, this price was too high to pay for the addition of 27,000 Bible Christians to the denomination's 182,000. At the 1895 Primitive Methodist Conference, some complained that the change to parity

---

[1] *Proceedings of the Second Ecumenical Methodist Conference Held in the Metropolitan Methodist Episcopal Church, Washington, October, 1891*, London, 1892, p. 122.

[2] *Primitive Methodist World*, 23 June 1892, p. 490.

[3] *P.M.W.*, 21 June 1894, pp. 475, 483.

[4] *Minutes of the Bible Christian Connexion*, 1895, p. 45.

was undemocratic and retrograde. In any event, over the past three years the Primitive Methodists had awakened to their position in the Methodist world. They would rather lead a great union of all liberal Methodists, succeeding where the other non-Wesleyans had failed for sixty years, than merely unite with the small and remote Bible Christian denomination. The Primitive Methodist Grand Committee was therefore authorized to approach the New Connexion and the Free Methodists.[1]

The Bible Christian Conference of 1895 did not know of this new departure in Primitive Methodist policy. Indeed, it was only on Bourne's specific request that the Conference paused in its ecumenical enthusiasm to debate the matter at all. But when Bible Christians discovered what the Primitive Methodists had done, they displayed a hostility almost unique in Bible Christian history. The Primitive Methodists, they complained, were 'shunting the lesser Union for the greater'.[2] [*sic*].

The New Connexion and the Free Methodists were both disturbed at the prospect of being swamped by the numerous but socially inferior Primitive Methodists. The New Connexion declared that no step towards union could be taken without bringing in the Wesleyans. The Free Methodists declined to comment before the next Assembly considered the matter. As the Assembly met later in the year than the Primitive Methodist Conference, the latter could not discuss the union question again till 1897.

But when the Assembly of 1896 met, it rejected the Primitive Methodist proposals. The Primitive Methodists, like the New Connexion in 1867, now had only the Bible Christians to fall back on. The Primitive Methodist Conference of 1897 received the 1895 report, with its recommendation of parity, and sent it to the district committees.[3]

Primitive Methodists now regarded union with the Bible Christians as rather below their dignity. Some leaders were completely hostile to the union. At the 1897 Conference, the Rev. John Smith, Secretary of the Primitive Methodist Missionary Committee, condemned the idea of departure from the 'Two to One Principle' as monstrous. 'He did not think', he said, 'that these were the times to limit the influence of laymen in the management of Churches in this country'.[4] Shortly

[1] *P.M.W.*, 19 December 1896, p. 988.
[2] *B.C. Mag.*, September 1895, pp. 577–8; January 1896, p. 12.
[3] *P.M.W.*, 1 July 1897, p. 529.
[4] *Ibid.*, 1 July 1897, p. 529.

afterwards Smith published an attack on the scheme called *Unity and Union*.[1] The district committees voted 60 per cent in favour of union in principle, but rejected parity. Smith was elected President of the Conference, a bad omen for ecumenicalism. But this did not restrict him to mere moral influence on the gathering. Vacating the chair, he urged that there could be no deviation from the 'Two to One Principle'. A motion to that effect was defeated by sixty-nine votes to thirty-seven. Another motion to refer the constitution back to the joint committee was then carried.[2]

The joint committee did not alter the constitution in any particular, partly because of Bible Christian hostility to 'Two to One', partly because Primitive Methodist unionists believed they could not hope to carry any larger union at a later date if they were committed to the principle. The constitution was returned untouched to the conferences of 1899. The Primitive Methodist Conference, meeting first, decided, in lieu of a better plan, to send it to the quarterly meetings. The Bible Christian Conference followed this lead, but their quarterly meetings which met in May did not discuss the union, for the Primitive Methodist quarterly meetings in January voted 74 per cent against the scheme. In 1901, Thomas Mitchell had to admit to the third Ecumenical Conference that, on the great union question, 'I fear that my church will be the last to fall into line.'[3]

### The Making of United Methodism

While Mitchell was confessing his failure to bring the Primitive Methodists into union, the Free Methodists were embarking on the first successful ecumenical project since 1857. The Free Methodists were still anxious for some victory over the Wesleyans. The 1899 Assembly copied Hughes' and Perks' Million Guinea Fund with a Twentieth Century Fund of 100,000 guineas. This, like the Wesleyan Fund, was mainly needed to build a new denominational headquarters. Just as the Westminster Central Hall was designed to impress the Anglicans, the Free Methodist Church House was designed to impress the Wesleyans. It had to be 'something arrestive, something that will appeal to the imagination, something that will remind others that we have an existence as a Denomination'.[4]

[1] *P.M.W.*, 7 October 1897, p. 795.
[2] *Ibid.*, 30 December 1897, p. 1034; 9 June 1898, p. 458; 23 June 1898, pp. 515–17.
[3] *Proceedings of the Third Oecumenical Methodist Conference Held in City Road Chapel, London, September, 1901*, London, 1901, p. 134.
[4] *M.M.*, 1901, p. 318.

The negotiations which led to the formation of the United Methodist Church were conducted by the Rev. William Redfern, a Free Methodist minister, assisted by Alderman Robert Bird of Cardiff, the Free Methodist Perks. Like other ecumenicalists, Redfern was a 'guiding star' of advanced theology. In 1906, he published *Modern Developments of Methodism*, under the auspices of the National Free Church Council. This book expressed the hostilities of liberal Methodists toward Wesleyanism. Though Wesleyanism had greatly extended lay power since 1850, it still reserved many powers to the ministers sitting in the all-ministerial Pastoral Session of Conference. Having many schools of its own, the denomination also refused to support liberal Methodists grouped under the National Council in open resistance to the Balfour government's education policy. This did little to win their affections. Wesleyans took Redfern's book very seriously. Much contemporary protest was followed by the appearance in 1911 of J. Robinson Gregory's history of Methodism, virtually a two-volume refutation of Redfern.[1]

At the third Ecumenical Conference, David Brook, current Free Methodist President, Redfern and Bird, sounded Bible Christian and New Connexion delegates about the possibilities of a union of liberal Methodists.[2] 'Much earnest conversation in private' followed the closing of the Conference, noted the *Free Methodist*, in October 1901. It felt that the union cause 'might best be served at present by private and informal consultations rather than by public discussion'.[3]

The Free Methodist Assembly of 1902 seemed unaware of Redfern and Bird's policies. A resolution was carried empowering the Connexional Committee to enter into negotiations for Methodist union with whatever body should choose to communicate with it; but Bird failed to carry a motion limiting the field of negotiation to Free Methodists, New Connexion and Bible Christians.[4]

But this was unimportant. The Primitive Methodists had just disgraced themselves, the Wesleyans were impossible. Only the three denominations mattered–and since this was so, all three mattered. The Bible Christians were enthusiastic, the New Connexion was not. Redfern proposed to gain the support of the latter by first approaching the former. He could use the Bible Christians to convince the New

[1] William Redfern, *Modern Developments in Methodism*, London, 1906; J. Robinson Gregory, *History of Methodism*, London, 1911; *United Methodist Magazine*, January 1924, p. 17.
[2] *F.M.*, 19 July 1906, p. 454.
[3] *Ibid.*, 31 October 1901, p. 733.
[4] *Ibid.*, 24 July 1902, p. 489.

Connexion that a union of liberal Methodism, with or without them, was inevitable; to avoid the direct Free Methodist-New Connexion confrontation that had long proved so disastrous; and to allay New Connexion fears of being absorbed into an unadulterated Free Methodist union.

After the Free Methodist Assembly, Redfern, who had been elected President for 1902, visited the Bible Christian Conference on 31 July 1902. Redfern made a long, enthusiastic, and detailed speech in favour of union. He insisted that 'the negotiations must not be unduly protracted'. He himself would like to see the fiftieth anniversary of the United Methodist Free Churches, in 1907, marked by the formation of a yet larger union. A Free Methodist correspondent at the Conference believed that 'if a vote had been taken then and there an overwhelming majority would have determined on union with the United Methodist Free Churches'.[1] The *Bible Christian Magazine* solemnly announced that, 'there is reason to believe that the morning of 31 July 1902 will become memorable in the annals of Methodist history'.[2]

In October, the union movement was further advanced by the conversion of the *Free Methodist* into an interdenominational paper, serving the smaller two denominations which had no weekly of their own. This move created a very strong impression that union was already agreed upon or had indeed in some aspects taken place.

The New Connexion Conference of 1902 debated union *in camera*. It passed an 'open door' resolution, framed, as Henry Smith put it, so that, though another denomination could come in, the New Connexion could not go out.[3] The resolution simply authorized the Annual Committee's reception of such communications on Methodist union as should reach it from other denominations. In October, Redfern and Bird made their appeal to the denomination in the form of letters in the *New Connexion Magazine*. Redfern put it bluntly:

'the only way to attain Methodist union ultimately is to secure as soon as possible, Union between the smaller Methodist bodies. Who can expect the Wesleyan body with its 500,000 members, even if it were heartily in favour of Methodist Union, to make concessions—say to the Methodist New Connexion body? And how can the smaller body, with its century of noble history, its record of

[1] *F.M.*, 7 August 1902, pp. 519, 523.
[2] *B.C. Mag.*, September 1902, p. 407.
[3] *M.N.C. Mag.*, October 1902, p. 327.

worthy men and its love of freedom, consent to be swallowed up without trace?'[1]

Instead it should unite with the other liberal Methodists, a term evidently applying to the three denominations only, in a free and equal partnership.

Although the New Connexion Annual Committee had no real authorization to do so, it met delegates of the other two denominations in the early autumn of 1902. The joint meeting agreed upon parity of representation and adopted the crucial sections 5 (e) and 5 (f) of the draft constitution of 1890. It resolved

> 'That as a matter of expediency in the transaction of Church business, the Superintendent Minister shall preside at all Circuit and Quarterly Meetings . . . and Church Meetings at which he may be present – all proper safeguards against possible abuse being duly provided. In his absence the meeting shall elect its own Chairman and dispose of its business.'[2]

The 1903 Methodist New Connexion passed an act of oblivion to exculpate its Annual Committee's transgression of the 'open door' resolution. Indeed the majority of ministers in the Conference apparently 'had assembled with fixed minds' in favour of the scheme.[3] All three denominations agreed to put the matter before their quarterly meetings between January and May 1904.

The sudden appearance and rapid success of Redfern's union bid dismayed many Wesleyans. One of Hughes' last editorials was an appeal to the three denominations to wait for a Wesleyan initiative, at some unspecified future date. 'We are still of opinion', he wrote, '. . . that the most satisfactory method of securing Methodist union is for the "Mother Church" . . . to take the lead.'[4] George Jackson feared that 'If the minor bodies are left to unite among themselves, there is always the peril . . . that some concessions may be made on one side or other which would eventually bar the way to the larger union.'[5] The liberal Methodists should wait for the Wesleyans to lead them into an anti-Anglican united church based on the Wesleyan constitution in its entirety; and not form a Free Methodist led anti-Wesleyan union, in which the minor denominations nearest to the Wesleyans would be assimilated to the Free Methodist system.

[1] *M.N.C. Mag.*, October 1902, p. 332.
[2] *Minutes of the Methodist New Connexion*, 1903, pp. 39–41.
[3] *M.N.C. Mag.*, July 1903, p. 240.
[4] *M.T.*, 4 September 1902, p. 644.
[5] George Jackson, *The Old Methodism and the New*, London, 1903, p. 22.

There was strong pressure for action. In March 1903, Percy Bunting, Hughes' successor as editor of the *Methodist Times*, wrote, 'We feel most strongly that a deplorable mistake will be committed if our own Church stands aside, and permits these bodies to draw together without at least endeavouring to promote a wider union which shall embrace both mother and daughter communions.'[1] At the Wesleyan Conference of 1903, John Bond, Secretary of the inter-denominational Methodist Committee for Concerted Action, proposed the appointment of a committee to meet representatives of the three denominations 'to enquire further as to the possibility of union between two or more of the several Churches'.

The right wing condemned this proposal. The Rev. J. S. Simon asked if they were willing 'to throw the whole of their constitution into the melting pot again?' and Rigg warned delegates without his length of experience that Methodist union was 'one of the most complicated questions in the world'. The resolution was modified to create a committee of inquiry debarred from discussing union. The committee was to be headed by Rigg, who had been abusing Methodist reformers for rather more than half-a-century.[2]

The committee of inquiry met representatives of the three denominations in the Memorial Hall, Farringdon, on 3 December 1903. Rigg made a considerable impression on the liberal Methodists. The *Free Methodist* happily commented that 'The effect of the interview was to prove to the Committee the uselessness of hoping for any union at present with the Wesleyans, and to cement the smaller bodies together to an extraordinary degree.' The *Methodist Times* correspondent found the leaders of the three denominations saying, ' "How could the Wesleyans meet us? They are at one extreme and we are at the other. They cannot give up points in their constitution, nor can we. The Mother Church has shut the doors, bolted the locks and even pulled down the blinds against us, and after all we cannot see exactly how she could do otherwise." '[3]

The encounter with Rigg, whose polemic against the reformers had been too severe for Bunting and Jackson,[4] was particularly traumatic for the New Connexion. New Connexion opposition to the union scheme received a severe blow. This opposition had been growing since the New Connexion Conference of 1902, after which Henry

[1] *M.T.*, 4 September 1902, p. 644; 12 March 1903, p. 177.
[2] *Methodist Recorder*, 23 July 1903, p. 3; 30 July 1903, p. 101.
[3] *F.M.*, 10 December 1903, p. 817; *M.T.*, 10 December 1903, p. 879.
[4] John Telford, *The Life of James Harrison Rigg*, London, 1910, p. 86.

Smith had argued that the New Connexion, possessing the *via media*, should seek to bring together non-Wesleyans and Wesleyans alike rather than accept Redfern's initiative.[1] But the opposition lacked its traditional centre, Ranmoor College, since the new Principal, J. S. Clemens, was decidedly in favour of union with the Free Methodists. But James Crothers, the son, and E. F. H. Capey, the son-in-law, of Clemens' predecessor, T. D. Crothers, were as strongly opposed to union with any denomination but the Wesleyans as Crothers himself had been.

Townsend vacillated. He was still advocating union with Wesleyan Methodism in December 1903. But in January 1904, shortly after the Farringdon Hall meeting, he declared that any interruption of the current negotiations by an attempt to unite with the Wesleyans would be 'disastrous'.[2] Though he continued to hesitate, Townsend was virtually useless to the New Connexion opposition, and he was shortly commissioned to write the semi-official story of Methodist union in connection with the coming amalgamation.

But the opposition was not impotent. It attacked the poverty of the Bible Christians and the Free Methodists in comparison with the New Connexion. It claimed that, as the Rev. James Payne put it, the New Connexion ministry was about to be sacrificed on the altar of Free Methodist anti-clericalism.[3] Crothers himself circularized the Connexion in an effort to influence the quarterly meetings of 1904,[4] and the opposition possessed a periodical, the *Methodist Evangelist*, which apparently advocated Wesleyan–New Connexion union. In 1904, E. F. H. Capey could command thirty or forty votes in the New Connexion Conference, which was probably about 150 strong; and even in 1904, forty-eight votes were cast out of 154 to refer the question of ministerial chairmanship back to the committee.[5]

'In spite of determined efforts to confuse the issue', as the New Connexion section of the *Free Methodist* put it,[6] the quarterly meetings voted massively in favour of union in 1904. It was fairly certain that union would now be achieved. But, at the Wesleyan Conference of 1904, despite this vote and the failure of the committee of inquiry to win friends for Wesleyanism among the liberal Methodists, Perks proposed a direct approach to the New Connexion. Possibly, as was

[1] *M.N.C. Mag.*, October 1902, p. 327.
[2] *M.T.*, 10 December 1903, p. 878; *M.N.C. Mag.*, January 1904, p. 9.
[3] *M.N.C. Mag.*, January 1904, p. 9; May 1905, p. 203.
[4] *Ibid.*, February 1904, p. 69.
[5] *F.M.*, 30 June 1904, p. 405; 22 June 1905, p. 394.
[6] *Ibid.*, 14 January 1904, p. 21.

said by other and disillusioned Forward Movement men at this time, Perks had been reading too much of the *Methodist Evangelist* and was simply misinformed of the true state of New Connexion opinion; possibly seeing his project for a Wesleyan-led anti-Anglican union being destroyed by the advent of an anti-Wesleyan union led by the most vigorous living opponent of Wesleyanism, he felt something had to be done however inadequate.[1]

In any event, his resolution, for an offer of union to the New Connexion, was made ridiculous by the addition during the debate by Mr. John Cooper of the proviso that the Pastoral Session of Conference, the symbol of Wesleyan sacerdotalism, should remain intact in any such union. Rigg strongly opposed the whole scheme, which was, he said, beneath the dignity of the Conference: 'A great body like theirs to ask a little body like that! . . . To invite a minor body to separate itself from the Committee and join with them would be an utterly unheard of and unworthy proposal.' Further, he warned, 'The differences between the New Connexion and themselves were absolutely radical, as they might yet live to find out.'[2]

But the Perks–Cooper resolution was duly forwarded to the New Connexion. Henry Smith, who, two years before, had been counselling a general union including the Wesleyans, and who strongly advocated acceptance of the Pastoral Session fifteen years later, now denounced the resolution. He declared

'we are asked to surrender the very contention for making which our fathers were thrust out of the Wesleyan Church, the one principle that alone justifies our origin and history . . . the right, the principle . . . that the people of Christ, whether laymen or ministers, have alone the authority to determine all things in the Church of God, in submission to the Divine Head, whether they be matters of doctrines, of discipline, of the stationing of ministers. . . . I cannot think that the Church of my fathers, the Church of my boyhood's and my manhood's choice, the Church that has been to me as the very angel of God, is capable of so great, so unworthy, so ignoble a surrender.'[3]

Smith's confidence was not misplaced. The Rev. H. Rowe proposed a committee of inquiry to meet the Wesleyans. This scheme, which would have set back the current negotiations at least a year, was

[1] *M.T.*, 8 September 1905, p. 657.
[2] *M.R.*, 7 July 1904, p. 8.
[3] *M.N.C. Mag.*, September 1904, p. 329.

rejected by 138 votes to thirty-two. The tone of the debate was that of the speaker who said that the invitation was 'too late . . . too late by 108 years'.[1] The committee resolution was carried by 146 votes to sixteen. This rejected the offer since it 'would involve the surrender of duties and privileges of which our laymen have been in rightful possession for 108 years'. The 'foundation principle' of the New Connexion, Wesleyans were reminded, was that ' "the Church itself is entitled, either collectively in the person of its members, or representatively by persons chosen out of and by itself, to a voice and influence in all acts of administration and legislation" '.[2]

The New Connexion's stand finally answered Free Methodist accusations of 'sacerdotalism'. Redfern said, 'they had been wonderfully encouraged during the year' by the New Connexion's attitude.[3] By 1905 Redfern was deeply committed to the project of a united 'liberal Methodism'. He was not a constitutional lawyer like Chew, but an ideologue who saw liberal Methodism as the vehicle of progress bringing freedom and enlightenment to Wesleyan darkness. His great interest was doctrine. He abandoned the formal Free Methodist commitment to Wesley's teachings, and secured a modernist doctrinal formula for the new church. This stated that 'The Scriptures of the Old and New Testaments, through Divine Inspiration, contain a revelation of the will of God to man, and furnish a sufficient rule of faith and practice.' In case this revelation materially altered, he also obtained provision for the decennial revision of the doctrinal basis, an arrangement he described as 'the glory and crown of our polity'.[4]

To gain these advantages and to obtain a united church, whose mere existence was expected to revolutionize Methodism, Redfern was willing to make major concessions to the New Connexion. Perhaps he was encouraged to do so by the confidence that these concessions would strengthen the position of ministers in the united church, thus assisting the enlightenment of more old-fashioned laymen. Perhaps too the New Connexion's vigorous rejection of the Wesleyan initiative strengthened the Connexion's reputation and bargaining power with the Free Methodists.

Though Free Methodists insisted on an *ex officio* seat in the leaders' meeting for the local preacher, they were willing to concede changes in the ministerial chairmanship clause. New Connexion scruples were

---

[1] *F.M.*, 22 June 1905, pp. 393–4.
[2] *Minutes of the Methodist New Connexion*, 1905, p. 34.
[3] *F.M.*, 18 May 1905, p. 313.
[4] Edwin Askew, *Free Methodist Manual*, London, 1895, p. 17; United Methodist *Minutes*, 1907, p. 40; *United Methodist*, 10 July 1913, p. 525.

met by deletion of the qualification 'as a matter of expediency'; and by the concession that in certain circumstances ministers other than the superintendent of the circuit could take the chair, an arrangement which underlined the *ex officio* right of ministers as such to lead the proceedings. Bird reassured the Free Methodists that 'the superintendent minister should take the chair . . . but if he declined to do any business, or put any resolution, or did not favour anything before the meeting, he must either keep his mouth closed or get out of the chair and let somebody else go in'.[1]

Free Methodist leaders made another and more important concession. Up to the conferences of 1906, the joint committee of the three denominations remained loyal to a slightly amended version of clauses 5 (e) and (f) of the 1890 scheme. Conference could levy the circuits for 'the maintenance of the Ministry and the obligations of the Connexion'. Outside this area the conference would only have 'the right of appeal to the circuits for the loyal fulfilment of their obligation to sustain all institutions and funds of a distinctly Connexional character'.

In December 1905 and January 1906, the quarterly meetings voted on the details of the proposed scheme, and accepted this section. But after the 1906 Conferences, the formula was privately amended, without even a formal record in the minutes of the joint committee. The conference of the united church acquired the right 'to take such action as it may deem necessary or expedient to induce the circuits loyally to fulfil in any manner which the Conference may think desirable their obligations to sustain all institutions and funds of a Connexional character'.[2] Circuit independence had died a quiet death.

Redfern was rewarded in September 1907, when, at Wesley's Chapel, in City Road, the Bible Christians, Free Methodists and New Connexion merged into the United Methodist Church.

[1] *Minutes of the United Methodist Free Churches*, 1905, p. 316; *F.M.*, 23 February 1905, p. 114.

[2] *Methodist Union. Minute Book, December 18th, 1902, to September 18th, 1907; Minutes of the United Methodist Free Churches*, 1907, p. 51.

# CHAPTER EIGHT

# The Making of the Methodist Church

## Ecumenical Projects, 1907–17

'The most sanguine among us must admit that the immediate result of the triple alliance will be to retard our final union,' the Rev. William Wakinshaw warned the New Connexion in 1907.[1] But Wakinshaw and other Forward Movement Wesleyans determined to ignore the filial ingratitude of the New Connexion and the challenge presented by the United Methodist Church. Despite the unfortunate initiative of 1903 many Wesleyans insisted that union was now 'practical politics'.[2]

Primitive Methodists also continued to think about union, after the disastrous negotiations of the 1890s. Their famous lay theologian, A. S. Peake (1865–1929), was an ardent ecumenicalist, prepared, for the sake of union, to jettison the 'Two to One' principle so dear to Primitive Methodist laymen in 1900.[3] Many agreed. ' "Two laymen to one minister", to keep us from a possible career in the larger scope of God's purpose,' exclaimed the *Primitive Methodist Leader*, in 1916, '–it is preposterous', especially as 'Primitive Methodism . . . has lost its exuberant vigour.'[4]

United Methodist opinion also shifted slightly after 1907. At the fourth Methodist Ecumenical Conference, Redfern was 'deeply impressed' by 'the strong progressive thought' of some Wesleyans, and felt that 'the union sentiment' had taken 'immense strides'. But general United Methodist opinion was probably accurately reflected by the Rev. Arthur Jones, who asked, 'have we not really had enough of Union to last us for a little while?' Jones added, 'And, further, I must frankly say that I, for one . . . do not see that we are particularly near our Wesleyan friends.'[5]

[1] *Methodist New Connexion Magazine*, February 1907, p. 61.
[2] *Methodist Recorder*, 9 December 1909, p. 5.
[3] John T. Wilkinson (ed.), *Arthur Samuel Peake, 1865–1929*, London, 1958, p. 42.
[4] *Primitive Methodist Leader*, 9 November 1916, p. 729.
[5] *United Methodist*, 1 May 1913, p. 354; 25 September 1913, p. 731.

The major Wesleyan development during these years was the replacement of the *Methodist Recorder*'s high Wesleyan editor, Nehemiah Curnock, by Mr. J. B. Watson, an ex-Presbyterian, who was later appointed manager, although he was never formally recognized as editor. Watson's personal views are obscure. But under his regime (1906–34), the *Recorder* joined and even surpassed the *Methodist Times* in its ecumenicalism. The accession of Watson changed the face of Methodism.[1]

The 1911 Ecumenical Conference encouraged Wesleyan unionists to a new initiative. The Rev. James Lewis introduced a motion on union in the Wesleyan Conference of 1912. There was no time to debate it, and it was withdrawn. The *Recorder* noted, 'much disappointment has been felt, and in some quarters freely expressed, that the recent Conference . . . made no pronouncement on the subject of the reunion of Methodism'.[2]

But Perks carried through the 1913 Conference a resolution appointing a committee 'to collect information' on union 'and to report to the next Conference'. In reply, the Rev. R. Bevan Shepherd moved, but failed to carry, an inquiry into the possibility of 'union . . . with the Mother Church of England'.[3] Perks' committee had several advantages which his initiative of 1903 had not. Wesleyanism had now suffered a more prolonged loss of members than at any time in its history. The committee was supported, where in 1903 Perks was opposed, by the *Recorder*; and the committee had the services of a very able Secretary and Convenor, the Rev. E. Aldom French (1868–1962).

French was a strong evangelical, whose youthful attitude to the sacraments was essentially 'quaker'.[4] He was a great advocate of action and organization, who made his reputation by launching the Brighton Mission. He made his first speech in the 1911 Conference, and spoke 'remarkably well'. In December 1911, French informed the *Recorder* that 'A closer alliance of Methodists', was 'inevitable'. In April 1912, he contributed a striking article to that paper. 'The time has come', wrote French, 'when, at all costs, Methodism as a whole must deal with the accusations and complaints as to its condition, which are so incessantly pouring forth.'[5] The appointment of this able,

---

[1] *M.R.*, 7 December 1905, p. 3; 15 September 1910, p. 3; 6 April 1961, p. 16.
[2] *Ibid.*, 15 August 1912, p. 3.
[3] William Wakinshaw, *Gleanings from My Life*, London, 1931, p. 83; *M.R.*, 24 July 1913, p. 19.
[4] *M.R.*, 22 July 1920, p. 8.
[5] *Ibid.*, 20 July 1911, p. 17; 28 December 1911, p. 5; 4 April 1912, p. 5; *Methodist Times*, 13 January 1921, p. 4.

but very junior man may suggest Perks' personal intervention. It certainly suggests that, in 1913, Conference thought the committee quite unimportant.

The committee, a safe majority of whose members were against union,[1] compiled a 'Questionnaire' on the doctrine and polity of the different denominations. But the committee ran into a curious difficulty. It believed that the main virtue of union would be to make Methodism 'a greater evangelistic force'. This meant rationalization, and that meant reduction of overlap. The scale and character of overlap was unknown.

In April 1914, the committee adopted a ten-column analysis of overlap statistics which the Rev. Henry Carter was to collect: a large assignment, as there were about 16,500 Methodist chapels. The task was particularly difficult since, as the committee noted with a touch of surprise, on 5 March 1915, 'In the section dealing with Overlapping, it has been found that no statistics whatever were in the possession of the other Methodist Churches.' The Wesleyan attitude was summed up in a letter from F. L. Wiseman, Home Missions Secretary, to French. In reply to French's request for information as to the whereabouts of Wesleyan chapels, Wiseman said he had no information, and could not see his way to obtaining it, for 'The work of compilation would be enormous', and 'the utility of the whole is not obvious to me'. There was little the committee could do. The scale and character of overlap, the problem union was supposed to solve, remained unknown.[2]

Non-Wesleyans were unenthusiastic about the committee. The Primitive Methodist Conference even ordered a rival inquiry, apparently in vain. The *United Methodist* reacted to the Wesleyan committee by denouncing the doctrine 'that questions of the pastorate belong exclusively to the pastors', and to the Primitive Methodist initiative by warning that United Methodists could not 'take any active part' so soon after 1907.[3]

The situation shortly changed. By raising moral pressure, the war gave new impetus to old projects. In 1916, J. H. Shakespeare, the Baptist leader, advocated Free Church Federation to respectful but

[1] *M.T.*, 13 May 1920, p. 6.

[2] Meetings of 17 October 1913; 13 November 1913; 1 April 1914; 5 March 1915, and 3 November 1916; F. L. Wiseman–E. Aldom French, 30 December 1919 (insert), in *Minutes of the Wesleyan Methodist Union Committee, 17 October, 1913 to 18 December, 1919.*

[3] *P.M.L.*, 8 August 1913, p. 565; Primitive Methodist *Minutes*, 1914, p. 247; *U.M.*, 7 August 1913, p. 613; 9 July 1914, p. 522.

indifferent audiences in all three Methodist Conferences. The Rev. David Brook criticized the scheme in the United Methodist Conference. 'They were consolidating Union, and they would be glad to have been left alone for a little while', he said. He personally thought Methodist Union 'would be more effective'.[1] A. T. Guttery's notable dictum of 1916, 'We are not going to clear out of any village for the Baptists, still less for the Wesleyans,' had two edges and Free Church federation felt one of them.[2] Perks was shocked by any suggestion that 'the distinctive features of Methodist usage and polity . . . and the Methodist name' might be 'obliterated'.[3]

War assisted another project. High Wesleyans and certain Anglicans had long desired union of Wesleyanism and the Church of England. In 1917, unofficial Wesleyan-Anglican discussions began in the Kingsway Hall. The leading figure on the Wesleyan side was the Rev. J. Ernest Rattenbury (1870–1963), Superintendent of the West London Mission, and a college friend of French's. Over Rattenbury's study desk was a portrait of his grandfather, who had seconded Everett's expulsion. Rattenbury 'had no greater ambition than to be true to his old family heritage and tradition in the service of Methodism'. In his opinion, Bunting turned 'Methodist preachers into Wesleyan ministers', and 'The creation of a real ministry, necessary to a real Church, was perhaps worth the trouble and schism it caused'. Although Rattenbury admired the Primitive Methodists for their fervour and success, he was contemptuous of United Methodism, 'a syncopation of several movements of revolt', the reason for whose 'separate existence had passed away', and which now had no 'specific system to stand for'. Rattenbury believed that Wesleyanism was the '*via media* between Anglicanism and Nonconformity', although 'There is a clearer kinship between many Wesleyans and Anglicans than with either of the junior Methodist Churches'. Inside Wesleyanism, Rattenbury was suspect, before the war as a Christian Socialist, after it as a ritualist.[4]

The Kingsway Conference dismayed Methodists. Mr. W. A. Lupton of Ilkley declared, 'It is high time that the Bishops . . . were told what

[1] *U.M.*, 20 July 1916, p. 366.
[2] *P.M.L.*, 22 June 1916, p. 399.
[3] *M.R.*, 2 January 1908, p. 5; R. W. Perks, *The Re-union of British Methodism*, London, 1920, pp. 11–12; *M.R.*, 27 July 1916, pp. 6–7; 19 April 1917, p. 3.
[4] *M.T.*, 16 August 1917, p. 9; *M.R.*, 30 July 1914, p. 4; J. Ernest Rattenbury, *Christian Union and Methodist Fusion*, London, n.d., pp. 27–31; J. Ernest Rattenbury, 'The Wesleyan Opposition to Methodist Union', manuscript, in Rattenbury Papers; *M.R.*, 9 December 1909, p. 6; 22 January 1920, p. 4; 29 January 1920, pp. 13, 15.

most Methodists think of them, and their attempts to seduce us from our own Church.'[1] The *Recorder* strongly condemned the conferences. The Anglo-Catholics, it said, were 'entirely inflexible in essentials'.[2]

Shakespeare and Rattenbury gave a sudden new impetus to a third old project, Methodist Union. By 1917, the French committee had almost ceased to matter.[3] But with Methodism now threatened by Free Church federation on one side and absorption in the established Church on the other, French and Perks carried a motion enlarging the committee and empowering it to meet committees of the other Methodist denominations. An unexpected and decisive change had taken place.[4]

The committee, which now had a majority for union, decided that its task was 'to . . . discover what Methodist Union would involve'. A sub-committee, led by the Rev. John Hornabrook, promptly jettisonned the 'Questionnaire' and drafted twenty-eight questions for the other denominations. The questions hinted at an old-fashioned Wesleyan evangelicalism. They wanted a Pastoral Session with exclusive control over 'all matters pertaining to Doctrine, Stationing and Discipline', an anachronism even in Wesleyanism. The minister was to be *ex officio* chairman of all meetings and to nominate all lay officials. Non-Wesleyans were asked, 'Would your people be prepared fully to accept the Connexional principle?' and 'Would your Conference accept our Standards as to the guarantees of the Evangelical doctrinal position of Methodism?' i.e. Wesley's *Sermons* and *Notes on the New Testament*. The questions were duly forwarded to the Primitive and United Methodists.[5]

Liberal Methodists had not been idle. In the 1916 Primitive Methodist Conference, the Rev. Samuel Horton (1857–1949) secured the appointment of a committee 'to inquire into the advisability and practicability of organic union between the United Methodist Church and our own'. But the Conference, uneasy over this move, prohibited communication between the committee and the United Methodists, thus pleasing the latter but killing the former.[6]

But many Primitive Methodists were enthusiastic about the project. The *Primitive Methodist Leader*, fearing that 'union of all the Method-

---

[1] *M.R.*, 26 July 1917, p. 8.
[2] *Ibid.*, 12 July 1917, p. 3.
[3] *M.T.*, 19 July 1917, p. 3.
[4] *M.R.*, 26 July 1920, p. 6; 21 June 1917, p. 3.
[5] *M.T.*, 13 May 1920, p. 6; *M.R.*, 22 July 1920, p. 8; Meetings of 11 October 1917; 30 October 1917, and 7 December 1917, in *Minutes* . . .
[6] *P.M.L.*, 29 June 1916, p. 424.

ists . . . may not yet be practicable', concluded 'What lies nearer to us is the union of at least two of the Methodist denominations.' The United Methodist constitution was believed to come 'almost identically into line with our own': and, where it diverged, it diverged in directions Primitive Methodist leaders wished to go.[1]

When the Primitive Methodists appointed their committee, the *United Methodist* indicated that it preferred 'the Mother Church of Methodism . . . to prosecute with vigour the investigations already begun as to the practicality . . . of a reunion of Methodism in this country'. The constituent denominations of the United Methodist Church had either rejected or been rejected by the Primitive Methodists in the previous two decades and, if union was inevitable, United Methodist leaders desired some larger project than mere coalescence of liberal Methodism. In any event, calling for a Wesleyan initiative served both to postpone a decision and to get rid of the Primitive Methodists. In November 1916, French told the Wesleyan committee that 'He had reason to think that . . . the other Churches would prefer . . . the Wesleyan Methodist Church to give the lead.' Horton would not have given him such 'reason', perhaps Brook had. Once French was willing to oblige the United Methodists, the Primitive Methodists could only fall into line. On 9 January 1918, representatives of the three denominations met for the first time to discuss the reunion of Methodism.[2]

*The Evolution of the* Tentative Scheme *of 1920*

The United Committee soon discovered that nobody knew what the reunion of Methodism meant. Should the Wesleyan Reform Union and the Independent Methodists be included? In March 1919, the Committee decided against further 'discussions' with the Wesleyan Reform Union.[3] It simply ignored the Independent Methodists. With even less hesitation the Committee shelved inquiry into overlap. It resolved 'that the elimination of unnecessary chapels would have to be a gradual process, but that there was no insuperable difficulty to complete Union'.[4]

The Committee hoped these fundamental problems would solve themselves, and turned to the more interesting task of planning a

[1] *P.M.L.*, 24 February 1916, p. 115; 16 March 1916, p. 162.
[2] *U.M.*, 20 January 1916, p. 31; 22 June 1916, p. 315; Meeting of 3 November 1916, in *Minutes* . . .
[3] Meeting of the United Committee, 3 October 1918, and 27 March 1919, in *Minutes* . . .
[4] Subcommittee of the United Committee, 6 February 1918, in *Minutes* . . .

united church. This raised another problem. If union was to make Methodism 'a greater evangelistic force', the Committee needed a scheme which would be 'of intrinsic value in serving a new age'. But it had to adopt another course, that of 'concessions in order to secure union'. In fact the Committee could never decide whether it was resolving the controversies of the past or looking, under divine guidance, to the new age.[1]

The subsequent constitutional negotiations were dominated by Wesleyan insistence on what was discreetly renamed the *Ministerial Session* of Conference. Acceptance of the Ministerial Session was, as Primitive Methodist leaders privately recognized, 'the honourable understanding with which negotiations were commenced', without which 'Methodist Union will not be accepted by the Wesleyan Methodist Church'. But the more Wesleyans insisted on the Ministerial Session, the less they could insist on anything else. The polity outlined in the 'Questions' of October 1917 virtually disappeared.

Wesleyans agreed that the Representative Session should elect the President, have extensive control over doctrine, and 'recognize' ministers, concessions they had denied their own laymen for forty years. After the Primitive and United Methodist delegates urged that 'acceptance of a Pastoral Session would be greatly eased if the Stationing Committee could consist of ministers and laymen', Wesleyans reluctantly conceded this point, on the understanding, 'The final reading of Stations to be taken in the Ministerial Session, but no change to be made unless all parties are agreed'. Wesleyans even agreed to surrender the minister's exclusive power to nominate lay officials, a basic principle of Wesleyanism since Wesley's death.[2]

Wesleyan unionists knew that, to carry the major Wesleyan vested interest, the ministers, they had to allow them, under whatever limitations, to go on meeting annually alone and together as they had done for nearly two centuries. Consequently non-Wesleyans could make drastic inroads on the rest of the Wesleyan constitution. Peake believed this was a process which led to 'a compromise between the two systems at present in vogue'.[3] It could also be described as a holocaust, the end product of which bore little resemblance to either of the

[1] United Committee, 9 January 1918, in *Minutes* . . .; *M.T.*, 15 July 1920, p. 15.

[2] Meetings of the London Members of the Primitive Methodist Committee on union, 31 January 1923 and 6 April 1923, in *Primitive Methodist Committees on Union, 1917–1932*; Meetings of February 1918–March 1919, in *Minutes* . . .

[3] *P.M.L.*, 9 November 1922, p. 715.

'systems' that fuelled it. By the end of 1919, the 'at all costs' school of unionists, headed by French, Peake and Lidgett, had devastated Wesleyan polity where generations of reformers had failed, while securing from liberal Methodists a recognition of pastoral authority Bunting had never been able to extort.

The proposed Methodist Church was to be ruled by a two-session Conference, modelled on the Wesleyan, in which a mixed Representative Session, with general sovereignty in the Church, preceded a Ministerial Session, with oversight of ministers, the second and last reading of Stations, and final responsibility for doctrine. District synods were similarly divided. The local courts would not be composed of ministerial nominees and society representatives, on the Wesleyan model, but of a self-perpetuating oligarchy of officials plus society representatives on the non-Wesleyan model. These courts were to be presided over by ministers *ex officio*.

This system could be expanded or altered only by mutual concession. When the Wesleyans, troubled by completely open nomination in the quarterly meeting, proposed that the meeting should appoint a special mixed committee to do its nomination for it, the United Committee assented. At the same time, it accepted a Primitive and United Methodist demand for a lay Vice-President of Conference. While discreetly rejecting the *exclusive* ministerial judiciary characteristic of Wesleyanism since Aldersgate, the United Committee rejected any lay share in the trial of ministers: a bargain calculated to offend both Wesleyan and reformed susceptibilities. At the same meeting, the United Committee rejected both a Wesleyan attempt to exclude laymen from discussing changes in Stations at the second reading, and a United Methodist demand for *ex officio* seats in the leaders' meeting for local preachers.[1]

All this made sense enough at the negotiating table; and advanced Wesleyans, contemplating the ruin of their heritage, could at least convince themselves that liberal Methodist raids on the Wesleyan constitution brought it more into line with the democratic spirit of the age. But more conservative Methodists, reformed and Wesleyan, could only look on the *Tentative Scheme*'s constitutional proposals as a series of deals which made nonsense of the past.

Conservative Methodists were also disturbed by the *Scheme*'s doctrinal proposals. The non-Wesleyans were strong Protestants, who wanted to base their belief on the Bible alone; and, often, strong modernists, who wanted to reinterpret the Bible in the light of modern

[1] Meetings of March 1919–April 1920, in *Minutes* . . .

thought. They did not want, as United Methodists put it, to commit themselves to the doctrines of Wesley 'or any other man'.[1] The opposition to 'Wesley's Standards', as required by the 'Questions' of October 1917, was led by Peake.

The United Committee's Standing Committee on Doctrine accepted 'Wesley's Standards' on 2 February 1919. Peake's price for accepting Wesley was the formula, 'That the evangelical doctrines entrusted to Methodism, as held by the three Conferences and as generally contained in Wesley's Notes on the New Testament and the First Four Volumes of his Sermons, shall be the doctrinal basis of the United Church.' Peake believed that 'generally' provided the necessary 'elasticity'. Primitive Methodists saw the word as 'a door that opens outwards, and will lead to new realms of truth that come with enlarging days'.[2]

But 'generally' still left Wesley in possession of the field, and in March 1920, Peake raised the price of surrender. The doctrines of the united church were to be 'generally contained in Wesley's Notes . . . and . . . Sermons, subject to the authority of Divine Revelation recorded in the Holy Scriptures'. Wesley was no longer supreme, nor were the Scriptures. Peake told French, 'it is to secure elasticity that we do not say "the Holy Scriptures" but "Divine Revelation recorded in the Holy Scriptures"'. Wesleyans were disturbed by these developments, but secured no revision of the doctrinal formula before the publication of the *Tentative Scheme*.[3]

They had relatively little success, either, on the question of administration of sacraments. Both Primitive and United Methodism allowed lay administration, Wesleyanism did not. Wesleyan attitudes on the sacraments varied. Rattenbury held that ordination was necessary to administration. Wesleyans, he claimed, 'do not like the methods employed by the other Denominations'. They treated the sacraments with indifference and administered them casually. Against this behaviour, Rattenbury usually argued the 'Order not Orders' theory: that church order and decency, not special grace in ordination, required that ministers only should administer.[4] But many Wesleyans on the United Committee, including French and Perks, had much lower views on sacraments.

---

[1] Meeting of 20 April 1920, in *Minutes* . . .
[2] *P.M.L.*, 19 February 1920, p. 121.
[3] A. S. Peake–E. Aldom French, 29 December 1921, in Peake Papers; Meetings of February 1919–April 1920, in *Minutes* . . .
[4] Rattenbury, *loc. cit.*; Rattenbury, *Christian Union and Methodist Fusion*, pp. 26, 38–9.

Peake was lukewarm on lay administration, but recognized that it was necessary if the major non-Wesleyan interest, the lay officials, were to accept union.[1] Other liberal Methodist leaders prevaricated. Samuel Horton told the Wesleyans in 1919 that 'As to Lay Administration of the Sacrament, all are agreed that if a minister can preside he should, and only the paucity of ministers has forced the question to the front.' But the doctrine of *expediency*, that the supply of non-Wesleyan ministers could not meet the sacramental demands of the far-flung chapels, was for Wesleyan consumption only. Horton assured the Primitive Methodist Conference that he hoped 'the time would never come when a Methodist Conference would decide that the sacrament should only be administered by a minister'.[2]

Wesleyans had to concede lay administration if they wanted union. But if they were willing to accept lay administration, they could specify the conditions. The United Committee's basic understanding on ministry and sacraments was defined in two resolutions moved by a Wesleyan, the Rev. William Bradfield, on 19 February 1919. The first resolution, seconded by French, called for acceptance of imposition of hands in ordination, a rite foreign to Primitive and United Methodists alike, on the rather 'representational' ground that it expressed merely 'the Church's endorsement of the minister's personal call'. The second resolution, seconded by a Primitive Methodist, the Rev. Henry Pickett, called for acceptance of lay administration, not because, as Pickett himself put it, 'We repudiate the claim of a separated priesthood as possessing spiritual authority not equally open to every member of the household of faith', but because lay administration was 'urgently necessary in order to provide for the administration of the Lord's Supper in our numerous smaller churches, and also . . . on general grounds'.

Qualified imposition of hands and qualified lay administration were verbal concessions of principle to secure practical gains. Although this compromise was essential to union, it left many dissatisfied. A year's pressure from the Wesleyans led the Committee to draft two alternative clauses on the sacraments in March 1920. Both recognized that 'general practice' of the three denominations had been ministerial administration. But the 'non-Wesleyan' alternative clause stated that lay administration to obtain 'more regular and frequent administration . . . is not to be regarded as contrary to the principles of discipline of the Methodist Church'. In other words, lay adminis-

[1] *P.M.L.*, 10 April 1924, p. 234.
[2] *M.T.*, 11 December 1919, p. 4; *P.M.L.*, 19 June 1924, p. 399

tration was to be accepted *on principle*, and not merely as a matter of expediency.

The 'Wesleyan' alternative clause required Conference authority for the practice, and put the matter in negative and rather slighting terms: 'If in any area provision be required owing to inadequate staff, etc., the Conference is to be responsible for the appointment of persons duly authorized.'

In April 1920, the United Committee accepted this latter clause in modified form. Non-Wesleyans got the reference to 'inadequate [ministerial] staff' eliminated and the doubting 'If in any area' replaced by the more positive 'In any area'. The Wesleyans got the statement that the persons authorized or appointed would be 'set apart' for the purpose, a phrase which definitely suggested that they would be in some sense ordained ministers. The *Tentative Scheme* stated that:

'The general usage of the three uniting Churches whereby the Sacrament of the Lord's Supper is administered by ministers shall continue to be observed. In any area where provision for the regular administration is required, Conference shall be responsible for the authorization of duly qualified persons set apart for the purpose.'

This subtle formula required ministerial administration, while defining it as a 'general usage' only: and allowed laymen to administer, while suggesting they would be 'set apart', thus making them virtually indistinguishable from ministers. Conservative Wesleyans remained gloomy, but the formula might well satisfy everyone else.[1]

*Methodist Union and Methodist Opinion, 1918–21*

The Methodist public knew little of these negotiations before June 1920. But, despite the advantages of 'secret diplomacy',[2] a majority on the United Committee, and the support of the Methodist press, unionists could only advance their own cause, they could not stop opposition. This first appeared in organized form in Wesleyanism, where a higher level of education made it more difficult for Conference leaders to dominate opinion. In 1913, the Rev. R. Bevan Shepherd had opposed Perks in Conference. The first lay opposition came

[1] *P.M.L.*, 9 November 1922, p. 718; Meetings of October 1918–May 1920, in *Minutes . . .*; and *Minutes of the Wesleyan Methodist Union Committee, etc., 1919–1921*.
[2] *M.R.*, 24 July 1919, p. 8.

from a group in Lancashire and Cheshire, organized, after the war, by Mr T. W. Clucas.[1] Co-operation between these two men may have begun in 1919.

In 1919, ministerial anti-unionists had control of the *Methodist Times*. But in January 1920, Benjamin Gregory took over as editor, and the anti-unionists gradually lost influence on the paper.[2] They then tried other methods of publicity. In January 1920, Bevan Shepherd launched a ministers' manifesto against union, which, by April, had received signatures from 815 ministers, just under one-third of the total. This was startling success. The manifesto urged exclusively ministerial administration of sacraments and a fully autonomous Ministerial Session. It demanded protection of the 'Pastoral Office', and rejected the view that ministers were mere 'employés of the Church'. Finally, it insisted that nothing be done which would jeopardize 'wider reunion', *i.e.* with the Church of England.[3]

Anti-unionists now gained a label, 'The Other Side'—ecumenicalists' euphemistic description of opposition to God's will and the Conference majority. They also gained a leader. In June 1920, Rattenbury denounced the *Tentative Scheme*. 'This scheme', he wrote, 'is and will be challenged by organized opposition which is prepared to fight to the last ditch.'[4]

The Other Side was partly composed of high church Wesleyans who had 'recently shaken hands with a Bishop',[5] as W. Russell Maltby put it, or who were disturbed by rumours of non-Wesleyan communion services conducted with biscuits and water.[6] Partly they were conservative evangelicals, such as G. Armstrong Bennetts, who declared,

'The Church Reunion craze . . . is one of the arch-devices of Satan by which he is seeking to destroy Christian doctrine. . . . Destroy all the bulwarks of the existing churches, and pulverize their messages into dust . . . and let them be scattered abroad by the wind of gassy declamations about the magnificence of Union, and you will have Union–the Union of Negation, the Union of Vacuum, the Union of *Agreement about Nothing*.'[7]

---

[1] *The Wesleyan Methodist*, November 1922, p. 1.
[2] *M.T.*, 2 January 1919, p. 4; 6 January 1919, p. 3; 20 March 1919, p. 8; 3 April 1919, p. 7; 1 January 1920, p. 2; 20 May 1920, p. 11.
[3] *M.T.*, 5 February 1920, pp. 10–11; 12 February 1920, p. 6; *M.R.*, 22 January 1920, p. 6; 5 February 1920, p. 6; 1 April 1920, p. 13.
[4] *M.R.*, 15 April 1920, p. 5; 24 June 1920, p. 13.
[5] *Ibid.*, 25 March 1920, p. 4.
[6] *Ibid.*, 15 April 1920, p. 5; 6 May 1920, p. 4.
[7] *Journal of the Wesley Bible Union*, January 1920, p. 19.

But all were agreed upon the necessity of preserving the Wesleyan heritage from the unionists' depredations.

Non-Wesleyan opposition long remained unorganized but vocal. Many Primitive and United Methodists preferred the United Methodist constitution to that of the *Tentative Scheme*.[1] They were also aggrieved by the doctrinal proposals. One Primitive Methodist minister denied that 'the New Age demands a reversal to the interpretations of John Wesley. . . . Frankly, many of us DON'T believe what John Wesley believed, and for all the Conferences in the world we are not going to pretend that we do.' Such liberals were also dissatisfied by the proposed immutability of the Methodist Church doctrinal formula.[2]

Their opposition was supplemented from the conservative wing of Primitive and United Methodism. Mr. John Whittaker, a Primitive Methodist of Baildon, in attacking union, declared, 'The desire for latitudinarianism has wrought untold mischief in our Church. Theosophy, Swedenborgianism, Unitarianism and even Agnosticism are rampant to-day within our borders. It is time the Church was purged.'[3]

Opposition was also expressed to the sacramental proposals. The United Methodist, Councillor H. W. Surtees, confusing, as some tended to do, previous and present denominational allegiance, declared, 'Free Methodism has always held that whatever was done by a minister could be equally done by a layman. . . . The vital objection to the proposed scheme from a Free Methodist point of view is that it confers on the ministry a power and exalts its authority at the expense of the heritage of the Church.'[4]

The criticism drew much from the democratic ideology of reformed Methodism. Methodism united, said Guttery, had to be 'a great spiritual democracy', which proclaimed 'the spiritual identity of all men before the Atoning work of our Lord'. A Primitive Methodist layman, Mr. Thomas Tompkins, claimed that

'The Primitive Methodist Church believes in the right of all believers. The Sunday-school teacher, local preacher, and class leader, can be as much called of God as the minister. The agricultural labourer and chimney sweep may become saints and equal in power to the President and Secretary of Conference.'

[1] *P.M.L.*, 20 June 1918, p. 349; *U.M.*, 25 April 1918, p. 193.
[2] *P.M.L.*, 8 January 1920, p. 23; *United Methodist Magazine*, May 1920, pp. 131–2.
[3] *P.M.L.*, 3 March 1921, p. 329.
[4] *U.M.*, 14 September 1922, p. 440.

But 'the present scheme of union denies this'.[1]

The 1920 Conferences had the *Tentative Scheme* before them. The United Committee also provided them with an ingenious resolution declaring that 'the scheme . . . affords ground for hope that a satisfactory basis of Union can be found', and requiring the districts to vote on the details of the *Scheme*, but not on the principle of union, a procedure calculated to commit the denominations to union before they even voted on it. Horton recommended the *Scheme* to the Primitive Methodist Conference, saying that it was 'an amalgamation of the best in all the three constitutions. It had not been won by the employment of dexterous little diplomacies, nor by the spirit of the market-place, but by the spirit of the Upper Room . . . not one section of the three Churches was sacrificing a single vital principle.' There was little opposition in either the Primitive or United Methodist Conferences. The *Scheme* went to the districts.

Feelings were high in the Wesleyan Conference. French spoke 'with little excitement and few adjectives', but Rattenbury was 'keen, hot and red-faced'. The opposition offended the unionists as wreckers and crypto-Romanists. The unionists offended the opposition by the sleight of hand of their resolution. For the Other Side, Sir George Smith carried a notable amendment, eliminating all reference to 'a satisfactory basis'. The *Scheme* went naked to the synods.[2]

The United Committee now busied itself with propaganda. A set of ten pamphlets was produced and distributed to the districts. The newspapers strongly advocated union and a series of public meetings was held. French spoke to at least twenty-three between October 1920 and April 1921.

Although liberal Methodist opposition was still weak, Wesleyan anti-unionists were stirred into action by the coming synods and the new possibilities of union with the Church of England held out by the Lambeth Appeal.[3] The Wesleyan opposition met at the Kingsway Hall on 26 November 1920. The meeting, which the *Methodist Times* found 'bellicose', formed itself into the 'Other Side' organization. The Rev. J. H. Rider, Chairman of the Cornwall District, was made chairman, his brother, Mr. James Rider, treasurer, and Bevan Shepherd and Clucas, secretaries. Rattenbury sat on the committee. The Other Side raised a propaganda fund and, by February 1921, had head-

[1] *P.M.L.*, 7 October 1920, p. 578; 19 January 1922, p. 39.
[2] *P.M.L.*, 24 June 1920, pp. 395–7; *U.M.*, 15 July 1920, pp. 348–9; *M.R.*, 22 July 1920, pp. 14–16; 29 July 1920, p. 7.
[3] *M.R.*, 16 September 1920, p. 13; *U.M.*, 14 April 1921, p. 173; 5 May 1921, p. 212; 26 May 1921, p. 247.

quarters in London and Liverpool. By November 1922 it had secretaries in 75 per cent of circuits.[1]

Some Wesleyans thought reconciliation necessary. The Rev. Rowland Major and Mr. Arnold Williams, moderate critics of the *Scheme*, produced an 'Eirenicon', in December 1920, advocating some form of Methodist federation. After perfunctory respects were paid to it, the 'Eirenicon' disappeared.[2] The purpose of the Other Side was to agitate the Connexion and this it did.

The districts voted in May 1921. Despite the efforts of the Other Side, which was largely ministerial in complexion and 'conferential' in outlook, Wesleyan laymen found the *Scheme* much more acceptable than their less articulate and organized liberal Methodist fellows did. A minority of Wesleyan laymen shared the concern of conservative ministers, and rejected the *Scheme*'s attacks on the Ministerial Session, ministerial stationing and ministerial nomination of lay officials. But the majority of delegates to the Wesleyan synods at least acquiesced in the *Scheme*'s proposal to confer large new powers on them. A majority of Primitive Methodist districts rejected an autonomous Ministerial Session and Conference authorization of lay administration. United Methodists strongly supported Primitive Methodist criticisms, and also called for local preachers to be *ex officio* members of the leaders' meeting. Doctrinal questions and traditional slogans such as 'Two to One' seemed relatively uninteresting.[3]

The districts were severe enough with the *Scheme* to make the United Committee decide to postpone a similar vote in the quarterly meetings, especially since the parts of the *Scheme* the districts found most offensive were those essential to union. Non-Wesleyan leaders did their best to minimize this. David Brook insisted that 'the suggestions from the United Methodist synods were amendments which they would like to see carried out, but their Church liked Union better . . .

---

[1] *M.T.*, 2 December 1920, pp. 3–4; *The Other Side. Methodist Union*, n.d.; *Methodist Union–Manifesto of Progressives*, n.d., p. 2; *M.R.*, 10 February 1921, p. 3; *W.M.*, November 1922, p. 11.

[2] *M.R.*, 13 January 1921, p. 13; *M.T.*, 16 December 1920, pp. 3, 11; 23 December 1920, p. 6; 30 December 1920, p. 6; 6 January 1921, p. 6.

[3] *Methodist Union. Analysis of the Suggestions of the Wesleyan Synods; Methodist Union. Analysis of the Amendments of the Primitive Methodist Synods; Findings of the Primitive Methodist District Committees and Synods on Methodist Union; Methodist Union. The United Methodist District Meetings (May, 1921) and the Tentative Scheme of Union; Methodist Union. Suggestions for Amendments of the Scheme from the United Methodist District Meetings.*

and they were not to be regarded as fatal to the acceptance of Union'.[1]

The Primitive and United Methodist Conferences voted 97 per cent and 99·6 per cent for the Committee to continue work, despite the districts' extensive criticisms. One observer justly complained that the Primitive Methodist Conference did not 'reflect the true feeling throughout the Connexion'. The Wesleyan Conference was again more critical. 31·3 per cent of the Representative Session supported Rattenbury when he moved that 'the time is not yet ripe for Organic Union of the type set forth in the tentative Scheme', and urged that the committee consider alternative proposals. But 60 per cent of the Session voted for Hornabrook's amendment replacing the substantive resolution's hope 'that a satisfactory basis will be found', with the hope that the 'difficulties are not insoluble'. The Session voted 85·8 per cent for the Committee's resolution thus amended. The Pastoral Session discreetly acquiesced in this.[2]

## Concessions and Criticisms, 1921–4

Primitive and United Methodist delegates now tried to get some concessions for their districts. But Wesleyan delegates rejected a plea for subordination of the Ministerial to the Representative Session, and obliged their colleagues to rewrite the doctrinal clause in Wesley's favour. 'Wesley's Standards' were no longer to be described as 'subject to the Divine Revelation recorded in the Holy Scriptures', but as 'based upon' this revelation. This change positively raised Wesley's status by asserting that he was 'based upon' the Bible.

But a type of compromise was reached on the sacramental proposals. The Wesleyans wanted conference authorization or even ordination of lay administration, which would thus cease to be lay. Non-Wesleyan opinion strongly demanded continuation of informal appointment by the quarterly meeting. The Committee came upon 'a happy deliverance': Dedication in Synod. The term could suggest ordination or not according to preference; the court stood midway between quarterly meeting and conference. One commentator noted that 'the ardent unionist' suddenly found 'more blue in the sky than he has ever seen before'.[3]

[1] Meetings of 2 and 3 June 1921, in *Minutes of the Wesleyan Methodist Union Committee, etc., 1919–1921.*

[2] *P.M.L.*, 23 June 1921, p. 394; 14 July 1921, p. 447; *U.M.*, 21 July 1921, pp. 348, 356; *M.R.*, 21 July 1921, pp. 4–5; 28 July 1921, p. 5.

[3] *P.M.L.*, 28 July 1921, p. 480; *U.M.*, 5 February 1920, p. 62; *M.T.*, 16 February 1922, p. 5; Meetings of 31 August 1921 and 28 September 1921, in *Primitive Methodist Committees . . .*; Meetings of October 1921–January 1922, in *United Committee Minutes, etc., 1921–1925.*

Despite internal difficulties, the Committee's public relations were highly efficient. 'Throughout the length and breadth of the land meetings were held, impassioned pro-union speeches were delivered in a setting replete with massed choirs and old Methodist hymns and tunes, with a Press reporter at each who . . . made as much of his job as he could.' Meetings were supported by a press campaign, some of it allegedly subsidized, and the Committee itself issued a great deal of literature.[1]

But all this propaganda did not remove liberal Methodists' increasing and not unjustified distrust of 'our representatives on the Committee'. In July and August 1922, Surtees, Sir Walter Essex, the wallpaper manufacturer, and the Rev. John Higman appealed for United Methodist action against 'government by the priest' and 'Mandarin Methodism'.[2] The new group, largely and self-consciously ex-Free Methodist, called itself the 'Progressives'.[3]

The Progressives had a simple case. As Higman put it,

'There are two distinct types of Methodism in England–the specific Wesleyan type and that for which the United . . . and Primitive Methodist Churches have stood since their origin . . . the two types cannot be fused without sacrifice of principle on both sides. . . . Surely we ought not to go back on our history. Our founders did not fight for mere expediency. They gave up much for freedom, for the principles of true democracy in Church government, and for the principle of the "priesthood of all believers".'

The greatest surrender of all in Progressive eyes was acceptance of the Ministerial Session, which meant that 'The voice of Christ in the general body of his people will be subject to the uncontrolled decisions of a ministerial aristocracy'. Progressives expressed some interest in union, but their ecumenicalism was probably defined by 'Local', who wrote, 'I suggest we scrap the Scheme and join up with the Primitive Methodists only.'[4]

[1] *The Wesleyan Methodist Gazette*, April 1927, p. 1; *M.R.*, 16 November 1922, p. 3; *The Schedule Indicating the Changes in the Scheme for Union as Compared with the Existing Constitutions and Financial Statement* (Methodist Archives copy); *W.M.*, 17 May 1923, p. 10.

[2] *U.M.*, 31 August 1922, p. 416; 9 January 1913, p. 101; 11 November 1920, p. 550; 20 July 1922, p. 346; 23 February 1922, p. 89; *M.U. Protest of Progressives*.

[3] *U.M.*, 27 July 1922, pp. 357, 369.

[4] *Methodist Union. Manifesto of Progressives*, p. 6; John Higman, *Ought We to Accept a Ministerial Session and The Case against Methodist Union on the Proposed Basis*, n.d., pp. 5, 31–2; *U.M.*, 21 August 1924, p. 412.

The vigour of the unionist campaign also stimulated the Other Side. The Committee of the Other Side met in the Oak Room at the Kingsway Hall on 9 February 1922, in a mood of 'unqualified opposition'. Speakers 'felt they were up against Methodist wealth, the Methodist Press and the Conference platform', and demanded 'a fair and general hearing among the Methodist people'. The committee probably now hoped to start a newspaper.[1]

As a short-term measure, it returned to manifestos. Bevan Shepherd and seventy-five other ministers issued a manifesto denouncing the *Scheme* and declaring that 'the viewpoint of Wesleyan Methodism is essentially different from that of the other Methodist Churches in regard to doctrinal standards, the Sacraments, forms of worship, the ministry, party politics, and other matters'. By June 1922, the manifesto had received nearly 800 signatures from Wesleyan ministers, almost as many as had signed Shepherd's first manifesto.

The blue suddenly vanished from the unionist sky. In the spring of 1922, unionists apparently planned to take the amended *Scheme* through the 1922 Conferences, allow the quarterly meetings of March 1923 to vote for or against union itself, ratify this vote at the following Conferences and unite in 1925 or 1926. 'But the Manifesto had revealed so much opposition that it was considered that unless our people were more enlightened the success of the venture might be imperilled. It was therefore decided to prolong the educative process,' in other words, to make a second postponement and extend the propaganda campaign.[2]

The bluntness of Shepherd's manifesto caused great offence. Shortly after it appeared, Samuel Horton wrote to Rattenbury to protest at this development and to threaten him with an anti-Wesleyan coalition. 'It has been, and will . . . continue to be my policy', wrote Horton,

'to try to keep the atmosphere sweet between the two parties, for it will be a great calamity if we are driven into hostile camps . . . I think what you, and our Wesleyan friends generally, should make up your mind to, *is that Union is coming*: if not the larger Union that of the three lesser bodies,'

presumably Primitive and United Methodists and the Wesleyan Reform Union. '. . . I am perfectly certain', he concluded with a

[1] *M.R.*, 16 February 1922, p. 15; 23 February 1922, p. 15.
[2] *Ibid.*, 27 April 1922, p. 4; 15 June 1922, p. 14; 1 June 1922, p. 5; *M.T.*, 1 June 1922, p. 6.

nostalgic glance at 1916, 'that the negotiations which were going forward of another Union would have fructified ere this.'[1]

Peake took the manifesto as a personal insult. 'With hot indignation' he accused the manifesto of hinting that he took the 'grovelling view' of the minister as 'the paid agent of the Church', and told the United Committee that the manifesto's claims 'must be elucidated and substantiated', or else 'withdrawn', for 'If they represent real fact, they were fatal to Union, at any rate for the present.'[2] The Other Side were glad of an opportunity to attack the Primitive Methodists' famous modernist lay theologian. Rattenbury cited many 'essential differences', including Wesleyan use of liturgy, the Ministerial Session, and liberal Methodist lay administration of sacraments. Peake failed to answer Rattenbury's case.[3] Fortified by this victory, the Other Side proceeded to its autumn campaign. Funds were raised, five leaflets printed, and a nonce newspaper, *The Wesleyan Methodist*, made a one issue appearance in November 1922.[4]

'A world vision' of union in the 1922 Primitive Methodist Conference stimulated a 'weird thrill' of 'emotion, enthusiasm and assent', in which lay grievances virtually disappeared. Delegates could be seen 'breathing heavily with relief' when the Conference unanimously sent the *Scheme* to the December quarterly meetings with the benediction 'that neither on doctrine, nor on financial grounds, nor on questions of Church government, are there any obstacles to Methodist Union which, with goodwill, cannot be overcome'. The United Methodist Conference was only slightly less pliable.[5]

In the Wesleyan Conference, 31·7 per cent of the Representative, and 27·6 per cent of the Pastoral, Session opposed union. To Primitive and United Methodist disgust, French once more agreed to an amendment of the Committee's resolution, this time to allow the quarterly meetings to vote on the principle of union as well as the details of the *Scheme*.[6]

The quarterly meetings voted in December 1922 and January 1923. The meetings closely followed the districts' criticisms of 1921. French

---

[1] Samuel Horton–J. Ernest Rattenbury, 25 February 1922, in Rattenbury Papers.

[2] *P.M.L.*, 8 June 1922, p. 356; Meeting of 24 May 1922, in *United Committee Minutes* . . .

[3] *M.R.*, 8 June 1922, p. 6; 15 June 1922, p. 14.

[4] 'The Other Side', Nos. 1–5; *W.M.*, November 1922; *The Other Side. Methodist Union.*

[5] *P.M.L.*, 22 June 1922, p. 399; 29 June 1922, p. 418; *U.M.*, 20 July 1922, p. 346.

[6] *M.R.*, 27 July 1922, pp. 4–6; 3 August 1922, pp. 4–5.

calculated that 46·2 per cent of Wesleyan meetings accepted the *Scheme* without reserve. Non-Wesleyans were substantially less enthusiastic. After five years' work the United Committee had achieved very little.[1]

Public reactions to the votes varied. The *Recorder* declared, 'We have reason to congratulate ourselves . . . on the decisiveness of the vote.' Conference now had a 'popular mandate' for union, despite 'organized opposition and propaganda'. But the *Primitive Methodist Leader* did not feel so happy. 'Some advocates of Union profess a conviction that the returns are eminently satisfactory', it stated; 'but, at the moment, we cannot share that view.'[2]

Committee members recognized the seriousness of the situation. After an Other Side appeal for delay, Hornabrook carried through the Wesleyan Representative Session Committee on union a resolution stating that, because 'a considerable number of quarterly meetings are either opposed to union or not prepared to consent to it at present', a year's delay was desirable in order to consider 'certain amendments'. The United Committee would then report to the 1924 Conferences – 'by which time it is hoped that a satisfactory basis of Union may be found'. The Primitive *Methodist Leader* expressed 'keen disappointment' at the prospect of delay, but the Primitive Methodist Union Committee agreed that a year's delay was desirable.[3] It urged 'that the Ministerial Session should meet first and submit its findings to the Representative Session'. But the Wesleyans were unlikely to agree to this.[4]

The quarterly meeting votes pleased the Other Side. They soon demonstrated their confidence and strength. Regular weekly publication of the *Wesleyan Methodist* newspaper began on 10 May 1923. With the realization of this old Other Side ambition, union receded almost to the horizon. The newspaper would 'stand for great Wesleyan

---

[1] *Methodist Union. Wesleyan Methodist Church. Amendments and Suggestions from the Quarterly Meetings, December, 1922; The Methodist Union Scheme, 1922–1923. United Methodist Church Findings of the December Quarterly Meetings; The Methodist Union Scheme, 1922–1923. Primitive Methodist Church. Findings of the December Quarterly Meetings;* Meeting of the Representative Session Committee, 19 June 1923, in *United Committee Minutes . . .*

[2] *M.R.*, 14 December 1922, p. 3; 18 January 1923, p. 12; *P.M.L.*, 21 December 1922, p. 828.

[3] *M.R.*, 8 March 1923, p. 3; Meetings of February–April 1923, in *United Committee Minutes . . .*; *P.M.L.*, 8 March 1923, p. 152; Meetings of January–April 1923, in *Primitive Methodist Committees . . .*

[4] Meetings of April 1923, in *United Committee Minutes . . .*; *Primitive Methodist Committees . . .*

principles': 'the great evangelical doctrines of John Wesley', 'Wesleyan Methodism as the *via media* between Anglicanism and Nonconformity', and 'the policy', presumably the polity, 'of Wesleyan Methodism'.[1]

Peake expressed ecumenicalist gloom when he told the 1923 Primitive Methodist Conference 'they were now simply marking time' on union. Horton assured that gathering, 'The greatest difficulty for Primitive Methodists gathered about the idea of a ministerial session. Frankly, their representatives were not enamoured of it.' The delegates, reassured, voted unanimously for negotiations to continue. The *Wesleyan Methodist* commented sourly that the delegates 'have voted, as is their custom, according to the direction of their platform'. The United Methodist Conference had greater difficulties. Essex moved a lengthy resolution for a new and specifically 'reformed' scheme. Nine per cent of the Conference supported him, a considerable advance on 1922.[2]

The Wesleyan Conference was noisy and excited. When Mr. R. Wilberforce Allen condemned 'this "all or nothing" policy–the Scheme, the whole Scheme, and nothing but the Scheme', disorder was such that the President had to say 'I must ask the Conference to be quiet. Of course the Conference may express approval or disapproval but it is possible to overdo it.' Allen's amendment for 'alternative proposals' got 32·4 per cent, a slight improvement on the Other Side vote of 1922. In the Pastoral Session, Rattenbury and Rider repeatedly heckled French. The Session voted 36·6 per cent for 'alternative proposals', a considerable advance on the Other Side vote of the previous year, and the first occasion in which Pastoral Session opposition surpassed Representative.[3] The Other Side were now 'very well satisfied with themselves'.[4]

Unionists were now in a cautious mood. Despite their exuberant propaganda, opposition was gaining ground. The Other Side had more enthusiasm despite the illness of Rattenbury, and his absence in Italy from December 1924 to April 1925.[5] Anti-unionist ranks were strengthened by the emergence of an organized Primitive Methodist opposition.

The Rev. James Thorp regretted the absence of such an organization, in July 1923. The *Leader* declared, 'Our people may feel assured

[1] *W.M.*, 10 May 1923, p. 1; 17 May 1923, p. 1.
[2] *P.M.L.*, 21 June 1923, p. 399; *W.M.*, 28 June 1923, p. 1; *U.M.*, 19 July 1923, p. 348.
[3] *M.R.*, 26 July 1923, pp. 9–11; 2 August 1923, p. 6.
[4] *W.M.*, 26 July 1923, p. 13.
[5] *M.R.*, 24 July 1924, p. 6.

that the representatives of the Primitive Methodist Church' on the United Committee 'are pressing their views to the utmost'. But Primitive Methodists doubted, as United Methodists had doubted a year before. On 24 January 1924, Thorp, the Rev. Thomas Auty and Mr. John Whittaker advertised for support. The organization they led, which usually called itself 'The Primitive Methodist "Other Side"', was a vote of no confidence in Horton. Auty said that organization had been delayed 'in the hope that such action might be rendered unnecessary by the strong insistence of our representatives on the things for which as a Church we have stood'. The Primitive Methodist Other Side, centred in London, chiefly criticized the Ministerial Session, and other attacks on the privileges of Primitive Methodist laymen.[1]

*The* Scheme *Amended, 1923–4*

The quarterly meetings had reinforced the districts' demands for thorough amendment of the *Scheme*. But lay opposition would only be satisfied by elimination of those items of the *Scheme* which were essential to the union compromise: the Ministerial Session, 'Wesley's Standards' and lay administration. Ecumenicalists could either satisfy the laymen or secure union. They could not do both. But if these lay demands could not be satisfied, unionists all the more needed to satisfy enough denominational leaders, ministerial and lay, to present recalcitrant localities with a firm conference decision for union.

This necessity gave the union negotiations a curious twist. If ecumenicalists had sought to conciliate the laymen, they would have been most concerned with Primitive and United Methodist grievances, since these denominations' district and quarterly meetings were most critical of the *Scheme*. But as unionists were obliged to conciliate denominational leaders instead, they were bound to concentrate on Wesleyan grievances, since Primitive and United Methodist ministers and conference laymen were almost without exception for union, while a large minority of Wesleyan leaders were extremely hostile to union.

But Wesleyan unionists were willing and able to make small gestures to the non-Wesleyans. Probably in October 1923, the Wesleyans agreed on a 'Reasoned Statement as to the Necessity of the

[1] *P.M.L.*, 12 July 1923, p. 455; 25 October 1923, p. 690; 1 November 1923, p. 711; 15 November 1923, p. 743; 24 January 1924, p. 56; Meetings of 1 February 1924 and 26 March 1924, in *Primitive Methodist Committees . . .*; *P.M.L.*, 3 April 1924, p. 217; T. R. Auty, M. H. Bainton and W. Usher, *Methodist Union. The Case against the Scheme*, n.d., *passim*.

Representative Session . . . Meeting before the Ministerial Session'. The 'Statement' argued that priority of the Ministerial Session only made sense if the Representatives were to scrutinize its findings, and this would prevent the Representative Session from concentrating on 'great moral and religious questions of the utmost moment'. This scarcely satisfied liberal Methodist laymen, who preferred the opportunity to veto the Ministerial Session's decisions. But the 'Statement' enabled non-Wesleyan delegates to offer *some* reason for their refusal to secure priority of the Ministerial Session.[1]

In March 1924, Wesleyans made a more important proposal. The United Methodists still urged that local preachers like ministers should have *ex officio* seats in the leaders' meeting. Wesleyans agreed that the leaders' meeting could co-opt local preachers as members. As long as a local preacher remained in an ex-United Methodist chapel in the united church, he could be sure of a seat in the leaders' meeting. This compromise destroyed the last vestige of Eckett's reformed polity, and finally demoted the local preacher, but it did preserve the existing rights of thousands of United Methodists.[2]

Wesleyans were not willing to compromise on 'Wesley's Standards'. '*Generally* contained in Wesley's Notes . . . and . . . Sermons' continued to offend the Other Side, although Peake told French that, without the word, 'I shall find' the doctrinal clause 'much more difficult to defend to our people.' In December 1923, the Executive of the United Committee finally eliminated 'generally'. Non-Wesleyans were somewhat luckier in 1924. The draft doctrinal clause had long contained the phrase 'The Evangelical Doctrines which Methodism . . . holds'. High Wesleyans now objected to this. The phrase seemed either too vague or too narrow: either Methodism held other, unspecified doctrines; or it only held those doctrines which might properly be called 'evangelical'. In January 1924, they proposed to delete 'Evangelical'. By October the United Committee settled for a compromise offered by Peake and F. L. Wiseman: 'The doctrines of the Evangelical Faith which Methodism . . . holds.'[3]

While Wesleyans gained the alterations they wanted, at very little

[1] Meeting of 26 March 1924, in *Primitive Methodist Committees* . . .; *P.M.L.*, 20 December 1923, p. 833.

[2] *W.M.*, 3 April 1924, p. 1; 10 July 1924, p. 2.

[3] A. S. Peake–E. Aldom French, 29 December 1921, in Peake Papers; Meeting of 13 December 1923, in *United Committee Minutes* . . .; Meetings of Pastoral Session Committee, 10 January 1924, and of Representative Session Committee, 2 October 1924; A. S. Peake–E. Aldom French, 1 April 1924 (insert), in *United Committee Minutes* . . .

cost, non-Wesleyans struggled for some concessions to their denominations. Since the Ministerial Session seemed unshakeable, they were particularly eager to improve the future of lay administration, and in October 1923, the United Committee agreed that, whatever else, the 'existing exceptions to ministerial administration should not be interfered with'. In December, the Committee made a further apparent concession to non-Wesleyan opinion, replacing the unpopular provision for synod dedication with the formula, 'N.B. In certain exceptional cases where there has been a departure from the general usage' of ministerial administration 'it is recognized that time must be allowed for the attainment of uniformity of practice'. Wesleyans thought the new clause 'meets the position of all save the most recalcitrant'. But the 'N.B.', while postponing a decision on the sacraments obviously envisaged a decision in favour of 'uniformity' of ministerial administration.[1]

In March 1924, Hornabrook replaced the 'N.B.' with a very broad statement that 'The general usage of the three uniting Churches whereby the Sacrament of the Lord's Supper is administered by ministers shall continue wherever practicable to be observed.' He also introduced a formula on the ministry, written by G. G. Findlay. This declared that ministers had 'a principal and directing part' in shepherding the flock, but 'no exclusive title to the preaching of the gospel or the care of souls'. Conveniently, it made no reference to sacraments. It proved very popular.

Hornabrook's own sweeping formula did not. The three denominational secretaries produced a new draft in March 1924, which recognized that ministerial administration was and would be 'general usage'. 'Exceptions' were to be left 'until the Conference' of the united church 'is able to determine how best to provide for all the Methodist people to partake of the Sacrament with regularity and frequency'. The new clause did not guarantee the permanency of lay administration, but it did not exclude it either. With this non-Wesleyans had to be content.[2]

*The Quarterly Meetings, December 1924*

By the Conferences of 1924, unionists were depressed. Now all three

---

[1] Meeting of 13 December 1923, in *United Committee Minutes* . . .; *M.T.* 17 January 1924, pp. 3, 5.

[2] *P.M.L.*, 3 April 1924, p. 217; *U.M.*, 3 April 1924, p. 163; *P.M.L.*, 28 April 1921, p. 260; 7 July 1921, p. 425; 29 May 1924, p. 340; Meeting of 27 March 1924, in *United Committee Minutes* . . .; *M.T.*, 25 March 1920, p. 4; Meeting of 19 May 1924, in *United Committee Minutes* . . .

denominations had organized opposition. Negotiation in committee was slow, intricate and dispiriting. 'It has been suggested', noted the *Recorder*, that ' "Methodist Union is dead".' The paper felt this was 'The Crisis'. The drift had to be stopped and 'disunion', which was contrary to 'the mind and will of Christ', ended. It had to be ended soon, for 'The Church of Christ cannot wait until all are agreed.'[1]

But the crisis did not materialize in the Primitive or United Methodist Conferences which sent the *Scheme* to the quarterly meetings for the decisive vote, with the declaration that 'the Scheme . . . affords a basis of Union which would ensure harmonious working without the sacrifice of any principle which is vital to Methodism'.[2]

The Wesleyan Conference made up for this lack of fireworks. Amos Burnet, a leading anti-unionist, was President. Lidgett and W. Russell Maltby delivered speeches of great feeling to the Representative Session. Defeat of union would be 'the deadliest blow to Christian Reunion all over the world', said Maltby. He added, 'I shall know quite well in my soul that if this thing goes on and is defeated, sometimes by argument and sometimes by delay – I shall know that I belong to a Church that made the refusal. That is what it means and I do not know in the end quite where it will lead us.' Thirty-one per cent voted for the Other Side's amendment, slightly less than the previous year. The *Wesleyan Methodist* was disappointed. Looking to the Pastoral Session, it declared severely, 'It is time that the matter was taken seriously by the ministers of Methodism. The fear of differing from the representatives has been emphasized repeatedly at past Conferences and timid souls have not given utterance to all that was in them.'[3]

The 'timid souls' responded to the challenge. The Rev. W. H. Armstrong moved an amendment declaring 'that the present scheme must be amended in important particulars'. After a short debate a vote was taken. Two hundred and twenty-five votes were cast for the amendment, 223 against, an Other Side majority of 50·2 per cent. The crisis had come. Unionists panicked. Maltby 'on a point of order asked the President whether he, as President, could not find some way of deferring the decision. This was quite the most heated and confusing atmosphere he had ever known in Conference.' Burnet 'said Mr. Maltby had exhausted his point of order. He could find no way.' But Hornabrook could. 'No greater disaster' could be imagined than persistence with Armstrong's amendment, he said, and moved a re-

[1] *M.R.*, 15 May 1924, p. 12.
[2] *P.M.L.*, 19 June 1924, p. 399; 3 July 1924, p. 439; 2 October 1924, p. 647.
[3] *M.R.*, 24 July 1924, pp. 4–8; *W.M.*, 24 July 1924, p. 1.

assuringly vague resolution that 'the judgement of the Local Courts in all three churches must be ascertained' before any final decision.

This amendment apparently *excluded* Armstrong's. It was moved and carried; and then the substantive vote, with this addition, but with no reference to Armstrong's amendment, was itself given a final vote. The Other Side vote suddenly collapsed to 20·2 per cent. An observer commented, 'I do not think that the "Other Side" really wanted to carry the thing as far as it went. There was a certain drawing back – at once.'[1] The Other Side did not want union, but they were afraid to reject it. Might they not, as ecumenicalists claimed, be opposing 'the mind and will of Christ'? Such doubt was fatal to the Other Side.

In the autumn the unionists launched a new propaganda campaign. The great virtues of union were proclaimed: 'The whole Methodist Church will enter upon a new era of extension which will rival the early days.' Doubtful liberal Methodists were told that the *Scheme* was 'liberal, democratic and comprehensive. . . . A liberal Methodism has been the ideal of the Union Committee.' Anxious members and officials of all denominations were reassured that 'Should Methodist Union be consummated there need be no misgiving concerning its effect on local Churches. The Union of local Churches will only take place where this is desired by the local Churches themselves. . . . There will be no coercion from any quarter.'[2]

In December 1924 and January 1925, the quarterly meetings voted on the question, 'Are you in favour of Organic Union of the Wesleyan Methodist and the Primitive Methodist and the United Methodist Churches on the basis of the Scheme now submitted?' Primitive Methodist officials voted 71·2 per cent in favour; United Methodist officials, 66·1 per cent; Wesleyan, 67·1 per cent.[3] Despite its vastly greater strength, the Other Side had no bigger following in the country than the feeble non-Wesleyan opposition groups. The Other Side was dominated by ministerial concerns and, as the votes of 1922–3 had shown, Wesleyan laymen cared little for the preservation of ministerial privileges. United Methodist and Primitive Methodist laymen cared a good deal for the preservation of their privileges. But faced with near unanimous conference decisions for union, many were

[1] *M.R.*, 31 July 1924, pp. 5–6, 15; *W.M.*, 31 July 1924, p. 1.

[2] *M.R.*, 23 October 1924, p. 8; *P.M.L.*, 27 November 1924, p. 776; *Primitive Methodist Church. Methodist Union Committee. Issued by the Authority of Conference. The Liberal Basis of the Scheme*, n.d., *passim* (insert in *Primitive Methodist Committee* . . .).

[3] Calculations based on official returns.

willing to acquiesce. The result was the same in each denomination; a considerable majority of lay officials accepted union, a considerable minority did not.

*Conciliation, January–September 1925*

The 30 per cent minority in Primitive and United Methodist quarterly meetings paled beside the 90 per cent majority in conference. But the 30 per cent minority in the Wesleyan quarterly meetings and the Wesleyan Conference confirmed and reinforced each other. The (mainly ministerial) Primitive and United Methodist unionists did not intend to be kept out of a large and dramatic union project by the obscurantism of lay officials. Wesleyan unionists, especially the ministers, felt less happy about alienating a large section of their colleagues and acquaintances backed, as Rattenbury liked to claim, and the votes seemed to suggest, by a section of Wesleyanism as big as the entire United Methodist Church.

Unionists were divided. 'Vigilant', in the *Primitive Methodist Leader*, rejected the idea of 'any new conditions of peace'. Negotiations with the non-Wesleyan minority would wreck the *Scheme*; and further concessions to the Other Side, the only other feasible course, 'would be the signal for new opposition in the minor bodies'. Perks, who was now seventy-six, had no sympathy with the Other Side, and was eager to see Methodism united. Rider told Rattenbury, still in Italy, in January 1925, 'Perks has had a luncheon with some of his cronies and he seems determined to push the matter through.' Perks probably hoped for union in 1928.[1]

But many Wesleyans disagreed. John Hornabrook claimed to be dispassionate about union. He had 'tremendous hold . . . upon the hearts and imagination of Primitive Methodism', but was greatly respected by Other Side leaders.[2] Hornabrook's advocacy of conciliation was supported by two successive Wesleyan Temperance Secretaries, the Rev. J. Alfred Sharp, and the Rev. Henry Carter. Sharp was a strong evangelical sympathetic to Anglicanism. Although a friend of French's, he had Armstrong as his biographer.[3] Carter, a moderate unionist, had advocated conciliation since 1920.[4]

The possibility of conciliation was increased by the Other Side's

---

[1] *M.T.*, 5 February 1925, p. 4; *P.M.L.*, 12 February 1925, p. 99; J. Herbert Rider–J. Ernest Rattenbury, 24 January 1925, in Rattenbury Papers; *M.T.*, 10 September 1925, p. 6.

[2] *P.M.L.*, 28 October 1920, p. 614; *M.R.*, 17 June 1926, p. 7.

[3] Walter H. Armstrong, *John Alfred Sharp. A Memoir*, London, 1932, p. 83.

[4] E. C. Urwin, *Henry Carter*, London, 1955, p. 21; *M.R.*, 8 July 1920, p. 14.

unease after the Armstrong amendment. The momentary triumph of the Other Side revealed its dilemma. Persistent obstruction of the unionist majority might end in an open split. John Rattenbury had opposed the reformers' onslaughts. Could his grandson divide Wesleyanism in the attempt to resist the reformers' descendants? Hornabrook warned Rattenbury early in 1925, 'It behoves those of us who attempt to guide the opinion of the Church, to act with great caution, otherwise in our endeavour to preserve what in the judgement of many of us is not vital to Methodism, as we know it, Methodism will be wrecked.' Rattenbury assured Carter he would be sympathetic to anything which 'will make for peace'.[1] Conciliation also made tactical sense. The Other Side had been obliged to close the *Wesleyan Methodist* on 1 January 1925. This did not eliminate financial difficulties. Rider told Rattenbury at the end of January, 'Money is coming in very slowly and this worries me a lot.'[2]

By the end of March, Hornabrook had converted Perks to gradualism, and again advocated the cause of those who urged 'further delay in the hope of practical unanimity'. Non-Wesleyans were 'a shade disappointed'. But Hornabrook won them over with 'a masterly speech'.[3]

Informal discussions with the Other Side began in March 1925 and lasted at least until July.[4] Perks and French offered the Other Side an understanding. Taking an idea from the United Methodist Church Act, which required a 75 per cent vote for union with any other denomination, they proposed Methodist union should be conditional on such a vote. In effect unionists offered to wait for union till they could satisfy enough Other Siders to reduce the minority's vote to 25 per cent. Many moderate Other Siders accepted this, though extremists strongly disapproved.[5]

But the Other Side wanted to alter the *Scheme* as well as delay union. On 30 April, Rattenbury appeared at the United Committee. The Committee proposed that the Conferences should declare in favour of union; while it continued with 'further consideration' of the

---

[1] John Hornabrook–J. Ernest Rattenbury, 3 April 1925; J. Ernest Rattenbury–Henry Carter (draft) in Rattenbury Papers.
[2] *W.M.*, 1 January 1925, p. 1; J. Herbert Rider–J. Ernest Rattenbury, 24 January 1925, in Rattenbury Papers.
[3] John Hornabrook–J. Ernest Rattenbury, 16 January 1925 and 30 March 1925, in Rattenbury Papers; *M.T.*, 12 February 1925; p. 11; *M.R.*, 7 May 1925, p. 3.
[4] *M.T.*, 26 March 1925, p. 3; 30 July 1925, p. 10.
[5] *Ibid.*, 30 September 1926, p. 5; *M.R.*, 28 July 1927, p. 5; 21 July 1927, p. 5; *W.M. Gazette*, April 1927, p. 2; *M.R.*, 23 July 1925, p. 8.

*Scheme*, consistent with the 'general principles' already accepted, and studied 'the methods and stages by which Union . . . may be carried out'. Rattenbury was expected 'to bury the hatchet'. Instead, 'To the general surprise and dismay, he made one of the most uncompromising speeches of the whole controversy.'[1] The speech demonstrated, as Rattenbury intended, that the *Scheme* would have to be recast.

Opposition scarcely troubled the Primitive and United Methodist Conferences which both voted by 93 per cent to accept Methodist Union and the 75 per cent formula; and to hold a district vote on an Enabling Bill to give the necessary legal sanction to union.[2] The Wesleyan Representative Session debate was vigorous and protracted. Burnet moved that 'the Conference is quite unable at the present moment to declare in favour of Methodist Union on the basis of the only Scheme before it', but was only supported by 27·3 per cent. The committee resolutions were carried – that in favour of union by 75·8 per cent vote. According to the 75 per cent formula, the Representative Session had in fact just voted in favour of union by five votes in 523. The pastors had recovered some of their confidence since the Armstrong amendment. The Pastoral Session voted in favour of union, but by a mere 64 per cent. It had fallen 11 per cent short, and was now in direct and open conflict with the Representative Session.[3]

Wesleyan obduracy heightened non-Wesleyan unease. Elimination, or even subordination, of the Ministerial Session, was evidently impossible. Some accused non-Wesleyan leaders of deception. Richard Pyke wrote in the *United Methodist*,

> 'It has frequently been stated that somehow it was not made known to our people generally that a Pastoral Session was a *sine qua non* on the part of the Wesleyans. We were thought to have agreed to a condition generally obnoxious. . . . A little group of eager officials, it was said, had secretly sold the pass; the people were committed but not informed.'

Pyke quoted the printed report of 1919, which provided for 'a session of the ministerial representatives to Conference', and claimed that 'at the first possible moment, we made known what was supposed to have been kept secret'.[4] Nobody doubted that the Ministerial Session was

---

[1] *M.T.*, 7 May 1925, p. 8.
[2] *P.M.L.*, 18 June 1925, p. 399; *U.M.*, 16 July 1925, pp. 342–3.
[3] *M.R.*, 23 July 1925, pp. 4–8; 30 July 1925, pp. 4–7.
[4] *U.M.*, 13 March 1925, p. 121.

in the *Scheme*, after all, thousands had voted against it. But they now knew that it was a '*sine qua non*', and their votes had been wasted. The Progressives could expect little more.

Primitive Methodist leaders went a little farther in conciliating their defeated opponents, whom they met at Abbeydale, Sheffield, on 18 September 1925. The union committee agreed that informal facilities would be available for ministers conscientiously contracting out of the united church, but they refused to give legal commitments. Unionists cited both the pledge that no existing 'exceptions' to ministerial administration of sacraments would be interfered with, and the provisions of the Three Secretaries' Clause.[1] 'Assurance was given that the present practice in each Church is maintained, and the liberty of the laymen in no way endangered.' The anti-unionists also wanted the Representative Session to have 'the last word'. The unionists agreed that this should be definitely assured. After the Abbeydale meeting, two opposition leaders joined the Primitive Methodist Union Committee.[2]

*The Two Clauses, 1925–6*

But unionists now concentrated on conciliating the Other Side. Since the Other Side was willing to accept the constitutional provisions, this meant rewriting the doctrinal and sacramental clauses of the *Scheme*. (See Appendix 2.)

The doctrinal clause was strengthened by a reference to Wesley's doctrine of scriptural holiness or Christian perfection. This was finally adopted in the form: 'The Methodist Church . . . ever remembers that in the Providence of God Methodism was raised up to spread Scriptural Holiness through the land by proclamation of the Evangelical Faith and declares its unfaltering resolve to be true to its Divinely appointed Mission.'

A disciplinary statement, that the Methodist preachers, both ministerial and lay (no doubt a provision with Peake in mind) were pledged to 'Wesley's Standards', was added; although the Pastoral Session Union Committee softened this provision by the inclusion of a statement by the Wesleyan Conference of 1919. This statement, which Brook and Peake favoured, declared that the 'Standards'

'were not intended to impose a system of formal or speculative theology on our preachers, but to set up standards of preaching and

[1] See p. 271 above.
[2] Abbeydale Meeting (insert) and Meeting of 2 October 1925, in *Primitive Methodist Committees* . . .

belief which should secure loyalty to the fundamental truths of the Gospel of Redemption, and insure the Church's continued witness to the realities of the Christian experience of Salvation.'

The Wesleyans attempted to strengthen the Scriptures also. Sharp suggested replacing the modernist formula that Methodism holds 'The Doctrines of the Evangelical Faith . . . based upon the Divine Revelation recorded in the Holy Scriptures' with the stricter formula, 'The Methodist Church . . . holds the doctrines of the Christian faith as set forth in the New Testament Scriptures.' Peake and Lidgett rejected this.

Apparently on behalf of the Other Side, Sharp also proposed a formula setting the united church in the context of Christianity. This began: 'The Methodist Church' inherits 'the historic faith of Christendom which found expression in the Ecumenical creeds of the early and undivided Church'. Sharp, who was known for 'sturdy Protestantism', is unlikely to have drafted this exceedingly 'Catholic' formula, although he may have been responsible for the statement which followed it, that the Methodist Church emphasizes 'those Evangelical truths which are generally held by the Reformed Churches'.

Lidgett and Peake could not stomach 'the early and undivided Church'. After some vicissitudes this section was rewritten to read: 'The Methodist Church claims and cherishes its place in the Holy Catholic Church which is the Body of Christ. It rejoices in the inheritance of the apostolic faith.' Sharp's general but fairly unexceptionable 'Reformed' section was replaced by Lidgett and Peake with the declaration that the Methodist Church 'loyally accepts the fundamental principles of the Historic Creeds of the Protestant Reformation', a curiously thoughtless formula literally committing Methodism to both Arminianism and Calvinism.

Thus the position of Wesley was greatly strengthened in the new doctrinal clause, while the Methodist Church was firmly if clumsily set in the wider Christian context, but the attempt to reduce the modernist tone of the doctrinal formula failed.[1]

While Sharp was reorganizing the doctrinal clause, Rattenbury was attempting to reconstruct the clause on sacraments and the ministry under the surveillance of a committee consisting of Brook, Hornabrook and Peake. When the new clause emerged, it contained an

[1] Pastoral Session Committee of 18 November 1925, in *United Committee Minutes, etc., 1925–1928*; *P.M.L.*, 19 February 1920, p. 121; *U.M.*, 22 October 1925, p. 518; *M.R.*, 6 May 1926, pp. 1, 16; Meetings of December 1925–February 1926, in *United Committee Minutes* . . .

attempt at a general theory of the ministry. Armstrong proposed a brief summary of Findlay's 1908 statement which, successively refined by Rattenbury and Brook, Hornabrook and Peake, read: 'The Methodist Church holds the doctrine of the priesthood of all believers and consequently believes that no priesthood exists which belongs exclusively to a particular order or class of men.' This summary co-existed tautologously with the 1908 statement itself, and was meant perhaps as a specific 'setting' for the sacramental question.

Rattenbury's draft also included the 'Order not Orders' theory in the words, 'not because of any inherent priestly virtue in the office, but for the sake of Church Order, the ministers of the United Church are set apart by ordination to the ministry of Word and Sacrament'.

A third element in the theoretical section of the new clause read, in Rattenbury's draft, 'But in the exercise of its corporate life and worship our Church demands special qualities for the performance of special duties and thus acknowledges the principle of representative selection.' Such a 'Protestant' and liberal Methodist formula is unlikely to have come from Rattenbury and is probably a concession to the non-Wesleyans written by Peake, whose considered statement on the ministry in 1921 concentrated on the idea of representation. The formula is crudely drafted, especially in the Brook–Hornabrook–Peake stage of its development, in which the final phrase reads, 'and thus the principle of representative selection is recognized'.

Despite the formula's logical and semantic difficulties, centred on the meaningless 'thus', the 'representative selection' section is probably simply a needlessly bemusing way of saying, 'The tasks of the ministry require expertise, and therefore a body of full-time experts. The Church selects these experts. They are its representatives.' Thus translated, the formula summarizes the non-Wesleyan doctrine of the ministry from Cooke to Peake, but has little in common with the rest of the theoretical section.

Rattenbury followed his version of the theoretical section with a disciplinary clause comparable to that on doctrine. The Brook–Hornabrook–Peake draft read, that the 'preachers, itinerant and lay, are examined, tested and approved before they are authorized to minister in holy things'.

Rattenbury also attempted to eliminate the 'Exceptions to the general usage' of ministerial administration. He attributed them, as the alternative clause of 1920 had done, to 'inadequate' 'Ministerial supply'; stated that they would continue during the 'transitional' period of the united church's life; and declared that, when the new church was entirely united in each locality and overlap was altogether eliminated, 'the general usage of administration by ministers will continue'. The Brook–Hornabrook–Peake draft merely eliminated the reference to ministerial supply. But while Rattenbury thought lay administration would be terminated, non-Wesleyans were confident that it would continue, despite their acquiescence in Rattenbury's formula.

The Primitive Methodist Union Committee declared, on 23 February 1926, 'the continuity of Lay Administration is secured in the United Church'. According to the *United Methodist*, on 13 October 1925, in the United Committee, Brook

> 'made it very plain that not only must laymen be as free to administer the sacrament as an ordained minister, but that this is not to be conceded as a favour, or as a temporary provision . . . there can be no mistake that the question of a layman administering the Sacrament of the Lord's Supper is one of principle.'

In July 1926, Brook was allegedly 'glorying in the coming of lay administration in the largest non-Episcopal Church'. The programme of union and reform had done very little about the Ministerial Session, but Brook might well 'glory', for despite Rattenbury's efforts, lay administration was to survive, as a matter of principle, in the united church.

Rattenbury had little more success in trying to control the operation of lay administration. In his scheme, the circuit would nominate 'persons', and Conference would 'authorize', this act being 'expressed by a certificate signed by the President'. Later Rider carried an amendment making this authorization annual. The presidential certificate, clearly intended as an act of quasi-ordination by the 'chief pastoral officer', as Rigg called him, was neatly amended, probably by Hornabrook, by adding the secretary of conference to the certification process. The secretary was also a minister, but one to whom no one attributed episcopal functions. This slight change turned certification from quasi-ordination to administrative routine.[1]

The introduction of 'representative selection'; the non-Wesleyan refusal to accept Rattenbury's interpretation of the 'exceptions' formula; and the secretary's share in certification, indicated the limits on the Other Side's attempt to eliminate lay administration, and the

[1] *U.M.*, 22 October 1925, pp. 515, 518; *P.M.L.*, 7 July 1921, p. 425; 25 March 1920, p. 201; *M.R.*, 29 July 1926, p. 4; Meetings of November 1925–February 1926, in *United Committee Minutes . . .*; Meeting of 23 February 1926, in *Primitive Methodist Committees . . .*; *U.M.*, 22 April 1926, p. 186.

doctrines that lay behind it. But the new version of the sacramental clause was decidedly more respectable, more ministerial, more Wesleyan than the old. Just as the Wesleyans could have the Ministerial Session, on non-Wesleyan terms, the new clause finally demonstrated that the Primitive and United Methodists could have lay administration, on Wesleyan terms.

Non-Wesleyans believed they had lost ground in these crucial sections. The Primitive Methodist Union Committee resolved on 11 June 1926, 'We have accepted the foregoing amendments and additions to the Sacramental and Doctrinal Statement on the distinct understanding that our doing so will be regarded as a step towards reconciliation of the "Other Side" in the Wesleyan Methodist Church.' However, Wesleyans and non-Wesleyans alike believed these concessions would suffice. A Wesleyan claimed that 'the acceptance' of 'the two clauses' would 'make a great difference' to the Other Side. In February 1926, Peake hoped that 'by the end of July the question of Methodist Union will be definitely settled one way or the other'.[1]

*Union by Stages, 1926–8*

When unionists offered the Other Side delay, the Other Side demanded alterations to the *Scheme*. Now the *Scheme* had been altered, the Other Side demanded delay. The Other Side had a lively sense of the differences between denominations, and feared disaster if they were suddenly and thoroughly amalgamated. These fears were exaggerated, while the time-span of any remotely acceptable period of delay and preparation for union, say ten years, was far too short to enable thorough convergence and reconciliation of differences. But the basic assumption underlying this view, that unification of diverse religious traditions was a very slow process, was more realistic than some of the assumptions of ecumenicalism.

In April 1926, Armstrong, Rattenbury and Rider published a statement which recognized the value of the new draft of the two clauses, but insisted that 'there must be much clearer evidence of the general desire for Union among Methodists before steps that virtually commit us to Organic Union can be taken'.[2] Later, Rattenbury stated his personal dilemma: 'I love Methodism and don't want to see her wrecked. In my opinion the adoption of the Union Scheme at the

---

[1] *M.T.*, 7 May 1925, p. 8; Meeting of 11 June 1926, in *Primitive Methodist Committees* . . .; *U.M.*, 2 April 1926, p. 186; *M.R.*, 15 April 1926, p. 9; Peake–?, 10 February 1926, in Peake Papers.
[2] *M.T.*, 29 April 1926, p. 11.

present time or its withdrawal would be a tragic blunder.'[1] Rattenbury had come a long way since his 'last ditch' declaration of 1920. But he was not yet willing to accept the *Scheme* outright. Instead he proposed a 'third way' between outright opposition and outright acceptance. The three denominations should at once enter on a scheme of 'unification by stages', involving amalgamation of departments and theological colleges, and encouragement of local unions 'especially in regard to the closing of superfluous chapels'. Union should be completed in twelve years, by 1938.[2]

The third way was propounded for the benefit of the May synods of 1926, which were to vote on the Enabling Bill necessary for union. Once the synods had given the necessary 75 per cent vote for the draft Bill further opposition was hopeless. Non-Wesleyan synods dutifully returned large majorities in favour of the Bill. But the delegates in the various Wesleyan Representative Sessions voted 65·9 per cent in favour, while those in the Pastoral Sessions voted 57·0 per cent in favour. Seventy-five per cent was nowhere in sight.[3]

When the Wesleyan Representative Session Committee on union met on 19 May 1926, 'a thin, chilling and depressing mist pervaded the room'. 'The long months of discussion, persuasion and mutual concession seem to have left things pretty much where they have always been', wrote the *United Methodist* despairingly. Non-Wesleyans felt they had been deceived. Dr. Joseph Lineham, a United Methodist ex-President, told the United Committee with 'great emotion', 'They had met the Wesleyan Other Side . . . on the . . . Doctrinal and Sacramental Clauses, and yet the Other Side had led the opposition to Union in the Synods as though nothing had happened.'[4]

Unionists approached the 1926 Conference in gloom. They proposed that the Conferences should now 'pronounce definitely upon the question'. At the Primitive Methodist Conference, 'Speaker after speaker . . . emphasized the claim that the Wesleyan Conference shall now declare itself irrevocably.' If that body did not do so, it was felt, 'then there will be trouble'. But the Primitive Methodist Conference voted 86·5 per cent to accept the *Scheme*; and although the Progressives got 12·5 per cent of the vote on one amendment in the United

[1] *M.T.*, 27 May 1926, p. 7.
[2] *Ibid.*, 5 May 1927, *Methodist Union Supplement*, p. ii; *M.R.*, 27 May 1926, p. 14.
[3] *M.R.*, 17 June 1926, p. 17; 22 July 1926, p. 4; *M.T.*, 27 May, 1926, p. 10; 19 May 1927, p. 7.
[4] *M.T.*, 27 May 1926, p. 4; *U.M.*, 10 June 1926, p. 243; *M.R.*, 10 June 1926, p. 8.

Methodist Conference, it voted 95 per cent for union and *Scheme*.[1] All now depended on the Wesleyan Conference. Unionists determined to avoid a debacle. The Rev. H. Paynter Boase organized payment of expenses for at least thirty-one reliable ministers, who would not otherwise have attended the Pastoral Session. The Representative Session provided just adequate support of *Scheme* and union, 76·9 per cent.

The Other Side slumped in the Pastoral Session, which voted 70·4 per cent for the Committee resolution. This vote was inadequate but encouraging for unionists. A naïve reporter commented, 'The majority is much greater than I expected, and certainly the vote did *not* correspond with the shouting. The volume was overwhelmingly anti-Unionist.' Though they did not shout much, Boase's recruits had voted. If they had been a few dozen more, they would have ended the matter. As it was, despite ultimate detection, and some unionist loss of face, the stratagem was quite successful.[2]

Wesleyan unionists now had to take the Enabling Bill back through synod. They were encouraged by signs of division in the Other Side. In March 1927, the Other Side launched a three-issue monthly for the forthcoming synods, called *The Wesleyan Methodist Gazette*. Rattenbury wrote an article for the May issue, stating that he was voting against the Bill '*at present* . . . because I am convinced that the time is not ripe for Union'. He dissociated himself from 'those members of the "Other Side" whose opposition is uncompromising and unaltering'.[3]

But the synods pleased the Other Side not the unionists. The Representative Sessions voted 68·4 per cent, the Pastoral Sessions 60·5 per cent, for the Bill. At this rate the synods might take five or six years to reach a 75 per cent majority. Brook told the United Committee on 31 May 1927, that 'the smaller Churches could not wait indefinitely for union', but 'wondered if there was anything they could do to lessen the minority'. Perks did his best to cheer up the Committee with the old slogans. Once united, he said, 'The Methodist Church . . . would help to save England from Roman Catholicism and Anglo-Catholicism.'[4]

But the cruellest blow had yet to come. The Wesleyan Methodist Representative Session debated union on 14 July 1927. It voted 71·5

---

[1] Meeting of 1 June 1926, *in United Committee Minutes . . .*; *M.R.*, 17 June 1926, p. 7; *U.M.*, 5 June 1926, pp. 308–9.
[2] *M.R.*, 24 March 1927, p. 17; 22 July 1926, pp. 4–7; 29 July 1926, pp. 4–5.
[3] *U.M.*, 2 December 1926, p. 555; *W.M. Gazette*, May 1927, p. 2.
[4] *M.T.*, 19 May 1927, p. 7; *P.M.L.*, 2 June 1927, p. 343.

per cent for the *Scheme*, 70·7 per cent for the Bill. Its 75 per cent vote had disappeared. That the Representative Session had failed was particularly disturbing: with both Sessions united, one could not be used to put pressure on the other; and Wesleyan opposition could not be dismissed as hierarchical obscurantism.

Demand for Primitive Methodist-United Methodist union was again heard. Mr A. Hawthorne of Stoke-on-Trent warned that the Primitive Methodists' 'patience has become exhausted and their pride in their Church has become imperilled. If Wesleyan Methodism desires Union it will have to move quickly, or the "time glass will have run out".'[1] When the United Committee met on 29 September 1927, 'The reverse . . . seemed to hang over the meeting like a pall.'[2]

But the Representative Session's vote alarmed Rattenbury as much as the unionists. He was convinced that another failure to reach 75 per cent in the Wesleyan Conference would defeat union 'for another generation and perhaps altogether'. 'I should feel it for the rest of my days if I shared in such a responsibility,' he said. Unionists had to exploit Rattenbury's growing alienation from the Other Side extremists, if the union movement was not to end in fiasco.[3]

In September 1927, the Representative Session Committee on union appointed a strong ' "Business" Committee'. After discussion, proposals by Hornabrook were made 'the basis of a draft of an agreement'. This was referred to a committee of four, Carter, Hornabrook, Rattenbury and Rider. When the Business Committee met on 30 November 1927, they presented 'A Policy of Three Stages': acceptance of the Enabling Bill in 1928; a final vote for union in 1931, and the uniting Conference in 1932; the first Conference of the United Church in 1933. The interim period was to be devoted to active preparation, and the 75 per cent formula was to be observed throughout.

According to Rattenbury, the Business Committee adopted the proposals largely because of 'the magnanimity of Sir Robert Perks'. When French agreed to a Synod vote in 1931 on the question, 'Is the Church now ready for Union?', Rider, Armstrong and Rattenbury committed themselves to the new proposals.[4]

The Other Side held a committee meeting on 10 January 1928, presumably with Rider still in the chair. He, Armstrong and Rattenbury made a brief prepared statement. Two others, one of whom was

[1] *U.M.*, 21 July 1927, pp. 345–7, 349; *M.R.*, 21 July 1927, pp. 4–7; 28 July 1927; pp. 5–6; *M.T.*, 20 October 1927, p. 17.
[2] *M.R.*, 6 October 1927, p. 3.
[3] *Ibid.*, 26 April 1928, p. 7; 26 July 1928, p. 5; *M.T.*, 19 January, p. 14.
[4] Meetings, October–December 1927, in *United Committee Minutes* . . .

apparently Clucas, voted against continued opposition to the Enabling Bill. The five dissidents withdrew, the remainder of the committee voted to continue opposition, and Bevan Shepherd, veteran of 1913. was elected Chairman.[1]

The Executive of the United Committee met the following day. It was a lugubrious gathering. The Three Stages were outlined. Armstrong, Rattenbury and Rider dolefully pledged support. The Primitive and United Methodist delegates requested an adjournment. They met separately for forty-five minutes. There was little they could do. The Primitive Methodists returned with a long resolution that must have taken most of the forty-five minutes to draft. It declared,

'after careful consideration of the new situation that has been created by the statements and pledges of those who hitherto have been the representatives of the organized opposition to Union, stating that if these proposals are accepted they will wholeheartedly co-operate to promote Union; and further, we being persuaded of their deep sincerity and relying upon what amounts to a moral guarantee of Union being consummated, we accept the basic principles of the proposals.'

The United Methodists concurred in these sentiments.

The three leaders, and indeed the Wesleyan Methodist Church, being thus put upon their honour, the Committee proceeded to a decision. Sixty-eight voted on the Three Stages, and the Rev. J. J. Johnston of the Other Side was the only dissentient. The gloom of the meeting persisted. Peake, who had a year and a half to live, expressed 'sorrow that the delay was needful', but added, 'In the life of a Church two or three years did not mean much.' Pyke wrote, 'the proposed delay is a real disappointment to our own and to the Primitive Methodist Church. The annoyance arises largely from inability to see what precise advantage is to arise from putting off till 1932, what might as well be achieved in 1929.'[2]

Union in 1932 now turned on the ability of the three leaders to carry enough Other Siders with them to get the Enabling Bill through Conference on a 75 per cent vote. Johnston, busy rallying faithful anti-unionists, declared in April, 'It is evident that an agreed acceptance of the Enabling Bill in 1928 means that THE MATTER IS AT AN END.'[3]

[1] *M.T.*, 12 January 1928, p. 4; J. J. Johnston, *Circular*, 15 January 1928; A Methodist to Methodists, *The 'Methodist Union' Controversy. The Right Way Out*, n.d.
[2] *Methodist Leader*, 19 January 1928, p. 36; *U.M.*, 3 May 1928, p. 207; Meeting of 11 January 1928, in *United Committee Minutes . . .*
[3] *'The Other Side'. Methodist Union*, n.d.

The Representative Session debated union on 19 July 1928. French made a vigorous speech in the old style:

> 'The Church has no right to demand the utter destruction of social sins of war, destitution and vice, unless she believes in a Christ who can utterly destroy sin in her own heart. . . . We are threatened not only by the new paganism and secularism, but by the aggressiveness of Roman Catholicism and the growth of Anglo-Catholicism.'

Mr. Harold Jackson, speaking for the Other Side, said 'It is true that we have regretfully dropped a leader or two here and there. The mere defection of a few leaders does not matter.' Rattenbury made his first speech on behalf of union. 'I feel', he said, 'That the sort of opposition and criticism that many of us have given to the Union project in the past logically issues in support of the Scheme to-day.' 'The mere defection of a few leaders' split the Other Side in half. The highest Other Side vote was 15·6 per cent. The Session voted 86·3 per cent for the Three Stages; 88·4 per cent for the Enabling Bill.

The Pastoral Session debate took place eight days later, on 27 July. Six hundred and sixteen ministers voted on the resolution that 'Union of the three Methodist Churches is now the avowed policy of the Conference'. Four hundred and sixty-two, that is, precisely 75 per cent, voted in favour. About a dozen Other Side ministers had voted with Rattenbury. The vote was followed by uproar. 'The Conference was amazed,' wrote a reporter. 'Everywhere we express the same sentiment only varying the adjective: extraordinary, weird, unprecedented, impossible to have been faked, marvellous, miraculous, providential.'

The mythology of the vote soon accumulated: the missionary on furlough who got to Conference just in time to record his vote; the minister who left for home, missed his train and returned to the debate, and so on.[1] It was an occasion for celebrations. But the reality symbolized by the vote was not encouraging. After fifteen years, a third of Primitive and United Methodist officials were being carried into union against their will, while Wesleyans disliked union so much that its acceptance turned on one man's vote.

*Problems of Union, 1928–32*

Opposition did not stop with the 75 per cent vote. The Enabling Bill was opposed by four petitions, criticized by the *Recorder* as 'factious

---

[1] *M.R.*, 26 July 1928, pp. 4, 5; 2 August 1928, pp. 8, 18; *M.L.*, 2 August 1928, p. 508; Rupert Davies, *Methodism*, London, 1963, p. 152.

and at variance with the spirit of brotherly love'. Some resistance also continued in the country, notably the Primitive Methodist Defence League, which was active in Hull from 1924 till 1931. Not without foresight, the League declared, '*The Union Church will be the high road to Anglicanism.*'[1] But opposition ceased to count, and the Wesleyan synod vote of 1931 was a formality.

Area Committees prepared for union by means of public meetings. The United Committee offered Area Committees a 'common text for the Movement'.

'The "Methodist Witness" but expressed and applied so as to appeal to Young Methodism. The central point the "Experience of God" (the Witness of the Spirit) the world call and its implications (that Christ died for all)–our purpose is victory over all individual and social sin (Scriptural Holiness). Young men and women workers would be in the grandest of Movements, etc. Show how local co-operation will help new areas, etc.'

Opinions varied as to the value of this work. The Rev. Frank Hull told Samuel Horton that 'so far as Cornwall is concerned "the whole thing is a farce" '.[2]

Amid these preparations, the United Committee studied outstanding questions. In May 1930, Horton suggested an approach to the Wesleyan Reform Union. Perks said 'that while ultimately the inclusion of the Wesleyan Reform Union was very desirable it would be unfortunate to raise the question at this stage as it might delay Union through the necessity of considering new Financial obligations, etc. The proposal was therefore not pressed.'[3]

Rationalization remained the most important, yet the most delicate,

---

[1] *House of Commons Session 1929. Methodist Church Union. Petition of Ralph Eastman, Samuel Smethurst, W. J. Mason, James Rider, J. J. Johnston and Walter T. Penny; House of Commons Session 1929. Methodist Church Union Bill, Petition of Jabez Bell, Thomas Lill, Robert Woodmansey and Charles Hezekiah Ruse; House of Commons Session 1929. Methodist Church Union Bill. Petition of Sir R. W. Essex, William Samuel Welch, John Atack Burke, Wallace Edgar Southard, Frank Granville Stafford and Francis Henry Joseph Thornton*; typescript memorandum on cost of Methodist Church Union Bill, French Papers (Methodist Archives); *M.R.*, 4 April 1929, p. 3; *Methodist Union. A Protest, a Warning, a Comparison*, Cross Hills, 1931, p. 5; Meeting of 26 September 1924, in *Primitive Methodist Committees* . . .

[2] *M.R.*, 25 October 1928, p. 6; *Methodist Union. Suggestions to be Submitted to the Area Committees* (insert), in *Methodist Union Committees, 1928–1932*; Frank Hull–Samuel Horton, 12 September 1930 (insert), in *Primitive Methodist Committees* . . .

[3] Meeting of 16 May 1930, in *Methodist Union Committees* . . .

question. The Committee deliberately drew back from it. The Three Stages originally required the Area Committees to 'carefully study the question of overlapping, and note places where new erections or enlargements are needed'. In March 1928, the words, 'the question of overlapping', were replaced by 'the local situation'. When the Committee studied its draft report of June 1929, it amended the sentence, 'The Committee is emphatically of the opinion that the Methodist Churches must cease to build against one another or independently of one another and co-operate in obtaining sites and erecting churches,' to read, 'The Committee believes that in general the Methodist Churches are ceasing to build against one another and will increasingly co-operate in obtaining sites and erecting Churches.'[1] By January 1932, with six months of the preparation period left, no overall plan for amalgamating circuits existed.

The Committee had good reasons for caution. Mere organization of circuits in united districts proved exceedingly difficult. Sharp warned the 1930 Wesleyan Conference, 'There is strong feeling, and there are many protests. You will not get a considered vote on the main principle if this goes on. . . . Local prejudices and feelings will easily run away with great principles.' Nevertheless, the debate on Union in the Representative Session of 1931 degenerated into a 'wrangle' over district boundaries.[2]

Eventually several special inquiries were necessary. Various Wesleyan circuits on the outskirts of the London districts were dismayed to find they were being grouped with the rural Cambridge and Peterborough, and Norwich and Ipswich districts, where (in contrast to the new London districts) non-Wesleyans were in a majority. 'All our associations', the Rev. Arthur F. Wolton told Sharp, 'both commercially, socially and religiously are with' the circuits of the London districts, 'whereas we have not the slightest connection with Cambridge – never have had; and we object most strongly to having these associations interfered with'. Wesleyan circuits in Cheshire and North Wales objected to inclusion in 'so overwhelmingly rural' a district as the new Chester and Warrington district, where non-Wesleyans were much nearer parity with the Wesleyans than they were in the Liverpool district. Conversely, the small Primitive and United Methodist minority in the Channel Isles wanted to be included in a mainland

[1] M.R., 28 January 1932, p. 6; Meeting of 13 March 1928, in *United Committee Minutes* . . .; Meetings of 20 September 1928, 25 January 1929 and 7 June 1929, in *Methodist Union Committees* . . .

[2] M.R., 27 July 1930, p. 4; 23 July 1931, p. 21; Arthur F. Wolton–J. Alfred Sharp, 1 February 1932.

district, rather than in the united Channel Isles districts, dominated by Wesleyans who had rejected union.[1]

Disenchantment with ecumenicalism added to these problems. 'Without doubt', declared a remarkable *Recorder* editorial, on 4 August 1932,

> 'the devotion displayed in the cause of Methodist Union has been largely inspired by the hope that, in some way, the accomplishment of Union will be followed by a revival of the essential spirit of Methodism. But the experiences of the other Churches which have recently united hardly justifies such an expectation. . . . There is nothing in the union of Churches, considered in itself, that inevitably or even probably leads to the new birth of the spirit.'[2]

The United Committee's policy decisions paralleled this incredible *volte face*. While public meetings proclaimed the ecumenical vision, some detailed planning for the future was being done. In January 1930, looking forward to the coming Church and the 'great forward movement on quite unprecedented lines' that it would bring, the Committee concluded that arrangements for ministerial training should assume the united church's requirements would equal the three separate denominations' average demand for ministers over the previous decade. This calculation assumed that 'local amalgamations' and 'developments in new Areas' would 'balance one another', hardly a forecast of a great forward movement. Later a Theological Colleges Committee cut this figure by 5 per cent; and a Sub-Committee on Candidates, by 14 per cent. These decisions were puzzling if in 1930 ecumenicalists seriously believed in the revival which they publicly claimed union would inaugurate. The cuts would make sense if denominational leaders had by this time concluded that the united church would not grow but decline. If they did believe this, they were right.[3]

---

[1] J. Alfred Sharp–Arthur F. Wolton, 11 February 1932; *Memorial to the Methodist Union Committee, May, 1931*, in French Papers (Methodist Archives); Meeting of 19 February 1930, in *Methodist Union Committees . . .*

[2] *M.R.*, 4 August 1932, p. 10.

[3] *Ibid.*, 17 January 1929, p. 5; Meetings of 13 January 1930; 9 April 1930. in *Methodist Union Committees . . .*

# Part Four
# Methodism and Ecumenicalism

# CHAPTER NINE

# Methodism and Ecumenicalism

*Union and Compromise*

Ecumenicalism demands compromise, but churches can seldom compromise safely. They claim to be committed to principles associated in some sense with a realm of absolute truth. These principles are often closely linked with the concrete details of church organization, since religious people seek to model the Christian community on their concept of Christianity. The two major ecumenical schemes so far completed in England have involved compromises in many of their constituent denominations' beliefs and practices.

The three uniting denominations of 1907 sought a common 'liberal Methodism'. This undefined desideratum proved to require concessions from all. The Free Methodists finally acknowledged the existence of a separate 'ministerial' estate by accepting lay-ministerial parity of representation in conference, and conferred a long-resisted privilege upon that estate by conceding to it *ex officio* chairmanship of the quarterly meeting. At the same time, they finally abandoned circuit independence. The New Connexion agreed, after seventy years' opposition, to allow local preachers to sit in the leaders' meeting *ex officio*, just as ministers did, while withdrawing from the minister the 'power of salutary control'[1] over church meetings by allowing his tenure of the chair to depend upon his obedience to the meeting's will. These changes were comparatively minor items in the ecumenical abandonment of convictions, but they were the first small stones of an avalanche.

The Methodist Church represents this collapse at a still more advanced stage. The Wesleyan ministry constituted an autonomous presbytery which could deploy itself free from chapel officialdom and lay patronage. Despite lay 'invitation', only ministers could station ministers. Reformed Methodists asserted lay right to share in station-

---

[1] *The Jubilee of the Methodist New Connexion*, London, 1848, p. 146.

ing decisions, as in all other acts of the Christian community. The Methodist Church admitted laymen to the stationing process but limited them to advising the ministers and vetoing their decisions. Both the Wesleyan ideal of a free presbytery responsible only to God, and the reformed Methodist ideal of genuine lay participation in all church acts, were compromised.

Many Wesleyans regarded the President of Conference as 'the chief pastoral officer' of the connexion, the head of the free presbytery of Wesleyan ministers whose office should be immune from secular influences. Many reformed Methodists believed the President, as representative of the whole church, should be chosen from the whole Church, ministry and laity alike. In the Methodist Church, ministerial and lay representatives together elected the President, but laymen were debarred from that office. Two significant constitutional systems, one based on a high doctrine of the ministry, the other on priesthood of all believers, were replaced by a meaningless amalgam.

The Methodist Church adopted a similar amalgam from the United Methodists when it made the minister *ex officio* chairman but denied him power to refuse resolutions. Wesleyans surrendered unrestricted *ex officio* chairmanship, Primitive Methodists abandoned free election to that office without distinction of ministry or laity. But although United Methodists preserved this section of their constitution, Primitive and Wesleyan Methodists refused to give local preachers *ex officio* seats in the leaders' meeting and would only allow that body discretionary power to co-opt local preachers as members. The United Methodist system vindicated co-pastorate of laity and ministry. The new compromise merely satisfied some local preachers' desire to go on sitting in the leaders' meeting.

The Wesleyan constitution gave ministers, with their high pastoral responsibilities, power to nominate lay officials and judge cases involving laymen; while the doctrine of the ministry as a free presbytery responsible only to God was recognized in exclusion of ministers from lay jurisdiction. Reformed Methodism's democratic propensities, its deep concern for co-pastorate and spiritual equality, led to free nomination and election of all officials, and co-jurisdiction of ministers and laymen over all members of the Church. The Methodist Church compromised both systems. Wesleyans surrendered exclusive ministerial jurisdiction and nomination in local meetings. Liberal Methodists surrendered all lay claims to a share in jurisdiction over ministers, although laymen were admitted to nomination and election of all circuit officials and to judgement of cases involving laymen.

The largest of these amalgams of mutually antagonistic systems was the new Ministerial Session. Non-Wesleyan acceptance of the reduced Ministerial Session meant drastic changes quite alien to their traditions. Laymen provided 50 per cent of representatives in the United Methodist legislature, 66 per cent of the Primitive Methodist, but only 41 per cent of the Methodist. These figures do not illustrate the full extent of lay retreat. Liberal Methodist legislatures were unicameral; the Wesleyan and the new Methodist legislatures, bicameral. Laymen had no power over matters reserved to the jurisdiction of the ministerial house in the Methodist legislature. But this ministerial house had power over all subjects dealt with by the mixed house, except such matters as election of the President. The sovereignty of the Ministerial Session has shrunk since 1932; but this should not obscure liberal Methodist laymen's surrender in that year.

The Methodist Church, like the United Methodist Church, represents a rightward shift for many of its constituents who abandon their substantial beliefs for the strange ecumenical limbo where people speak without sense of incongruity about 'The Catholicity of Protestantism'. Spiritual convictions are hybridized.

This is seen in the sacramental settlement. Wesleyans confined administration of sacraments to ministers, since they did not recognize a complete co-pastorate of ministry and laity. Reformed Methodism vigorously asserted co-pastorate and made no distinction between full-time ministry and laity in the ministry of the Sacrament, any more than it did in the ministry of the Word. The Methodist Church adopted lay administration, which Wesleyans had hitherto rejected, and restricted this administration in various ways, all of which were foreign to the practice and convictions of liberal Methodism.

The successive involutions of the sacramental clause of the union *Scheme* left its significance obscured. Some hoped they had isolated lay administration as a temporary matter of expediency. Others hoped they had secured enough loopholes for it to be interpreted as a principle.[1] Conflicting aims were also seen in the attempt at a specific and explicit doctrine of the ministry in the Deed of Union. On the reformed Methodist side, this attempt consists of the assertion that

[1] Fourteen years after union, the liberals who advocated lay administration as a principle were seen to have won. The 1946 Methodist Conference adopted a report which officially recognized that some Methodists 'very strongly held' lay administration 'as a principle', and not, as Wesleyans were continually assured in the 1920s, as a matter of mere expediency. Conference naturally allowed that, in view of this principle, no attempt should be made 'to exclude lay administration'. *Minutes of the Methodist Conference*, 1946, p. 203.

'The Methodist Church holds the doctrine of the priesthood of all believers'; and that, in this church, 'the principle of representative selection is recognized'. The Wesleyan section of this formula is: 'for the sake of Church Order . . . Ministers of the Methodist Church are set apart by ordination to the Ministry of the Word and Sacraments'.

Many Wesleyans rejected representative selection and priesthood of all believers, except in a modified form. Few if any liberal Methodists accepted the 'Order not Orders' theory, simply because they rejected the notion of 'Order' implied. The logic of this amalgamated Methodist doctrine of the ministry, that all Christians are priests, but that it is only 'Orderly' for a few of them to perform their priestly functions, lacks the virtue of cogency, especially since 1946. The 'representative selection' formula is probably literally meaningless. The 'Church Order' formula is vitiated by actual Methodist practice for successive Methodist Conferences have found no breach of 'Church Order' in some ministers being 'set apart . . . to the Ministry of the Word and Sacraments', not by ordination but by 'recognition' as local preachers to practise the ministry of the Word, and 'authorization' to practise the ministry of the Sacraments.

The Methodist Church's general doctrinal position shows similar vagueness. Non-Wesleyans accepted 'Wesley's Standards' with extreme reluctance. In so doing, the United Methodist Church abandoned its doctrinal formula of 1907, which made no reference to Wesley; and the Primitive Methodists reversed their policy of 1915–16, when they sought to eliminate Wesley from their own Deed Poll. Of course most non-Wesleyans knew little and liked less of Wesley, and unification with the Wesleyans did not convert them. The resulting doctrinal situation was comparable to that of the Articles in the Church of England.

The Methodist Church was made possible because the Wesleyans took a long step to meet liberal Methodists and liberal Methodists took a longer step still to meet the Wesleyans. Both surrendered much ground, in hope.

*Ecumenical Realities*

With few exceptions the rewards of ecumenicalism have not justified the sacrifices. Methodists sought various types of union, but none of these were particularly successful.

The earliest phase of ecumenicalism in Methodism was polemical, anti-Wesleyan or anti-Anglican. A polemical 'superdenomination' might prosecute interdenominational conflict more efficiently than several divided if mutually sympathetic denominations could. But neither the United Methodist Free Churches, the United Methodist Church nor the Methodist Church conducted more vigorous or successful polemic against their opponents than their constituents had done. On the contrary, liberal Methodist propaganda declined after 1857 and after 1907, and Methodist anti-Anglican propaganda declined after 1932. Free Methodists did engage in a costly building war with Wesleyans. But the United Methodist Church could not continue let alone increase this war. Perks' anti-Anglican schemes–rural Nonconformist schools and 2,000 new village chapels–were stillborn. In any event, the polemic of bricks and mortar had little effect. Small denominations could not build sufficient rival chapels to threaten their larger opponents. Even if they had, the result might well have been intransigence rather than capitulation.

Polemic unions might operate in other ways. They might, by mere size, impress opponents. But such arguments were wishful thinking. No possible Methodist union was more than a fraction of the size of the Roman Catholic Church, but that denomination's bulk and power led few Methodists to abandon their beliefs. No more success attended the argument that the united church's success in annexing the non-churchgoing millions would fatally enfeeble and discredit opponents. The Wesleyan Home Missions report of 1886 anticipated the day when Methodism would 'inevitably become in the hour of its victory, *the* church of England'. But no united church proved to have this dynamism.[1]

The Eckett-Walls-Redfern theory of ecumenicalism was more promising. This theory assumed the construction of ever larger ecumenical units. Union of similar organizations would consolidate the claims of some common denominator of their beliefs in eventual future negotiations with the present enemy. But the actual negotiating record of these sectional united churches is unencouraging. Free Methodists surrendered a great deal in 1907 in the hope of strengthening the liberal Methodist hand in a future Methodist union. But in the 1920s the united church achieved little that its constituents might not have achieved negotiating as separate bodies.

Even united, the three denominations were able to achieve very little without the support of the much larger Primitive Methodist Church. Free Methodists insisted on local preachers' *ex officio*

[1] Quoted in R. W. Perks, *The Re-union of British Methodism*, London, 1920, p. 7.

membership of the leaders' meeting, presumably the key item in their interpretation of 'Liberal Methodism' in 1907. They also then gained power to revise doctrine decennially, 'the glory and crown of our polity' as Redfern called it. These were the only two points at which the United Methodist interpretation of the demands of liberal Methodism diverged from the Primitive Methodist. Decennial revision of doctrine disappeared. Primitive and Wesleyan Methodists required United Methodists to be content with provision for the leaders' meeting to co-opt local preachers at its discretion. There is little here to commend polemical ecumenicalism.

Success or failure in the later stage of ecumenicalism, the 'ecumenicalism of mission', is difficult to evaluate. If a united church had a better growth record than its constituent denominations, this might be held to show that union advances mission. But denominational growth rates fluctuate over time in such a way as to suggest that they are influenced by factors external to the denomination. Mere improvement of the material or spiritual efficiency of the organization would not necessarily result in a higher growth rate, since the 'evangelization opportunities' afforded by the denomination's social context might change adversely. Conclusions about ecumenicalism and mission cannot be drawn from the fact that both the United Methodist and the Methodist Churches suffered very severe losses. These may be due to adverse changes in evangelization opportunities rather than adverse changes in the ability of the organization to utilize these opportunities. We cannot tell whether the constituent denominations in each case would have done better or worse if they had remained divided than they did when united.

But one of these problems may be partly solved. Analysis of Methodist growth rates suggests that the performance of one Methodist denomination is at least roughly comparable with that of another. This may enable some evaluation of the United Methodist experience. During the quarter century before their union, the Bible Christians and the New Connexion grew faster while the Free Methodists grew slower than any other major Methodist denomination. During the quarter century of the United Methodist Church's life, it had a worse growth rate than either the Primitive or the Wesleyan Methodists. Perhaps the ex-Bible Christian and ex-New Connexion sections of the United Methodist Church continued to grow quickly but their vigour was offset by Free Methodist feebleness; or perhaps the minority traditions of the united church lost the energy they had shown before union. Whatever explanation may be offered, the United Methodist

Church growth rate casts great doubt on the claim that ecumenicalism promotes mission.

A similar analysis of the significance of the union of 1932 would be useful. But no appropriate comparison exists. Between 1932 and 1964, the Methodist Church's membership has decreased by 140,000, i.e. 17·7 per cent. This is a substantially smaller percentage decrease than the Congregationalists and Baptists have suffered, but a substantially larger percentage decrease than that experienced by the Anglicans. The loss of members from the united church may have been smaller than the loss of members from the three separate denominations would have been had they survived into this period. But there is little in the performance of the Methodist Church to justify the ecumenical promise of 1929 that 'a Revival will coincide with the coming of Methodist Union . . . with the consummation of union a great forward movement on quite unprecedented lines is anticipated; is indeed inevitable'.[1]

Despite the comparatively similar failure of 'mission' in both united churches, their rationalization record differs markedly. The United Methodist record is one of complete failure as Table Eight shows.

TABLE EIGHT. *Overlap in the United Methodist Church.*

| | Chapels per Minister | Members per Chapel |
|---|---|---|
| 1907 | 3·0 | 59 |
| 1932 | 4·1 | 48 |

Source: Minutes.

According to the theory of rationalization, a situation of severe 'overlap', with members scattered through too many chapels served by too few ministers, is at least reduced, after union, to the point where there are on average *more* members per chapel, and *less* chapels per minister. The United Methodist Church, through failure to close chapels and to recruit ministers, was in the unhappy state of having *less* members per chapel, and *more* chapels per minister in 1932 than it did in 1907.

Rationalization in the Methodist Church is generally held to have been slow and inadequate. 'Overlap' or 'redundancy', as it is now called, allegedly still stands at a very high level. Mr. Alan Richer of Gomersal asked in 1963,

'is Conference really aware of the scandal of redundancy that has been dragging on in this area for thirty years?; thirty years during

[1] *M.R.*, 17 January 1929, p. 5.

which countless numbers have, for a short time, savoured the dusty, drab, declining, unheated, uncared for churches ... only ... kept open by a loyal two or three families who between them hold every office from society steward to caretaker. The image of Methodism with its cracked tea-cups must go.'

Concern is expressed at the highest level of Methodism. In 1960, the Secretary of Conference, Dr. Eric Baker, declared that 'redundancy ... is steadily strangling our effectiveness'. Three years previously, speaking on behalf of the General Purposes Committee, Dr. Baker rejected a memorial to Conference, 'that the Silver Jubilee of Methodist Union should be observed ... this year'. Dr. Baker 'said that the committee felt that it would be hypocritical in view of the partial implementation of Methodist Union, and proposed the reply that the best way to celebrate the occasion would be for the union to be made effective in those quarters where hitherto there had been reluctance to do so. The Conference agreed.'[1]

A more cheerful note might have been struck, as Table Nine shows.

TABLE NINE. *Overlap in the Methodist Church.*

|  | Chapels per Minister | Members per Chapel |
|---|---|---|
| 1932 | 3·5 | 58 |
| 1960 | 3·2 | 62 |

*Source: Minutes.*

Doubtless there are still far too many Methodist chapels for general administrative convenience; and, in particular, too many 'overlapping' chapels in the same area. But there are now more members per chapel and less chapels per minister than there were in 1932. The Methodist Church, partly by more closures, partly by recruiting more ministers, has a far better rationalization record than the United Methodist Church. Perhaps the Silver Jubilee might have been celebrated modestly.

If it had been celebrated, the modern ecumenicalists of Methodism should have taken the opportunity to examine the history of rationalization and evangelization in Methodism. In the 1920s, ecumenicalists expected much from rationalization. But those who looked for the revitalization of mission to follow the better stewardship of resources, and therefore pressed the advantages of rationalization, can be seen in retrospect to have demanded a far more elongated time-span than was

[1] *M.R.*, 1 August 1963, p. 4; 30 June 1960, p. 1; 11 July 1957, p. 7.

then even imagined or suspected. Rationalization policies have yet to be completed, and schemes confidently propounded in 1920 have yet to show results nearly fifty years later.

Long-term policies are not intrinsically bad policies, but ecumenicalists urged 'almost headlong haste' to stop the 'drifting from the churches': the short run dominated their thinking.[1] Rationalization involved two major assumptions: that it could be achieved in a relatively short time-span – which evidently it cannot; and that within this time-span, the social situation, the church's evangelization opportunities, would remain relatively constant. Even if ecumenicalists had offered a cogent argument that rationalization would promote mission in the 1920s, this argument would not show that the same effect could be secured by the same policy, say, fifty years later. The social situation of the Church becomes ever less favourable, and its evangelization opportunities ever sparser. A policy which might have been successful, could it have been realized in the 1920s, will not necessarily be successful when it is realized in the 1970s, 1980s or 1990s.

Both pronounced failure to rationalize in the United Methodist Church and modest success at rationalization in the Methodist Church, have accompanied severe losses. Those of the Methodist Church exceed in number the total membership of the United Methodist Church in 1932. This suggests that rationalization has very little to do with success or failure in evangelization; and that the belief that reducing the number of church buildings will promote religion in the twentieth century is as fallacious as the belief that increasing the number of church buildings would promote religion in the nineteenth. If this is so, ecumenical theory is severely weakened.

But religious organizations do not exist merely for evangelization or mission. Besides recruiting new members, they should have something to offer existing members. Methodism united has failed to recruit as ecumenicalists predicted. It has also failed to satisfy many of the members it took over from the three constituent denominations in 1932. The refusal to celebrate the Silver Jubilee symbolizes a general disenchantment.

Uncertainty and even apparent deception on the closure of chapels and other issues, and a well-founded suspicion that local opposition was not being expressed or even acknowledged at denominational level, left many laymen, especially those of the smaller churches, deeply dissatisfied. An East Anglian Methodist wrote in 1963,

[1] *M.R.*, 4 April 1912, p. 5.

'I was Primitive Methodist when it came about and the whole thing is still fresh, perhaps too fresh in my memory. . . . What caused most resentment was the fact that no individual member had a voice in the matter or was allowed a say in anything. The highlights arranged everything to suit their own convenience and the Church members were kept in the dark till everything was fixed up. Feeling was strong against Union. . . . Some were willing to give it a trial, but very few were keen on it. . . . What we, as ex-Prims, sadly miss is our old time freedom, something almost unknown in Wesleyan circles . . . if you want to give a true picture of what took place in 1932, you cannot paint it in bright colours. There are some wounds which take a long time to heal.'[1]

For some Methodists, 1932 has become a date as traumatic as 1849. Life in the united church has been disheartening. The raids on chapel and denominational loyalties foreseen by anti-unionists have materialized. On average a couple of chapels have been closed every week since union. Each closure is accompanied by a decrease in membership, partly due to removal of dead wood from the membership roll, partly due to alienation of members. A Liskeard Methodist wrote of the closure of Greenbank Chapel, Liskeard, in 1955, 'I would prefer going to Hell my own way than to go to Heaven along the road our advisers offer.'[2] Even without closures, members are dissatisfied with the outcome of the Wesleyan-non-Wesleyan confrontation in the united church. In December 1955, a group of Cornish local preachers warned, 'Some of us already have cause to regret Methodist Union when we see ritualistic and sacerdotal tendencies growing.' But Mr. R. F. Martin of Hounslow retorted, 'Many Methodists regret the lower standard of worship that many of our churches have carelessly drifted into since Union. We have been too willing to surrender the full use both of our Hymn Book and our Book of Offices.'[3]

Defence of Methodist Union is rare. Dr. R. F. Wearmouth, an ex-Primitive Methodist, strongly criticized it in 1957. Dr. Wearmouth observed that 'the high initial hopes have not been fulfilled, statistically speaking. The decline in Methodism . . . has not been arrested; it has been accelerated. . . . Judged by the declared purpose, the open and manifest record is of non-success.' He attributed this failure partly to aspects of the united church itself.

Dr. Wearmouth's often expressed dedication to 'the little chapel by

[1] Letter in author's possession.
[2] *M.R.*, 8 September 1955, p. 7.
[3] *Ibid.*, 8 December 1955, p. 22; 15 December 1955, p. 7.

the wayside at Oxhill', indicated his commitment to chapel society. This society, he claimed, was jeopardized by Methodist Union. The united church has a 'remote and cumbersome' bureaucracy. The customs of the smaller churches have been effaced. 'In Methodism as now united, the customs, conventions, prejudices, and traditions deriving from the Wesleyans may have inhibited the genius of the Primitives and the United Methodist,' he warns. The Methodist landscape may be 'more symmetrical . . . more uniform', but it is 'less fertile and fruitful and familiar'. In particular, united Methodism has relentlessly closed the chapels. 'The closing of churches, encouraged on economic grounds, may have been unwise psychologically,' Dr. Wearmouth wrote,

> 'because the poorer and weaker places have been among the first to be sacrificed, most of them Primitive Methodist in origin. Every individual Church is entwined by emotions, and personal histories, by remembrances and tokens of diligence, loyalty and love, and care needs to be exercised as doubtless it is, before the axe is applied to the tree and the knife to the tendrils.'[1]

The smaller constituent denominations of a united church lose their chapels, accept alien customs and contribute relatively little to church leadership. The Rev. Rupert E. Davies commented in 1961, 'every now and again the cry goes up, more and more muted as time goes on, that the representatives of such-and-such tradition are being passed over in appointments to important posts'.[2] Such complaints are justified. Free Methodists contributed 53·6 per cent of the United Methodist membership of 1907, Wesleyans 59·6 per cent of the Methodist membership of 1932. Unless a rigid quota system of appointments is adopted – and such a system would have considerable disadvantages – the majority group will tend to elect church leaders from among itself.

The United Methodist presidency circulated fairly freely among members of the three constituent denominations. But other official posts did not. In 1907, an attempt was made to appoint equal numbers of denominational officials from each group, thus over-representing the two smaller churches. But during 1908–32, two Bible Christian (9·1 per cent), fifteen Free Methodist (68·9 per cent), and five New Connexion (22·7 per cent) officials were appointed. Both smaller

---

[1] Robert F. Wearmouth, *The Social and Political Influence of Methodism in the Twentieth Century*, London, 1957, pp. 218 ff.

[2] W. S. F. Pickering (ed.), *Anglican–Methodist Relations. Some Institutional Factors*, London, 1961, p. 74.

denominations had less officials than their numbers deserved. In particular, the Bible Christian the smallest of the three denominations, was grossly under-represented. Whatever the merits of individual appointments, this situation was unhealthy.

A worse situation arose in the Methodist Church. Table Ten illustrates the marked over-representation of Wesleyanism in the presidency of the Methodist Church, and the way in which the

TABLE TEN. *Presidents of the Methodist Conference by Denomination, 1932–1965 (per cent).*

|  | Percentage of 1932 Membership | Presidents 1932–65 | 1932–39 | 1940–57 | 1958–65 |
|---|---|---|---|---|---|
| PMC | 23·8 | 17·7 | 25·0 | 5·6 | 37·6 |
| UMC | 16·6 | 8·9 | 25·0 | 0·0 | 12·4 |
| WMC | 59·6 | 73·4 | 50·0 | 94·4 | 50·0 |

Sources: *Minutes*; *Ministers and Probationers of the Methodist Church* (various editions).

smallest constituent denomination of 1932 tended to do worst of all, as the smallest constituent denomination of 1907 had done. In the first eight years of the Methodist Church a definite system of rotation was maintained: two Wesleyans were followed by a Primitive and then a United Methodist. In the eighteen years, 1940–57, this was completely abandoned. With one exception in 1947, every president was ex-Wesleyan. The majority elected its own members to, and excluded the minority from, the highest position in the church. As 'ex-Presidents', these men constituted an overwhelmingly ex-Wesleyan informal leadership in conference. Not till 1957, a generation after union, did party labels cease to count in presidential elections. The effect of this trend was virtual elimination of liberal Methodism from the leadership of the united church in the 1940s and 1950s.

This was true not merely of the presidency. Each appointment to the all-important post of secretary of conference in the Methodist Church has been Wesleyan. Table Eleven shows distribution of offices

TABLE ELEVEN. *Percentage Distribution of Offices among ex-Ministers of Constituent Churches, 1965.*

|  | Percentage of 1932 Membership | Offices held by ex-Ministers of Constituent Churches | | |
|---|---|---|---|---|
|  |  | Departmental Offices | District Chairman-ships | Theological College Offices |
| PMC | 23·8 | 7·7 | 21·4 | 0·0 |
| UMC | 16·6 | 15·3 | 7·2 | 10·0 |
| WMC | 59·6 | 77·0 | 71·4 | 90·0 |

Sources: *Minutes*; *Ministers and Probationers of the Methodist Church* (various editions).

in 1965, thirty-three years after union, among men who had been ministers in a constituent church. Wesleyans heavily predominate in the bureaucracy, in the districts and in the theological colleges. The minor traditions have been largely excluded from the local and central administration of the united church, and from the training of its ministers. It is perhaps not surprising that 'every now and then the cry goes up'. The experience of the united church has been that majority tradition gets stronger, and minority traditions are largely squeezed out.[1]

Ecumenicalists lay great emphasis on variety in unity and on the special contribution each tradition can make to the united church. Distribution of offices in two Methodist united churches suggests there is relatively little room for minor traditions. The tendency for subordinate elements to lose their buildings quicker also accelerates the progress of the united church towards uniformity. At the same time these elements lose their organs of opinion. In 1932, Methodism had four denominational weeklies, the Wesleyan *Methodist Recorder* and *Methodist Times*, the Primitive Methodist *Methodist Leader* and the *United Methodist*. The *United Methodist* ended with the United Methodist Church. The *Leader* merged with the *Times*. Thus the United Methodist tradition immediately lost any separate voice, the Primitive Methodist tradition preserved merely part of an ex-Wesleyan paper to express its views, while the Wesleyan tradition kept both its papers. For a while the *Times and Leader* seemed likely to become the organ of left-wing Wesleyan and liberal Methodist opinion. But it did not survive the thirties and was merged with the *Recorder*. This scarcely promoted variety in unity.

Despite a few and temporary successes, protestant or reformed ideas have been damaged rather than strengthened by polemical ecumenical projects: the Methodist Church has no more 'met the bill'[2] against Anglo-Catholicism than the United Methodist Church met the bill against Wesleyanism. The great claims of the ecumenicalism of mission have been largely disproved by Methodist experience. Revival was promised; decline ensued. Varying degrees of success in rationalizing resources, especially by eliminating overlap, have had no apparent effect on evangelization. The members of a united Methodism are highly dissatisfied. Its leaders refused to celebrate the twenty-fifth anniversary of 1932.

[1] Henry Smith, John E. Swallow and William Treffry, *The Story of the United Methodist Church*, London, 1932, *passim*; Methodist *Minutes, passim*; *Ministers and Probationers of the Methodist Church*, London, 1963, *passim*.
[2] *M.R.*, 27 July 1922, pp. 4–5.

Great sacrifices have been made. Since 1900, half-a-dozen de-nominations have surrendered both convictions and existence to make the present Methodist Church possible. Since 1932, thousands of private members have been evicted from their chapels. Minority traditions have been overwhelmed by the majority. But the 'great forward movement' which might justify these sacrifices has never come.

## The Ecumenical Imperative

Ecumenicalists always look forward. When the United Methodist Church failed to meet the promises of its makers, they amalgamated it with the Wesleyans. When the Methodist Church disappointed all the expectations of its advocates, its leaders proposed to unite it with the Church of England. Since the United Methodist Church was originally an anti-Wesleyan project, and the Methodist Church originally anti-Anglican, this process is the more striking. An ecu-menical imperative drives the churches towards union.

Since 1956, Methodists have been negotiating with Anglicans. In 1963, two 'stages' of closer relations were proposed. In a 'Service of Reconciliation' at Stage One, then hoped to be in 1967 or 1968, an Anglican bishop would lay hands on Methodist ministers with the words, 'Take authority to exercise the office of priest'; and a Method-ist minister would lay hands on Anglican bishops and priests, and say, 'Take authority to exercise the office of a minister.' After, and apparently because of, this rite, Anglican bishops would consecrate some Methodist ministers bishops, and Anglicans would receive the sacraments from Methodist ministers. After a period of fifteen or twenty years, Stage Two, 'The achievement of organic union', would begin. Anglicans would get what they have long wanted, 'complete self-government'; but the fate of Methodism is obscure apart from the fact that Conference 'in its present form will disappear'.[1]

Some Methodists have strongly opposed this scheme, arguing that the Service of Reconciliation is 'reordination', and consequently requires Methodist ministers to renounce their existing ministry. A new 'Other Side' has arisen: the Voice of Methodism, formed in 1963, and the National Liaison Committee, formed in 1965. In 1965, Methodists voted whether to continue negotiations on the basis of the 1963 scheme. Forty-four per cent of quarterly-meeting members voted

---

[1] Harold Roberts, *Anglican–Methodist Conversations*, London, 1963, pp. 28, 33; *Conversations between the Church of England and the Methodist Church*, London, 1963, pp. 37, 43, 47, 52–3, 57–63.

against continuation, although the double indirect representation system cut the minority to 22 per cent in Conference.[1] With these votes, Methodist leaders found themselves in the position of the non-Wesleyan leaders in 1923: a considerable section of their lay officials and members rejected the leadership's union proposals and challenged the very items which were essential to the scheme.

The Service of Reconciliation raises anew the perennial problems of Church and ministry. Anglicans will not recognize Methodist sacraments unless Methodists 'take episcopacy into their system', as Archbishop Fisher put it. This provides the rationale of the Service. Mr. David Foot Nash, the leading lay Methodist advocate of union, observes, 'The Reconciliation Rite *is* a rite of episcopal ordination.' The Service will revolutionize, indeed end, the Methodist doctrine of the ministry. As recently as 1959, Dr. Eric Baker, the Secretary of Conference, described this doctrine as 'a matter of order and not of orders'; while, in 1958, Mr. Foot Nash declared that the 1932 Deed of Union 'blows episcopacy skyhigh'. If Methodism accepts episcopal 'orders', it abandons its traditional doctrines.[2]

But the price of union is episcopal orders. The Rev. Dr. Harold Roberts, the Methodist spokesman on union, claimed that the 1963 proposals rested on two assumptions, 'First . . . a recognition of the reality and spiritual effectiveness of our respective ministries. Secondly, full communion could only be achieved if Methodism took episcopacy into its system.'[3] The logical congruity of these two assumptions is not readily apparent: if the Methodist ministry is already spiritually effective, why alter it? But the significance of the statement is clear. Episcopacy is essential to union, and union is essential. If Methodist leaders want union they must alter the character of their ministry, just as non-Wesleyan leaders had to accept the Ministerial Session.

The Anglican-Methodist Unity Commission, appointed in 1965, sought to mitigate this difficulty. In 1967 it published proposals for overcoming the reordination problem. These proposals involved a new terminology and a new formulation of the commitment to doctrine required of members of a religious organization.

The language of the Service of Reconciliation was now amended.

---

[1] *M.R.*, 17 October 1963, p. 3; 14 November 1963, p. 1; 21 November 1963, p. 1; 30 September 1965, p. 2; *The Methodist Conference, Plymouth. Representative Session. Agenda. 1965*, pp. 125 ff.

[2] *Conversations*, p. 7; David Foot Nash, *Their Finest Hour: Methodists and Anglicans*, London, 1964, p. 72; Eric W. Baker, *Fathers and Brethren*, London, 1959, p. 30; *M.R.*, 10 July 1958, p. 7.

[3] *M.R.*, 7 March 1963, p. 3.

The Bishop, laying hands on '*each of the Methodist Ministers*', was to say 'Take authority for the office and work of a Priest'; and then the Methodist 'Presiding Minister', laying hands on '*each Bishop and Priest*', was to say 'Take authority for the office and work of a Minister'. But both ordaining Bishop and Presiding Minister were also to say to those on whom they laid hands, 'We welcome you as fellow Presbyters with us in Christ's Church'.

The Commission states that the words 'priest' and 'presbyter' are 'synonymous'. It does not extend this synonymity to 'minister', which, it says, is included 'as being the language of the Methodist . . . Book of Offices'. Nor does it deny that 'overtones' exist in the case of 'priest' which make it a word 'of division' while 'presbyter' is 'a word of reconciliation'; though, curiously, in the Service of Reconciliation Methodists are not to be spared the divisive word 'priest'.

The Commission did not clarify its reasoning on this point. It seems to have been convinced that Methodist ministers must be ordained 'priest'. Once ordained 'priest', though not before, Methodist ministers can call themselves 'presbyters' and Anglican priests are willing to share the title with them. A semantic and chronological asymmetry seems to remain. Could the Service of Reconciliation be reversed, so that, before the Presiding Minister is made 'priest', he can himself make Anglican priests 'ministers' and speak of himself as a 'fellow Presbyter' with them?[1]

The terminology of the 1967 Service of Reconciliation seems to raise many problems, though these may be removed by the Commission's next report. Certainly in 1967 the Commission did not rely on terminology alone. It sought a more radical solution to its problems by rejecting all possible interpretations of what occurs in the Service of Reconciliation as uncharitable and divisive:

'If some see the Service as a conditional or unconditional ordination of Methodist ministers to a priesthood not hitherto exercised, others in both Churches are sure it is no such thing. . . . And if either a "catholic" or an "evangelical" understanding of the Service appears to be taken . . . many at the opposite extreme will feel that their own convictions about priesthood would be compromised if they took part. . . . So, if the Service is not to be intolerable for some, neither Church must officially define its significance for Methodist ministers. . . . The common intention

[1] *Towards Reconciliation. The Interim Statement of the Anglican-Methodist Unity Commission*, London, 1967. pp. 41, 44, 53, 64ff.

which the Service requires ... is ... this: to commit our continuing differences to God, and ... to commit ourselves, with our differences, to each other.... this intention has a higher justification than expediency.... not only is a measure of disagreement about priesthood ... "not intolerable" in a united Church, but a united Church is the best context for continued exploration of the differences that remain.'[1]

In short, the attempt to give significance to the Service of Reconciliation is 'to judge an issue which some would settle one way and some another, but which we can all agree is properly left in God's hands'.[2] The Commission appears to hold that unity comes first, the discovery of what has been united comes later. This doctrine must greatly complicate the Commission's task both in drafting Services whose significance it cannot define and in advising Methodists and Anglicans whether they are being reordained in submitting to these mysteries.

Whether Methodist ministers will be newly ordained, Methodist laymen must cease to administer the sacraments. In 1958, Dr. Roberts insisted that 'acceptance of Episcopacy does not mean the abandonment of a lay ministry or apostolate'. But the 1963 report declared, 'Because we believe that the position of the laity in the spiritual life of the Church is one of the great contributions Methodism has to make to the Church of the future, we anticipate no interference with the position they now hold.... The only change will be in the lay administration of the sacrament of Holy Communion, which would cease.'[3]

Ministers who value Methodism above union, and laymen who believe in a full, operative priesthood of all believers, are dissatisfied. Others are disturbed by the prospect of forming part–perhaps a quarter–of a united Church whose leaders and members will have alien doctrines, modes of worship and traditions. Anglican-Methodist union, said Dr. C. Kingsley Barrett in 1963, meant 'the Methodist Jonah in the Anglican whale'.[4] Others fear inevitable closure of chapels. Mr. Ralph Whitlock writes,

'Although in any such union there may be a flourishing future for the suburban churches and central halls of Methodism, there can be no doubt about what it will mean for most village causes. As the years go by, with union becoming a reality, the question of redun-

[1] *Ibid.*, p. 15.
[2] *Ibid.*, p. 29.
[3] *M.R.*, 21 August 1958, p. 7; *Conversations*, p. 55.
[4] *M.R.*, 7 March 1963, p. 3.

dancy will certainly arise. It will . . . seem as wasteful and stupid to have Anglican and Methodist Churches in one small village as, a few years ago, it did to have Wesleyan and Primitive Methodist Churches within a stone's throw of each other. There will be one difference that, when the closure of one of them comes up for consideration, there can be no doubt which will be shut–the Methodist chapel. The Anglicans have an architectural advantage. Who would dream of closing a lovely Early English church and transferring the parish worship to a Victorian Gothic chapel?'[1]

Some Methodists also fear the social implications of union; the antithesis of church and chapel retains much significance.

Similar obstacles to union have been overcome in the past. Ecumenicalism continues to offer fresh and alluring prospects. Despite the drastic surrender required in Anglican-Methodist union, a surrender greater than that any Methodist denomination made for Methodist Union, a polemical ecumenicalism persists. Professor Torrance has urged Methodists not to miss 'this great opportunity of capturing the spiritual citadel of the Church of England'.[2] The Rev. Frank Pritchard has advocated the union because 'There is . . . good reason to hope that' Anglicans 'will ignore our refusal to believe in' episcopacy 'if we will only practise it. And if we do agree to practise it, and thereby increase the measure of communion between us and the Anglicans, have we not enough faith in the truth of Reformation principles to believe that they rather than Catholic errors will prevail?'[3] Larger schemes have also been aired. Dr Snaith notes that Anglican-Methodist union has been urged as 'our best bulwark against Rome'.[4]

The ecumenicalism of mission also persists. 'Unity . . . is the will of God for His Church', declares Dr. Roberts.[5] The moral language of the twenties is revived. 'Our young people. . . . will not forgive us if we put artificial barriers in the way of progress', states Lord Soper in support of union.[6] All the claims made for Methodist Union are now made for Anglican-Methodist union. Dr. Rupp claims that the proposals offer 'A new kind of Church for a new kind of world, and a new kind of ministry for a new kind of Church'. This new Church, Dr. Roberts suggests, will 'change the image of the Church' in the mind

[1] *M.R.*, 4 April 1963, p. 11.
[2] *Ibid.*, 21 November 1963, p. 1.
[3] *Ibid.*, 10 November 1955, p. 7.
[4] *Ibid.*, 25 May 1967, p. 12.
[5] *Ibid.*, 11 July 1957, p. 3.
[6] *Ibid.*, 13 July 1967, p. 19.

of 'the man in the street' by showing that Christians take seriously 'the message of reconciliation we are commending to the world'. At the same time, unity promises rationalization. 'Our disunity means inefficiency', says Dr. Roberts. '. . . What a difference it would make if together in every area we could plan for Christian advance and use to the full our common resources!'[1]

The underlying theme is the same now as it was half-a-century ago. Dr. Roberts points to 'the painful impotence of the Church in its disunity in face of the forces ranged against it'. Dr. Leslie Davison, Methodist Home Missions Secretary, said in 1965, 'They were fighting for the life of the Church. Time was not on their side.' Union is the answer. 'We must . . . ask ourselves, *why* . . . God is not visiting us,' wrote Mr. Foot Nash in 1964, *'why* in so many places He is allowing our societies to die on their feet. . . . Is it that He cannot bless us *on our own*? Is it that He has waiting for us, just around the corner, a Pentecostal outpouring upon this nation which just cannot be channelled into a number of different denominations?'[2]

The fears and hopes enacted on the Methodist stage are now given a repeat performance before a wider audience. Ecumenical displays continue to fascinate their promoters, even though their history is one of short runs and empty houses. Methodist experience may elucidate this phenomenon.

Religious organizations, like other institutions, generate divergent doctrines, vested interests, and disputes over scarce resources, power and prestige. Despite the ecumenical language of unity, peace and concord, the age of ecumenicalism has modified, not eliminated, conflict. 'Polemical ecumenicalism' presumes a situation of conflict; and the 'ecumenicalism of mission' can be interpreted as a function of conflict between denomination and society. But ecumenicalism does modify conflict. An over-riding 'ecumenical imperative' has united Methodism and involved it in the continuing process of church unification.

Factors promoting conflict were present in Methodism from the beginning. Wesley recruited members with divergent ideas, aspirations and expectations. His discipline of members and direction of the elite of travelling preachers provided further sources of conflict. Because involvement in the organization was high, propensity to engage in conflict was high. But during Wesley's lifetime the level of conflict was low. Great disparities existed between the educational

---

[1] *M.R.*, 8 July 1965, p. 18; 11 July 1963, p. 12; Roberts, *op. cit.*, p. 14.
[2] *M.R.*, 11 July 1957, p. 3; 8 July 1965, p. 17; Nash, *op. cit.*, p. 25.

level of laity and leadership and between the incipient ministerial elite and its leader, both in terms of general education and of knowledge about the organization. This discouraged insubordination. The strength of Wesley's leadership also checked conflict: his charisma evoked intense veneration of his person and complete loyalty to his directives. The 'method' by which members sought 'perfection' stressed obedience and total commitment to the process of moral improvement. This tended to legitimate the existing structure of the organization, and the existing distribution of power within it.

Intra-organizational conflict rose rapidly after Wesley's death. The leader's demise acted as a short-term factor accelerating long run increase in conflict. Educational levels began to converge, by dissemination of general education and knowledge about the organization. The charismatic leader was succeeded by the elite. It lacked his self-authentication, and was challenged by opposition liberated by his death. General interests developed through the organization: men began to think of themselves as laymen or ministers rather than as brother followers of the leader. This development was hastened by the emergence of local lay interests in the form of the chapel community.

Various other factors were associated with these changes. But religious organizations seem liable to develop one major and cumulative conflict between laity and hierarchy over the disposal of power in the organization. Positively, this leads to articulation of lay and ministerial roles; negatively, to the disruption of the organization. Such disruptions may be assisted by intra-hierarchical conflicts. But the ability of lay dissidents to detach sections of the hierarchy and recruit them as leaders was strictly limited in Methodism. Available ministerial leadership was usually temporary and limited.

The disruptive power of lay-hierarchical conflict during the period of very high involvement of members in the organization translated intra-organizational into inter-organizational conflict. The hostilities of rival denominations, created in this way, need not affect the parties adversely. Juxtaposition in conflict may strengthen the groups involved, defining and identifying loyalties and calling forth apologetic material to defend each group's position and to condemn its rivals. Conflict of this sort may also be advantageous to the parent body by transferring dissidents to separate denominations. This too makes for greater intra-organizational peace, at the expense of a (relatively harmless) inter-organizational warfare.

Changes in the character and expectations of the organizations involved superseded this overt, legitimated and universal conflict between religious organizations. Rival denominations usually fail to reform or eliminate each other. After a brief period of fluctuation, such organizations stabilize. In Methodism, as in Christianity as a whole, the parent church from which organizations have split off, remained incomparably larger and more powerful than all other groups. Smaller, radical groups, originating in schism, were unable to end the dominance of the parent body. This stimulated interest in amalgamation of different radical groups to strengthen some general 'radicalism' vis-a-vis the parent body. Coincident modification of that body's position disclosed the possibility of future reconciliation, and this also stimulated an interest in amalgamation among seceded groups eager to strengthen the future bargaining power of their common ideas.

As the tactical and strategic problems of interdenominational conflict became evident to participants, this conflict was itself reduced by the process of secularization. A rising standard of living, the emergence of interests and activities outside the religious community, the secularization of this community itself, all tended to lower members' involvement. As involvement decreased inter- and intra-organizational conflict also decreased. Rival doctrines and systems, and the disposal of power within the organization, ceased to dominate members' minds.

During this phase, complex social and cultural changes predisposed religious organizations towards ecumenicalism. Upward social mobility of religious groups has, in the last hundred years, been associated with erosion of loyalties to Christian doctrine and tradition. Looser commitments at the level of belief mean looser denominational commitments and muted interdenominational hostilities. Members are less confident that their organization possesses universal truth, if only because they are less confident about universal truth. Nonconformity, in particular, has experienced upward social mobility as a search for respectability. Much of the secularization process can be explained in social terms. Rigid belief systems, a strict coercive concept of the three-storey universe and pronounced denominational labels seem disreputable and outlandish. Ecumenicalism offers to institutionalize these changes, incorporating the discontented in organizations of superior social status.

A more general change accompanies this search for respectability. Secularization weakens commitment to the doctrine of hell, to a rigorous ethic and to the structures that promote it. These changes substitute an 'ethic of community' for an 'ethic of commitment'.

World-rejection and self-discipline are subordinated to community, happiness and niceness. To be nice, that is, to be cheerful, contented and inoffensive, has become a pervasive Christian ideal. This new ethic of community discredited older and more severe conflicts between priest and people. Hierarchical requirements have been modified, but they have been implemented more easily. Lay-ministerial conflicts persist and, since ecumenicalism tends to encroach upon lay rather than ministerial interests, may increase. But these conflicts must be concealed and restrained, according to the ethic of community. This tends to favour the *status quo*, i.e. ministerial power.

Most denominational divisions arise out of different solutions to the problem of hierarchical authority and power. The ethic of community discredits inter- as well as intra-denominational conflict. It is nicer to assert common Christianity than to denounce apostasy. Division becomes intrinsically disreputable. It is held to be no longer relevant or important. This strong pressure towards ecumenicalism is strengthened by the real convergence of religious organizations. Denominational structures grow more not less alike. Agreement on the theory of hierarchical rights and functions often precedes assimilation of practice. Such convergence evidently facilitates union.

Ecumenicalism develops as conflict declines and as religion declines. Failing to recruit, flourishing communities become sluggish, ageing and dispirited. Conversion of manifest success into manifest failure has nowhere been sharper than in Methodism. This change in fortunes has promoted an atmosphere of malaise. As tolerance of persistent decline fails, the organization seeks to replace missing 'frontal' growth from recruitment with 'lateral' growth from amalgamation. Responses to decline vary. Denominational leadership, the young, the optimistic, the relatively successful, accept the ecumenical option. Rank and file, the old, the pessimistic, those who are worst hit by decline, tend to reject it. But religious organizations are relatively undemocratic and give little weight to minorities; while declining involvement of members also limits resistance. In the long run, members acquiesce in leaders' decisions, however unwillingly.

The ecumenical option is hierarchical in origin. Its perspective is that of the denomination rather than the chapel, of ministerial rather than lay concerns. Ecumenicalism defines advantage and disadvantage in denominational not local terms: general survival of the general aims of the group, not the preservation of local communities, predominates. Lay-ministerial divergence is as apparent here as in the age of schism. The minister thinks in large religious terms, the member more in terms of immediate personal associations. The minister's sphere of action is not threatened by the ecumenical option, local lay society is.

Ecumenicalism resolves past conflict, often by drastic conflations. Whether the context is one of interdenominational conflict, or of religious decline, the ecumenical process embodies adoption of a common denominator of the doctrines and systems involved. Since 'optimistic', forward-looking elements in denominations are usually foremost in organizing amalgamation, denominational tradition is given peculiarly little attention in ecumenical negotiations. Ecumenical activity, unlike schism, is 'official' activity; and the official element in denominations tends to be hierarchical, especially in the ecumenical period when lay members' involvement is low. While schism is especially a lay activity, church union is especially ministerial, and past conflicts tend to be resolved in hierarchical terms. Few ecumenical settlements are monotone, but their complexion is generally ministerial.

Another factor has a similar effect. Ecumenicalism may involve, and institutionalize, upward social mobility. Radical schismatic groups generally have low social status, the conservative parent body a higher status. The doctrines and systems of these low status groups are at a social disadvantage. Members are glad to rid themselves of older democratic notions, as of rigid belief systems, a strict ethic and an outlandish denominational label.

While past conflicts are superseded in the ecumenical process by conflation of differences and the establishment of some 'common denominator', fresh conflicts may arise. Since ecumenical schemes tend to reflect ministerial interests, general lay acquiescence in ecumenicalism may be disturbed by new lay-hierarchical conflict, as small but vigorous minorities develop in opposition to amalgamation. Intra-hierarchical conflict may also occur, for example, over demands for 'reordination'.

But the ecumenical imperative can overwhelm new conflicts as well as old. Ecumenicalists achieve their aims, even if the united churches thus constructed display considerable alienation, especially the persistence of aggrieved minority traditions, denied legitimate expression of their interests and concerns by the ecumenical ideology of unity, peace and concord. So strong are the social and organizational forces that constitute the ecumenical imperative, that even manifest failure of united churches to fulfil ecumenical promises does not deter ecumenically minded leadership, itself alienated by this failure, from pursuing ever larger ecumenical policies. Rational considerations and assessment of past experience seem irrelevant.

Ecumenicalism is advocated as the solution of the churches' problems. Official interpretations of the movement suggest youthful enthusiasm and boundless prospects. But close examination of the process of reunion shows that in advanced societies ecumenicalism is the product of an ageing religion. It arises out of decline and secularization, but fails to deal with either. The strength of the ecumenical imperative can be seen in the apparent inability of denominational leadership to devise alternatives to already discredited policies that abolish crumbling convictions and leave little in their place. This inability is lamented by many Christian leaders. But it is lauded as the divine will by many more. A more critical appraisal is overdue, for the hope that ecumenicalism will be the salvation of Christianity seems illusory.

# Major Dates in Methodist History, 1791-1932

1791    Death of John Wesley.

1795    Plan of Pacification.

1897    Leeds Regulations.
          Methodist New Connexion established.

1801    William O'Bryan begins evangelistic work.

1803    William Bramwell gathers a group of 'Revivalists' at Leeds.

1803–4  Jabez Bunting reorganizes the accounts of the Wesleyan Missionary Committee.

1806    First Annual Meeting of the Independent Methodists.
          Band Room Methodist secession in Manchester.

1807    Camp Meeting on Mow Cop.

1812    Hugh Bourne and William Clowes adopt the name 'Primitive Methodists'.

1813–14 Unrest among Wesleyans in Cornwall.

1814    Start of the Tent Mission in Gloucestershire.
          Bunting elected to Legal Hundred.

1815    O'Bryan and James Thorne adopt the name 'Bible Christians'.

1816–17 Unrest among Wesleyans in London.

1819    First Bible Christian Conference.
          Preliminary Meeting of the Primitive Methodists.

1820    Tent Methodist secession in Bristol.

1822–3  James Everett works in the Wesleyan Book Room.

1827    Leeds Organ Case.
          Protestant Methodist secession.

1830    *Circular to Wesleyan Methodists* launched.

1832    Secession of Arminian or Faith Methodists in Derby.

1833    Bunting permanent General Secretary of the Wesleyan Missionary Committee.

1834    Samuel Warren condemns the Buntingites' scheme for a Theological Institution.
          Grand Central Association formed.

1834    *Watchman's Lantern* launched.

1835    *Watchman* launched.
First Delegate Meeting of the Grand Central Association.
Robert Eckett expelled from Wesleyan Methodism.

1836    First Assembly of the Wesleyan (Methodist) Association.
'Circuit independence' adopted.
Negotiations for union between the Methodist New Connexion and the Wesleyan Association.

1837    Negotiations for union between the New Connexion and the Association fail.
Warren leaves and Eckett gains control of the Association.
Arminian Methodists, Independent Primitive Methodists of Scarborough and Protestant Methodists join the Association.

1838    Independent Wesleyans of North Wales join the Association.

1839    Scottish United Methodist Churches join the Association.
Centenary of Methodism. Centenary Hall built for Bunting.

1840    Everett publishes the *Wesleyan Takings*.

1841–2  Teetotal controversies in Bristol and Lincolnshire.

1842    Teetotal Wesleyan Methodists secede in West Cornwall.

1843–8  Everett's preaching tours.

1844    *Wesleyan and Christian Record* launched.
*Wesleyan Chronicle* launched and amalgamated with the *Wesleyan*.
First *Fly Sheet* published.

1845    James Buckle's attack on the spirit vaults of the Centenary Hall.
Jacob Stanley elected 'liberal' President of the Wesleyan Conference.

1846    First *Fly Sheet* reprinted.
Second *Fly Sheet* published.
'Liberal' candidate, William Atherton, elected President of the Wesleyan Conference.

1847    Third *Fly Sheet* published.
*Christian World* article attacking Buntingism.
'Liberal' candidate, Samuel Jackson, elected President of the Wesleyan Conference. George Osborn introduces test on authorship of the *Fly Sheets*.

1848    Fourth *Fly Sheet* published.
'Liberal' candidate for the Presidency, Joseph Fowler, defeated by the Buntingites.

| | |
|---|---|
| 1849 | *Wesleyan Times* launched. |
| | James Everett, William Griffith and Samuel Dunn expelled from Wesleyan Methodism. |
| | Local Preachers' Mutual Aid Association formed. |
| 1850 | Mass expulsion of Wesleyans. |
| | First Delegate Meeting of the Wesleyan Reformers. |
| | General Reform Committee set up. |
| | Eckett advocates 'Question by Penalty'. |
| 1852 | The 'Law of 1852' brings slight concessions to Wesleyan laymen. |
| 1853 | General Reform Committee commissions Everett to compile a hymn book. |
| | Methodist New Connexion Conference, under the leadership of William Cooke, invites Reformers to join the New Connexion. |
| | Eckett finally defeats his opponents in the Association and argues for the essential similarity of Reform and Associationist principles in the *Wesleyan Times*. |
| 1853–4 | Many Reformers favour union with the New Connexion. |
| 1854 | Delegate Meeting of the Reformers seeks union negotiations with the Association and the New Connexion. |
| | New Connexion rebuffs the Reformers. |
| 1855 | Last year of net decrease in Wesleyan membership. |
| | General Reform Committee in financial difficulties. |
| | Association and Reformers' representatives issue a joint circular on union. |
| 1856 | Reformers vote to unite with the Association. |
| 1857 | United Methodist Free Churches formed. |
| 1859 | Minority of Reformers form the Wesleyan Reform Union. |
| 1861 | *Methodist Recorder* launched. |
| 1862 | Death of Eckett. |
| 1863 | Cooke seeks Free Methodist-New Connexion union. |
| 1866 | Samuel Hulme's letters to the Presidents of the Methodist Conferences. |
| 1867 | Abortive Free Methodist-New Connexion discussion of union at Leeds. |
| 1868 | Cooke seeks Bible Christian-New Connexion union. |
| 1869 | Bible Christian-New Connexion negotiations. |
| | Cooke and Hulme propose 'Federal Union' of the two denominations. |
| 1869–70 | James Stacey and W. J. Townsend oppose this scheme. |

1870    New Connexion Conference rejects union with the Bible Christians.

1871    T. P. Bunting advocates lay representation in the Wesleyan Conference.

1872    Richard Chew and Samuel Barton's resolutions in the Free Methodist Assembly on the Cleckheaton case.

1876    Wesleyan Conference accepts lay representation.

1878    First meeting of the Representative Session of the Wesleyan Conference.

1881    First Methodist Ecumenical Conference.

1883    Primitive Methodist Committee on 'Districtism'.

1885    Hugh Price Hughes launches the *Methodist Times*.

1886    Hughes' Olive Branch to the Bible Christians and the New Connexion.

1887    The Wesleyan Conference rejects the Olive Branch.
Alienated by this, Townsend seeks Free Methodist-New Connexion union.

1889    James H. Rigg prevents drastic reform of Wesleyanism by the 'Rigg Sandwich'.

1890    Free Methodist Foundation Deed amended.
Free Methodist-New Connexion negotiations on union. Draft constitution proposed.
Stacey prevents New Connexion Conference accepting the draft constitution.

1891    New Connexion Conference rejects union with the Free Methodists.
Thomas Mitchell seeks a Primitive Methodist initiative on Methodist Union.
Second Methodist Ecumenical Conference.

1892    Primitive Methodist Conference considers Bible Christian-Primitive Methodist union.
Chew's opinion on the Bristol North Circuit case.
Wesleyan quarterly meetings allowed to send delegates to synod.

1895    Bible Christian-Primitive Methodist negotiations.
Primitive Methodist Conference proposes union with the Free Methodists and New Connexion.
Free Methodists and New Connexion decline this union.

1897    Primitive Methodists return to the scheme of Bible Christian-Primitive Methodist union.

| | |
|---|---|
| 1898 | R. W. Perks and Hugh Price Hughes launch the Wesleyan Twentieth Century Fund (Million Guinea Fund). |
| 1899 | Free Methodists launch Hundred Thousand Guinea Fund. |
| 1900 | Primitive Methodist quarterly meetings reject union with the Bible Christians by large majorities. |
| | Representative Session of the Wesleyan Conference first meets before the Pastoral Session. |
| 1901 | At the Third Methodist Ecumenical Conference, David Brook sounds Bible Christian and New Connexion leaders on Bible Christian-Free Methodist-New Connexion union. |
| 1902 | Free Methodist Assembly approves the start of negotiations. William Redfern and Robert Bird address the Bible Christian Conference. |
| | *Free Methodist* newspaper becomes newspaper for all three denominations. |
| | New Connexion Conference passes 'open door' resolution on union. |
| 1902–7 | Bible Christian-Free Methodist-New Connexion negotiations on union. |
| 1903 | New Connexion *Methodist Evangelist* advocates New Connexion-Wesleyan union. |
| | Perks seeks Wesleyan initiative on union. |
| | Wesleyan Committee of Inquiry meets representatives of the three denominations. |
| 1904 | Perks secures Wesleyan initiative for Wesleyan-New Connexion Union. |
| 1905 | New Connexion Conference rejects Wesleyan proposals. |
| 1906 | Bible Christians, Free Methodists and New Connexion agree to unite. |
| | Nehemiah Curnock retires as editor of the *Methodist Recorder*. |
| 1907 | United Methodist Church formed. |
| 1911 | Fourth Methodist Ecumenical Conference. |
| 1912 | James Lewis introduces a motion on Methodist Union in the Wesleyan Conference. |
| 1913 | Perks secures appointment by the Wesleyan Conference of a Committee of Inquiry on Methodist Union. |
| 1916 | J. H. Shakespeare advocates Free Church Federation. |
| | Samuel Horton secures appointment by the Primitive Methodist Conference of a Committee on Primitive Methodist-United Methodist union. |

# APPENDIX ONE

1917     Kingsway Conference on Wesleyan-Church of England union.

Wesleyan Conference empowers the Union Committee to meet representatives of the other denominations.

1918–32 Primitive Methodist-United Methodist-Wesleyan Methodist negotiations on union.

1919     T. W. Clucas organizes Wesleyan opposition to union.

1920     Publication of the *Tentative Scheme* for Methodist Union.

R. Bevan Shepherd's first Manifesto against union.

J. E. Rattenbury announces 'last ditch' opposition to union on the basis of the *Scheme*.

The three Conferences send the *Scheme* to the district meetings for consideration of details.

Wesleyan opposition organizes itself as 'The Other Side'.

1921     District meetings strongly criticize the *Scheme*.

Unionists decide on delay.

Fifth Methodist Ecumenical Conference.

1922     John Higman, R. W. Essex and H. W. Surtees organize United Methodist opposition to union under the name 'The Progressives'.

Bevan Shepherd's second Manifesto against union.

The Peake-Rattenbury debate.

1922–3 'December' quarterly meetings strongly criticize the *Scheme*.

1923     The Other Side launch the *Wesleyan Methodist*.

1924     'The Primitive Methodist Other Side' organized against union.

On an amendment by W. H. Armstrong, the Wesleyan Pastoral Session of Conference votes 50·2 per cent against union on the basis of the *Scheme*. Armstrong amendment subsequently abandoned.

1924–5 Two-thirds of the members of the 'December' quarterly meetings in favour of union on the basis of the *Scheme*.

1925     John Hornabrook delays a final decision.

Informal talks between Wesleyan Unionists and the Wesleyan Other Side.

The 75 per cent formula adopted.

Primitive Methodist and United Methodist Conferences accept union.

Primitive Methodist leaders meet the Primitive Methodist Other Side at Abbeydale, Sheffield.

1925–6   Major revision of the doctrinal and sacramental clauses of the *Scheme*.

1926     Wesleyan synods fail to vote 75 per cent for the Enabling Bill necessary for union.

Wesleyan Representative Session of Conference accepts Methodist Union on the basis of the *Scheme*.

1927     Wesleyan synods again fail to vote 75 per cent for the Enabling Bill.

Wesleyan Representative Session of Conference withdraws its support for union.

Rattenbury decides that compromise is necessary. 'A Policy of Three Stages' proposed: Union in 1932.

1928     The Other Side splits. Rattenbury accepts the Three Stages. A majority of the Other Side Committee decides to continue opposition to union.

Primitive Methodist and United Methodist leaders accept the Three Stages.

Wesleyan Representative Session returns to the support of union.

Wesleyan Pastoral Session finally accepts Methodist Union, by one vote.

1929     Methodist Church Union Act passed.

1931     Sixth Methodist Ecumenical Conference.

1932     Methodist Church formed.

# Clauses Thirty and Thirty-one of the Deed of Union

30. *Doctrine.* – The doctrinal standards of The Methodist Church are as follows:

The Methodist Church claims and cherishes its place in the Holy Catholic Church which is the Body of Christ. It rejoices in the inheritance of the Apostolic Faith and loyally accepts the fundamental principles of the historic creeds and of the Protestant Reformation. It ever remembers that in the Providence of God Methodism was raised up to spread Scriptural Holiness through the land by the proclamation of the Evangelical Faith and declares its unfaltering resolve to be true to its Divinely appointed mission.

The Doctrines of the Evangelical Faith which Methodism has held from the beginning and still holds are based upon the Divine Revelation recorded in the Holy Scriptures. The Methodist Church acknowledges this revelation as the supreme rule of faith and practice. These Evangelical Doctrines to which the Preachers of The Methodist Church both Ministers and Laymen are pledged are contained in Wesley's Notes on the New Testament and the first four volumes of his sermons.

The Notes on the New Testament and the forty-four Sermons are not intended to impose a system of formal or speculative theology on Methodist Preachers, but to set up standards of preaching and belief which should secure loyalty to the fundamental truths of the Gospel of Redemption and ensure the continued witness of the Church to the realities of the Christian experience of salvation.

Christ's Ministers in the Church are Stewards in the household of God and Shepherds of His flock. Some are called and ordained to this sole occupation and have a principal and directing part in these great duties but they hold no priesthood differing in kind from that which is common to the Lord's people and they have no exclusive title to the preaching of the gospel or the care of souls. These ministries are shared with them by others to whom also the Spirit divides His gifts severally as He wills.

It is the universal conviction of the Methodist people that the office of the Christian ministry depends upon the call of God who bestows the gifts of the Spirit the grace and the fruit which indicate those whom He has chosen.

Those whom The Methodist Church recognizes as called of God and therefore receives into its Ministry shall be ordained by the imposition of hands as expressive of the Church's recognition of the Minister's personal call.

The Methodist Church holds the doctrine of the priesthood of all believers and consequently believes that no priesthood exists which belongs exclusively to a particular order or class of men but in the exercise of its corporate life and worship special qualifications for the discharge of special duties are required and thus the principle of representative selection is recognized.

The Preachers itinerant and lay are examined tested and approved before they are authorized to minister in holy things. For the sake of Church Order and not because of any priestly virtue inherent in the office the Ministers of The Methodist Church are set apart by ordination to the Ministry of the Word and Sacraments.

The Methodist Church recognizes two sacraments namely Baptism and the Lord's Supper as of Divine Appointment and of perpetual obligation of which it is the privilege and duty of Members of The Methodist Church to avail themselves.

31. *Doctrinal Standards Unalterable,*–(a) The Conference shall not have any power to alter or vary in any manner whatsoever the clauses contained in this Deed which define the doctrinal standards of The Methodist Church.

(b) The Conference shall be the final authority within The Methodist Church with regard to all questions concerning the interpretation of its doctrines.

(From: Harold Spencer and Edwin Finch, *The Constitutional Practice and Discipline of the Methodist Church,* London, 1958, pp. 264-5.)

# Index

*For abbreviations see Table One, page 87.*

327

156, 164–5; UMFC, 148–9; WMC, 164–5; Wesleyan Reform Union, 148–9

Leaders' meeting, Bible Christian, *see* elders' meeting

League of Nations, 187

Leakage, Methodist, 98–100

Leeds, 62, 68, 107, 151, 204; Ebenezer Chapel, 217; Lady Lane Circuit, 203; MNC-UMFC meeting at, 231; Missionary Meeting at, 31–2; Organ Case, 52, 60, 62, 74, 218, 317; Quarry Hill Chapel, 46; Regulations, 28–9, 317; Stone Chapel, 46; Bramley Circuit, 212; Wesleyan Reformers' Delegate Meeting at, 230

Legal Hundred, 150; and President, 161–4; foundation of, 25–6; reform of, 32–3, 317

Lewis, James, 249, 321

Liberal Methodists, union of, 174–5, 185, 230, 293

Liberal Party, 180, 184–5

Liberal theology, 121

Lidgett, John Scott, 255, 272; on ecumenicalism, 187–8, 195; on God, 122; on Methodist doctrine, 165–6, 278

Life, Christian concepts of, 17, 138–9, 141

Lincolnshire, 45, 207, 209; ecumenicalism in, 202–3; Methodism in, 104–5; PMC in, 104–5; teetotalism in, 70, 318; WMC in, 104–5

Lineham, Joseph, 282

Liskeard, 302

Liverpool, 47, 210, 288; and the Other Side, 262; Carveth at 226; North Circuit, 62–3; Mission, 211

Local preachers, 25; and leaders' meeting in the Methodist Church, 270; and ministers, 52–3, 293; and reform, 52–3; and superintendents, 53; *ex officio* seats of, in UMC local meetings, 156, 293;

*ex officio* seats of, in UMFC local meetings, 147, 156, 293; *ex officio* seats of, in WMA local meetings, 147, 220

Local Preachers' Mutual Aid Association, 53, 70, 319

Lockhart, James, 130

Lomas, Mary, 125

London, Albion Street Chapel, 53, 73, 222; and Methodist union, 196, 228; and Other Side, 262; and Primitive Methodist Other Side, 269; controversy in, 61, 318; Hinde Street Chapel, 49; Methodism in, 104–9, 131, 209–10; PMC in 104–9; WMC in, 104–9; East Circuit, 48, 61; South Circuit, 48; West Circuit, 60, 63

Longbottom, William, 234

Loss, Methodist, 98–100

Love-feast, 130, 132

Luke, John, 200

Lunn, Henry, 181

Lupton, W. A., 251–2

Luther, Martin, 18–20

Luton, 46, 137

McKechnie, C. C., 237

McOwan, John, 47

Magic, 135

Magic Methodists, 57

Major, Rowland, 262

Mallinson, Joah, 46

Maltby, W. Russell, 186, 259, 272

Man, Isle of, 21

Manchester, 104; and Band Room Methodists, 56, 317; and WMA assembly, 230; Everett and, 66; Grand Central Association and, 218; Methodist Ministers' Fraternal, 204; Warren and, 64

Mann, Horace, 222

Mansfield, 128

Margate, 212

Martin, R. F., 302

Martin, William, 227–9

Mason, J. A., 47

Mather, Alexander, 27

Matthews, J. E., 182, 188

Membership-attendance ratios, 198 and n.

Membership-population ratios, 89–93

Methodism, *passim*

Methodist Archives, 14

Methodist Church, and Wesleyan Conference, 254–5; and Wesley's Standards, 252, 255–6, 263, 269, 296; conference of, 254–5, 262–3, 269–71, 294; decline of, 299; Deed of Union of, 307, 324–5; distribution of offices in, 304–5; district synod in, 255; doctrine in, 255–6, 277–8, 295–6, 324–5; formation of, 248–89, 323; judicial proceedings in, 255, 294; lay-ministerial relations in, 254–5, 269–70, 294–6, 324–5; ministerial chairmanship in, 255, 294; Ministerial Session of conference of, 254–5, 269–70; ministry in, 254–5, 294, 324–5; nomination of lay officials in, 254–5, 294; President of conference in, 254, 294, 304; proposed union of with Church of England, 11, 306–11; quarterly meeting in, 254–5; Representative Session of conference of, 254–5, 269–70; sacraments in, 256–8, 269, 271, 277–81, 295–6, 324–5; society meeting in, 255; stationing in, 254–5; Vice-President of conference in, 255

Methodist Church Union Act, 282–7, 323

*Methodist Evangelist*, 244–5, 321

*Methodist Monitor*, 58–9, 62

*Methodist Monthly*, 123

Methodist New Connexion, 54, 76, 141–51, 155–6, 168, 200, 206–8, 217–47, 293–4, 317–21; and Band Room Methodists, 60; and BCs, 207–8, 232–3, 319–21; and biblical criticism, 113–4; and critical size, 88; and 1837 scheme of union, 220; and 1869 scheme of union, 232–3; and 1890 scheme of union, 154–6, 243, 247; and

entertainment, 132–4; and evolution, 114–7; and *ex officio* seats for local preachers in local meetings, 147, 156, 246; and games, 132; and hell, 119; and idealist theology, 123; and Kilham, 58–9, 217; and Leeds Organ Case, 60, 218; and liberal theology, 120; and the novel, 135–6; and personality of Christ, 124; and philosophy, 132; and PMC, 206, 238, 320; and Protestant Methodists, 60, 218; and Theological Institution, 65, 218–20; and Thom, 59, 217; and UMC, 155–6, 240–7, 321; and UMFC, 206, 208, 231–2, 240, 319–20; and WMA, 219–20, 318; and WMC, 58–9, 206, 230–1, 233–4, 243–6, 248, 320–1; and Wesleyan Reformers, 222–30, 319; attempts of to recruit Wesleyans, 59–61, 65, 217; Barkerite controversy in, 92, 222; Book Room of, 60, 193; chairmanship in, 149, 156; committees in, 193; conference of, 142, 144–5; death rates of, 100–1; Deed Poll of, 150; district meeting in, 146; elite of, 208; formation of, 58–9, 217, 317; foundation principle of, 141, 246; growth rates of, 95, 298; Guardian Representatives of, 150; lay-ministerial relations in, 141–9, 151, 231; leaders' meeting in, 148; 'leakage' in, 98–100; 'loss' in, 98–100; membership figures of, 87, 217; membership-population ratios of, 90–3, 103; parity in, 78, 142; preachers' certificates in, 150; quarterly meeting in, 147-8, 231; representation in, 141, 143; vote on union of 1904, 103, 244; vote on union of 1905–6, 103, 244

*Methodist New Connexion Magazine*, 116, 119, 136

Methodist Publishing House, 14

*Methodist Recorder*, 108, 161, 197, 201, 305; Curnock and, 162, 321; formation of, 158, 319; on Church

lay appointments, 29; and local preachers, 52; and members, 29; and Methodist reform, 75–6; and tent mission, 57; Bunting's theory of, 40–1; disciplinary powers of, 29; judicial role of, 29, 75–6, 118–119
Supremacy, pastoral, 165, 175–6
Surrey, 21 n., 107, 209
Surtees, H. W., 260, 264, 322
Sussex, 107
Swedenborgianism, 260
Swinburne, Joseph, 67
Synod, district, see District synod

Tamar, 131
Taylor, E. R., 36
Teetotalism, 70, 131, 132, 318
Teetotal Wesleyan Methodist, 69–70, 318
*Tentative Scheme, The*, 253–8, 259, 262, 269, 322
Tent Methodists, 54–6, 77, 317; district meeting in, 146; district representation in, 143; formation of, 54–7; leaders' meeting in, 148; lay-ministerial relations in, 143–9
Tetzel, John, 81
Theological college, WMC, 113, 158
Theological Institution, WMC, 48, 60, 64–7, 218–19, 317
Theosophy, 260
Thom, William, 59–60, 217
Thompson, E. P., 49
Thompson, William, 27
Thorne, James, 56, 232, 317
Thorp, James, 268–9
*Times*, 73
Todmorden, 199
Tompkins, 260
Torrance, T. F., 310
Tottenham, 106, 212
Townsend, W. J., 232–6, 244, 319–320
Tractarianism, 176
Troutbeck, Samuel, 45
Truro, 61
Trustees, 24–5, 28, 50, 52–3

Tunstall, 151
Turnover, Methodist, 98–100
Two-to-One principle, 78, 142–3, 151, 237–9
Tyne, 131

Ulverston, 212
Union Committee, BCs–MNC–UMFC, 163
Union, Deed of, Methodist, 307, 324–5
Unitarianism, 260
United Committee on Methodist Union, PMC–UMC–WMC, 269; and Area Committees, 287; and delay of union, 275–6, 283–5; and doctrine, 255–6, 263, 277–8; and Independent Methodists, 253; and ministerial candidates, 289; and Ministerial Session of conference, 254–5, 263; and overlap, 253, 273, 282–6; and President of conference, 254; and propaganda, 261, 264, 273; and purpose of Methodist union, 254; and quarterly meeting, 254–5; and Representative Session of conference, 254–5, 263; and sacraments, 256–258, 263, 278–80; and society meeting, 254–5; and Stationing Committee, 254–5; and the Three Stages, 284–5; and Vice-president of conference, 255; and Wesleyan Reform Union, 253, 287; formation of, 253; on *Tentative Scheme*, 261
United Kingdom, 26
*United Methodist*, 250, 253, 282, 305
United Methodist Church, 13, 54, 86, 108, 164–5, 191, 195, 198–9, 240, 247; and ecumenicalism, 190–5, 198–200; and MNC–UMFC scheme of union of 1890, 155–6, 242, 247; and Methodist union, 248–89, 321–3; and PMC, 252; and PMC–UMC union, 252–3, 264, 284, 321; and *Tentative Scheme*, 259; and WMC, 253, 321–3; Book Room of, 193;

sonality of Christ, 124; and Plan of Pacification, 28–9; and PMC, 173, 202–3, 205, 207, 211–12, 248–89, 322–3; and progress, 121–2; and secessions, 58–82; and sin, 119; and social class, 205–13; and the theatre, 133; and UMC, 208, 212, 250–89; and WMA, 218–19; and Wesleyan Reformers, 65–76, 223–4; Bands of Hope in, 133–4; central halls in, 211; chapels in, 24, 44–53; class meeting in, 125–9; conference of, 22, 40–1, 150, 159, 160–4; death rates of, 100–1; decline of, 87, 90–103, 191; district chairman in, 28; district representation in, 158–9; district synod in, 28–9, 37, 62, 160–1, 164, 262–3, 282–3, 287, 320, 323; doctrine of the ministry in, 38–43, 165–8, 169–72; finances of, 30, 224; geographical distribution of, 104–9; growth rates of, 94–8; inquisition in, 19, 22, 36, 125–9; itinerancy in, 23; laity in, 41–3, 46; lay-ministerial relations in, 30–1, 38–43, 46–53, 150, 164–165; lay officials in, 46; lay representation in, 159–60, 233, 321; leaders' meeting in, 164–5; 'leakage' in, 98–100; liturgy in, 30, 302; local preachers in, 25, 52–3; 'loss' in, 98–100; losses to MNC, 58–9, 65; losses to WMA, 65; losses to Wesleyan Reformers, 223; love-feast in, 130, 132; membership-attendance ratios in, 198; membership figures of, 87, 223, 319; membership-population ratios of, 90–3, 102; memorials in, 35, 159; ministerial elite in, 209–10; mixed committees in, 35–36; preachers of, 23–5; President in, 22–3, 25, 34, 71–2, 161–3, 195; quarterly meeting in, 28, 35, 144, 159, 164–5, 321; recruitment in, 98–100; sacraments in, 25, 28, 59, 130–1; society meeting in, 164–5; Stationing

Committee of, 32, 34; stewards in, 23; superintendents in, 40–1; trustees in, 24–5, 50; vote on union of 1924, 102, 108–9, 198–200, 203–5, 210–13, 273–4; worship in, 129–31

*Wesleyan Methodist Gazette*, 283
*Wesleyan Methodist Magazine*, 115, 119–21, 135
*Wesleyan Methodist Penny Magazine*, 224
*Wesleyan Reformer*, 224
Wesleyan Reformers, 54, 76, 319; aims of, 73–4, 76–80; Albion Street Chapel meeting of, 53, 73, 222; and Buntingites, 224; and Cooke, 224–8; and connexionalism, 227–8; and Everett, 73, 222–230; and MNC, 222–30, 319; and UMFC, 230, 319; and WMA, 206, 222–30, 319; and WMC, 222–30; and Wesleyan Reform Union, 230, 319; Declaration of Principles of, 229; Delegate Meeting of, 223, 225, 229–30, 319; doctrine of, 76–80; finances of, 223–4; General Reform Committee of, 222–4, 226, 229–30, 319; hymn book of, 224; membership of, 87, 92, 222–3; policy of, 74; religious egalitarianism of, 78–80

Wesleyan Reform Union, 54, 157, 231; and Methodist union, 253, 287; annual meeting of, 143–4; circuit representation in, 143; formation of, 230; lay-ministerial relations in, 143–9; leaders' meeting in, 148; quarterly meeting in, 147–8; Wesleyan Reformers and, 230, 319

*Wesleyan Times*, 67, 72, 227–8, 319
Wesley's Chapel, 203, 247
*Wesley's Ghost*, 60–1, 69
Wesley's Standards, 252, 255–6, 263, 269, 276–7, 324
Westerdale, T. E., 161
West London Mission, 129, 181, 211, 251